# TIME FOR CHANGE

## PSYCHOANALYTIC IDEAS AND APPLICATIONS SERIES

# TIME FOR CHANGE

## Tracking Transformations in Psychoanalysis—The Three-Level Model

Edited by

*Marina Altmann de Litvan*

Routledge
Taylor & Francis Group
LONDON AND NEW YORK

First published 2014 by Karnac Books Ltd.

Published 2018 by Routledge
2 Park Square, Milton Park, Abingdon, Oxon OX14 4RN
711 Third Avenue, New York, NY 10017, USA

*Routledge is an imprint of the Taylor & Francis Group, an informa business*



British Library Cataloguing in Publication Data

A C.I.P. for this book is available from the British Library

ISBN 9781782201816 (pbk)

Edited, designed and produced by The Studio Publishing Services Ltd
www.publishingservicesuk.co.uk
e-mail: studio@publishingservicesuk.co.uk

## *CONTENTS*

## PART IV
## THE 3-LM: A CASE, REPORT, AND DISCUSSION



## PART V
## CLINICAL CONCEPTS



## PART VI
## AN APPLICATION OF THE 3-LM AT THE END OF ANALYTIC TRAINING

## PART VII
## FURTHER DEVELOPMENTS OF THE 3-LM IN CHILD ANALYSIS

# *ABOUT THE EDITOR AND CONTRIBUTORS*

**Marina Altmann de Litvan**, PhD, psychoanalyst, Master in Psychoanalysis, and children and adolescent psychoanalyst (IPA). She is a full member and training analyst of the Uruguayan Psychoanalytic Association and Member of the International Psychoanalytical Association. She is Chair of the Clinical Observation Committee since 2010 (until 2017) and member of the Clinical Research Subcommittee of the Research Committee of the IPA (2014).

She has been a member of the Education Committee (2010–2013), Co-Chair of the Education-Research Subcommittee of (2007–2009), and Co-Chair of the Research Committee (2003-2006) of the Psychoanalytic Federation of Latin America (FEPAL).

She is a research fellow of University College London, Third Annual Training Programme (1997), and visiting professor at University College London, Research Training Programme of the IPA, (2005–2006).

She was President of the Society of Medical Psychology (1997–1999).

She won the Biannual Exceptional Contribution Award from the Research Committee of the International Psychoanalytical Association (2001) for her research in verbal and non-verbal interactions in the mother–baby psychotherapeutic process. She has published chapters in books, and papers in both Spanish and English. She is a member of evaluating boards for psychoanalytic journals, scientific publications, and research projects. Her research fields are: clinical research in psychoanalysis, psychoanalytic training, child analysis, mother–infant interaction, and psychotherapeutic process.

**Ricardo Bernardi**, PhD, is a medical doctor and psychiatrist at Facultad de Medicina, Universidad de la República, UdelaR, Uruguay). He holds a Masters in Psychoanalysis (Asociación Psicoanalítica del Uruguay, member of the International Psychoanalytic Association) and a PhD in Psychology (Universidad de Buenos Aires, Argentina). He is former Head Professor and Chairman of the Department of Medical Psychology at the Medicine School (UdelaR). He has won the following awards: FEPAL (1992), 2º award from the National Academy of Medicine (1997), Mary S. Sigourney Award (1999), *International Journal of Psychoanalysis* Best Paper Award (2003), and the PEP Author Prize. In addition, he is acknowledged to have the most downloaded articles during the years 2010 and 2011. He has served as Regional Editor for Latin America of the *International Journal of Psychoanalysis* (from 2008 to 2011), and is Vice Chair of the International Research Board of the International Psychoanalytical Association (since 2009). He has been a member of the Clinical Observation Committee of the International Psychoanalytical Association since 2009, is a researcher of the ANII, Uruguay, consultant and reviewer for the UdelaR, MEC, and ANII, member of the editorial boards and reviewer for numerous journals. He is Emeritus Professor of the Medicine School (UdelaR).

**Beatriz de León de Bernardi** is a Uruguayan full member and training analyst of the Uruguayan Psychoanalytic Association (APU). She is Past President of the APU, and is an Editorial Board member of the *International Journal of Psychoanalysis*. Currently, she is a representative for Latin America in the International Psychoanalytical Association Board and member of the IPA Education Committee. She has published papers and books in different languages, mainly about the patient–analyst interaction and the analyst's contribution to the analytic process, the notion of countertransference in Latin America (*International Journal of Psychoanalysis*, 2000), the thought of Madeleine and Willy Baranger (*International Journal of Psychoanalysis*, 2008). She has researched and published about implicit theories in psychoanalytic practice and about metaphors in the analytic field. She has received the Award of the Latin-American Psychoanalytical Federation (FEPAL) and the Training Today Award.

**Margaret Ann Fitzpatrick Hanly**, PhD, is a training and supervising psychoanalyst in the Canadian Institute of Psychoanalysis, in private practice in Toronto, Canada. She is Past President of the Canadian Psychoanalytic Society, Associate Director of the Toronto Institute of Psychoanalysis, and member of the International Psychoanalytic Association Committee on Clinical Observation. Margaret Ann Fitzpatrick-Hanly is on the Executive Editorial Board of the *Psychoanalytic Quarterly*, and on the Editorial Boards of the *International Journal of Psychoanalysis* and the *Canadian Journal of Psychoanalysis*. Her publications include *Essential Papers on Masochism* (Editor, New York University Press, 1995); "Narrative, now and then: a critical realist approach" (*International Journal of Psychoanalysis*, 1996); "Aesthetic ambiguity and sibling jealousy in Austen's Pride and Prejudice" (*Psychoanalytic Quarterly*, 2009).

**Liliana Fudin de Winograd** has full membership of the International Psychoanalytical Association, and is a training analyst, Sociedad Argentina de Psicoanalisis. She is a founding member of the Sociedad Argentina de Psicoanálisis, and Director of Training of Sociedad Argentina de Psicoanálisis. She is also a teacher of mental health at the Facultad de Medicina, Universidad de Buenos Aires, and a member of the Asociación Argentina de Epistemología del Psicoanálisis.

**William C. Glover**, PhD, is a training and supervising analyst, and Chair, Psychoanalytic Education Division, San Francisco Center for Psychoanalysis.

**Siri Erika Gullestad** is Professor of Clinical Psychology at the Department of Psychology, University of Oslo, Norway, where she is the leader of the Clinic for Dynamic Psychotherapy. Gullestad is a training and supervising analyst of the IPA. She is former president of the Norwegian Psychoanalytic Society, and former Head of Department of Psychology. She is the author of numerous books and articles within the psychoanalytic field. She has been a member of the Clinical Observation Committee of the International Psychoanalytical Association since 2012, and is currently a member of the IPA Research Committee.

**Charles Hanly** is a psychoanalyst in private practice, a training analyst at the Toronto Institute of Psychoanalysis, and Professor Emeritus (philosophy) at the University of Toronto. Since 1985, Professor Hanly has been active in the International Psychoanalytical Association (IPA), having a leadership role in enabling independent psychoanalytic societies in the USA to become Component Societies of the IPA and in the redevelopment of psychoanalysis in Eastern Europe. He has been elected to the Executive Council of the IPA for three terms as Vice-President North America, and to the Board of Representatives for two terms as Global Representative for North America. He was elected President-elect of the IPA in 2007 and served two terms as IPA President 2009–2013. Professor Hanly is the author of four books, and more than eighty clinical, theoretical, and applied papers in journals and books.

**Silvana Hernández Romillo** is a psychologist. She has a Master's Degree in psychoanalysis, and is an associate member in training functions in the Uruguayan Psychoanalytic Association. She was a member of the Board of Directors of the Uruguayan Psychoanalytic Association 2008–2010, and Director of the Exchange Center of the Uruguayan Psychoanalytic Association 2008–2010. She is a training analyst at the Latin American Institute of Psychoanalysis (ILAP) FEPAL – IPA, and was President of the Latin American Federation of Analytic Psychotherapy of Groups (FLAPAG) 2001–2009. She is a postgraduate in family, couple and group psychoanalysis.

**Marvin Hurvich**, PhD, is a recently retired professor and past Chair, Department of Psychology, LIU, a member of the faculty and training/supervisory psychoanalyst at IPTAR, NYU P-D, and the Contemporary Freudian Society. Diplomate in Psychoanalysis, ABPP, IPA Fellow, and member of the Clinical Observation Project Group. He is a member of the PDM Task Force Adult SX Group, and is the author of over forty publications, including *Ego Functions in Schizophrenics, Neurotics and Normals* (Wiley, 1973), with Bellak and Gediman. Most recent publications are a chapter, "New developments in the theory and clinical application of the annihilation anxiety concept, in *A New Freudian Synthesis*, edited by Druck, Ellman, Freedman, and Thaler (Karnac, 2011), and a co-authored book, *Another Kind of Evidence*, by Freedman, Hurvich, and Ward (Karnac, 2011).

**Judy L. Kantrowitz**, PhD, is a clinical associate professor at Harvard Medical School, and a training and supervising analyst at Boston Psychoanalytic Institute. She is the author of two books, *The Patient's Impact on the Analyst*, and *Writing about Patients: Responsibilities, Risks, and Ramifications*, and papers on the patient–analyst match and outcome of psychoanalysis and others on impasses in analysis. She has served three times on the Editorial Boards of *JAPA* and is currently on the board of the *Psychoanalytic Quarterly*. Her latest book is *Myths of Termination: What Patients Can Teach Psychoanalysts about Endings* (2014).

**Adela Leibovich de Duarte**, PhD (New York University, 1972), is Professor Emerita (since 2007), Facultad de Psicología, Universidad de Buenos Aires; a training analyst (since 2000), and past President (2003–2005) of the Sociedad Argentina de Psicoanálisis (Argentine Psychoanalytic Society) and Honorary Member (since 2012) of the Asociación Psicoanalítica de Buenos Aires (Buenos Aires Psychoanalytic Association). She is Co-chair of the IPA Psychoanalysis and University Committee (since 2012). She is a member of the IPA Project Committee on Clinical Observation (since 2013); of the IPA Committee on Evaluation of Research Proposals (since 2010); of the FEPAL Professional Committee (since 2012), and of the Society for Psychotherapy Research, Research Grant Awards Committee, (since 2012). She was the recipient of the 1973 Founders Day Award from New York University, of the 2007 Psychoanalytic Research Exceptional Contributions Award from the International Psychoanalytical Association, and of the 2010 Poster Award, II Congreso Internacional de Investigación y Práctica Profesional en Psicología, Buenos Aires. Her publications include book chapters and papers in both Spanish and English. Her research interests focus mainly on the clinical inferential process.

**Marianne Leuzinger-Bohleber**, Prof. Dr. Phil., is Director of the Sigmund-Freud-Institut in Frankfurt am Main, Germany, and a professor of psychoanalysis at the University of Kassel. She is a training analyst of the German Psychoanalytical Association and member of the Swiss Psychoanalytical Society and the International Psychoanalytical Association. She was Chair of the Research Subcommittees for Conceptual Research of the Internationalen Psychoanalytischen Vereinigung (IPA) (2001–2009, and, since 2010, is Vice Chair of the Research Board of the IPA. She is a Visiting Professor of the University College London, and a member of the "Action Group" of the Society for Neuropsychoanalysis. Her research fields are clinical and extra-clinical research in psychoanalysis, psychoanalytical developmental research, prevention studies, interdisciplinary dialogue between psychoanalysis and literature, educational sciences, and neurosciences. She has been a member of the Clinical Observation Committee of the International Psychoanalytical Association since 2009.

**Delfina Miller**, PhD, is Director of the Department of Clinical and Health Psychology, Academic Coordinator of the Postgraduate and Master Course in Child and Adolescent Clinical Psychology, Professor of Psychopathology, Diagnosis and Psychotherapeutic Interventions at the Catholic University of Uruguay, Tutoring Director of final dissertations of Master and Licenciate degrees, and consulting technician of the Culture and Education Ministry of Uruguay. She was awarded "Best research paper on depression" of the International Psychoanalytical Society (2013) and also won the "Best Academic Paper" award, Catholic University (2010, 2012). She is a researcher on child affective regulation, and a psychoanalytic therapist and supervisor.

**Michael Šebek**, PhD, CSc, is a clinical psychologist and senior lecturer at the second faculty of medicine at Charles University, Prague, Department of Medical Ethics and Human Studies in Medicine. He is a training and supervising analyst at the Czech Psychoanalytic Society, and has twice been elected as its president. He is the Director of the Psychoanalytic Institute of the Czech Psychoanalytical Society (since 2012). He was, in 2000–2002, the Secretary of the IPA President (D. Widlocher) for Europe. From 1993 to 2010, he was a member of the International Board of the US journal *Psychoanalytic Inquiry*. In 1999, he was Erikson Scholar of the Erikson Institute of the Austen Riggs Center in Stockbridge, MA. Since 1995, he has been involved in the training activities for the Han Groen Prakken Institute for Eastern Europe.

**Virginia Ungar**, MD, is a full member and training analyst at the Buenos Aires Psychoanalytical Association. She is a specialist in child and adolescent psychoanalysis. She also teaches at the University Institute of Mental Health of Buenos Aires Psychoanalytical Association and on the Post-Graduate Course on Child and Adolescent Psychoanalysis at the Buenos Aires University (Argentina). She is also member of Faculty of the Psychoanalytic Institute of Northern California (PINC), and of the International Institute for Psychoanalytic Training (IIPT). She has also taught in Porto Alegre, Brazil, and in Santiago, Chile. She has been teaching the Infant Observation seminars on Esther Bick–Tavistock Clinic Method for the last fifteen years. She has published numerous papers in journals and chapters in some books. She was a former Latin American Representative on the Board and the Executive Committee of the IPA (2005–2009), member of the IPA Clinical Observation Project group (2009–2013) and the former Chair and current consultant on the Committee of Child and Adolescent Psychoanalysis of the IPA (COCAP). She is Chair of the IPA Integrated Training Committee, and member of the Latin American Board of the *International Journal of Psychoanalysis*.

**Robert White** is a member of the faculty of the Western New England Psychoanalytic Institute in the state of Connecticut, USA. He is a founding member of the North American Clinical Comparative Method Working Party. In the past year, he has joined the North American Clinical Observation group. He is a former associate editor for *JAPA* and has published papers and book chapters in the areas of Bion studies and intersubjectivity. In his local society, he chairs the psychotherapy training programme and teaches in the psychiatry training programme at Yale University.

## *IPA PROJECT COMMITTEE ON CLINICAL OBSERVATION AND TESTING*

Members (in alphabetical order):

Altmann de Litvan, Marina (Chair)
Bernardi, Ricardo
Fitzpatrick-Hanly, Margaret Ann
Glover, William
Gullestad, Siri
Hurvich, Marvin*
Leibovich de Duarte, Adela*
Leuzinger-Bohleber, Marianne
Ungar, Virginia*

*Hurvich, Marvin: Member 2009–2013. Consultant since 2014.

Leibovich de Duarte, Adela: Chair 2009–2010. Consultant 2011–2013. Member since 2014.

Ungar, Virginia: Member 2009–2013.

# *SERIES EDITOR'S FOREWORD*

The Publications Committee of the International Psychoanalytical Association continues, with this volume, the series "Psychoanalytic Ideas and Applications".

The aim of this series is to focus on the scientific production of significant authors whose works are outstanding contributions to the development of the psychoanalytic field and to set out relevant ideas and themes, generated during the history of psychoanalysis, that deserve to be known and discussed by present psychoanalysts.

The relationship between psychoanalytic ideas and their applications has to be put forward from the perspective of theory, clinical practice, technique, and research, so as to maintain their validity for contemporary psychoanalysis.

The Publications Committee's objective is to share these ideas with the psychoanalytic community and with professionals in other related disciplines, in order to expand their knowledge and generate a productive interchange between the text and the reader.

*Time for Change. Tracking Transformations in Psychoanalysis—The Three-Level Model*, edited by Marina Altmann de Litvan, is a multi-authored book which summarises the work of the Clinical Observation Committee of the International Psychoanalytic Association carried out between 2009 and 2013. It represents the fruit of a research work on transformations in psychoanalysis and tries to improve clinical observation of changes in psychoanalysis, comparing, by means of a strict methodology based on the "three-level model", the different points of view of one group of psychoanalysts from all over the world and from different psychoanalytical cultures and backgrounds. The volume explores this interesting subject from both theoretical and clinical points of view, thus providing readers interested in the methodology of research in psychoanalysis with the results of an excellent work in this difficult field.

Special thanks are, therefore, due to the editor and to all the contributors to this volume, which enriches our "Psychoanalytic Ideas and Applications" series.

Gennaro Saragnano
Series Editor
Chair, IPA Publications Committee

# *FOREWORD*

## *Charles Hanly*

When, at the Chicago Congress, I devoted my IPA presidency to validating and strengthening confidence in clinical observation as the primary source of psychoanalytic knowledge, I did not dare to hope that as much could be accomplished as has been towards this end by the dedicated colleagues who took up the challenge. It is these colleagues who have developed a methodology, created IPA Work Groups on clinical observation, and have put together this important book.

For some time, it had been my view that many analysts had become despondent about clinical psychoanalysis and its evidential value for theory building. One factor in this despondency has been the difficulty analysts have been having in finding patients. Another factor has been the postmodern epistemological critiques of the objectivity of psychoanalytic clinical observation, which have implicitly called into question the evidential reliability of clinical psychoanalysis by announcing its irremediable subjectivity (Hanly, 1995, 1999; Hanly & Hanly, 2001). In order to address this situation, I thought that it would be useful to create opportunities for colleagues, including colleagues of different theoretical and technical orientations, to explore together the reliability of psychoanalytic clinical processes and the observations on which interpretations are based. If interpretations bear the crucial part of the burden of therapeutic benefit (or the absence thereof) (Hanly, 1994), then interpretations and the observations of the analytic process on which they are based form the bedrock of psychoanalytic therapy. If so, then the observation of what happens in the analytic process after interpretations are made is essential to evaluating the therapeutic efficacy (or inefficacy) of interpretations. Only in this way can the soundness of interpretations be evaluated. Using observation of the analytic process in this way is an essential part of the evaluations analysts make of their ongoing clinical work. Groups of analysts conducting enquiries into the clinical work of colleagues could provide useful knowledge of how psychoanalysis works. These enquiries would be in a position to investigate, for example, the assumption concerning the therapeutic role of interpretation that forms one premise of the argument I have just elaborated. Such enquiries need to be "open" and without adherence to unquestionable orthodoxies.

The task was entrusted to a Project Committee on Clinical Observation and Testing, which received IPA Board authorisation at the Chicago Congress. The committee took up the challenge of developing and testing a methodology that groups of analysts in our component societies could use to carry out clinical enquiries of this kind. One could characterise their work as a "Freudian return to Freud". It is a return to Freud in the sense that the crucial step in Freud's discovery of infantile sexuality and unconscious phantasy was the clinical observations that revealed to him the inadequacy of his seduction theory. Freud used clinical observation to test the validity of the seduction theory and to discover how he needed to modify it (1) to account for what he was observing in his patients and (2) to fit the interpretations and technique he was using to help them heal. This return to Freud is also itself Freudian because the methodology it employs is only as good as it is useful; it invites evaluation and improvement. To be sure, Freud is often enough seen as a somewhat popish authority, sometimes reviled and sometimes venerated, but Freud, for the most part, relied upon the authority of observed clinical fact as the basis for psychoanalytic knowledge. This basic epistemological point is one that Kleinian analysts such as Britton (2004), Britton and Steiner (1994), Feldman (1993), Segal (1994), and Etchegoyen (1996, 2004) share with Freudian analysts. It is this spirit that has guided the work of the Committee on Clinical Observation.

The task is not made easier by the prevalence of alternative theories. However, it is not so much the alternative theories, as such, as it is the epistemological idea that experience and, hence, psychoanalytic clinical observation is invariably compromised by the ideas, values, and beliefs we bring to it. Indeed, even if our ordinary everyday experience might not always depend upon ideas, clinical observation does require ideas that provide focus, ideas that are treated as hunches and remain open to correction by clinical observation. These clinical formulations are no different than the ideas that guide scientific observation generally, for example, the ideas that led Harvey to the experiments that proved the continuity and circularity of the system of veins and arteries in mammals. Further entrenching and logically elaborating this subjectivist epistemological idea is the notion of co-creation: that is, that the observing analyst inescapably influences the affects and narratives of the patient's associations, including dreams reported in analysis, thus creating a version of his symptoms and their origins in his/her life peculiar to any given analytic dyad. The same would be true for transferences. This questioning of the objectivity of clinical observation (the intersubjectivity of clinical observation in the common sense and scientific meaning of the term) has had a long history, beginning with the problem of suggestion. Freud (1916–1917, 1923c, 1937d) had already raised and discussed these epistemological questions. By bringing analysts of different theoretical and technical persuasions to study and discuss clinical process notes, the IPA Work Groups on Clinical Observation are designed to test the extent to which theoretical and technical persuasions compromise clinical observation. What happens in the work of the Work Groups will bear evidentially on an important epistemological controversy in contemporary psychoanalysis that needs to be resolved experientially and technically as well as philosophically (Hanly & Hanly, 2001). Are there facts about an analytic process that bear on questions of interpretation, theory, and technique upon which adequately trained analysts can agree despite theoretical and technical differences among the discussants and the presenters of clinical cases?

The Project Committee on Clinical Observation and Testing's methodology focuses primarily on change or transformation in the patient in the course of an analysis. Of course, changes/transformations in the functioning of a patient involve somewhat complex processes developing over time; they include changes that occur in the dynamics of the analytic work itself which have a potential for beneficial or adverse changes in the conflicts that cause symptoms and inhibitions, for example, changes in dream patterns, changes in the transference, including such developments as "transference cures", and shifts in the working alliance. By beginning with a diagnostically sound description of the patient's symptoms and inhibitions prior to analysis, the Work Groups can establish a bench mark against which estimations of functional improvements, lack of improvements, and deteriorations can be made with a reasonable and useful degree of ordinal accuracy, as in the following description: the patient's obsessional anxiety, which had prohibited his use of a public urinal, has abated. He is able to use public urinals, although he still has to take special care in washing his hands even when using his own toilet without which he remains somewhat worried about infections. The fate of this residue of anxiety can be detected in later segments of the analysis. The observation of the causes can be detected in the details of the process and the responses of the patient to the interpretations of transference and associations as they develop. These observations, in the long run, open up the prospect of an evidential clinical basis for evaluating interpretations and the theories they imply. This type of enquiry promises to be able to realise the three objectives of the formation of IPA Work Groups on Clinical Observation: (1) to provide opportunities for on-going professional development; (2) to enable clinical and theoretical enquiries; (3) to foster publications when warranted by results.

From a semantic point of view "change" and "transformation" are used interchangeably in naming and describing the object of this enquiry. Neither of the terms includes the extreme meanings attached to "transformation" in English, for example, "transubstantiation", as in the transformation of wine and bread into the blood and body of Jesus, or "denature", cited as synonym and antonym for "transformation", which is itself acknowledged to be a synonym for "change" (*Roget's Thesaurus*, 1961). In English, the ancient animistic idealism of Platonic and Aristotelian metaphysics still cause "substance" and "nature" to cling associatively to certain compound words using the word "form". In this context, "transformation" does not have these associative connotations. "Transformation" and "beneficial change" would identically apply to the reduction of severely inhibiting obsessional anxieties, as in a patient who once again was able to drive his car with only ordinary caution and courtesy for other drivers after having had to give up driving altogether, at great inconvenience to himself, because of anxiety about causing an accident (although earlier symptoms about checking his stove and locking the door of his condo remained in a greatly attenuated form at the level of the psychopathology of everyday life). Symptom and inhibition amelioration need not be total in order to qualify as a "transformation".

The focus on change (transformation) has a further potential long-term benefit for psychoanalysis. Given the diagnostically sound benchmark at the beginning of an analysis (which could be rendered additionally convincing by employing a competent diagnostician to make an independent diagnosis), and given the detailed study of portions of clinical material over the course of the analysis, the Work Groups on Clinical Observation offer a way of providing an evidential basis for gauging the efficacy of psychoanalytic treatment. If one or more IPA Work Groups using similar methods were formed in numerous component societies of the IPA, then their data could be used for large-scale studies of the efficacy of psychoanalysis supplemented with neutral party reliability checks at a cost that could be within reach of the IPA. Other studies also become possible using this methodology or adaptations of it, for example, the study of the efficacy of telephone or Skype analysis by comparing initial periods of "in the office" analysis followed by telephone or Skype analysis, the efficacy of frequency, the importance of endogenous as compared with exogenous causes of neurosis, etc.

For all of these reasons, this publication, focused on the methodology and first results of a method for enquiries in psychoanalytic process, merits your thoughtful attention. It is important to the continuity and advancement of psychoanalysis. It invites your study and your participation in this new psychoanalytic venture.

## References

Britton, R. (2004). Subjectivity, objectivity, and triangular space. *Psychoanalytic Quarterly, 73*: 47–61.

Britton, R., & Steiner, J. (1994). Interpretation: selected fact or overvalued idea? *International Joournal of Psychoanalysis, 75*: 1069–1078.

Etchegoyen, R. H. (1996). Some views on psychic reality. *International Journal of Psychoanalysis, 77*: 1–14.

Etchegoyen, R. H. (2004). *Epistemología y psicoanálisis* [Epistemology and psychoanalysis] by Gregorio Klimovsky Buenos Aires: Biebel. 2004. Vol. I: 313 pp; Vol. II: 316 pp. *International Journal of Psychoanalysis, 85*: 1291–1297.

Feldman, M. (1993). Aspects of reality, and the focus of interpretation. *Psychoanalytic Inquiry, 13*: 274–295.

Freud, S. (1916–1917). *Introductory Lectures on Psychoanalysis. S.E., 16.* London: Hogarth.

Freud, S. (1923c). Remarks on the theory and practice of dream-interpretation as a whole. *S.E., 19*: 109–124. London: Hogarth.

Freud, S. (1937d). Constructions in analysis. *S.E., 23*: 255–270. London: Hogarth.

Hanly, C. (1994). Reflections on the place of the therapeutic alliance in psychoanalysis. *International Journal of Psychoanalysis, 75*: 457–467.

Hanly, C. (1995). On facts and ideas in psychoanalysis. *International Journal of Psycho-Analysis, 76*: 901–908.

Hanly, C. (1999). On subjectivity and objectivity in psychoanalysis. *Journal of the American Psychoanalytic Association, 47*: 427–444.

Hanly, C., & Hanly, M. A. (2001). Critical realism: distinguishing the psychological subjectivity of the analyst from epistemological subjectivism. *Journal of the American Psychological Association, 47*: 515–533.

Roget, P. (1962). *Roget's International Thesaurus* (3rd edn). New York: Thomas Y. Cromwell.

Segal, H. (1994). Phantasy and reality. *International Journal of Psychoanalysis, 75*: 395–401.

# Introduction

*Marina Altmann de Litvan*

The richness of the work with patients and the importance we have attributed to clinical material as a source of knowledge since the birth of psychoanalysis as such are unquestionable for psychoanalysts. Nevertheless, we need to explain how transformations are produced in our practice, a process that may seem quasi-magical and is difficult to show to the non-specialist. This feature has posed obstacles to the acknowledgement of the scientific status of psychoanalysis, an issue that has been extensively discussed in the literature produced both within and outside the psychoanalytic community.

A problem for psychoanalysis is that, unfortunately, the quality of observations is often lacking. For instance, the clinical material is not described in sufficient detail, not enough information is provided about the context of this material (e.g., phase of treatment, diagnostic considerations), or there is no reflection on potential distortions in its description (produced by scotomisations of the author's perception, such as those due to projection or to countertransference reactions). Analytic narratives are constructed according to latent psychodynamic presumptions, and it is often impossible to recognise the analyst's contribution; only a few interpretations are selectively described, and there is no way to know what has been omitted.

Over the past years, great efforts have been made to understand analysts' implicit theories and the different ways of treating patients that may be found in different psychoanalytic cultures (Canestri, 2006; Tuckett, 2008), thereby building bridges and developing understanding among psychoanalysts of different schools and orientations (e.g., the EPF working parties).

Promoting transformation in our patients (by way of therapeutic action leading to changes in their inner world) is a goal shared by all psychoanalysts. The illustration of transformation processes should, thus, be a priority in clinical writing. Therefore, qualified documentation and communication of such processes in various patients and groups of patients remain major aims of clinical psychoanalytic papers. Knowledge about transformation processes experienced by patients in psychoanalysis is critical to achieving progress in our field (internal document written by the committee, Copenhagen, April 2011). The quality of clinical observations may be improved. We are convinced that a careful study of the exchange between patient and psychoanalyst is essential to advance psychoanalysis and foster a dialogue with other disciplines.

The IPA Project Committee on Clinical Observation and Testing is part of the New Scientific Initiatives promoted by IPA President Charles Hanly as an attempt to "address some of the significant challenges of psychoanalysis which we have talked of and written about at great length over many years" (Hanly, 2010, IPA website). The aim of the Committee has been to refine the criteria for reliable clinical observations made over the course of clinical work. In our meeting in Copenhagen on 17 April 2011, committee members agreed on the following goal: "to make a contribution to the improvement of clinical observation, its documentation and its communication by clinical papers or other forms of sharing clinical insights".

Our committee saw the need to work with what was happening to a particular patient with a particular analyst in the context of their work, taking as a reference not ideal theoretical models, but what takes place in real practice. The three-level model for observing patient transformations was developed with the following challenges in mind: assessing transformations, focusing on the patient, looking at what happens to analyst and patient from a close perspective, and refining clinical observation and communication.

The model centres on patients as persons in their context. We ask once again, along with the analyst, what was the reason that brought them to analysis, and we ask ourselves how and in which ways patients' answers were heard and explored at different moments of their analysis. While working with this model, we have faced both actual problems posed by patients in analysis and the difficulties encountered by analysts while performing their work. We have also shown analysts' willingness to share this work with others so that the group could develop alternative hypotheses based on the analytic process.

Group work following the model leads participants to analyse and to deconstruct this particular and unique analyst–patient relationship through different lenses. We deconstruct the clinical material so as to reconstruct it in our minds. Transformations are observed in various specific dimensions, a procedure that allows analysts to identify precisely what changes have or have not occurred.

Psychoanalytic literature often shows different moments of change and develops different hypotheses about this change, but we still know little about its impact throughout the analysis and over the course of patients' lifetimes. The three-level model seeks to acknowledge the richness of clinical experience by considering conflicts, defences, the transference, and other aspects that influence the context of the analysis (such as changes related to developmental factors, somatic illnesses, medication, and acute or chronic stressors or traumatic situations), as well as patients' ability to cope with them.

As we are well aware, clinical observations are never independent of the concepts and theories "in the back of the analyst's mind". The strategy we have developed helps analysts examine the explicit and implicit theories they have applied with patients and consider if other approaches would be better to promote patients' transformations of the aspects that are worked on in analysis.

With the three-level model, the group of analysts discussing the clinical material acts as a "consensus of experts" that validates or not the analyst's observations and systematically documents convergences and divergences with clinical observation (method developed in the DPV follow-up study; see Leuzinger-Bohleber et al., 2010). Thanks to the discussion of a clinical material with other analysts, we transcend the individual realm. Other listeners appear who confirm or contradict our hypotheses, thus providing different perspectives on the material.

The work we have developed has proved to be very useful for many reasons. First, it fosters the presenter's (the analyst's) thoughtful consideration of the patient and the analytic process. Second, it offers a "second look" at the process itself, allowing us to find blind spots, successes, and mistakes in our work as analysts. Finally, it creates a space to share different theoretical approaches in a manner that feels comfortable and provides a good opportunity for open discussion.

More than 600 analysts have already participated in groups working with this model in many cities in different regions: Buenos Aires, Mendoza, Sao Paulo, Pelotas, Campo Grande, Lima, Montevideo, New York, San Francisco, Toronto, Frankfurt, Tel Aviv, and Prague. Group discussions evince diverse ways of applying the model regarding participants' interests, geographical contexts, cultural backgrounds, and so on. We believe that such diversity, made possible by its flexibility, is one of the model's strengths. We would like to share our experience through this book.

Every chapter is the result of an ongoing process; the three-level model, as well as the group work it promotes, is constantly improving. Without downplaying this vitality, I can state that this publication gathers the most important aspects of our work. It is my wish and that of all committee members to offer readers a way to apprehend an issue that, despite its significance for psychoanalysis, is seldom discussed in the current literature.

In the first part of the book, "Introducing the three-level model for observing patient transformations", Ricardo Bernardi presents in Chapter One, titled "The three-level model for observing patient transformations (3-LM)", the model he developed in the IPA Project Committee on Clinical Observation and Testing. This instrument, critical to the Committee's work, aims to enhance and refine clinical observation and the description of transformations that occur during lengthy periods of analysis or over the course of a complete treatment by examining the clinical material from diverse angles or perspectives. In his chapter, Bernardi describes each of the three levels, illustrating the specific questions asked by the model with clinical material and the results of group discussion. He also addresses the 3-LM's difficulties and limitations as well as its potential for development, underlining the great theoretical and practical importance of a refined description of clinical changes for psychoanalysis.

The patient presented by Bernardi was in an ongoing analytic treatment, and the same group discussed clinical material from this patient a year later. In her chapter, "Leticia one year later: the emergence of questions about herself", the analyst Silvana Hernández shows how the 3-LM and group discussion helped her to work with a difficult patient.

Chapter Three, "Irina. Usefulness of the three-level model for observing patient transformations", gives an account of the first clinical material examined by the Clinical Observation Committee using the 3-LM. This discussion served the group to test and discuss the questions and dimensions proposed in an attempt to see how the analyst's mind identifies the different motivations that bring a patient to therapy, how the analyst understands what happens in the transference and countertransference relationship during the analytic process, and how all these issues bring about positive changes, negative changes, or no change at all.

The second part, "Observing and working with the 3-LM", begins with Chapter Four, "Tracking patient transformations: the function of observation in psychoanalysis", by Virginia Ungar and Margaret Ann Fitzpatrick-Hanly. The authors study the potential use of observation to track transformations experienced by a patient during a psychoanalytic or psychotherapeutic treatment. Anchor points can be thought of as "starting points" (often presented in the patient's words) that condense complex problems in the patient's psychic functioning. When no transformations are observed, anchor points (symptoms, inhibitions, or anxieties) can reflect those aspects of the patient's dynamics and the analytic process that are the hardest to change. Analysts in the Work Groups implementing the 3-LM can return to the hypotheses about core problems that are explicit or implicit in these points, moving back and forth between earlier and later sessions. Reflecting on anchor points serves to further understand their dynamic meanings and their vicissitudes in the later phases of the analysis.

In her chapter, "Depression and trauma. The psychoanalysis of a patient suffering from chronic depression: an exemplary case study based on the three levels of clinical observation" Marianne Leuzinger-Bohleber explains how the 3-LM, and the steps proposed to work with it, can be articulated with the "psychoanalytical expert validation" method applied in the ongoing LAC Depression Study (see, among others, Fischmann, Russ, & Leuzinger-Bohleber, 2013; Leuzinger-Bohleber & Teising, 2012; Leuzinger-Bohleber, Engels, & Tsiantis, 2008). The three levels of the model were used to support reflection on the analysand's transformation processes, focusing on a specific topic to write up the case, and resort to group members' views as "psychoanalytic expert validation" to cope productively with one's own blind spots.

Chapter Six, "Close-to observation: some reflections on the value of the three-level model for observing patient transformation to study change", by Siri Gullestad, recalls Freud's dictum concerning the need to adopt a principled attitude towards psychoanalysis as a discipline, and offers a research approach characterised by openness, flexibility, and fundamental respect for unbiased observation. In this way, the author establishes that theory is the servant of clinical practice. She underscores the widespread tendency to ignore questions related to the validity of our clinical observations and of clarifying the distinction between observation and conceptualisation. In addition, Gullestad points to the relevance of argumentation to documenting clinical papers and comments on Marianne Leuzinger-Bohleber's clinical case.

In Chapter Seven, "Working with the third level of the three-level model. The incidence of our theoretical model on our clinical thinking", Adela Leibovich de Duarte brings up the inferences stemming from the discussion of a case based on the model, a case that is presented in this book in Chapter Three. The author refers to the different explanatory hypotheses regarding transformations that the group developed after having addressed different markers of change in Levels 1 and 2, including the analyst's explicit and implicit theories as well as alternative hypotheses. We need certain dimensions to describe changes and transformations because the abstraction of metapsychological concepts may lead us to use the same theoretical terms to describe diverse clinical phenomena or to ascribe different names to the same clinical facts.

In Chapter Eight, "A traumatised patient in analysis: observing patient transformations", Margaret Ann Fitzpatrick-Hanly presents a traumatised patient who suffered psychotic episodes and several hospitalisations. The application of the three-level model to this clinical material was carried out simultaneously in two different IPA work groups—a group of training analysts, and a group of recently graduated analysts and senior candidates. Members of these two IPA

Work Groups came independently to very similar conclusions about kinds of change and absence of change in the patient and in the analytic process. One of the questions the groups discussed in greater depth was whether conflicts, which called for interpretations, or structural problems, which needed other kinds of interventions, were predominant.

In Part IV, "The 3-LM: a case, report, and discussion" shows the process of the discussion of a clinical case. It describes the presentation by the analyst and the working group's report, and adds a fruitful discussion by Judy Kantrowitz.

Chapter Nine, "Transformations in Paula with 'no history'", by Michael Šebek, shows the psychoanalytic process at different stages: the first interviews, and after eight months, sixteen months, and three years of treatment. The difficulties experienced by the analyst during this process are narrated in an honest way. Moreover, we can feel the wall behind which the patient is hiding in the analyst's words, and the latter's commitment to help her; we can see how the patient's feelings, memories, and thoughts start emerging. Then the author comments on the analysis of the case by means of the 3-LM conducted by Clinical Observation Committee members at the 48th IPA Congress and on the major conclusions of group discussion reports. This is followed by Robert White's account of this discussion (Chapter Ten) to inform readers and to show how group discussions are summarised when implementing the model.

White describes participants' exchanges in each level. In Level 1, the first task of the group is to choose anchor points. These are phenomenological descriptions of key aspects of the patient's personality or behaviour that can be tracked over time. In Level 2, the group analyses changes in the patient according to diagnostic dimensions described in a language close to experience and theoretically unsaturated. Given the group's time constraints, participants choose to concentrate on those dimensions that seem more relevant to that particular clinical case. Finally, the report presents the group's debate of Level 3, "Explanatory hypotheses of change".

Judy Kantrowitz thoroughly discusses the clinical material presented by Michael Šebek and its analysis at the 48th IPA Congress. The author stresses very important issues that the 3-LM aims to assess. She begins by addressing the project and the model, stating that tracking transformations in psychoanalysis is a method that can systematically trace change. The model expects us to conceptualise the problem from the standpoint of each patient. What is the patient struggling with? This question is not posed at a theoretical level, but, rather, at the level of observed phenomena. The patient is his or her own baseline. The model asks us to avoid jargon and document our perceptions with data from the sessions. Then Kantrowitz highlights the analysis of Michael Šebek's case done by Bernardi, Fitzpatrick-Hanly, and Leuzinger-Bohleber to illustrate the process, and closes with her own observations.

Part V, "Clinical concepts", presents two chapters reflecting on important aspects of the 3-LM. These aspects are clinical observations and generalisations, and the assessment of change.

In his chapter, "Some reflections on the three-level model: organising psychoanalytic knowledge through clinical observations and generalisations", Marvin Hurvich highlights an important question: how the 3-LM findings are organised, and how this organisation relates to methodological issues, especially reliability and validity.

Ricardo Bernardi's chapter, "The assessment of changes: diagnostic aspects", analyses the relationship between diagnosis and psychoanalysis and stresses the relevance of diagnostic categories to track changes in patients over the course of the psychoanalytic process. The author discusses the need for operational definitions and theoretical content, and how this issue was tackled in the design of the 3-LM.

Part VI, "An application of the 3-LM at the end of analytic training", addresses two implementations of the 3-LM in analytic training. In their chapter, "The three-level model in psychoanalytic training" Beatriz de León de Bernardi and Marina Altmann de Litvan recount an experience of partial application of this model in the field of psychoanalytic training. In Chapter Fifteen, "The use of the 3-LM to teach candidates to observe transformations in clinical cases", Liliana Fudim and Adela Leibovich de Duarte narrate their training experience at the Argentine Psychoanalytic Society (SAP).

In Part VII, "Further developments of the 3-LM in child analysis", Marina Altmann de Litvan, Delfina Miller, and Ricardo Bernardi developed an application of the model for children taking specifically those aspects that clearly differentiate child analysis, presented in Chapter Sixteen. The child analyst works not only with the reconstruction supported by regression and analysis of conflict, but also with the construction of a psychism and certain patterns of development which are influenced by external and internal factors and that, simultaneously, interact with the dynamic unconscious. Family and school factors have an important role and the child's play is central, because it is a natural form of expression in the child as well as a privileged means of exchange with the analyst, where, through the display of desires, anxieties, phantasies, defences, and object relationships, the level of development, abilities, and organisation of personality can be evaluated. It is through play that growth and emotional development of the child is promoted.

In the Appendices, readers will find guidelines to start a clinical observation group, as well as an example of a report presented by William Glover. A list of suggested questions to work in the groups is proposed, and a survey to be completed before and after group discussions is included. Finally, you will find a listing of the clinical observation working groups made during years 2011–2013.

To conclude, I would like to ask the readers to linger for a moment over the title we have chosen for this book, as it denotes the relationship between the time-frame of the analytic process and the changes that patients achieve throughout this process. Usually, we observe different moments or sequences of change by looking at patients' responses to our interpretations during a session. With the three-level model, we seek to offer a longer view of the analytic process that focuses not only on the analyst's mind, but also on how that mind perceives the patient's needs and desires. This goal drove us to find dimensions in which we could track and compare modifications occurring at different stages of the analysis. Such dimensions were developed as comprehensive questions drafted in a language that remains close to experience. Questions are self-explanatory for all trained clinicians, regardless of their theoretical background.

The title also refers to the challenge faced nowadays by psychoanalysis as a discipline. We hope to contribute to a positive change that will help us focus and strengthen our work with our patients. If we cannot understand what is happening with our patients, we will not find answers to many of our questions. Understanding is the only way to respond to the following questions: what happens to patients in our practice? Why does it happen? How can we use our analytic tools to help them?

Psychoanalysis is an opportunity, a possibility to relieve human pain. If we avoid the real challenges, we will fail in our purpose to address human problems and suffering and help patients improve their lives.

## *References*

Canestri, J. (2006). Implicit understanding of clinical material beyond theory. In: J. Canestri (Ed.), *Psychoanalysis. From Practice to Theory* (pp. 13–28). Chichester: John Wiley.

Fischmann, T., Russ, M., & Leuzinger-Bohleber, M. (2013). Trauma, dream and psychic change in psychoanalysis. A dialog between psychoanalysis and the neurosciences. *Frontiers in Human Neuroscience, 7*: 1–15.

Hanly, C. (2010). From the President. Furthering Freud's Dream. *International Psychoanalysis, the News Magazine of the IPA, Centenary Special Edition, 18.*

Leuzinger-Bohleber, M., & Teising, M. (2012). "Without being in psychoanalysis I would never have dared to become pregnant": psychoanalytical observations in a multidisciplinary study concerning a woman undergoing prenatal diagnostics. *International Journal of Psychoanalysis, 93*: 293–315.

Leuzinger-Bohleber, M., Bahrke, U., Beutel, M., Deserno, H., Edinger, J., Fiedler, G., Haselbacher, A., Hautzinger, M., Kallenbach, L., Keller, W., Negele, A., Pfenning-Meerkötter, N., Prestele, H., Strecker-von Kannen, T., Stuhr, U., & Will, A. (2010). Psychoanalytische und kognitivverhaltenstherapeutische Langzeittherapien bei chronischer Depression: Die LAC-Depressionstudie. *Psyche-Z Psychonal., 64*: 782–832.

Leuzinger-Bohleber, M., Engels, E. M., & Tsiantis, J. (Eds.) (2008). *The Janus Face of Prenatal Diagnostics: A European Study Bridging Ethics, Psychoanalysis, and Medicine.* London: Karnac.

Tuckett, D. (Ed.) (2008). *Psychoanalysis Comparable and Incomparable: The Evolution of a Method to Describe and Compare Psychoanalytic Approaches.* London: Routledge.

# PART I

# INTRODUCING THE THREE-LEVEL MODEL FOR OBSERVING PATIENT TRANSFORMATIONS

CHAPTER ONE

# The three-level model (3-LM) for observing patient transformations

*Ricardo Bernardi*

## *Introduction*

The description of the transformations or changes that occur in patients over the course of their analysis is of great theoretical and practical importance. A guide or heuristic is proposed below for observing and describing these changes, using three successive levels of analysis and named, for this reason, "three-level model for observing patient transformations" (3-LM). Each of these levels, which will be described in this paper, suggest specific questions, which are intended to serve as a guide for group discussion or for the analyst's personal reflection. From the heuristic point of view, the 3-LM is expected to enhance and refine the clinical observation and description of transformations that occur during lengthy periods of analysis, or through a complete treatment.

A wider and more detailed description of patient transformations offers a better basis for understanding the analytic process and its mechanisms of change. The word "process" refers to a succession of states whose transformations or changes will be better identified and understood the longer the time and the wider the context taken into account. Analytical papers frequently study in depth especially meaningful moments of analysis. This inescapable perspective could usefully be complemented by the clinical observation of patient changes over prolonged periods of time, to which less attention has been paid in the literature. Psychoanalysis owns conceptual and clinical tools to envisage these kinds of descriptions, but it is not easy to integrate them because they belong to diverse and sometimes conflicting theoretical and technical points of view. However, when core aspects of these concepts are put together in a complex and coherent way, the result is highly challenging and enriching. This chapter examines and discusses the concepts that are most useful to answer the key questions: to what extent has the patient clinically improved (or worsened) during analysis? What are the main dimensions of the changes and what are the hypotheses that can best explain them?

The changes psychoanalysis aims for are still subject to the polarities, oscillations, and paradoxes that were described decades ago by Wallerstein (1965):

> The first seeming paradox is that between goallessness (or desirelessness) as a technical tool marking the proper therapeutic posture of analytic work and the fact that psychoanalysis differentiates itself from all other psychotherapies, analytically oriented or not, by positing the most ambitious and far-reaching goals in terms of the possibilities of fundamental personality reorganization. (p. 749)

The second paradox was, in Wallerstein's opinion, between the goals observed at a clinical level and their diverse metapsychological conceptualisations. The third paradox concerned whether an optimistic or pessimistic position was adopted regarding the degree of change achieved (p. 765). In the years that have followed Wallerstein's analysis, diverse ideal models of psychoanalytic process have been consolidated, based on the works of influential authors (Klein, Bion, Winnicott, Lacan, and Kohut, among others) whose descriptions acquired a paradigmatic value; as a result, the discussion of patient transformations has become more complex and too often theory-driven (Bernardi, 2001). Today, it is not simple to determine to what degree these different theoretical approaches are coincidental, contradictory, or complementary, or if they are incommensurable because they refer to different aspects of clinical facts (Bernardi, 1989, 1992). In addition, it is not easy to know whether the degree of the analyst's adherence to one or another of these different models really leads to different effects on the patient. This situation suggests not only the necessity for a more detailed and systematic investigation of the relationship between the analytic process and the changes that occur in the patient, but also argue for the use of a different, though complementary, perspective. Bleger rightly stated that what really matters is to be able to establish the aims of psychoanalysis based on its results in practice and not from previous formulations of a theoretical and normative nature (1973). He highlights that "a patient finishes his analysis with success in conditions that another patient may start it". As a consequence, the central question is no longer a prescriptive one—how an analysis has to be—but rather a factual one: what effects does analysis produce in the analysts' real practice? This is the perspective adopted by the 3-LM, hoping that a better description of patient changes could give more information for discussing what specific analytic process is associated with what changes in which kinds of patient.

The study of transformations of the patient currently has two wide avenues available for its progress: clinical observation and systematic empirical research of processes and results. Empirical research has provided firm evidence in favour of the effectiveness of psychoanalytical treatments (Fonagy & Target, 1994, 1996; Fonagy, Roth, & Higgitt, 2005; Leichsenring, 2009; Leuzinger-Bohleber, Stuhrast, Rüger, & Beutel, 2003; Sandell, 2012; Sandell et al., 2000; Shedler, 2010) and even result in changes in brain functioning (Beutel, Stark, Pan, Sibersweig, & Dietrich, 2010; Etkin, Phil, Pittenger, Polan, & Kandel, 2005). It has not yet succeeded, however, in convincing many clinicians that these results capture what is essential and specific about the psychoanalytical process (Eagle & Wolitzky, 2011; Hoffman, 2009; Walls, 2006).

Paradoxically, while systematic empirical research based on standardised instruments has been able to provide evidence of the effectiveness of psychoanalysis, there is still a lack of consensus regarding the best way to describe patient transformations over long periods of analysis. The challenge is to find concepts for describing long-term changes that, being fully psychoanalytic, at the same time reflect the meaningful changes that occur in the patient's life and in his/her mental and interpersonal functioning.

### *The three-level model (3-LM)*

The stimulus for the development of the 3-LM originated during Charles Hanly's presidency of a committee of the International Psychoanalytical Association (Project Committee on Clinical Observation, chaired by Marina Altmann de Litvan), which was asked to promote different modes of clinical observation. The 3-LM constitutes one of the proposals presented to the committee. This chapter essentially reflects the original proposal I submitted to the committee in May 2011. The committee developed this proposal and implemented group experiences applied in different regions and diverse psychoanalytic cultures (Altmann, 2013; Altmann, Fitzpatrick-Hanly, & Leuzinger-Bohleber, 2012a,b; Bernardi, 2013). The 3-LM as presented here reflects the core of the initial proposal and does not have an exhaustive or definite nature, since it is open to include modifications or new developments suggested from its application in diverse contexts and regions.

The 3-LM proposes to observe and analyse changes through three consecutive steps, each of which is based on the adoption of a specific point of view on the material. The first level adopts a phenomenological perspective and intends to describe the changes as they appear to the observer, whose observation is informed by his/her previous analytic experience. The second level intends a more precise description of several dimensions or categories that provide a more systematic profile of changes. In the third level, possible interpretations or explanatory hypotheses of these changes and their nature are examined, starting from the foci on which the analytical work was centred according to the analyst's explicit or implicit hypotheses. These hypotheses are then compared with alternative hypotheses that could arise from other clinical or theoretical approaches. These three levels are the three components of clinical judgement. However, the 3-LM model seeks to momentarily separate them in order to examine each of them more carefully.

The order of the levels purposely puts the phenomenological level in the first place of the discussion, aiming at carefully exploring and describing the phenomena before trying to explain them. Each level proposes the analysis of the observed changes from a specific and complementary angle. Discrepancies among levels are a signal that further analysis is required. The participants frequently need to move backward and forward among the levels, for example, returning to questions that have been discussed at level 1 or 2, when the discussion of the theoretical hypotheses at level 3 suggests new perspectives on the clinical material that calls for revising what has been previously discussed. The aim of moving back and forth is to refine clinical observation.

Freud (1914c, p. 77) stated that observation constitutes the foundation of psychoanalytic concepts, while theoretical notions of a speculative nature have to be substituted when new observations demand it. Today, we know that there are no theory-free observations, because our theoretical concepts shape the complex perceptual and inferential processes that lead us to clinical judgements (Leibovich de Duarte, 2000). The 3-LM invites analysts with different theoretical backgrounds to discuss together, illustrating how their theoretical assumptions inspire new ways of looking at the material. The aim is to strengthen a space of reflection and questioning in which the clinical observations may become, to a certain degree, autonomous, and even challenge the theoretical premises that shaped them. Put in another way, the aim is to distinguish the selected facts as clues or meaningful configurations emerging from the material, from other ideas, sometimes overvalued, that do not manage to shed light on the understanding of the material (Bion, 1967; Britton & Steiner, 1994). For that reason, the 3-LM aims to compare different moments of a treatment, continuously referring to the material, and using a clinical language close to experience that can be shared, or at least understood, by analysts with different theoretical approaches.

The use of a shared clinical language coincides with the suggestion of not losing sight of the experiential origin of analytic concepts (Bleger, 2012; Klein, 1976; Wallerstein, 1988). This does not mean adhering to a naïve realism or empiricism, but simply recognising that analysts from different traditions can indeed share clinical observations and they can also discuss to what extent their diverse theoretical hypotheses match or remain incompatible or insufficient (Bernardi, 1989). To become aware of the limits of our theoretical assumptions and to prevent hurried interpretations, the 3-LM proposes to come back again and again to the clinical material, looking for nuances that challenge our assumptions.

Although the 3-LM may be used for individual reflection, it is especially useful for group discussion. For that purpose, the IPA Committee on Clinical Observation designed a model to guide group discussions in which clinical material is examined in small groups for a prolonged time (ten or twelve hours). At the end of the meeting, a reporter summarises the discussion. The analyst is invited to present material from different periods of the analysis. The first interviews provide the anchor points whose transformations will be studied in at least two later moments of the analysis—months or, preferably, years later—which are supposed to provide the transformation points. The choice of the material, as well as the registration mode (notes or recordings) is left to the discretion of the analyst, who participates in the group discussions and may, if it is found useful, provide clarifying comments about the material. The experiences undergone with the 3-LM show a high degree of group consensus in the estimation of the changes in the patient, especially at the first and second levels. In some groups, participants were asked to fill out questionnaires before and after the group discussion in order to more precisely evaluate the degree of agreement among participants.

## *Observing the observations*

Participants of the 3-LM working groups make three kinds of observations. In the first place, they have what the patient perceives and says about him/herself. At the same time, they rely on the analyst's perception, enriched by his/her attitude of alert receptivity to the unconscious and intriguing aspects of the patient (Ungar et al., 2009). In the third place, they count on the observation of the participants of the group, including their own reactions and group manifestations such as parallel processes. All of them need to be listened to with the analytic "third ear", Reik's (1968) name for the instrument the analyst puts into play for his perception of unconscious communication, which reaches its greatest depth when the analyst can listen to his own voice in reaction to what the patient says. Certain psychoanalytical communications manage to reach the "third ear of the reader" (p. 18). This is the kind of listening that is sought in the working groups of the 3-LM.

Clinical reasoning is largely based upon the recognition of iterative patterns through a process that is difficult to trace and reproduce (Leibovich de Duarte, 2004; Ridderikhoff, 1993; Shedler & Westen, 2004). Clinical intuition, as it goes from the known singular to the unknown singular, is similar to Pierce's abduction (Hoffmann, 2005;

Leibovich de Duarte, 2010) and it opens the way to later inductive and deductive reasoning. In psychoanalysis, observations are made from the particular subjectivity of each observer. In this aspect, it differs from systematic empirical research, which aspires to a greater control of the subjective variables, even in the simple case studies. (Kächele, Schachter, & Thomä, 2008). The 3-LM exploits the strengths of the clinical method of participant observation. The analytic experience can only be grasped through the inner resonance of the clinical material and it can frequently be expressed only through metaphors, some of them co-created in the analytic field (de León de Bernardi, 2013), or quasi-artistic procedures (Altmann, 2008; Birksted-Breen, 2012). That is why, at level 1, the model asks the participants to identify the anchor points and those parts of the material that most resonated in them, using an experiential language that keeps their metaphoric potential alive. The resonance of the material among participants adds a new dimension to the clinical process, which could be named "observation of observations" because, as with a prism, that which initially resonated in the analyst is repeated with its own colouring in each participant and in group process. Questions from the 3-LM aim at making this internal resonance explicit, using the group discussion as a triangulation procedure that puts together observations from diverse observers and theoretical perspectives.

Participants are invited to listen to the material with the "third ear" and then to adopt a "second look" (Baranger, Baranger, & Mom, 1983) on the material. This second look is not opposed to the first look, in the same way as Bion's grid is not detrimental for analytic listening. The second look that the 3-LM proposes aims to identify significant clinical patterns that can be used as markers of long-term change. They include the analytic field, the patient's psychopathology, and a temporal perspective on the patient's evolution.

1. Regarding the second look on the analytic field, M. and W. Baranger and Mom (1983) note that in certain moments the "first look", based on free floating attention, must be left in suspense to leave room for a "second look", which, more broadly, includes what is happening in the analytical situation between patient and analyst. For that reason the 3-LM especially investigates the use that the patient makes of the analyst (Winnicott, 1969) and of his/her interpretations (Etchegoyen, 1991; Faimberg, 1996). The

3-LM requests the analyst presenting the material to include in it his/her countertransference, and to make clarifications about the context of the analytic situation that can contribute to better understanding the changes of patients in relation to the foci of the analyst's interpretations. In this regard, the 3-LM is complementary to other modes of clinical discussion (e.g., Tuckett et al., 2008) that aim to raise awareness of the analyst's working models.

2. The 3-LM attempts to broaden the comprehension of the psychopathology of the patient. Green (2002), reflecting upon the flow of psychoanalytic clinical thought, states that the free-floating attention at moments has to be replaced by an attitude of investigative sharpness, which enables the analyst to reorganise and broaden his/her understanding of the patient, going from the comprehension of the specific transferential position to a more global image of his/her conflicts. Moreover, the markers usually employed to assess moment-to-moment transformations are not necessarily useful for tracking long-term transformations. The second level of the 3-LM is devoted to proposing the core dimensions that could be more useful for this task (see below).
3. The long term temporal dimension is a specific contribution of the 3-LM perspective, whose central aim is to describe the transformations that occur over time, comparing material from different periods. The discussion of the material moves from the first interviews forward, but the 3-LM also enables an *a posteriori* look at the analysis, because, from the changes produced, it is possible to review what happened in the initial stages in the light of what happened later. It is interesting to note that changes do not occur only during the sessions, but also between them and after treatment termination (Shedler et al., 2010). It is also possible that phenomena occur in the patient which are similar to that which Freud (1918b) called "a posterior" effects or "deferred action" (*nachträglich*), which cause certain events to acquire new efficacy and psychic meaning when they are in a new context.

### *Level 1: phenomenological description of transformations*

The list below displays the questions that guide the discussion of the first level. During the discussion, at this level as at other levels, participants can select those questions that they consider most appropriate to the material. New questions may also emerge during the discussion.

### *Questions about Level 1: phenomenological description of transformations*

1. What aspects of the material suggest the existence of positive changes, negative changes, or the non-existence of changes? Which prevail?
2. Are there changes that may be noticed in the course of one session? And through time, between different sessions? In which areas is it possible to observe changes? (E.g., (a) capacity to love and sexuality; (b) family and social relationships; (c) occupation and leisure; (d) interests and creativity; (e) symptoms and subjective well-being.) Which is the patient's perspective regarding his changes?
3. Do changes exist in the analytic process regarding (a) how the patient uses the analyst and her interventions; (b) how the patient uses his/her own mental and bodily resources during the session?
4. Which parts of the clinical material had a special resonance for the participants of the group and can be considered as anchor points that make it possible to track changes in the patient? What is the relation of these anchor points to the foci of the analyst's interpretations?

The initial question aims to gather global impressions about changes in the patient from the perspective of an informed observer. Analysts are aware that certain apparently positive changes might be defensive, or that greater awareness of painful problems may provoke a temporary worsening. As negative therapeutic reactions show, adverse effects also may occur in psychoanalytic treatment, just as they do in any other treatment.

The third question refers to the use that the patient makes of the analyst and her interpretations. This question, inspired by Winnicott (1969), includes aspects that are central in one session (e.g., transferential fantasies, countertransference) but goes further, asking how the patient is making use of the analysis for the changes he/she is facing at different stages. This requires that attention be paid to the conscious and unconscious reactions of the analyst. This third question also asks about changes in the patient's use of her own mental and bodily resources in analysis (which is related to core dimensions of mental functioning that will be considered in Level 2). Question 2 also asks about the use of these resources in everyday life, outside analysis.

Participants discuss in point 4 what parts of the material have special conscious or unconscious resonance for them. Parallel processes allow the perception of unconscious resonance in the group through the repetition of the patient's conflicts in the group. This resonance is a guide to identify, in the first meetings with the analyst, the anchor points that will be the landmarks used later to track changes in the patient. These anchor points will be compared with the foci of the analyst's interpretations, in as much as they reflect the analyst's perception of the problems that generate or maintain the patient's suffering.

### *Level 2: identification of the main diagnostic dimensions of change. Relevant questions*

Level 2 aims to identify the most important dimensions transformations. Freud summarised the distinction between health and neurosis using two words: *Genuss*, meaning capacity for enjoyment, and *Leistungsfahigkeit*, effectiveness, which means the capacity to produce (Freud, 1916–1917, p. 457). The current concept of quality of life related to health heads in a similar direction, combining the criterion of the subjective perception of well-being with the criterion of personal functioning (Fleck, 2008). However, these concepts are too general and need to acquire greater diagnostic precision to be useful in evaluating the changes of the patient. Several authors are advanced in the diagnostic use of psychoanalytical concepts (Freedman, Geller, Hoffenberg, Hurvich, & Ward, 2011, the Hampstead Psychoanalytic Index, 1981; the Propositional Method of N. Freedman and M. Hurvich (Hurvich, 2003); the Structural Interview (Kernberg, 2006; Stern et al., 2010)). (See Chapters Twelve and Thirteen, this volume.)

More recently, two psychodynamic diagnostic systems have been proposed: the *Psychodynamic Diagnostic Manual* (*PDM*, 2006) and the *Operationalized Psychodynamic Diagnosis (OPD)*, version 2 (OPD Task

Force, 2008). Both of them aim to operationalise definitions using a categorical–dimensional approach. In 2013, the *DSM-5* (American Psychiatric Association, 2013) included in its Section III (Emergent Measures and Models) a Level of Personality Functioning Scale (LPFS) that has great interest for psychoanalysis. The three diagnostic systems have an amazing coincidence in the core content of the indicators used for evaluating personality functioning. These similarities have been underlined in two panels held during the 47th IPA Congress (Mexico, 2011), and the 48th IPA Congress (Prague, 2013), see Bernardi (2013).

The three systems pay special attention to the self–other polarity of mental life. The 3-LM borrowed the axes and categories of the *OPD-2*, which evaluates mental functioning (structure axis) according to four capacities: (1) to adequately perceive the self and objects; (2) to regulate affects related to the self and the relationship with others; (3) to communicate emotionally and symbolically, both internally and externally; (4) to develop attachment to internal and external objects. The 3-LM also included dimensions from the *PDM* and the *DSM-5*. The *PDM* contains nine capacities for evaluating mental functioning, while the LPFS of the *DSM-5* group them in a self domain: identity and self direction, and an interpersonal domain: empathy and intimacy. In spite of the different groupings, the three systems point to similar capacities. The convergences between the content of the three systems, which emerge from their conceptual comparison (Bernardi, 2010), have been corroborated from the empirical point of view between the *OPD-2* and the LPFS. Zimmermann and colleagues (2012) found a very high correlation between descriptors of mental functioning level of the *DSM-5* LPFS and the levels of structural integration of the *OPD-2* ($r = 0.93$, $p < 0.001$).

It is important to note that the three diagnostic systems aim at operationalising their concepts, making them user friendly for clinicians from different traditions. The *OPD-2* states that a challenge in doing this is not to lose conceptual content in order to gain consensus, and, therefore, proposes to use the "smallest common multiple" among the different meanings of these concepts (p. 14). (See Chapter Thirteen.) Building upon these convergences, the 3-LM has selected, based on intuitive clinical criteria and with practical aims, a series of questions inspired by the three systems. The items selected were those that seem most relevant to tracking changes. It has also considered the items from the Heidelberg Structural Change Scale (HSCS), included in the *OPD-2* (p. 286). The questions were formulated in a way that is self-explanatory for psychoanalysts and does not require special training. To what extent they are reliable and have concurrent validity regarding their original source is a question left to empirical research.

The Level 2 questions are listed in the next section, below. The first dimension refers to the changes in the patient's experience of his/her suffering. This is supposed to change as a consequence of new insights during analysis. The questions about the degree of acknowledgment of problems and foreseeing new ways of experiencing and behaving were inspired by the HSBC. Recent research (Grande, Dilg, Jakobsen, Keller, & Krawietz, 2009) corroborates that if patients, when finishing a psychotherapy, have managed to see themselves and their problems "under a different light", this fact better predicts the permanence of the positive effects of therapy three years after having finished treatment than immediate symptomatic improvement.

The second group of questions has its origin in the classical notion of transference and countertransference, to which changes in relational patterns outside analysis is added. In consequence, the questions cover the way in which the patient sees others and him/herself in his/her meaningful relationships, and the way in which others see him/her and themselves in those relationships. A developmental perspective is included, as well as the consideration of verbal and non-verbal aspects, and differences among them (Altmann de Litvan, 2007).

In the third group of questions, the prevailing conflicts are considered. Changes expected at this level are those that traditionally have been highlighted by psychoanalysis. Change is supposed to be accompanied by a more flexible use of defences, especially those that distort or restrict internal or external experience. It is also of interest to differentiate the way in which conflicts are presented in patients with a well-integrated psychic structure from what occurs in patients with a lower level of integration (such as in borderline organisation). In the latter, we find, instead of stable conflicts that present like a drama that unendingly repeats itself, several oscillating conflicts, like fragments of different narratives that take place upon a shaky stage because of the inadequate availability of structural functions (*OPD*, pp. 158–159).

Structural functions are explored in the fourth group of questions. These questions aim at exploring further what is described as vulnerabilities, fragilities, deficits, or developmental arrests of the patient. Four dimensions are taken into account, following the *OPD-2* criteria. The first dimension refers to the patient's capacity to perceive what occurs in his own mind and to build, based on that, an integrated and differentiated sense of his personal identity and of his capacity to project towards the future (as the *DSM-5* LPFS highlights). Analysis is supposed to improve mentalization, which means the capacity to understand through the reflecting function what happens in the analysand's own mind and in the mind of others (Allen & Fonagy, 2006; Fonagy, Gergely, Jurist, & Target, 2002). The second dimension refers to the capacity to regulate impulses mood affects, and self-esteem, as well as establishing an adequate emotional balance between the needs of one's self and the needs of the others. The third dimension, internal and external communication and the capacity for symbolisation, is crucial for the psychoanalytic process because these functions enable the psychic and interpersonal processing of lived experiences and their integration, contributing in this way to mental growth and the elaboration of the psychoanalytic work. Lived experiences need to be processed through fantasies, dreams, and mental representations in order to give greater depth and consistency to the processes of thought and to interpersonal relationships. The fourth and last of the structural functions considered is the capacity to have deep bonds with internal and external objects, something that implies the ability to initiate, preserve, and end relationships, to tolerate separations and to acknowledge the place of a third. These four capacities, as explained in Chapter Thirteen, are those that permit the functions evaluated in the LPFS regarding the possibility of self-identity and self-direction regarding the self domain, and empathy and intimacy regarding the interpersonal domain.

It can be easily noticed that the questions are not essentially about symptomatic or well-being effects, but, on the contrary, that beneath them are the core concepts of psychoanalytic theory. However, they intend to be expressed in the most theoretically unsaturated way, referring to what has to be explored in the clinical material, but without impeding that analysts with different traditions reframe the answer according to their theoretical preferences.

The fifth and last question raises the discussion as to whether there is a kind of identifiable disturbance, as well as the level of personality organisation. The generalised severity of the disturbances in personality functioning is considered the most important predictor of concurrent and prospective dysfunction (Bender, Morey, & Skodol, 2011; Skodol et al., 2011; Skodol et al., 2011a,b; Tyrer, 2005). The levels of mental integration of *OPD-2* and the *DSM-5* LPFS are correlated and it would be interesting to compare those with the clinical assessment through the 3-LM.

The questions of level 2 include many, if not all, of the core concepts that can contribute to assessing psychic change from a psychoanalytic perspective.

### *Questions about level 2: dimensions of change*

1. Subjective experience of illness and contextual factors.
   (a) What are the patient's subjective experience, beliefs, and expectations about his/her problems and treatment? How much does s/he recognise his/her problems? How much does s/he foresee possibilities of change? To what extent do patient and analyst agree regarding the expected transformations?
   (b) Do contextual factors exist which affect the therapeutic process? (For example, crisis situations, traumatic experiences, somatic illnesses, drugs, etc.? How capable is the patient of facing these situations?)
   (c) How have these aspects changed? How has the patient's modified his/her understanding of his/her problems and therapeutic possibilities?
2. Patterns of interpersonal relationship.
   (a) How are the interpersonal relationships of the patient, especially in connection with the bonds that imply closeness and intimacy?
   (b) How does the patient experience others and how does s/he experience him/herself in relation to others? How do others experience the patient and how do they experience themselves in relation to the patient? (Both in transference–countertransference and in other meaningful bonds.)
   (c) To what extent can the patient relate his/her current relational patterns to the experiences lived in his/her childhood and the transferential relationship.
   (d) How have these aspects changed?

3. Main intrapsychic conflicts.

(a) What are the main conflicts (e.g., individuation *vs.* dependency; submission *vs.* control; need for care *vs.* self-sufficiency; self-worth, guilt, oedipal conflict, identity conflict). Which are the dominant unconscious fantasies that can be inferred from conflicts and relational patterns?

   (b) The prevailing defences are adequate and flexible or dysfunctional, distorting or restraining internal and external experiences?

   (c) How have these aspects changed?

4. Structural aspects of mental functioning.

   (a) What is the level of mental functioning in the following areas?

      - Perception of self and others' identity.
        How capable is the patient of adequately perceiving his/her own internal states and those of others? Is s/he able to empathise, tolerating and understanding different points of view? Does s/he have an integrated feeling of his/her own identity, open to the possibility of unconscious aspects? What are the characteristics of identifications (especially pathological ones)? Does s/he manage to connect with his/her past and give direction to his/her life with a sense of agency and short- and long-term wishes and goals?
      - Affective regulation: Is the patient able to regulate his/her impulses, affects, and self-esteem adequately? Do his/her ideals and values help him/her to handle his/her emotions? Does s/he manage to regulate his/her for self-esteem when facing internal and external demands? How often does s/he achieve an adequate balance between his/her own interests and those of others?
      - Internal and external communication. Symbolisation. How rich is the dialogue with him/herself and others, based on affective experiences, bodily self, fantasies, dreams, sexuality, symbolic representations, and capacity to play and for creativity?
      - Attachment with internal and external objects. How deep,stable, and differentiated are the relationships with internal and external objects? How much can s/he start

and finish relationships and tolerate separations? How does s/he handle relationships that imply the existence of a third one?

   (b) How have these aspects changed?

5. Type of disorder
   (a) Is it possible to identify a type of personality disorder or other kind of mental or bodily disorder?
   (b) How severe are the disturbances of personality functioning? How much is analytic work conditioned by the structural vulnerabilities of mental functioning?
   (c) How have these aspects changed?

### *Level 3: explanatory hypotheses of change. Relevant questions*

While the two previous levels intend to describe what has changed, the aim of the third level is to understand how and why changes occurred (or did not occur). Therefore, it discusses the explicit and implicit theories (Bleger, 2012; Canestri, 2006; Sandler, 1983) by which transformations can be explained, starting with those that manifest in the analyst's interpretations.

Participants are asked to propose alternative hypotheses or points of view that come from their own theoretical and technical frames. The different approaches themselves are not under discussion, but their contribution to proposing alternative ways to interpret the material is considered. From the heuristic point of view, these new hypotheses may suggest revising the discussion of previous levels, checking how convincing and fruitful the diverse hypotheses are.

The nature of the changes is the last point to be discussed. In this chapter, "changes" and "transformation" have been used as equivalents, but, while "transformation" suggests the metamorphosis of the same elements, "change" has a more general and broad meaning. These and other related terms, such as "shift", "modification", "development", "evolution", etc., can be used as equivalents or might mean something more specific when they are defined according to a given theoretical frame. Patients' change probably involves diverse processes, some of them implying development or transformation of the personality that allows new ways of experiencing, while others are more limited switches among diverse coping and defence mechanisms or the finding of other ways of bypassing inner structural limitations or external conflictive situations. Some recent contributions propose models of psychoanalytic changes from a dynamic system theory perspective (Boston Change Process Study Group, 2005; Galatzer-Levy, 2009). The 3-LM aim is not to choose among these different theoretical views, but to ask them to provide clinical markers or hypotheses that can better help to assess the depth and stability of the changes described in the previous levels.

### *Questions about level 3: explanatory hypotheses of change*

1. On which aspects did the interventions of the analyst mainly focus? Has his/her explicit or implicit hypotheses and interventions changed during treatment?
2. Could there be other theoretical hypotheses or interpretative strategies? In what ways are each of them convincingly adjusted to the material?
3. What is the nature of the observed changes, their depth, and expected stability?

## *Example: group discussion of Leticia*

The brief synthesis of a group discussion can illustrate the way the model works.

Leticia's material was selected by the analyst for discussion in a 3-LM working group because the analyst wanted to examine to what extent the patient was improving. At the time of the discussion, Leticia had been in three-times-a-week analysis for two and a half years. The group met for nearly ten hours and was moderated by the myself and Marina Altmann de Litvan. After some introductory remarks from the co-ordinators about the model, the analyst (Hernández) presented material from different moments of Leticia's analysis, introducing the group discussion. Both will be very briefly summarised here

### *Leticia*

When Leticia, aged thirty, entered the office, the analyst's attention was drawn to her huddled position, her robot-like way of walking, and her slow and monotonous voice.

She sat and said,

> "I don't know where to start from . . ," [Silence.] Invited to continue, she adds, "I am a little like this . . . bad . . . There are cycles . . . they last some months and they go away . . . a little depressed . . . insecure by the responsibility at my job. I manage to solve problems . . . but always in an insecure way." [Silence.] "That's my biggest problem now, I never know if I'm doing things right." [Silence.] "I don't know what to talk about. I'm afraid of not knowing what to talk about . . . I don't know . . ." [Silence.]

Silences and the expression "I don't know" are repeated in interviews initially during the analysis, especially when she attempts to refer to what she feels or thinks.

> "I have a friend . . . I don't know how to call it . . . [Silence.]

> "Nothing special happened in my childhood. I don't know what else to say . . ."

After a period of face-to-face, twice-a-week analysis, patient and analyst agreed to use the couch and to raise the frequency to three times a week.

Early in analysis, Leticia came punctually to the sessions and described her current life in a realistic way, with neither conflict nor emotions, except her concern for doing things in the proper way. She behaved towards the analyst as if their relationship was merely professional, with the latent fear of being disapproved of by the analyst. Attempts to explore these feelings led Leticia to remain silent or to answer from reality, and to insist that the problems were in her and not in the relationship with the analyst.

The analyst focused on helping Leticia to explore her inner feelings. However, even if there was a clear improvement in her capacity to communicate emotions to herself and to the analyst, the analyst was, at moments, surprised by the way in which Leticia distorted her perception of situations. For example, at the end of one session, the following dialogue occurred.

> *L*: I have also wondered about the analysis. I thought that I've been coming for two years. . . . I don't know why I am afraid of coming and not talking. [She has not stopped talking and crying since she arrived at this session.] [Silence.] But coming to analysis, seriously, it seems to

me that I will arrive and I will stay mute all the time, that's why I say that, I don't know, I don't know if I feel like coming.

*A*: But you are talking, and you have come anxious, you have cried, maybe you needed to come.

*L*: Yes, it seems so, but I had not realized. [Silence.]

Leticia begins to communicate dreams. In one of them, she had not awakened in time and then she could not retrieve her belongings from her parents' home (no associations). In another session, she remembered a painful episode from her childhood. Once, in a game with her parents, she hid from them, expecting them to look for her, but was very disappointed when they did not pay attention to her.

Leticia slowly became more communicative. However, the analyst commented that many times she felt uncomfortable and disconcerted. Regarding Leticia's silences, the analyst said, "I felt as if I were the one who was left associating instead of her. It was as if analytical work happened inside myself more than between the two of us." At a certain moment, she was surprised by an enactment, in which she answered a request from Leticia in an unusually obliging way.

### *The discussion group*

I shall summarise the group comments, based on the report of the discussion made by one of the participants (Beatriz de León de Bernardi).

#### *Level 1*

Global changes were perceived as "slightly positive" by some participants and as "moderate" by others. Her distress has diminished, and, more than that, she is in better contact with her emotional life and can transmit it with greater bodily participation (e.g., crying), showing a subtle but valuable change in the way she uses her own mind and body during the session.

An issue widely discussed was the way Leticia "uses" the analyst. At the beginning of the discussion, several participants proposed theoretical explanations which implied concepts like container, projective identification, holding, mirroring, symbiosis, etc. The moderators then proposed to postpone these theoretical aspects until the third level discussion. The group returned to the level 1 questions and asked why transference and countertransference seemed so intense, yet, at the same time, it was difficult to say what kind of object the analyst represented for Leticia in her fantasy life. Participants then focused on the parts of the material with greatest resonance in themselves. Some of them pointed at the dream about recovering her belongings that she had left at her parents' house. The group considered this a metaphor of the analysis, concluding that the analyst was expected to be the depository of certain psychic functions that were difficult for her to recover at the moment.

All participants agreed on the strong resonance of Leticia's memory when she hid expecting to be found, but her parents did not look for her. The analyst felt this was a reference to transference, but preferred to wait instead of interpreting. This brought the discussion to what extent Leticia would benefit from more active interpretations—and of what nature—or from a waiting attitude, allowing her to find her own pace, letting her decide the moment to be found. Theoretical considerations were also raised regarding these options and postponed again to Level 3.

*Level 2*

2.1. A subtle change was mentioned regarding Leticia's subjective experience of her suffering: she started asking herself questions about her "I don't know". For example, she said, "I don't know why I *then* felt *so* distressed . . ." It was more a change in her attitude towards herself than a display of fantasies or beliefs about her problems.

2.2. Her patterns of relationships were repetitive at the beginning of the analysis. Descriptions of others were blurred; they appear as pale figures always expecting more from her and never being sufficiently pleased. She seems to tell herself, "I get depressed because I will fail and nobody will accept me. If I hide, they don't come to look for me. I'd better make them see that I will behave as they want, even if I feel so distressed inside." This pattern seems to slowly change with the analyst and later in the outer world. In the second year of analysis, she started a relationship with a boyfriend. This was the first time she felt that someone was kind and content with her.

2.3. Initially, the most visible conflicts were those related to dependence, self-esteem, and guilt. These conflicts were scarcely developed in her strongly inhibited fantasy life. She seemed terrified of not accomplishing what was expected of her. Based on biographical data not presented here, the group discussed the factors that could lead her to avoid emotions and inhibit her inner communication. The discussion turned to the question of how little her conflicts were represented and if her narrative appeared faded and discoloured because of structural functions (especially symbolisation and inner communication) having been affected either as a defence to avoid conflicts or as a developmental consequence of some biographical circumstances. These questions led the group to pay special attention to the next set of questions.

2.4. The group agreed that increasing confidence in analysis helped Leticia to be more aware of her inner states. She started asking herself questions about her own feelings and those of others, that is, her reflective function increased. This seemed to be fundamental to enabling analytic work.

Regarding affective regulation, Leticia's mood fluctuations seemed to be related to her difficulty perceiving and modulating emotions and self-esteem, which she could only express as distress or depressive mood, and not as differentiated feelings or changing ways of behaving in social life. She could only maintain an interpersonal balance by ignoring her own demands, which was detrimental to her self-esteem. She seemed to ask the analyst to do the same, to be only a function and not a person. The group discussed how the analyst might make use of her intense countertransferential feelings to further the analysis, but there was not a clear agreement about this.

Regarding symbolisation, the group considered the initial impoverishment in internal and external communication as a key feature in Leticia's analysis. She treated her body as a robot, inhibited her imagination, and turned off the processing of many emotions and feelings. The analyst's attitude of helping her, little by little, to communicate with herself seemed to have been effective and improved her affective life.

*Level 3*

Participants agreed with the analyst that the focus of the analytical work should be on Leticia's need to make greater contact with her emotional experience and this was the anchor point identified in the first interviews. The analysis of the dimensions of mental functioning in Level 2 confirmed in a consistent way the core importance of this point.

There was a smaller degree of agreement regarding the factors that limited Leticia's understanding of herself and others. Some understood her difficulty in metabolising her emotional experiences in terms of Bion's concepts, such as the probable flaws in the maternal "reverie" function, supporting these hypotheses with biographical data omitted here. Other participants, including the analyst, suggested Leticia's need of a "transformational object" in Bollas's sense (1979). Other participants remarked on the similarity of Leticia's initial functioning with Marty's descriptions of operational thought and essential depression (1985), or with Sifneos's alexithymia (1996).

For other participants, closer to a more classical Freudian perspective, Leticia's conflicts had a more evolved level, but were not easy to explore because of the strength of her defences. The fear of the loss of the love of the object led her to over-adaptive behaviour in the external world and an avoidant attitude regarding her internal world. From this perspective, Leticia's "I don't know" could mean "I know, but I must hide".

These different considerations reopened the discussion about the nature of core problems and whether they should be linked to conflict and defence (suggesting more classical interpretations from the analyst), or to structural difficulties which require a different kind of intervention. The group concluded that both hypotheses were plausible and that it was not possible to decide between them until the analysis progresses and provides new evidence.

In an anonymous questionnaire, the group agreed about the usefulness of the experience. The analyst commented that she felt enriched by the experience and reported later that some of the opinions suggested new ideas to her. The group agreed to gather one year later in order to discuss the new material. (See Chapter Two.)

## *Discussion and conclusions*

The 3-LM proposals, as a guide or heuristic for refining and enhancing psychoanalytic observation of patient transformations, presents potentialities and also limitations that are discussed here.

The 3-LM calls attention to an area of observation that is not sufficiently taken into account by current literature. Are there psychoanalytic criteria which enable us to say whether a patient is improving or not, in which aspects the patient has changed, and what the meaning of those changes is? Our experiences using the 3-LM allow us to state that questions proposed by the model are interesting to analysts and their discussion enriches the analysts' understanding of the patient. It was also confirmed that these questions may be shared by analysts with very different theoretical background. Cases are not selected based on their agreement with certain models of psychoanalytic practice, but intending to get closer to real analytic practice, inviting analysts to discuss those cases that interest them. Very often, the interest is raised by the difficulties that cases present and they greatly represent situations where real practice exceeds the postulates of ideal models.

In that sense, the 3-LM does not attempt to be a supervision, or a method to decide among different theoretical models, but to be a tool for enhancing the observation of the analysis as it took place. The Level 2 dimensions help to show which kind of changes have taken place that are relevant for a psychoanalysis, and the level 3 questions invite reflection about different interpretative strategies that might emerge from other theoretical approaches. The abstract comparison of different theoretical hypotheses does not often lead to a dialogue that is useful for the advancement of psychoanalysis (Bernardi, 2002). This comparison becomes more fruitful when these hypotheses are expressed as mini-models or metaphors (Leuzinger-Bohleber & Fischmann, 2006) that adjust to the singularity of the patient and that may be discussed on the basis of concrete examples. In that sense, when the discussion about Leticia leads the group to imagine the different ways in which the interpretative strategies of the analyst may or may not facilitate the changes of the patient, the group is conducting a mental experiment which has aspects in common with eliminative inductivism (Edelson, 1983), in which the weight of observations that support a certain hypothesis is compared with the weight of those that support the rival hypotheses. This enriching group discussion may also take place in the inner forum of the analyst and be beneficial for the training and the production of psychoanalytic papers (see Chapter Fourteen).

The 3-LM does not aspire to be a method for the direct validation of psychoanalytic hypotheses. Neither is it a method of empirical research, and, therefore, it does not intend to comply with its demands, such as eliminating biases. The selection and recording of the material is left to the analyst's choice. The initial interviews vary greatly according to analysts, and they combine in different degree exploratory moments with those that are left to the free association of the patient. Rather than avoiding biases, the 3-LM intends to acknowledge and examine them. The 3-LM is a clinical tool and not a research procedure. It cannot answer the question of to what extent conclusions would be different if the analyst had selected different sessions. However, it does attempt to clarify the way in which the analyst who presents the material is involved in the analytic process and in the selection of the material. The analyst him/herself is the one most interested in understanding his/her own role as observer and frequently during the discussion he/she spontaneously provides new material that increases participants' understanding. Clinical observation seeks to support itself on complexity, rather than reducing it.

During Leticia's discussion, as said above, diverse theoretical and technical alternatives were suggested. For example, let us consider the discussion of whether the analyst should interpret some key aspects in the transference. For example, Leticia's hiding and her wanting the analyst to feel anxious about not finding her. This question could be answered "top down", taking for granted the assumptions of one of the current psychoanalytic theories, but it can also be tackled from a different angle, trying to get closer to the patient's vantage point (Schwaber, 1981, 1992). When a little girl hides and wants to play with her parents, it is not at all the same if her parents—or the analyst's interpretation—say, "There you are", than if they ask "Where are you?" and let the girl appear when she decides to be found. The analyst's countertransferential anxiety reveals the intensity of the underlying feelings, probably fear, aggression, narcissism, and sexuality. However, the clinical problem is not only to identify these feelings, but also to find the best way and moment when they can enter the dialogue between analyst and patient. The 3-LM can only determine the effects the analyst's attitude had and to discuss, in a conjectural way, the predictable effects of other possible strategies; it cannot ascertain with certainty the best interpretative strategy. For example: is Leticia's difficulty in perceiving herself due to structural deficits (e.g., insufficient development of certain functions) or to structural vulnerabilities that transitorily prevent the functioning of capacities already acquired, but inhibited by internal and/or external factors? But even if we choose this second option as more plausible, it does not automatically allow us to ascertain which is the best interpretative strategy. Participants of working groups often feel that the discussion helps them get closer to the patient's vantage point ("I feel as if I had a personal contact with the patient") and this helps to empathically anticipate the way the patient will receive the interpretations. In so far as Leticia felt safe with the analyst, and this more tolerant "auxiliary superego" (Strachey, 1969), this diminished her "failure to mentalize" (Brown, 2008). This, in turn, reinforced her capacity for affect regulation and opened the way to a better internal and external communication and a stronger sense of agency. However, as said, many questions and controversial issues remain open. The discussion helps to acknowledge the limits of the observation. In a clinical case, it is important to perceive what we manage to know with a certain degree of evidence and also to perceive what is not yet observable or understandable. Often, divergent hypotheses did not find sufficient support in the available material for a choice to be made between them, enabling us, as Freud said (1918b), to conclude the problem "non liquet" at this time. To perceive with greater clarity how much the available theoretical interpretations are satisfactory and how much they are not, and where it is necessary to wait for new clinical evidence must be seen as a strength of the model, because it leads to the search for both new clinical and new theoretical improvements.

The 3-LM is open to the modifications and new developments that might arise from its use. During the discussion, participants alternate between focusing their attention on the internal resonance of the material (mainly in level 1), and a second look trying to identify and conceptualise the changes (mainly in level 2 and 3). The model includes both directions, but, as a matter of fact, some participants are more interested in one of them than in the other. For example, one participant said that what she especially appreciated was the effect of hearing the material's resonance in the other participants; she said that it was like opening the mind to the primary process. Other participants underline the necessity of a clearer definition of the dimensions used to identify the changes in order to increase their diagnostic value (see Chapters Twelve and Thirteen). Some aspects of the 3-LM may be further investigated, the first being interrater agreement among the participants of the groups, because expert consensus has value in establishing the degree of validity of the group's conclusions. Questionnaires to be applied before and after the group discussion have already been designed to measure these effects. It is also possible to study the degree of concurrent validity of 3-LM questions in relation to categories of the above-mentioned diagnostic systems or other evaluation instruments. Other bridges to empirical research may be established, but the existence of these bridges does not modify the clinical nature of the 3-LM. For a bridge to make sense, there must be two sides to communicate. That is why the 3-LM is not intended to transform itself into systematic empirical research, but to continue as a tool in the clinical field, trying to complement other methodologies when the nature of the questions suggest it.

## *References*

Allen, J. G., & Fonagy, P. (Eds.) (2006). *Handbook of Mentalization-Based Treatment*. Chichester: John Wiley.

Altmann, M. (2008). *Cómo se da el nacimiento del paciente en la mente del analista*. XVI Jornadas de Psicoanálisis de APU. Desafíos del psicoanálisis contemporáneo. Asociación Psicoanalítica del Uruguay (APU). Montevideo, Uruguay.

Altmann, M. (2013). Tracking transformations in a psychoanalytic process: unconscious and explicit. *International Journal of Psychoanalysis, 94*: 1191–1193.

Altmann, M., Fitzpatrick-Hanly, M. A., & Leuzinger-Bohleber, M. (2012a). Reports of Panels held at the 47th Congress of the International Psychoanalytic Association, Mexico City, 3–6 August 2011. *International Journal of Psychoanalysis, 93*: 504–506.

Altmann, M., Fitzpatrick-Hanly, M. A., & Leuzinger-Bohleber, M. (2012b). Project committee on clinical observation panels. *International Journal of Psychoanalysis, 93*: 748–750.

American Psychiatric Association (2013). *Diagnostic and Statistical Manual of Mental Disorders, 5th Edition (DSM-5)*. Arlington, VA: American Psychiatric Association.

Baranger, M., Baranger, W., & Mom, J. M. (1983). Process and non-process in analytic work. *International Journal of Psychoanalysis, 64*: 1–15.

Bender, D. S., Morey, L. C., & Skodol, A. E. (2011). Toward a model for assessing level of personality functioning in DSM-5, Part I: A review of theory and methods. *Journal of Personality Assessment, 93*(4): 332–346.

Bernardi, R. (1989). The role of paradigmatic determinants in psychoanalytic understanding. *International Journal of Psychoanalysis, 70*(Pt 2): 341–357.

Bernardi, R. (1992). On pluralism in psychoanalysis. *Psychoanalytic Inquiry, 12*(4): 506–525.

Bernardi, R. (2001). Psychoanalytic goals: new and old paradoxes. *Psychoanalytic Quarterly, 70*(1): 67–98.

Bernardi, R. (2002). The need for true controversies in psychoanalysis: the debates on Melanie Klein and Jacques Lacan in the Rio de la Plata. *International Journal of Psychoanalysis, 83*: 851–873.

Bernardi, R. (2010). DSM-5, OPD-2 y PDM: Convergencias y divergencias entre los nuevos sistemas diagnósticos psiquiátricos y psicoanalíticos. *Rev Psiquiatr Urug, 74*(2): 179–205.

Bernardi, R. (2013). Observing transformations in patients: the assessment of mental functioning. *International Journal of Psychoanalysis, 94*: 1170–1172.

Beutel, M. E., Stark, R., Pan, H., Sibersweig, D., & Dietrich, S. (2010). Changes of brain activation pre-post short-term psychodynamic inpatient psychotherapy: an fMRI study of panic disorder patients. *Psychiatry Research: Neuroimaging, 184*(2): 96–104.

Bion, W. R. (1967). *Second Thoughts*. New York: Jason Aronson.

Birksted-Breen, D. (2012). Taking time: the tempo of psychoanalysis. *International Journal of Psychoanalysis, 93*: 819–835.

Bleger, J. (1973). Criterios de curación y objetivos del psicoanálisis. *Revista de Psicoanálisis, XXX*: 317–350.

Bleger, J. (2012). Theory and practice in psychoanalysis: psychoanalytic praxis. *International Journal of Psychoanalysis, 93*: 993–1003.

Bollas, C. (1979). The transformational object. *International Journal of Psychoanalysis, 60*: 97–107.

Boston Change Process Study Group (2005). The 'something more' than interpretation revisited: sloppiness and co-creativity in the psychoanalytic encounter. *Journal of the American Psychoanalytic Association, 32*: 693–729.

Britton, R., & Steiner, J. (1994). Interpretation: selected fact or overvalued idea? *International Journal of Psychoanalysis, 75*: 1069–1078.

Brown, W. G. (2008). Failure to mentalize: defect or defense? *Psychoanalytic Social Work, 15*(1): 28–42.

Canestri, J. (2006). Implicit understanding of clinical material beyond theory. In: J. Canestri (Ed.), *Psychoanalysis. From Practice to Theory* (pp. 13–28): John Wiley.

De Litvan, M. A. (2007). Infant observation: a range of questions and challenges for contemporary psychoanalysis. *International Journal of Psychoanalysis, 88*: 713–733.

De León de Bernardi, B. (2013). Metaphor, analytic field, and spiral process. In S. Montana Katz (Ed.), *Metaphor and Fields. Common Ground, Common Language, and the Future of Psychoanalysis* (pp. 182–203). New York: Routledge.

Eagle, M., & Wolitzky, D. (2011). Systematic empirical research versus clinical case studies: a valid antagonism? *Journal of the American Psychoanalytic Association, 59*(4): 791–818.

Edelson, J. T. (1983). Is testing psychoanalytic hypotheses in the psychoanalytic situation really impossible? *Psychoanalytic Study of the Child, 38*: 61–109.

Etchegoyen, R. H. (1991). Psychoanalysis during the last decade: clinical and theoretical aspects. *Psychoanalytic Inquiry, 11*: 88–106.

Etkin, A., Phil, M., Pittenger, C., Polan, J., & Kandel, E. R. (2005). Toward a neurobiology of psychotherapy: basic science and clinical applications. *Journal of Neuropsychiatry and Clinical Neuroscience, 17*: 145–158.

Faimberg, H. (1996). Listening to listening. *International Journal of Psychoanalysis, 77*: 667–677.

Fleck, M. P. (2008). *A avaliação de qualidade de vida*. Sao Paulo: ARTMED.

Fonagy, P., & Target, M. (1994). The efficacy of psychoanalysis for children with disruptive disorders. *Journal of the American Academy of Child and Adolescent Psychiatry, 33*: 45–55.

Fonagy, P., & Target, M. (1996). Predictors of outcome in child psychoanalysis: a retrospective study of 763 cases at the Anna Freud Centre. *Journal of the American Psychoanalytic Association, 44*: 27–77.

Fonagy, P., Gergely, G., Jurist, E., & Target, M. (2002). *Affect Regulation, Mentalization, and the Development of the Self.* New York: Other Press.

Fonagy, P., Roth, A., & Higgitt, A. (2005). The outcome of psychodynamic psychotherapy for psychological disorders. *Clinical Neuroscience Research, 4*(5–6): 367–377.

Freedman, R., Geller, J. D., Hoffenberg, J., Hurvich, M., & Ward, R. (2011). *Another Kind of Evidence: Studies on Internalization, Annihilation Anxiety, and Progressive Symbolization in the Psychoanalytic Process*. London: Karnac.

Freud, S. (1914c). On narcissism: an introduction. *S.E., 14*: 67–102. London: Hogarth.

Freud, S. (1916–1917). *Introductory Lectures on Psycho-analysis. Part III. S.E., 16*. London: Hogarth.

Freud, S. (1918b). *From the History of an Infantile Neurosis. S.E., 17*: 1–124. London: Hogarth.

Galatzer-Levy, R. M. (2009). Good vibrations: analytic process as coupled oscillations. *International Journal of Psychoanalysis, 90*(5): 983–1007.

Grande, T., Dilg, R., Jakobsen, T., Keller, W., & Krawietz, B. (2009). Structural change as a predictor of long-term follow-up outcome. *Psychotherapy Research, 19*(3): 344–357.

Green, A. (2002). *La pensée clinique*. Paris: Odile Jacob.

Hampstead Psychoanalytic Index (1981). *Bulletin of the Anna Freud Centre, 4*: 217–220.

Hoffman, I. Z. (2009). Doublethinking our way to "scientific legitimacy": the desiccation of human experience. *Journal of the American Psychoanalytic Association, 57*: 1043–1069.

Hoffmann, M. (2005). ¿Hay una lógica de la abducción?

Hurvich, M. (2003). The place of annihilation anxieties in psychoanalytic theory. *Journal of the American Psychoanalytic Association, 51*: 579–616.

Kächele, H., Schachter, J., & Thomä, H. (2008). *From Psychoanalytic Narrative to Empirical Single Case Research: Implications for Psychoanalytic Practice*. New York: Routledge.

Kernberg, O. F. (2006). Identity. Recent findings and clinical implications. *Psychoanalytic Quarterly, 75*: 969–1003.

Klein, G. S. (1976). *Psychoanalytic Theory. An Exploration of Essentials*. New York: International Universities Press.

Leibovich de Duarte, A. (2000). Cómo construimos nuestras hipótesis clínicas. *Revista de la Sociedad Argentina de Psicoanálisis, 3*: 91–102.

Leibovich de Duarte, A. (2004). Cómo psicoanalistas y psicoterapeutas cognitivos construyen sus inferencias clínicas. Estudio empírico. Available at: www.aperturas.org.

Leibovich de Duarte, A. (2010). Psychotherapists at work. Exploring the construction of clinical inferences. In: R. Schwarzer & P. A. Frensch (Eds.), *Personality, Human Development, and Culture: International Perspectives on Psychological Science* (Vol. 2) (pp. 29–43). New York: Psychology Press.

Leichsenring, F. (2009). Psychodynamic psychotherapy: a review of efficacy and effectiveness studies. In: *Handbook of Evidence-Based Psychodynamic Psychotherapy* (pp. 3–27). Boston: Humana Press.

Leuzinger-Bohleber, M., & Fischmann, M. (2006). What is conceptual research in psychoanalysis? *International Journal of Psychoanalysis, 87*: 1355–1396.

Leuzinger-Bohleber, M., Stuhrast, U., Rüger, B., & Beutel, M. (2003). How to study the 'quality of psychoanalytic treatments' and their long-term effects on patients' well-being: a representative, multi-perspective follow-up study. *International Journal of Psychoanalysis, 84*: 263–290.

Marty, P. (1985). *L'ordre psycho-somatique*. Paris: Payot.

OPD Task Force (2008). *Operationalized Psychodynamic Diagnosis OPD-2. Manual of Diagnosis and Treatment Planning*. Cambridge, MA: Hogrefe & Huber.

*Psychodynamic Diagnostic Manual* (*PDM*) (2006). Silver Spring, MD: Alliance of Psychoanalytic Organizations.

Reik, T. (1968). Theodor Reik speaks of his psychoanalytic technique. *American Imago, 25*: 16–20.

Ridderikhoff, J. (1993). Problem-solving in general practice. Theoretical medicine and bioethics. *Historical Archive, 14*: 343–363.

Sandell, R. (2012). Research on outcomes of psychoanalysis and psychoanalysis-derived psychotherapies. In: B. E. Litowitz, P. Williams, & G. O. Gabbard (Eds.), *Textbook of Psychoanalysis*. Washington, DC: American Psychiatric.

Sandell, R., Blomberg, J., Lazar, A., Carlsson, J., Broberg, J., & Schubert, J. (2000). Varieties of long term outcome among patients in psychoanalysis and long term psychotherapy: a review of findings in the Stockholm outcome of psychoanalysis and psychotherapy project (STOPPP). *International Journal of Psychoanalysis, 81*(5): 921–942.

Sandler, J. (1983). Reflections on some relations between psychoanalytic concepts and psychoanalytic practice. *International Journal of Psychoanalysis, 64*: 35–45.

Schwaber, E. (1981). Empathy: a mode of analytic listening. *Psychoanalytic Inquiry, 1*: 357–392.

Schwaber, E. (1992). Psychoanalytic theory and its relation to clinical work. *Journal of the American Psychoanalytic Association, 40*: 1039–1057.

Shedler, J. (2010). The efficacy of psychodynamic psychotherapy. *American Psychologist, 65*(2): 98.

Shedler, J., & Westen, D. (2004). Refining DSM-IV personality disorder diagnosis: integrating science and practice. *American Journal of Psychiatry, 161*: 1350–1365.

Shedler, J., Beck, A., Fonagy, P., Gabbard, G. O., Gunderson, J., Kernberg, O., Michels, R., & Westen, D. (2010). Personality disorders in DSM-5. *American Journal of Psychiatry*, 167(9): 1026–1028.

Sifneos, P. E. (1996). Alexithymia: past and present. *American Journal of Psychiatry, 153*: 137–142.

Skodol, A. E., Bender, D. S., Morey, L. C., Clark, L. A., Oldham, J. M., Alarcon, R. D., Krueger, R. F., Verheul, R., Bell, C. C., & Siever, L. J. (2011). Personality disorder types proposed for DSM-5. *Journal of Personality Disorders, 25*(2): 136–169.

Skodol, A. E., Clark, L. A., Bender, D. S., Krueger, R. F., Livesley, W. J., & Morey, L. C. (2011a). Proposed changes in personality and personality disorder assessment and diagnosis for DSM-5, Part I: Description and rationale. *Personality Disorders: Theory, Research, and Treatment*, 2: 4–22.

Skodol, A. E., Clark, L. A., Bender, D. S., Krueger, R. F., Livesley, W. J., & Morey, L. C. (2011b). Proposed changes in personality and personality disorder assessment and diagnosis for DSM-5. Part II: Clinical application. *Personality Disorders: Theory, Research, and Treatment*, 2: 23–40.

Stern, B. L., Caligor, E., Clarkin, J. F., Critchfield, K. L., Horz, S., MacCornack, V., Lenzenweger, M. F., & Kernberg, O. (2010). Structured interview of personality organization (STIPO): preliminary psychometrics in a clinical sample. *Journal of Personality Assessment, 92*(1): 35–44.

Strachey, J. (1969). The nature of the therapeutic action of psychoanalysis. *International Journal of Psychoanalysis, 50*: 275–292.

Tuckett, D., Basile, R., Birksted-Breen, D., Böhm, T., Denis, P., Ferro, A., Hinz, H., Jemstedt, A., Mariotti, P., & Schubert, J. (2008). *Psychoanalysis Comparable and Incomparable: The Evolution of a Method to Describe and Compare Psychoanalytic Approaches*. Hove: Routledge.

Tyrer, P. (2005). The problem of severity in the classification of personality disorders. *Journal of Personality Disorders, 19*(3): 309–314.

Ungar, V., Koritar, E., Jacobs, T., Bolognini, S., Rolland, J., & Turgeon, A. (2009). The core of the analytic process. International Psychoanalytical Association Panel, Chicago, July 2009. *Canadian Journal of Psychoanalysis, 18*: 141–146.

Wallerstein, R. S. (1965). The goals of psychoanalysis—a survey of analytic viewpoints. *Journal of the American Psychoanalytic Association, 13*: 748–770.

Wallerstein, R. S. (1988). One psychoanalysis or many? *International Journal of Psychoanalysis, 69*: 5–21.

Walls, G. (2006). On being willing to sell your grandmother short: a reply to Wolitzky. *Psychologist–Psychoanalyst (Newsletter of Division 39 of the American Psychological Association), XXVI*: 20–22, 26.

Winnicott, D. W. (1969). The use of an object. *International Journal of Psychoanalysis, 50*: 711–716.

Zimmermann, J., Ehrenthal, J. C., Cierpka, M., Schauenburg, H., Doering, S., & Benecke, C. (2012). Assessing the level of structural integration using operationalized psychodynamic diagnosis (OPD): implications for DSM-5. *Journal of Personality Assessment, 94*(5): 522–532.

*CHAPTER TWO*

# Leticia: the emergence of questions about herself

*Silvana Hernández Romillo*

The case of Leticia, and its discussion in a working group that followed the three-level model for observing patient transformations (3-LM), was briefly introduced in Chapter One. As Leticia's analyst, I must say that everything related to her analytic treatment and its discussion greatly stirred my interest. This essay takes up again, and expands, the ideas shared by the group. In particular, I explore the initial difficulties I encountered, the effects of group discussion on my work and thoughts, and the subsequent progress of Leticia's analysis. (Asking Leticia for permission to publish this material also led to new developments that are worth including here, with her consent.)

## *The beginning*

Considered in the context of my twenty years as an analyst, Leticia's case posed difficulties I had rarely encountered before. In the first place, there was her peculiar reserve. As I stated in the material I presented to the working group, I was struck by her robot-like way of walking and her slow, monotonous voice, and especially by her silences and her recurring "I don't know" answer whenever she had to talk about her inner feelings. Beyond mentioning her insecurity or her sense of being unable to do things right, she felt she had very little to say. "Nothing special happened in my childhood," she would claim. It seemed as though she searched inside herself and found nothing valuable to communicate—or did not even experience anything valuable.

At the same time, Leticia seemed very engaged in her analysis, thanks to her trust in the psychoanalyst who had referred her to me, of whose prestige she was well aware. Yet, despite her firm decision to start treatment, she was laconic; she answered my questions with monosyllables. I noted that she was tense and anxious. She was asking for help in her own way, but at the same time was too withdrawn into herself—shy, aloof. Above all, her emotionality was very hard to grasp. I was having a hard time starting a dialogue that might allow me to explore what was going on with her and what she thought was going on with her, that is, why she was coming. She also seemed to mistrust me to a certain extent.

Leticia would say time and time again that she was afraid of making mistakes at work. This was the *leitmotif* of her manifest discourse. Our beginning was very hard, very arduous. At times, I even felt discouraged. I would say that she was showing me her inner world through a big pad of white paper with a few traces in shades of grey. In this way, different scenarios appeared with a small number of characters, pictures that showed a scarcity of elements and considerable discontinuity between them. Furthermore, a disquieting stillness prevailed in them. Her persistent "I don't know" answer when asked about her emotions made it very hard to reach her inner feelings. On other occasions, in response to an intervention where I referred to emotional issues, she would say, "It had never occurred to me to think of it like that."

During the first two months, then, darkness reigned amid an austerity of words. Up to now, we were far from developing an analysis. At least, this was not the type of analysis I was used to, where patients' associations enabled me to offer interpretations about their unconscious conflicts, about what was going on in their lives in relation to their history and to the transference–countertransference field. Of her intimate relationships, she also said very little. I could make just a few inferences based on very brief accounts of a love relationship where the patient was being constantly abandoned, almost ignored. Still, she did not complain or utter any criticism or self-criticism about it. Neither did she express love expectations, and much less passion, regarding her partner.

Now I wonder whether this is something she lacks, or something she cannot show, even in her analysis. Well into her treatment, she was finally able to tell me why she did not react to this man's behaviour. She said to me, "I didn't want to think of what was happening, I took it like that, and that's it, I didn't want to think because if I did, I knew that the avalanche would hit." This type of scene, where a feeling of being anaesthetised predominates, seems to be another strong metaphor for her relationships. This dynamic also developed in the transference bond; she would remain silent so that the "avalanche" would not hit.

During this period, I chose not to offer interpretations related to her resistance. I did not want to say, for instance, "Perhaps 'I don't know' means the opposite, that you do know but are afraid of saying more about yourself. You're worried that I will criticise you." My impression was that this kind of interpretation might further impede our dialogue. Analytic work became harder. Her silences, and especially her continual "I don't know" response, created a peculiar barrier that thwarted the analytic process and her ability to associate freely. In this sense, a serious question emerged regarding how to make progress psychoanalytically. I identified an ambivalence between this blockage and her simultaneous adherence to the treatment (she was never absent and paid on time, while her emotional attitude was one of insecurity interspersed with a neutral position).

I believe that in these first stages, the analytic process was beginning to surface, but in my own mind rather than in the analyst–patient work. From a theoretical perspective, Bollas's (1987) views about the relevance of the countertransference in these situations come to mind. I also think of Winnicott's and other authors' ideas on the use of the analyst as an object (Winnicott, 1969). There was doubtless a painful failure to connect emotionally, the meaning of which we would be able to find later in light of the patient's earlier failures of that sort. At the same time, I often thought of her between sessions. I would go over some of her phrases in my mind and keep asking questions. I was concerned about our as-yet-meaningless failure to connect emotionally.

With regard to the countertransference, I had the fantasy of being rejected by her—of her abandoning treatment or even seeking a different analyst. It should be stressed here that I could not identify anything Leticia said that might have caused this feeling to arise in me. She expressed neither reproach nor expectations. It is as though accepting the treatment were all she could expect of herself, even though I persisted in my wish to analyse her. In this sense, Bollas claims that analysands

> create environments. Each environment is idiomatic and therefore unique. The analyst is invited to fulfil differing and changing object representations in the environment, but such observations on our part are the rare moments of clarity in the countertransference. For a very long period of time . . . we are being taken into the patient's environmental idiom . . . This inevitable, ever-present, and necessary uncertainty about why we feel as we do gives to our private ongoing consideration of the countertransference a certain humility and responsibility. The most ordinary countertransference state is a not-knowing-yet-experiencing one. (Bollas, 1987, pp. 202–203)

Looking at her history and our work during the years of her treatment, I think that there might also have existed a projective identification component. The fear of rejection "for doing things wrong" (in the patient's own words) appeared in Leticia as one of the major aspects of her conflicts, which were connected with the superego (guilt, among others). While I had experienced this type of behavior in many other treatments, I was struck by the features it acquired in this case, the ways in which it touched my sensitivity and somehow produced this countertransference acting out, where a kind of inhibition of my analytic function also took place. At times, I also felt stuck, with too many "I don't know" answers, and somewhat confused.

In this same line, I wonder if this fantasy was an enactment of the beginning of the analysis (Bernardi, 1999), the working-through of which facilitated the treatment's progress. At the same time, I continued to reflect upon this experience in relation to the patient's need to make me undergo her painful emotional experiences—distance, confusion—such as she had done since early childhood. Leticia's memory (always a screen memory) that most resonated in me was that of a girl who would search for a hiding place every time they moved to a new house, fantasising that she would stay in that place and wait for someone to find her. It remained a fantasy until she finally did it and, painfully, stayed in the alleged hiding place for hours because nobody came searching for her. Perhaps this memory became a metaphor for her relationships. She would hide so that those close to her would worry about her absence (there was so much absence in her early sessions!) and go looking for her. In this way, she achieved her goal of being gazed at, loved, *found* in the deepest meaning of the word. I played this finder role, in a way, in my analytic function, as I describe later.

After a few months in this foggy zone I decided to make some changes. Given that free association had not developed, I would set aside my suspended attention at times and play a more active role than I usually do so as to explore the patient's inner world with her. Now, I think that I sought to find nuances in her narrow repertoire of answers. It was I who offered the questions she could not produce in order to identify shades in the spectrum of her emotions that she was unable to perceive on her own. (Or we could also say that I provided a repertoire of words so that she would choose the ones that resonated with her and were closer to her feelings.) In plain language, I would say that in these sessions I spoke much more than I do with other patients.

I should add that this strategy had already been brewing in me and was encouraged by the working group. Group members considered that this attitude would best promote the progress of the analysis in a way that followed the patient's emotional labyrinths. The group saw the need for an analytic relationship that stressed the analyst's capacity for reverie, as well as her daydreaming and imagination, as a major tool for treatment. None the less, I would also like to highlight that a fertile, rich dream production had started to unfold. I analysed these dreams from a Freudian perspective, and they became an important resource for the analysis.

## *A session after group discussion (two years and eight months)*

*L*: I didn't dream last night. [Silence] My friend Damián called to discuss some work stuff.

*A*: What does it mean to you that you didn't dream before coming to the session?

*L*: No, it's that sometimes it's easier for me to talk about what I dreamed.

*A*: And what is harder for you?

*L*: Well, talking about myself, not thinking of anything important to say.

*A*: What do you think? That those things are inside you and you don't think of them, or that they aren't there?

*L*: [With certainty] No, I think they are, but it's hard for me . . .

*A*: Is it always hard to talk about yourself, or only here?

*L*: No, it's hard, yes . . . [Silence] Yes, I don't know how, it's that I don't know . . .

*A*: And when you're with your closest friends, do you talk about yourself in an intimate, confidential way? Do you tell them what's going on with you?

*L*: Yes, there are people I can talk to. With Damián I talk. There are things I choose not to tell him, but it's like, I've talked to him often.

*A*: And with him, for instance, are there issues that are harder for you to discuss?

*L*: What seems harder for me is when I think I'm sick or something like that; when there's something wrong with me. [She had had a hard time naming her suffering. In the end we called it depression, but I have always thought that it was more complicated than that.] I told him when I started feeling down last year.

*A*: And what did he say?

*L*: He said to see a psychiatrist. But I didn't.

*A*: Now you don't feel depressed. It seems that the analysis has been enough so far.

*L*: Yes.

*A*: And how do you see yourself? Do you think you were depressed?

*L*: Well, at some point I saw myself as, yes, really depressed [laughs softly]. Because at times it's really hard for me to do what I need to do . . . [Pause] I think that this happens to me everywhere. Like when I have to go to a party, wow, so hard . . . And I like those kinds of things, but even going to choir rehearsal, which I always liked, at the end I had a hard time going. [Silence] If I had to describe what I'm like when I'm full of life, I have a hard time recognising myself.

*A*: Let's see, what does this mean to you . . .?

*L*: That I can't accept that this is happening to me, that I'm feeling so down. [She becomes distressed and starts crying softly.] I think of what I'm like, of everything I like to do, many things related to being with people, and then I don't recognise myself in this depressive attitude. It's as if I were waiting for it to be over. Indeed, I calculate the dates and say to myself, "Because by this day I should be better." [She cries.]

*A*: Do you think that the depressive aspects of your mother that you told me about are connected to this?

*L*: Yes. Sometimes I think that she went through the same thing. I realised when I was already a grown-up.

*A*: The other day you said it had occurred to you that your mother was depressed when you were born.

*L*: That's what I figure. She never told me anything.

*A*: Sometimes she seemed sad. And what made her happy?

*L*: When she was working, only when she was working was she happy. [Silence] I started to think of other things she would do. She always drove us to our after-school activities, gym, piano, but then she would go to another job and we would stay with my grandmother. But I don't have memories of my mother being sad. Like . . .. the other way around, in a way. If she saw that you were down she would say, "You shouldn't be sad."

*A*: But when you were young, were you sad?

*L*: No, no, I was demanding. I was always asking for things; asking them to buy me things.

*A*: And that phrase, "You shouldn't be sad," it's as if you were telling it to yourself now.

*L*: Yes. [Silence] I remembered that when I was young I had a lot of allergies, eczema behind my knees and in the creases of my arms, and it was awful. And I thought whether it could be related . . . Then it went away. Later I had hay fever for a long time. They would give me a shot once a week until I turned seventeen. [Silence] Another thing I remembered is that when I was young, if I was sad I would write, since I was seven. I wrote a lot, things about school, that I liked a boy . . .

*A*: Ah, then there was a writer of your emotional states, a writer of your intimacy.

*L*: Yes . . . [Silence]

*A*: And did you find things that scared you in your journal?

*L*: What scared me the most was what I wrote before going camping that time. A very depressive content, because after a while I read it and thought, "But here I was in really bad shape."

*A*: Then we could say that what happened to you that summer was the outbreak of something that had already been brewing?

*L*: Yes, like, I realised that before I had been very sad, very unhappy, as if I were just going through life, that's it . . .

## *Next session*

*L*: On Tuesday after the session I went to read the journal I wrote when I was very young, seven years old. You know what was the first thing I wrote in that journal? That I was going to have a sleepover at a friend's, that her father would drive me in their car, and that the next day I got homesick. And I told my parents, and I wrote, "But I don't know if they understood." [Silence] Then I wrote, "Today was a nasty day because my parents fought." "Today I'm happy because my parents made up." I talked to my journal. I wrote things that worried me.

*A*: I think it would be interesting for us to work on what you felt: "I don't think they understood." What comes to mind now?

*L*: I don't know. But . . . What I think is that I didn't want to tell them I was homesick because I was scared that they wouldn't let me have sleepovers any more. Because I often asked, and they would rarely let me. Especially my father; he didn't like me to be away from home.

*A*: I'm curious to know what it might mean that they didn't understand you. What could that mean to you?

*L*: Ah, yes, it made me think that I said I missed them, and displaying too much homesickness was not done in my family . . . I don't know. Being very sensitive was wrong.

*A*: Being weak. [We laugh]

*L*: Yes, something like that . . . [She laughs] Like, showing too much wasn't . . . Now it makes me think that my mother used to say, "You know that I love you," but she could never say it straight, "I love you."

She says, "The most important thing in the world are my daughters." Yes, but she doesn't say it to me.

*A*: And with Daniel, how do you feel about showing your feelings?

*L*: Sometimes it's hard. Because he's like, the total opposite.

*A*: And with your nephew?

*L*: Ah, with him I try to be more straightforward, yes. I tell him what I feel quite often, but I don't know . . .

The fact that she searched for this journal that she had been writing since she was seven years old tells us several things. Writing entails an ability to symbolise. In Leticia's case, being able to write about herself was a way of appropriating her subjectivity as well as her psychic pain, and of working through them. According to Kristeva,

> psychoanalysis and literature are the same . . . except one publishes and the other stores its discoveries in order to live better. Yet it is the same psychic dynamics, which consists in sweeping away everything that is tired words and boring ways of living, *narrating a new momentum, and changing the way we talk to ourselves and name things and tie ourselves to others*. Some are able to make room for this language experience and inscribe this recreation of intimacy and personal matters in a cultural tradition such as literature . . . Others do not take that step, and settle for getting married again, or changing professions, or giving up alcohol, or simply falling in love when they had thought they were incapable of loving. The lab where things click *is the same*. (Kristeva, 2011, translated for this edition, my italics)

In terms of the transference, we can say that in the session with Leticia described above, she responds with a rich symbolic material, a childhood production that stirs in both of us a marked interest in moving forward with the analysis.

## *The discussion experience with the three-level model: why I chose to present this case to the group, and the benefits of doing so*

I was particularly interested in working on this material with the group. As I have already mentioned, Leticia's treatment posed many challenges at the beginning and, at the same time, after two years I believed that she was starting to show very encouraging changes. I was sure that relevant psychic transformations were starting to develop, and was eager to explore them in depth and systematically. The fact that the treatment was under way was also an appealing feature, as it made it possible to examine the material at a later stage.

The most useful aspect of group work was the possibility of perceiving in a more nuanced way the patient's difficulties in communicating with herself. I am referring to her difficulties with coming into contact with her emotions and fantasies, in putting into words various aspects of her inner world, and in freely associating and, hence, in reaching insight. The group devoted much time to this issue, and, as I said, its input greatly contributed to my ability to continue working with the patient throughout the treatment. I would also like to stress the positive repercussions of my work with the three-level model on other treatments with so-called difficult patients, as well as on interviews where obstacles emerge clearly from the start. When I am at a crossroads between explicit and implicit theorisation, some of the model's topics come to my help as suspended theorisation (Aulagnier, 1998).

At the first meeting, I learnt that some group members believed that the case was more serious than I had thought. They even outlined a discouraging prognosis. Others, instead, suggested that I go on implementing the mirroring technique that I had already been using (in the same sense, they mentioned the analyst's capacity for reverie). In addition, they encouraged me to work on some conflicts, such as Leticia's relationships with her mother and her teenage years, which had not appeared in the material. Based on the changes that could be glimpsed in the last few months, these colleagues offered a better prognosis.

Two diagnostic positions were thus outlined. One focused on structural problems, claiming the existence of early deficits that indicated that Leticia's was a serious case. The other maintained that Leticia was a neurotic patient with a very severe inhibition. According to this point of view, a sadistic superego played the main role in her conflicts by generating guilt feelings and a fear of rejection that paralysed her. Other contributions were less useful because they were laden with theories that seemed to explain it all, but actually hampered my ability to study the case further. I believe that this is a common problem experienced by analysts when discussing clinical material. We choose a certain theoretical perspective and attempt clinical readings from that vantage point.

These types of exchanges, in my view, hinder rather than facilitate analysts' ability to relate clinical phenomena. The latter should be told in a way that enabled listeners to picture the sessions, the patient, the emotional climate, and preverbal elements. One of the goals of the three-level model is to develop a narrative as close to the clinical experience as possible so that participants can visualise psychic change. Fortunately, the theoretical discussion was postponed until the final stage of group work (the third level), and the co-ordinators always sought to refer this discussion to the clinical material.

## *A later stage*

In her third year of analysis, Leticia started to freely associate at times and brought to her sessions a fertile dream production. At other times, however, she still needed the analyst's active-enough attitude. I believe that with this patient, we must contemplate both diagnostic aspects, that is, structural problems and conflicts. In this sense, my attitude as an analyst involved being always alert to the patient's fluctuations. In some sessions, or parts of sessions, I worked with suspended attention and interpretation, as we do with neurotic patients in order to tackle their unconscious conflicts. In others, I put to work my daydreaming capacity and resorted to a form of mirroring that produces a surplus and thus leaves a mark, and provided words as well, probably performing the function of a transformational object.

According to Bollas, this object is

> experientially identified by the infant with the process of the alteration of self experience; an identification that emerges from symbiotic relating, where the first object is 'known' not by cognizing it into an object representation, but known as a recurrent experience of being—a kind of existential, as opposed to representational, knowing. (Bollas, 1979, p. 96)

It is worth recalling here Joyce McDougall's words:

> Might we not also suppose that this fragile flower-child gazing upon his own image is seeking a lost object in the pool that is not himself,

> but the *recognition of himself in the eyes of Another*? This recognition of oneself as a separate and unique being is sought by the infant's avid gazing at his reflection in his mother's eyes – a reflection destined to give him not only his mirror image, but also what he represents for his mother (Winnicott, 1971b). Only thus may he hope to recognize himself as having a personal value in the eyes of this Other who looks at him and talks to him. (McDougall, 1992, p. 300–1; original italics).

Below are some fragments of sessions that illustrate the foregoing discussion of this stage in the analysis.

### *Session from the third year*

*L*: The other day Lucía and I started the course, and then we had dinner. We spent three hours chatting. When I got home, I got a text from her that said, "It's been so long since I had such a good time talking to a friend." It felt good chatting with her, we have a lot in common. We're both in analysis three times a week . . . We talked quite a bit about therapy. It felt good. I said that you had told me that sometimes I was "gruff," and she said to me, "You, gruff?" And I thought that it is here, rather, that I'm like that, and I remembered other things we talk about here.

*A*: What other things?

*L*: I thought that it's as if I were afraid of talking here. I remember when I told you what happened to my friend with her psychologist . . . what you told me . . . that I might be scared of talking here . . . Now I remembered that I had a dream. I dreamed that I took my CV to several universities, like, I was excited about doing the Master's. Because I also talked about that with Lucía. At times I feel like doing it, especially taking courses with other people, like, you learn more. And I also felt better these last few days, my state of mind.

I had a dream where I was going to see a client. I interviewed him in front of my father, and then when I woke up I thought, "My father must have really influenced what happens to me with people I work with," that I don't know enough . . . The other day Lucía told me she was going to see a psychiatrist and I remembered that I didn't call . . .

*A*: Do you think you didn't because you trust your analysis, or because calling a psychiatrist is a hard thing to do?

*L*: Well, both . . . I trust the analysis, yes, that's why I say that I have a hard time realising why, what it is that doesn't let me talk, that makes me be like, defensive.

*A*: But you also talk to a friend for three hours. And you come here three times a week . . .

*L*: Yes, I'm talking quite a bit . . . And with Lucía, yes, we understand each other well . . .

[I decided to mention the transference aspect—three hours with her friend, three sessions—without interpreting it because I understood that transference work was already taking place.]

*A*: How does Lucía see you? What image do you think she has of you?

[I focused on how the patient thought others saw her because this was part of a major aspect of our analytic work concerning her relationships, as the latter had gone unnoticed in the sessions for a long time. She would go to parties and spend time with friends, but never knew how to talk about how others felt about her. I wondered if she adopted an attitude of placid friendliness that allowed her to feel loved for her silence, and therefore did not dare to disagree. This was part of an insight that occurred a couple of years later.]

*L*: She said to me, "Now you look good," because I had looked sad to her before, and also too happy.

*A*: Tell me more.

*L*: Once, at the beginning, she thought I was too happy, like, I was a bit over the top. Oh, and the other day she told me, "When you seemed more hyper, yes, you were more gruff," like you told me that day [I had used that word in a previous session].

*A*: Did you notice that of your hyper times we know less? It's a path we should explore, don't you think?

*L*: Yes. [Silence] Now I think about that stage and I think it's true, but when it's happening I don't realise. [Silence] Now I was thinking whether this would happen to me again. Because I wonder, do I identify feeling good with being hyper? [Silence]

I don't know. The other night I went to dinner with Alejandro and Lucía, after the monthly work meeting, and I felt good, I laughed heartily . . .

While pointing out the absence of a discussion of Leticia's dreams in this session would be a valid criticism, at this stage I used dreams as a guide to understand the patient's emotional state. I was particularly interested in both the fact that dreams were produced and the moment of the session when they appeared. It would be worth recalling here this statement from *The Interpretation of Dreams*:

> This, however, is the most common and the most striking psychological characteristic of the dream; a thought, usually the one wished for, is objectified in the dream, and represented as a scene, or – as we think – experienced. (Freud, 1900a, p. 535)

In this session I noticed that the patient started to ask questions about herself ("Do I identify feeling good with being hyper?"). This timid beginning—which provides the title for this article—seems to be a path that acquired increasing relevance in the analytic process. Leticia's questions became more complex and, hence, richer. This is the role of analysis: to generate questions that had not been there or had been concealed by defence mechanisms—to help patients become epistemologists of themselves in reference to the ever-fleeting sparkles of the unconscious.

Some time later, Leticia was able to discuss her conflicts, which were related to her childhood sexuality and the vicissitudes of the Oedipus complex, especially in relation to the maternal figure. At the same time, we started working on her unconscious conflicts concerning her brother. (Due to lack of space and to my choice of a specific cross-section of the treatment, I cannot discuss this aspect here.) What follows are other fragments of sessions from Leticia's fifth year of analysis, when these questions would become increasingly nuanced.

*L*: I was thinking of what you told me in my last session, something I didn't like . . . That when I'm with my friends I pretend I'm all goody-goody so that everyone will love me, or something like that . . . I didn't like it, that's not the way it is . . . Although, however, I remember that when I was very young my friends' parents, like, preferred me, because I always behaved, I wasn't a troublemaker . . . And you know what my friends would say to me? They would say, "You behave because you want them to like you, you're always trying to make a good impression" . . . Well, the truth is that it's similar to what you told me [she giggles]. And yes, it's something like that. I don't confront people, I listen to them, no problem, and I don't say anything. Maybe that's why they love me . . . [Silence] But I wonder: Could the problem be that I don't feel, or that I don't transmit what I feel?

*A*: Good question.

*L*: I think it's more that I feel but I don't dare convey what I feel because if I say something that people don't like, they will reject me. [Silence] And it's also a bit like that here . . . [Long silence]

*A*: What's it like here, with me?

*L*: Yes, I realise that I do watch what I say a bit, sometimes I don't tell you everything I feel, I don't know, like, I want to preserve my image here too, I don't know how to put it . . . [Silence]

*A*: Yes, a few times, like today, you do tell me that you didn't like what I told you in your session.

*L*: Yes . . . [She laughs softly.] I think I'm always trying to preserve my image so that people won't think I'm doing things wrong, or something like that.

*A*: Now we can understand what you told me at the beginning of the analysis—that you were scared of making mistakes at work, of what others would think about that, your fear of being considered incompetent.

*L*: Wow, yes, that's true, always, always . . . I don't know how to change that, it's always there . . .

Here we find a sharper style and, at the same time, an ability to inhabit the transference. The patient can verbalise her fantasies with me, travel smoothly toward the past, and associate freely. It is interesting to note her increased capacity to symbolise, which raises new questions about herself that lead to findings related to her defence mechanisms, already in the field of unconscious conflicts where the superego and guilt play key roles.

I believe that a significant part of the treatment shows changes in the patient's way of being with others, including the analyst. The construction of a new, more colourful narrative of herself can be glimpsed. None the less, questions persist about the work of the transference and countertransference, my active style, and issues related to the patient's sexuality and defences. Of the latter, inhibition seems to stand out the most. At this stage of the analysis, there is still more to do. In view of what has been discussed so far, we need to take on the compelling challenge of working towards Leticia's reunion with the writer–creator girl. When I say this to her, almost with the same words, she adds, "Yes, and my relationship with my body."

I have an optimistic feeling concerning my work with this patient. I think that analytic treatment is the best choice for her; changes achieved so far within and without the office are the basis for this conjecture. Yet, I also have a sense, which I can clearly recognise thanks to my analytic sensitivity, that Leticia has the potential to increase her inner capacity—verbalisation, transformations in her relationships, and insights related to her unconscious conflicts. The realisation of this potential will enable her to continue to rid herself of defences that still disrupt her everyday life.

To conclude, I shall go back to the origin of this chapter—the presentation of the clinical material so that it could be analysed according to the three-level model. My colleagues' opinions and discussions have remained within me as an ever-present sounding board. What is more, the disagreements that emerged from group discussions promoted my own internal debates during difficult times. In this way, I achieved greater freedom to think of the two major groups of hypotheses not as exclusive, but as occupying different moments of the analytic process, even within a session. Supporting patients in these fluctuations is, in a way, part of the art of psychoanalysis.

If someone were to ask me about my psychoanalytical affiliation, I would certainly answer that I am a Freudian, although I also integrate authors such as the ones I have quoted here (Winnicott and Bollas, among others). That is how I conduct my clinical practice. Incorporating the three-level model allowed me to add elements that are probably part of different theoretical developments, but are presented in the model in a systematic, detailed way. Such a presentation facilitates our delving into issues such as the ones discussed above, among them, patients' communication with themselves, intimate relationships, and relational patterns.

### *Epilogue (after asking for the patient's informed consent to the publication of her clinical material)*

At the beginning of the session where I ask for her consent, I invite the patient to sit on the couch and I explain my request in detail. She seems moved. "Yes," she says, and then, as she lies down on the couch, she adds, "It's clear that there is work, yes . . . since I started until now . . . yes." At the end of the session, I give her the paper to read.

In the next session she tells me that she read the paper. Reading about herself as a patient produced a sense of estrangement and stirred up many feelings, she says, some of them contradictory . . . and a need arose in her to write down her feelings in the notebook she always carries with her.

## References

Aulagnier, P. (1979). *Los destinos del placer. Alienación, amor, pasión* [The vicissitudes of pleasure: alienation, love, passion]. Buenos Aires: Paidós, 1998.

Bernardi, B. D. (1999). Attualitá di una polémica: le due dimensione dell'interazione analítica [The validity of a debate: the two dimensions of analytic interaction]. *Rivista di Psicoanalisi, 40*(1): 131–152.

Bollas, C. (1979). The transformational object. *International Journal of Psychoanalysis, 60*: 97–107.

Bollas, C. (1987). *The Shadow of the Object: Psychoanalysis of the Unthought Known*. New York: Columbia University Press.

Freud, S. (1900a). *The Interpretation of Dreams. S.E., 4*. London: Hogarth.

Kristeva, J. (2011). Psicoanálisis y literatura son la misma cosa [Psychoanalysis and literature are the same thing]. Interview by Mario Libertella. *Revista Ñ*. Available at: www.revistaenie.clarin.com/ideas/julia-kristeva-entrevista_0_589141333.html

McDougall, J. (1978). *Plea for a Measure of Abnormality*. New York: Brunner/Mazel, 1992.

Winnicott, D. W. (1969). The use of an object. *International Journal of Psychoanalysis, 50*: 711–716.

CHAPTER THREE

# Irina: an adolescent

## The usefulness of the three-level model for observing patient transformations

*Marina Altmann de Litvan*

### *Introduction*

The aim of this chapter is to use the three-level model for observing patient transformations to interpret specific clinical observations. I write from the perspective of the patient's analyst in order to describe the new insights about the patient that emerged from the group discussion following the model (Montevideo Focus Group: Marina Altmann de Litvan, Ricardo Bernardi, Beatriz De León de Bernardi, Nancy Delpréstitto, Alejandro Garbarino, Silvana Hernández Romillo, Adela Leibovich de Duarte, Evelyn Tellería, and Clara Uriarte, March 2011). My intention is to show how the model works, what transformations (as observed by the working group) occurred or did not occur during the analytic process in the case of this particular patient, and how the model contributed to achieving more accurate psychoanalytic observations.

As outlined in Chapter One (by Ricardo Bernardi), the 3-LM looks at clinical material at three different levels: phenomenological description, the different dimensions of change, and the theoretical hypotheses of the analyst (the third level is developed in Chapter Seven, by Adela Leibovich de Duarte). Our work aimed to assess (i) how the analyst's mind identifies the different reasons that bring a patient to therapy; (ii) how the analyst understands what happens in the transference and countertransference relationship in the analytic process; (iii) how these issues lead to positive changes, negative changes, or no change at all. The clinical material considered in this article, which focuses on an adolescent female, was selected to test the very first version of the 3-LM.

At the first level, the group attempts to give a phenomenological description of change. I refer to different topics regarding the patient in question: her body and how she experiences and expresses herself with it, the meaning of clothes, her self-destructiveness, her grievances, and her communication style.

At the second level, "main dimensions of change", I analyse most of the model's dimensions and outline how we observed them in this clinical material. The subjective experience of illness, patterns of interpersonal relationship, main intrapsychic conflicts, and structural aspects of mental functioning are illustrated with the clinical material highlighted by the group.

The model was later improved thanks to the group's enriching discussion, comments and observations, as well as to the feedback we received from many people who attended the Clinical Observation Committee's presentations.

## *Why study change?*

Change is an important matter for psychoanalysis and has been addressed by several authors. In 1980, Goldfried documented a growing discontent among therapists of varying orientations. Psychoanalytic, behavioural, and humanistically orientated clinicians were starting to raise serious questions about the limits of their respective approaches to change. Such questioning leads, in Goldfried's mind, to a more open attitude towards contributions from other paradigms.

Years later, when analysing the goals and special nature of psychoanalytic treatment, Bucci (1997) stated that patients enter treatment with a set of psychic structures that determine their emotional worldviews, and that analysts have their own emotional predispositions and views. The mental and emotional representations of both participants in the analytic process are internal, private, directly related to their experiences, and known only partially even to them. The change sought by psychoanalysis is in the patient's inner representational world. Bucci remarks that it is a great challenge to develop a science whose subject matter consists of mental and emotional representations that are private and sometimes inaccessible.

In 1975, Easkow and Parloff divided potential assessment methods to study change into four categories:

> (1) patient measures (tests, inventories, direct self-reports, behavioural measures, physiological measures, interviews and speech measures, cognitive and perceptual measures, projective techniques); (2) therapist measures (therapists' assessments and measures of outcome); (3) relevant others' measures (i.e., the use of estimates by relatives and other significant informants besides therapists and independent clinical evaluators); and (4) independent clinical evaluations. (Cited in Blatt & Ford, 1994, p. 20)

Luborsky, Singer, and Luborsky (1975, p. 233), in turn, noted that independent clinical evaluations "have an obvious advantage over the patient and therapist as judges of therapeutic outcome".

Blatt and Ford (1994) tried to assess therapeutic change occurring in hospitalised patients towards the end of these patients' participation in a treatment programme and prior to their discharge from the hospital. These authors considered it important to distinguish different types (or levels) of change, that is, to differentiate between the psychological and behavioural effects of treatment. In their own words,

> an essential first step in studying therapeutic change, however, is to demonstrate that treatment results in substantial change within the treatment context and to specify precisely the nature of that change for different types of patient. (p. 2)

Afterwards, research could be directed to determining "how, to what degree, and in what ways changes in different types of patients within the therapeutic process contribute to broader forms of adaptation beyond the treatment setting" (p. 2). For Blatt and Ford, "rather than searching for universal measures of change, it might be more productive to consider the possibility that different types of patients may change in different ways" (p. 18).

In their book, *Emotion, Psychotherapy and Change*, Safran and Greenberg (1991) focus on the emotional dimensions of psychotherapeutic change from a clinical and theoretical perspective. Fosshage (2005), instead, centres on therapeutic action and the battle waged in the history of psychoanalysis between interpretation/insight and relational experience as focal points. The ongoing paradigmatic shift within psychoanalysis from an intrapsychic to a relational (Greenberg & Mitchell, 1983; Mitchell, 1988) or intersubjective (Atwood & Stolorow, 1984) field model, where the analytic encounter is viewed as a co-constructed "intersection of two subjectivities" (Stolorow, Brandchaft, & Atwood, 1987), has accentuated the importance of relational experience for our understanding of development, pathogenesis, transference, and therapeutic action. Relational interaction is so important that exploratory/interpretative analytic work is best conceived as an aspect of analytic relational experience that can only be understood within the context of that experience. Fosshage affirms that "the foreground and background shifts that comprise the dance between the implicit and explicit systems provide an important key to understanding and facilitating the psychoanalytic process" (Fosshage, 2005, p. 535).

The Boston Process of Change Study Group (Stern et al., 1988) is a group of infant researchers working with experienced psychoanalytic adult clinicians to expand our understanding of the nature of the change process in psychoanalytic psychotherapy. They present new insights into the "something more" than interpretation that is needed to make conscious the unconscious. Their model emphasises that interpersonal "moments" between analyst and patient create change. Interpersonal factors are crucial in the generation of procedural aspects of personality functioning.

Awareness of the other is a prerequisite for articulation, differentiation, and flexibility. These relationship structures develop in the same way as the recurrent break-and-repair cycles of the mother–infant dialogue. As implicit relational knowledge structures arise out of developmental imbalance, it is to be expected that they will be emotionally charged and retain a spontaneous quality. The concept of implicit relational known is descriptively unconscious, unthought, but not unknowable. Both participants in the exchange are able to restructure their implicit relational systems in the light of their experience of the "scaffolding" (Vygotsky, 1966) of the other's mental organisation.

Fonagy (1998) states that clinicians are accustomed to "working with procedural memory". "Clinical sensitivity ... is mostly astuteness about the multiple meanings encoded into a single verbal message using stress, speech pauses, intonation, and other features of pragmatics, paradigmatically all expressions of procedurally stored knowledge" (p. 348). This feature of analytic work constitutes an important issue for the 3-LM. As the working group noticed, the analyst's verbal transmission of the clinical material to the group affects participants' understanding of what happened in the psychotherapeutic process.

Widlöcher (1970) studies the theory of change after revisiting Freudian structural theory. This author emphasises that while it is important to assess changes, it is also important to consider resistances. For Widlöcher, change is a transformation of the dynamic and economic equilibrium that regulates the reports of the ego, the superego, and the id. Resistances express conflicts in these three areas. One of the issues he highlights is resistance to change. Transformations are linked to what we consider "cure" in psychoanalysis. This author believes that change is a displacement of the charge of investitures. Libidinal investment in the object (marked by the conscious investiture of the desired object) is replaced, in the unconscious, by the investiture of representation. Widlöcher states that we can develop an equation in dynamic, topographic, and economic terms. The dynamic point of view does not change.

The quality and outcome of the therapeutic process can be greatly improved by understanding the modalities of change. From an epistemological point of view, Klimovsky (1994), connecting math and psychotherapeutic processes, claims that changes could either stem from an accumulation of ongoing micro-processes or happen abruptly, becoming an unavoidable discontinuity. The latter constitutes a real gap where the curve is interrupted and starts elsewhere assuming different values. Examples of this process could be Bion's "catastrophic change", Strachery's "mutative interpretation", or the "scientific revolutions" in epistemology highlighted by Kuhn.

It is crucial to know whether or not a transformation has actually occurred, as well as its impact on the evolution of the process. We must also take into account that there are different kinds (or levels) of change (Klimovsky et al., 1994). The first level manifests itself in patients' behaviours, actions, and material; the second corresponds to patients' knowledge about their own behaviour and problems; the third refers to judgements made by patients concerning their own knowledge; the fourth focuses on patients' own estimation of the treatment's progress and of the effects it is having on their lives and their suffering. The three-level model takes all these levels of change into account.

When we perceive a change in the patient, either during analytic work or after a session, we must understand whether it is the change we are hoping for or whether it will be detrimental to the analytic process. That is why we need to analyse the kinds of change that may take place in order to determine which are significant or desirable and which are inappropriate, and why. My opinion in the matter is that when we talk about transformations, we must take into account the relationship with both internal and external objects.

## *How do we observe change in psychoanalysis?*

Observation is a controversial issue in our field, and there are many different opinions about its relevance for analytic work. My own experience has led me to change my view on this subject over time. Currently, I approach this question through the synthesis of various perspectives: that of a practising analyst, that of a researcher in the field of infant mental health, and that of a professor at a psychoanalytic institute. In my professional life, analytic research and clinical practice have represented separate training processes that followed parallel paths for many years. As time went by, due to certain aspects of my clinical and teaching experience, areas of intersection and mutual enrichment emerged in my mind.

The definitions of the verb "to observe" and the noun "observation" have a very interesting dual quality. On the one hand, "to observe" means "to be or become aware of something", which suggests a passive action whereby the observer is witnessing something that is happening outside. On the other hand, it means "(to make) an inference or a judgment that is acquired from or based on observing" (see www.thefreedictionary.com). In this second sense, the same word is used to designate an active role that implies witnessing something and, based on what was witnessed, forming a judgement that is necessarily subjective. It is this duality that makes observation so difficult to work with and poses, as I see it, the most interesting challenge.

The object of the study of psychoanalysis is "the relationship that patient and analyst help create" (Nieto, 1965, p. 9). Accordingly, a "psychoanalytic fact" is a modification of the structure adopted by the interpersonal patient–analyst relationship—a variation that is grasped by the analyst in the transference bond. This psychoanalytic fact acquires meaning in relation to the context.

For many Uruguayan psychoanalysts, and particularly for me, it was Marta Nieto who stimulated our interest in research based on clinical material. Thanks to my experience as Chair of the IPA Project Committee on Clinical Observation and Testing and to many other opportunities I was offered over the years, I understand that a great number of the issues raised and examined in Marta's seminars are still valid today and deserve to be revisited. Rereading her work and discussing it with other colleagues represented a major contribution to my own work. I would like to focus here on some ideas that she discusses in her essay "Algunos problemas del analista como investigador" ["Some problems faced by analysts as researchers"] (Nieto, 1965).

Their interest *in a specific aspect of the analytic process* influences analysts' observation. The effects of this influence may range from the negative end of the spectrum, where the material is distorted, to the positive end, where it acts as a special training for observing a specific psychoanalytic matter. Another important issue is the *existence of blind spots* in the analyst. In this regard, we need to ask if these blind spots might invalidate observation. According to Nieto, *a priori*, we are justified to think that observation may be invalid if our blind spot overlaps with an important aspect of the patient's conflicts. We should also consider here another situation described by M. and W. Baranger (1961–1962): when analyst and patient coincide in their blindness (splitting). All these points must be taken into account when developing a clinical observation method that allows us to verify our hypotheses.

For Nieto, verifying consists in examining what type of modification occurs after an interpretation. This author describes the whole process as follows:

> ... we observe a modification and formulate a hypothesis that explains it. We translate this hypothesis into an interpretation and

> then observe again to see if this interpretation promoted a modification of such kind and exhibiting such signs that we can infer that the interpretation was accurate. (Nieto, 1965, p. 12)

Nieto questions the "evidence" analysts find in clinical material in terms of the lack of rigour of the verification process. "Sometimes", she claims, "there are almost no traces of the material that would serve as evidence . . . we [analysts] expressly present the material from the point of view of providing proof", without enquiring into it. "We offer a series of fragments where we may repeat the same mistake concerning the direction of our gaze that we made at the observation stage" (p. 13).

The aim of the Project Committee on Clinical Observation and Testing is precisely to improve the way in which we systematise and provide evidence for our clinical observations. The three-level model was developed with this aim in mind, and the clinical material used to test and discuss the first version of this model was Irina's.

## *How was the clinical material selected?*

Once the 3-LM had been designed, we needed to test it on a clinical material. Irina, a patient I had treated long ago, came to my mind. I had worked with her by focusing on the evolution of her dreams and on differences I found in her mental functioning. I recalled having observed some transformations, so I thought she might be an interesting case for our first test. She had finished her analysis nine years earlier and had left the country. I remembered the intense, comfortable relationship that had developed between us, with both pleasurable and painful moments. I had recorded some sessions with very extensive notes (I usually highlight those sessions that I find important for some reason). We used this clinical material to conduct a workshop that would test the effectiveness and usefulness of the 3-LM. The model requires that we examine the transformation process in the three levels. The clinical material was presented and discussed in a panel at the 46th International Psychoanalytic Association Congress (Altmann, Fitzpatrick-Hanly, & Leuzinger-Bohleber, 2012).

When we present a case, we select particular sections of the material, omit others, and ignore information that is not needed to understand the case. Consequently, we do not present it in a fully objective way; we purposely choose what to show (Messer, 1994, p. 3), and the vicissitudes of memory/recording also pose obstacles to objective reporting. The model aims to improve this situation by providing an initial phenomenological description of what happens in the session that should be as concrete as possible. In this case, I had notes from sessions I deemed critical to the group's understanding of the patient at those moments of the treatment.

## *How does the model work?*

The material was presented to the group in the raw so that participants could develop their own ideas regarding each level of observation. Furthermore, it was sent to them in advance so that they could read it beforehand. At the workshop session, the treating analyst read the material aloud in order to transmit her experience in a more vivid way. Her reading gave the group a more comprehensive view of what had happened with this analyst and this patient.

Irina's material was discussed first during a twelve-hour session, and then during a six-hour meeting held three months later; the group felt the need to work further on certain aspects of the case. Some participants pointed out the difference between the written material and its verbal transmission by the analyst. It had been hard for them to understand the patient when considering only the written text. Yet, thanks to the analyst's intonation and speech patterns, the oral presentation had provided greater depth and a more accurate image of the patient.

## *Working on Irina's case with the three-level model for observing patient transformations*

The first part of the clinical material observed with the three-level model comprises a brief presentation of the patient's background and the first interviews with the analyst. We call this the anchor point. As we started reading the material, we found that the group needed to read it all at once. The analyst chose to present the first and second sessions in full and two significant fragments of later sessions (at nine months and one and a half years after the analysis had started).

Irina started treatment because she was very depressed and anguished. She was a young teenager (sixteen years old) of average build who perceived her body as obese. She treated her body like a machine; she exercised excessively (dancing) and followed very strict diets in order to satisfy her internal ideal of plenitude and happiness, which was "being thin". This behaviour led her at times to binge eat and vomit compulsively (since she was twelve). Irina and her parents had requested some interviews when she was twelve years old. At that time, I had a meeting with her and her family but made no recommendation for treatment. When she was almost seventeen years old, she asked her parents to consult with me again. Her analytic treatment varied in frequency. Initially, she came twice a week, but there were periods when she was very distressed and needed a higher frequency. During these periods, we had three to five sessions a week.

Irina is clever and charming, and has quickly established a strong bond with me. She is very aware of my clothes and whether or not I wear matching accessories. Every session she spontaneously compliments or criticises me, as if she were assessing me. She measures and monitors my body as persistently as she does her own. It is within this unfolding of the transference that her different experiences of her body will gradually transform. What is striking is that she has chosen to work with me, an analyst who does not represent the body ideal that she seeks for herself.

When she recounts her dreams at a certain stage in the analysis, association is limited. However, in the analytic process itself these repetitive dreams intertwine with shifts in the transference that gradually take her symptoms in new directions.

## *Level 1: phenomenological description of transformations*

First, the group tackled Level 1, "phenomenological description of transformations". They studied the narrative of the clinical material to find evidence of change occurring between the anchor point and later sessions. The early associations selected as anchor points would return time and time again as the analysis proceeded, and would reveal greater depth and complexity when viewed through the relationship with the analyst in the transference and countertransference. These later associations and enactments would make change and its absence more accessible to observation.

The group analysed different aspects of the clinical material at the phenomenological level and identified several categories to study change that are discussed below.

### *The body: how she experiences her body, expresses herself with it, and attacks it*

The group deemed this category crucial in different ways. There is an unfolding and transformation of these aspects during the analytic process. One of the themes of interaction is the body in its fat/thin tension. For example, in the first interview the patient says,

> "I'm throwing up very often. Partly on purpose. It's a habit. I'm smoking a lot." [She talks very quickly, keeps talking and jumping between different conversation topics.]
>
> "My diet is a key issue . . . I have many ups and downs. I fast three days in a row and then I eat ten cupcakes. I'm seriously overweight. I suffer from hyperthyroidism and everything overwhelms me."
>
> "I love drinking. May I lie down [on the couch]?"

Her fat/thin tension is also expressed through other persons and in different dreams.

> "I dream about my grandpa being thin; I dream about my grandpa being fat, like he used to be. They asked me about food all the time . . ." (First session.)

This dream triggers no associations. Such lack of associations was an important feature of the first months of analysis. Later on, she mentions that she always dreams about very slim people, without breasts, as if they came from concentration camps. Even though she does not see their faces, she knows they are her parents, but their bodies are skinny. Body shape is always present—always thin. Her daily concerns appear in her dreams (manifest content) without much dream distortion.

Her body is also exuberant. It is in the second interview that she can say that she is unable to take proper care of it.

The body also appears as a vehicle for self-expression through dancing. When she dances, she feels good and graceful. She displays a sexual, vital body that must be admired by others:

"I like dancing. I like dancing with feathers, like a music-hall theatre. My father warned me not to act like a floozy."

"I can dance gracefully; it's a gift. I can dance to anything because I like dancing. I like vaudeville; I like the fact that dancing acts as a complement to the entire show. My gracefulness helps me!"

"Would I like to perform on Broadway?! Well, hold on. I wouldn't like to dance vaudeville, swinging your hips, and the moves . . . I wouldn't dare. It's kind of dirty . . . I see them as prostitutes, something between being abused and dancing."

Bulimic patients' active use of their musculature is considered a self-generated, narcissistic way of holding themselves together in the wake of severe anxiety. In this patient, there was a sense of un-integration and "catastrophic anxieties of the dead-end, falling through space, liquefying [and] life-spilling-out variety" (Bick, 1986, p. 298), and she needed to defend herself against them. Bick also mentions that the second skin "manifests itself as either [a] partial or total type of muscular shell or a corresponding verbal muscularity" (1968, p. 486). The type of skin described by Bick as "hippopotamus skin" (thick) corresponds to a way of functioning that is similar to this patient's—hyperactive, with a need to spend long hours in the gym and be constantly on the move, and unable to relax easily.

At the beginning of the treatment, Irina brings to therapy the manifestation of her symptoms in her own body (vomiting, binge eating). According to the group's observations, however, later the body takes a more mental dimension in the interaction with the analyst in the session. Thanks to this ability to interact, the mechanic, rejected, non-subjective body of the first interviews becomes less mechanical, and the patient tries to come into contact with it. Participants identified this more mental dimension in Irina's dreams from the ninth month of treatment:

"I ate the cake, and then I slit my wrists with my scissors."

"I become terribly anxious. I don't want to go out. My dad told me that I had lost three kilos in one week; I felt like locking myself in."

She tells me that she felt like taking a whole bottle of pills. She thought about having her tongue pierced so that she could spend two weeks without eating.

> "I want to get much thinner. I take aspirin all day long. I feel sick. I want to disappear. At night I had a crying fit. Nobody noticed. I stayed in the shower for a while, throwing up."

The dream of the beginning of the session is repeated, but is now linked to current events (the interruption of her analysis due to the holidays) and to other significant losses in her life. I convey this interpretation to her. She mentions thoughts of disappearing, running away, falling asleep, or being hospitalised. "I feel like being hospitalised or taking pills," she cries.

Later on she brings her perceptions and distortions of her body image—thin/fat—intertwined with conflicts in her mother–daughter relationship:

> "Same as always. Like, I get this terrible urge, it's an anxiety attack, it's like in a split second I ate a whole bag of cookies and as soon as I finished I threw them up, you know what I mean? It was at night, I felt kind of tired, I felt really fat because it didn't matter how much I weighed, I felt three times as fat! You know what I mean? I didn't feel like doing anything!" (9 months of treatment.)

> "On Saturday we were going to go dancing and in the end we didn't go because Maria had a fight with her mother. I spent the night at Maria's and that day I dreamed that I resumed ballet. And I was dancing ballet. I was actually very thin, and the teacher said to me, 'You're really fat. Keep losing weight.' I don't know what else . . . But it wasn't me; not even me when I was younger. And she said, like, I was doing everything wrong, and I woke up. The woman went like that with her back [Irina reproduces her expression], like she always did, but she wasn't my teacher. It was a teacher that hadn't taught me before."

Her dreams allow her to experience more of her internal world in a more symbolised way. At this time, she brings her problems with a woman teacher. Her dreams are not self-destructive; there is another person criticising her.

After a year and a half, she can make contact with her own body through her contact with and questions about the analyst's body. She asks the analyst, "Are you asthmatic?" The patient explains her question in her own way: "You're fat because you take steroids." She starts to realise that fatness does not only result from excess eating. She is learning that her problems are different from the body problems she attributes to the analyst. She wants to change, but feels hopeless because of the "malignant thoughts" that appear in her mind.

A topic that emerges in the psychotherapeutic process in connection with her body image is her wish to get a tattoo. One day she arrives and says, "Look, I got my belly button pierced." I am shocked; I did not expect this. The ring in her navel has two rhinestones. Aesthetically, it is very attractive. I see the navel as representing the trace of the first break between mother and daughter. I interpret this belly-button piercing as a sign of the patient's efforts to separate from her mother:

> "Do you remember the tattoos? Well, I thought that instead of getting a tattoo I could get a piercing. I feel I'm doing much better with my diet."

She links not having gained weight to having inserted a jewel into her navel.

Group members believed that getting a piercing instead of a tattoo, and the way the patient experienced this decision with the analyst in the transference, represented a significant change after a year and a half of treatment. "It makes me feel safe about my diet," Irina had said to me. "It makes me take care of myself. I talked to my mum about it and she liked the idea. My father told me, 'I'd rather you didn't do it, but it's better than a tattoo.' It hurt a little at the beginning, but not any more . . ." [Then she talked about dancing ballet and said that her mother was happy about that.]

Wanting to get a tattoo and having her navel pierced are ways of looking for a mark that will differentiate her. Tattoos and piercings function as bodily signs; they have an identification function. Irina was testing her parents' reaction and searching for a unique way of being herself.

### *The different meanings of clothes*

Irina's first interview when she was twelve years old was due to her compulsion to buy designer clothes. At that time, she would do anything to get the clothes she wanted. I connected her desire to buy these clothes to her desire to tattoo her body. Over the years, her interest shifted from wearing clothes from well-known brands to branding her body (like cattle), and later to the scars left on her body by implant surgery (after a year and a half): "My mum wants me to get buttock implants. My body and hers are very important to her."

For Irina's family—her grandparents and parents—clothes are a mark of social belonging, a feminine ideal that must be fulfilled somehow:

> "The clothes issue. My grandpa would supply me with clothes. I went to the mall with my grandparents, and suddenly there was a jacket that cost 4,000 pesos, super expensive. My grandpa thought about buying it but decided not to, because otherwise he would have to give the same amount of money to every grandchild . . . Because of the clothes? I think so. I went into a store and bought myself some jeans. I suddenly feel the urge to get something and I want it right now! If they don't give me the money, I can't pay for it myself. Not being able to buy something is one of the things that cause me the most anxiety!!"

Reilly (2004a) addresses the acts of dressing and the selection, shopping, purchasing, and wearing of clothes as expressions of unconscious meaning, focusing on the possibility of clothes being used by bulimic patients as psychic skin and second-skin substitutes (p. 161). She also states that, therefore, clothes can be viewed as a concrete form of containment: they surround the body, cover it up, adding an additional form of self-containment needed to ward off feelings of unintegration (Reilly, 2004a, p. 162).

The following fragment of clinical material corresponds to the third year of treatment and was not discussed by the group. Nevertheless, it enabled me to see how the patient had started experiencing her body through clothes in a different way, as well as the fact that now people might see her differently and how this change was reflected in her clothes. She was searching for her true self by differentiating herself from her mother and sister. Language, however, seems sub-symbolic in the sense used by Bucci when she talks about words that are still permeated by sensory experience.

When relating her choice of a dress for an important family event, the patient says:

> *P*: On the other hand, the weather was nice. We bought a dress for my sister's party . . . I told you before, I wasn't dying to go . . . First my mum and a friend of hers chose a dress for my mum . . . and they told me to try on one of the dresses my mum had tried on. I had already

picked three dresses I liked [she specifies colours, fabrics, and how the dresses looked on her body]. My mum and my sister wanted me to wear the one my mum had tried earlier, and it fit me, and I felt that I liked how my body looked in that dress, but it wasn't me, I didn't feel comfortable in it.

I bought the other one. The good thing about it is that you can wear it for any occasion; it's blue, it goes unnoticed, it's a traditional dress but not at all conventional. The other dress, the one my mother wanted me to wear, was really special ... it wasn't the one I chose ... It had a turquoise lining and the fabric was lavender, it looked like shot silk, and it was beautifully embroidered up here, but the neckline was way too low, I swear, and it was backless, and then my mum and my sister wanted me to wear it because it fit me so well, and I felt that I liked myself in that dress but it wasn't me, I wouldn't feel comfortable in it, I don't know.

Lately my mum has been asking me why I changed the way I dress so much. I told her, I don't know why I'm doing it, I didn't plan it. It had a huge cleavage. And what I don't like is when people ask you, "Why are you wearing that?" ... People question you, and I can't stand it ... To wear a cleavage like that, you must have a personality strong enough to say, "Just because!" ... I don't tend to answer, "Just because", I don't like that ... But I didn't like the idea of trying on a dress that my mother had already tried, because if the dress fit her it wouldn't fit me.

*A*: I think that when you chose that cocktail dress, you chose a way of showing your body, your personality through it, with neutral colours, blue-like, muted colours, and that way you differentiated yourself from your mum and from your sister.

You often live life in an intense, lively way, sometimes violently, but you chose a dress with muted colours. You decided to dress very simply, but with bright details that also showed an aspect of yourself.

*P*: It was the one I liked the most.

*A*: You were able to tell your mum that you no longer identified with the dress she had suggested, or that it made you feel so bad that you didn't want it. You gave yourself the chance to choose a dress you felt had more to do with you instead of choosing it just to satisfy or impress people. You were looking for your own self through dresses and dancing. You were searching for something that would show who you really are and would make you feel more comfortable with yourself ...

*P*: I loved the dress. To tell you the truth, I still feel that it's the perfect dress because everything about it is perfect . . .

Irina has switched from a more provocative way of dressing to one more consistent with her inner state. Both she and her mother perceive this change; the patient seems to feel more comfortable with herself.

### *Self-destructiveness*

Also linked to the body issue are her self-destructive thoughts and dreams. In the second interview, the patient says, "I have a friend who's dating a very successful athlete. He travels all the time. She tried to commit suicide; she slit her wrists. She has a psychiatrist who treats her and monitors her progress. What can I do to help her? I speak with her mother and visit her. I'm in charge of giving her her medication; she's not responsible enough to take it by herself. It's dangerous for her to do it by herself. She wanted a friend to give it to her."

I tell her that she does not come to therapy only to take care of others, but also to take care of herself, and she reveals that suicide has been a concern of her own.

*P*: To slit her wrists now that her boyfriend is very successful . . . It makes me very angry. "Don't you think you have a thousand things you should appreciate?" I said to her. She answered that she did.

*A*: Have you had suicidal thoughts at some point?

*P*: Once in a while. I never thought about slashing my wrists. I wouldn't dare. When I get angry I feel like taking some sharp object, but I immediately restrain myself. Once I was upset with my mum and took ten Tylenol . . . it wasn't going to do anything to me. My mum was very sad.

When I interviewed this patient, it seemed to me that she had many hysteric components.

*A*: I think that you like to make scenes.

Some of the analysts in the group pointed out that the patient's situation was serious because she was sixteen years old and wanted to kill herself. As her analyst, I did not consider the situation as worrying as they did. None the less, at some point during the treatment, we had increased the frequency of the sessions because of a need expressed and shown by the patient herself. She said she was feeling poorly both emotionally and physically and asked for help; she felt very fragile. She asked to be hospitalised (the word in Spanish is *internarse*, which also means "to go into" and stems from *interno*, internal), and I suggested that we work with her internal aspects. We decided to increase the number of sessions so that she could be more contained and work more deeply in her analysis.

Group members also observed that the patient was starting to show that her problems had to do not only with her body, but also with her mind. When she says to the analyst, "I don't understand how you can be both fat and happy", she is asking herself if she is the way she is or the way others see her. In the transference, she is capable of wondering what is going on in her analyst's mind. We observe both a movement toward the analyst and a differentiation from her.

This connection between body and mind can be clearly seen when Irina brings to the session what she calls her "malignant thoughts". Even in her third year, before leaving analysis and moving abroad, she wonders about the extent of the changes she has accomplished.

*P*: What's going on is that . . . maybe that day I hadn't eaten anything. So I kind of put an end to it and called Luciana [a friend] and told her that I wouldn't go dancing, that I wasn't feeling well. I quickly mentioned what was going on with me, but said that I wouldn't go because I didn't feel well. I kind of put myself first. I could have gone anyway, but I would have felt awful because I was having my malignant thoughts.

*A*: Your malignant thoughts . . . Tell me more about those malignant thoughts . . .

*P*: It's like . . . It's like this: my mood changes radically in a second. I'm doing well today, for example, today, so far, I'm doing really well, eating in a really good way . . . without wanting to throw up or not to eat. If I don't have malignant thoughts, if I behave well, then I have a positive outlook, I have plans, I plan to do this, I plan to do that. But if I binge and vomit . . . Recently what had happened to me with my eyes happened again with my nose, I had, like, a nosebleed, and I don't know how it got to my nose, and then I want to die, like, I can't make it on my own, and I want to say . . . "OK, I won't fight anymore, I don't give a damn, I'll kill myself.'"

*A*: You want to die, to kill yourself, just like that?

*P*: Yes, because I lose control, you know what I mean? Because suddenly I lose my voice, things like that happen to me, then, OK! After spending the whole weekend thinking that I, like, I thought I might, like, I kind of always tell you that I might look for one of those therapy groups, or maybe go to one of those places for people with eating disorders, because I don't know what to do any more . . . because by myself . . . I can spend two days without throwing up and . . . To me this is terrible, I come here, I say it . . . maybe I don't say it because last week I didn't say it, because it was happening and then I can't stop it. Everything was going fine, I was doing fine, and suddenly, for example, yesterday I got up, Karen called, we went for a walk and then I studied for a while, then Luciana came and then I studied again. I was doing great! Until 5 p.m., and suddenly I don't know what happened to me. It's like I'm suddenly left alone or something happens to me.

*A*: Let's see . . . If . . .

*P*: It really doesn't have to be like that. After all that the . . . this thing happened to my nose and I felt bad!

*A*: When you were by yourself, weren't your friends there? What happened?

*P*: Same as always. Like, I get this terrible urge, it's an anxiety attack, it's like in a split second I ate a whole bag of cookies and as soon as I finished I threw them up, you know what I mean? It was night time, I felt kind of tired, I felt really fat because it didn't matter how much I weighed, I felt three times as fat! You know what I mean? I didn't feel like doing anything!

### *Grief*

Another observation offered by one group member in particular was that the patient begins the psychotherapeutic process by describing different people in her life (the gardener, her grandfather) who had cancer and died. This analyst underlined that she observed a more symbolised mental functioning in this patient than the rest of the group did.

In the first interview, Irina says, "Then my grandpa died; I can't get over it. A high school teacher I loved very much died. I cry non-stop every time someone dies. I cried a lot as a child.

"If I had a written test at school when I was seven, I would start crying. I changed significantly. What moments marked my life? Grandpa's death . . . I'm very active. I go dancing every weekend. I'm scared because I'm fat; I eat, and then I throw up. Mum wanted me to come here and so did I."

Grief signs also appear in recurring dreams during the analytic process.

Later on, she brings body image perceptions and distortions—skinny/fat—intertwined with conflicts in the mother–daughter relationship.

> Yesterday I dreamed that my grandmother Anna was dying and was saying goodbye to me. She was dying angry . . . I woke up and thought of my grandfather, I wanted him to come back. If I lose my grandmother I'll die . . . I'm her favourite granddaughter!!!

> Same as always. Like I get this terrible urge, it's an anxiety attack, it's like in a split second I ate a whole bag of cookies and as soon as I finished I threw them up, you know what I mean? It was night time, I felt kind of tired, I felt really fat because it didn't matter how much I weighed, I felt three times as fat! You know what I mean? I didn't want to do anything!

> I was walking and I felt that my mother had died, and I promised her to get skinny. Or, I'm facing my father's grave; he died, and I think to myself, "I'm going to be a doctor." My parents always wanted me to study medicine, and I always dream about this. If my father dies I'll study medicine, but if my mother dies I swear I'll be really thin.

The dream she had at the beginning of her treatment comes back linked to current events (it appears near the summer holidays, when she will be away from her family and from her analysis for a longer period of time).

The deaths of both a close family member and of others around her act as traumatic events that render her more vulnerable to psychosomatic disruptions and more sensitive to separations (e.g., vacations). This reaction is an iteration of the contents of her dreams, where fixations and regressions can be observed as well as the blocking of the dream system (Marty & Parat, 1974). Recurring dreams containing the death of a loved one are associated with other deaths. "It has to do with the death of my grandfather. His death affected me and my mum very much. From one day to another, he disappears." We may also see the patient's hostile aspects. Aggressive elements emerge through a negation mechanism: "I dream that my grandma dies . . . I'm not angry with them [her family]".

### *Communication style*

The patient talks a lot, but in a very condensed way, particularly in the first interviews. A year and a half later, she engages in an open dialogue with the analyst where Irina can say things that are not meant to tease and provoke. Besides the content, what struck me about her speech was its hypomanic pace. It reminded me of her binge eating and vomiting; this was her way of presenting things, and also her way of thinking. Furthermore, she affirmed and denied things in the same speech sequence. When we vomit, we throw out both the good things and the bad things. With her analyst, the patient had the possibility of keeping some of the good things.

Reilly (2004a) quotes Bick's observation about the fact that patients with eating disorders also have a particular usage of language. Bick states that language is deployed in this way (silent freezing in anorexic patients and excessive speaking in bulimic patients) "not as a means of communication, but as a means of obliterating otherness" (Reilly, 2004a, p. 153). The author also mentions Anzieu and the functions of the skin as a metaphor for mental functioning, and as a barrier against greed.

A group member claimed that at the beginning, Irina's speech seemed to be divided into pieces ("she talks as if her speech were a piece of patchwork"), and that as the analysis advanced, the patient appeared to be more reflective and to have a greater capacity to interiorise. There was an increasing continuity in her speech and in her dialogue. The working group introduced a metaphor (which they all considered fitting) that helped us understand how this patient expressed herself: "She talks like a video clip."

The image of the video clip arose as a metaphor expressing the patients' way of communication (Altmann, 2008). The metaphorising process facilitates the passage from concrete observation to symbolisation and conceptualisation (de León de Bernardi, 2013; Wurmser,

1977) at the level of both individual and group work (see de León de Bernardi & Altmann de Litvan, Chapter Fourteen).

Regarding this communication style, Bick (1986)—working in the language as a second skin—says that bulimic patients have a tendency to flood the session with words, as this patient does, allowing little space for thoughts.

### *Major aspects observed and discussed regarding Level 2: identification of the main dimensions of change*

To share the analytic experience, instead of selecting just the significant moments of change in the session, the model proposes a longitudinal view that compares the initial sessions with sessions that took place when the process was more advanced (e.g., nine months and a year and a half). After the group has worked for a couple of hours and the reporter summarises the insights gained from the sessions, participants can ask for clarifications regarding the patient's history in the external world, in the analysis, and in her inner world, and request additional psychoanalytic diagnostic information.

#### *Subjective experience of illness: acknowledgment of her difficulties and hints of a new way of experiencing*

The patient comes to treatment because she needs help; she says she wants to change, although she shows difficulty in conveying her problems clearly. Has Irina presented transformations in her subjective experience of illness? It is expected that during the treatment this experience will change due to the analyst's interpretations and the patient's insights. The group observed that the patient's understanding of her difficulties had evolved. At the beginning of the therapeutic process, she felt different from her friends and family and experienced her mind and body as strange. As the psychotherapeutic process unfolded, by mirroring the analyst's body and mind, Irina became more trustful of her own image and self, which led to a more integrated feeling of self.

She also felt that she had problems in her relationships with her friends and with some family members (brother, father). In the sessions, she worked on the great rivalry and envy she felt, especially towards some friends and towards her brother. At the very beginning, these feelings were projected outside. Later on, she was able to realise that they were part of her. As a consequence, she became more confident and, thus, more independent. Her anxiety, depression, and unhappiness were less distressful. She experienced fewer mood oscillations and felt more optimistic about her future.

At the beginning of the analysis, vomiting was very frequent. It was a hidden ritual and had metabolic consequences. The patient felt ill and stated that she needed help. She viewed her throwing up as automatic; she accepted it as a habit, like smoking. It took her some time to feel confident enough to share her hidden rituals and lies in her analysis. Vomiting decreased at the end of the treatment, but did not disappear. It was present in her dreams, and she was able to relate the appearance of "malignant thoughts" to her impulsive vomiting.

As we saw earlier, Irina had a hard time accepting the death of people she loved (Holocaust family loss, the death of her beloved grandfather, and the recent death of the house gardener). Whenever someone died, she would "cry non-stop". "I cried a lot as a child," she told me. She could not understand why this happened to her. A year and a half later she was able to access this mental scene.

Her expectations of the analytic treatment were that the analyst would give her strength and help her feel happier; she would often feel overwhelmed by her "malignant thoughts". Unconsciously, she also expressed her wish to separate from her family figures in a healthy way—to become more independent.

Changes in this patient had to do with having greater ego control of her bulimic impulses.

*P*: Now it's harder for me to manage these aspects consciously, because before I would blame it on other problems, full stop.

*A*: You are doing so much better, even if you feel worse, because all the things you did, you would do automatically. While you still do things without thinking them through, it's different now. The work you do here leaves a mark in your psyche.

*P*: Sure, I know that now it's different, but before it was easier.

*A*: Do you think it was easier?

*P*: Because my mum always tells me, for example, "You're not a bulimic", as if I was forcing myself to be one.

*A*: Does it look like you want to be a bulimic?

*P*: That's it, my mum always tells me that, but right now I feel that if that's not the answer then I'm crazy, you know what I mean? Because if I feel that I try to stop vomiting but then I do it anyway, and this goes on for three months, it is something that is beyond me. And if this is not an illness I don't know what it is, you know what I mean? Because I consider myself to be pretty intelligent.

## *Patterns of interpersonal relationship*

How does the patient experience others, and how does she experience herself in relation to others? How do others experience the patient, and how do they experience themselves in relation to the patient (both in the transference–countertransference relationship and in other meaningful bonds)?

From the very beginning, Irina said to me, "I find problems where there aren't any." When she first mentioned this, I did not know what those problems were. Later on, however, I understood that she was referring to the way she related to others. "I've been needing help for a long time," she told me. In many cases, analyst and patient agreed on the problems that needed to be addressed. Still, there were other issues that the patient would bring to the session unknowingly, for example when she said, "I don't like being touched. When somebody hugs me . . . I feel like they are measuring my body fat . . ." This would happen to her with her peers, but later on she referred to this situation particularly in connection with her relationship with her father. Her father had wanted to touch her and she had rejected him, which had prompted him to say, "I'm not a rapist!" She brought this episode to the session without considering it a problem.

When group members introduced the main dimensions of change, they mentioned that the patient was able to see these changes and to share her problems with the analyst. Yet, for this to happen, the analyst must notice when she and the patient were not attuned to each other.

Regarding her relationship with the analyst, the group discussed the fact that the patient might have picked this analyst because of her body (she chose to come back to the same therapist who had interviewed her when she was twelve years old). Narcissistic aspects of both patient and analyst were explored. The patient was confident in her analysis because she trusted the therapist and thought that the latter would stand up for her. She used the analyst's body to reflect on the fact that a person can be chronically ill and fat, and happy at the same time.

The model also analyses how the patient uses the analyst. In this case, the group observed that the therapist was the place of the good and someone who helped the patient change her mental functioning: "I come here to share my problems," Irina would say; "I am talking to myself." The patient was looking for a haven in the transference relationship. This can be seen both in the transference and in her perception of change.

At the beginning of the treatment, Irina felt that people would not get close to her, would not value or notice her. She believed that she had trouble relating to her friends and to some family members (brother, father). Her brother belittled her; he would tell her that she was adopted and that she was not capable of leaving home and studying abroad. Her parents were always measuring her against others and trying to change her; they never accepted her as she was.

The group pointed to a relationship pattern: people did not notice, value, or get close to her, and she would respond by not letting others notice, get to know, or get close to her. She said she did not allow others to notice her or get close to her, and, as a consequence, she did not allow herself to forge close relationships. At first, these feelings were projected outside.

> "I am sixteen years old . . . It's hot in here! I don't feel like having a serious relationship with anyone. I like dancing, having a beer. I don't like to be conditioned by anyone. I move forward up to a point in the relationship, and then I stop.
>
> "I don't know why sometimes I feel kind of weird. I love studying. Everything confuses me. Sometimes I change friends a lot and people say I'm a 'total flirt'. Sometimes that's not good." (First session.)

A member of the group asked, "Why is it that at that her age she doesn't have any close friends?" I answered that the she did not have friends with whom she could share things; she had friends with whom she could go out dancing and drinking. I never felt that she had true friends. Then another analyst stated, "Now I can see her relationship pattern. 'If others underestimate me, I must be the brilliant one, the one who helps others.'" She felt she had to be brilliant in order not to feel inferior, and when she was not brilliant she fell apart.

When others coldly disapprove of her, the patient reacts by wanting to have a perfect body. "I went to a dance party. I drank a little. Someone threw a glass of whisky on my tits. How did I react? I made a scene with a very good [female] friend of my [female] cousin. I wanted revenge. I'm not vindictive until they get on my nerves; then I do want revenge". (First session.)

She dated young men but did not have a boyfriend; she had idealised figures, like her grandfather. As I mentioned earlier, during the treatment we worked on her strong feelings of rivalry and envy, directed especially towards some of her friends and towards her siblings. Realising that these projected feelings were actually inside her gave her greater confidence in herself. Later on, this behaviour was displayed in the transference. Her capacity to love improved during this year, and she was able to have a steady boyfriend.

Irina wanted to be perfect and felt that others were always measuring, criticising, and disapproving of her (her grandmother, her father, her mother, and her brother). There seemed to be no protective, affectionate figures in her close world, but, rather, figures that controlled and assessed her.

This dimension of the model helped me differentiate between her relationship with internal objects and her relationship with external objects. Participants' observations allowed me to come into contact with the patient's different relationship patterns. The group realised that this damaging pattern of not letting others notice, get to know, or get close to her had been broken. Analysis allowed Irina to do so by exploring how she felt about the analyst, and, thus, she was able to develop an intimate relationship. The group had told me, part as a joke and part as a criticism, that I had adopted the patient. I believe that the most important issue I identified in the analytic field was the need to generate this space of intimacy.

At the anchor point, the patient had shown an excessive proximity to her mother through her constant dieting. At the transformation point, she was able to experience her mother as a separate being and recognise that she had problems that were independent of her. Changes could also be observed in her relationships with male figures. At the beginning of the treatment, she did not feel comfortable with her father and did not want him to touch her. Moreover, she would quarrel frequently with her brother because he told her she had been adopted and looked down on her. Although no explicit transformations were seen in Irina's relationship with her father, she fought less with him and was able to establish more meaningful friendships.

At the beginning, she expressed the wish to study abroad. None the less, these plans were frustrated by her family; they did not believe in Irina's ability to be independent. The idea of separating from her family seemed impossible back then. Her separation anxieties were tackled in different ways during her analysis. She even worked abroad one summer, and when she came back she finally decided to study overseas and live alone.

At the end of our group work, we realised that this dimension was among those that had undergone transformations. These could be clearly seen in the transference with the analyst in the session at eighteen months.

## *Conflicts and defences: main intrapsychic conflict*

The group discussion helped the analyst by showing the co-existence of different conflicts that predominated at different times. As underlined in the *OPD Manual*, following Dührssen (1981), conflicts reveal themselves in essential areas of personal life: "choice of partner, bonding behavior and family life, domain in the family one is born into, the entire area of work and profession, behavior toward property, surrounding socio-cultural space, and experience of illness" (*OPD*, p. 88).

One of the patient's main conflicts was dependence *vs.* autonomy. Throughout the entire treatment, Irina expressed her desire to become more independent, but had severe difficulties pursuing it. She struggled to find her own thoughts, her own desires, because she felt she had to fulfil her family's ideals. Her intense separation anxieties made her feel very insecure.

These anxieties were especially addressed during short and long interruptions (due to vacations) in the analysis. Before every vacation, the patient expressed her desire to move far away from her parents, and described the obstacles posed by her anxiety and by the appearance of "malignant thoughts". The treatment ended when she decided to study and live abroad, after three years of treatment (in our country, adolescents live with their parents while they pursue their degrees. Young people usually leave their homes when they are almost twenty-seven years old). We should ask ourselves if this is a normal conflict for her age. To a certain extent, independence is a typical adolescent conflict, but Irina defended herself against these anxieties by way of projection.

Bulimia, and the fact that it typically begins during adolescence, has been linked to the instance of leaving home and the separation–individuation process (Reilly, 2004b, p. 376). Not being integrated into the total personality, aggression fuels a volatile emotionality and often-secret acting-out episodes. Reilly refers to this secrecy as an essential feature associated with omnipotence on the one hand and shame and humiliation on the other:

> Structurally all of this points to the important role played by the primitive ego-ideal within this pathology, as well as aspects of the primitive and mocking super-ego, which manifest themselves for example in the gaze, overt body-ego pathology and over-valuation of thinness, and accusatory sadistic and unremitting moralizing, respectively. (Reilly, 2004b, p. 380)

As we are dealing with an adolescent, questions regarding identity, dependence–autonomy, and her unconsolidated personality structure are expected to appear. Oedipal problems were displayed as well, but they did not have a central role for either patient or analyst.

Irina's self-esteem was also one of the major conflicts tackled in her analysis. She had poor representations. She needed to work on her body as a starting point so as to find and repair basic aspects of her feminine narcissism and self-esteem—to return a libidinal look to a body that was being experienced as "cut off".

At the transformation point, we observed more independence, better self-definition and self-esteem, and improved capacity to reflect and to express her ideas and thoughts. The activation of her mental resources was supported by the analytic process and accompanied by changes of different degrees in other key dimensions.

### *Structural aspects of mental functioning*

In this section, I identify changes in the patient's mental functioning, or the lack thereof, in the clinical material already presented. The group agreed that structural problems were predominant in this case.

*Perception of self and others: identity*

This sub-dimension aims to assess to what extent the patient is capable of adequately perceiving her own internal states and those of others, of empathising, and of understanding the existence of different points of view. The model also asks if the patient has an integrated feeling of her own identity and is open to the possibility of coming into contact with unconscious aspects, and examines the characteristics of identification (pathological ones in particular). The patient's connection with the past and her capacity to give direction to her life, including short- and long-term wishes and goals, are also observed.

At the very beginning of the treatment, Irina was unable to reflect about herself, did not discriminate her body from her mother's, and experienced difficulties in developing intimate relationships. She projected on to others what was happening to her. She was open to coming into contact with unconscious aspects of herself, although she did not have an integrated feeling of herself.

In a session at eighteen months of treatment, however, we could observe how she historicised her life in relation to different periods of her childhood.

> *P*: . . . everyone sees me as skinny, but I get "traumatised" about things in the same way I did when I was little . . . When I was in third grade we were asked to do a show about pre-Columbian times . . . I had to wear a very tight corset, and the whole class told me I was plump . . . It really traumatised me. Like, it made me very insecure. I was young and felt very insecure. When I was nine, I had to dance again and I was plump and they called me fatty. At eleven, I started going to a dietician. At my sister's age I already had eating disorders. My sister has my mother's metabolism and has already learnt to control how much she eats [both her sister and her mother are thin].
>
> I ask her if she had any dreams, and she answers,
>
> I dreamed something about my body, but I don't remember very well, it was like someone stole some food from me and I threw up, then I get up and eat, like I did four days ago . . . My mother worries a lot about things related to food, but she can't make my bum smaller.

Irina perceived herself as flawed and fat, and could not discriminate between herself and her mother—there was no bodily differentiation. At the beginning of the treatment, she had problems distinguishing between herself and both her mother and her sister. As the treatment progressed, a positive transformation occurred in this regard.

Empirical studies (Reich & Cierpka, 1998) have shown that bulimia occurs to varying degrees, and that it is a mistake, when confronted with the symptoms, to assume an "early", "narcissistic", or "borderline" disorder. Extensive bulimic symptoms develop as an expression of a "disorder of the self" in individuals who are otherwise relatively undisturbed, or may be part of a wider range of symptoms that suggests a more severe personality disorder (Reich & Cierpka, 1998, p. 385). We consider that these factors are complementary.

### *Affective regulation*

This item assesses whether the patient is able to regulate her impulses, affects, and self-esteem adequately, which enables her to control her self-esteem needs in the face of internal and external demands. It also considers if the patient's ideals and values help her to handle her emotions, and to what extent she achieves an adequate balance between her own interests and those of others.

If we focus on regulation, we observe that, at the beginning of the treatment, Irina shows difficulty in controlling her impulses and affects, which compromises everything related to her self-esteem. Her defences are dysfunctional, and she shows excessive idealisation of others. She acts out her evil thoughts: "I am sixteen years old . . . It's hot in here! I don't feel like having a serious relationship with anyone. I like dancing, having a beer. I don't like to be conditioned by anyone. I move forward up to a point in the relationship, and then I stop."

Irina's biological systems were compromised. Emotional regulation was also intertwined with impaired regulation of the sleep systems. She brings this topic to therapy.

> "Those days [when she ate and threw up] I had insomnia. I lay in bed and couldn't sleep until 2 a.m. At 4 a.m. I opened my eyes, and I wasn't sleepy at all during the day. I had my ballet presentation. I spent three days without being sick and I ate what I had planned to eat. I was focused. And I still felt insecure.
>
> "I believe that there was a part of me that wanted to dance and a part of me that felt frustrated, traumatised . . . Both parts were there! I had to go

out there and dance! I couldn't ruin everything!! Afterwards I met with my friend. And I was really hungry."

Irina very thoroughly and minutely recounts her hesitation between eating *alfajores* (chocolate-covered, caramel-filled cookies) and chocolate cake, as well as the different strategies she used to choose one or the other and the guilt feelings she experienced. She cannot regulate her impulse to eat or throw up.

*P*: I think so. I went into a store and bought myself some jeans. I suddenly feel the urge and I want it right now! If they don't give me the money I can't pay for it myself. Not being able to buy something is one of the things that cause me the most anxiety!!

She is unable to regulate her basic emotions; her mood changes dramatically from one moment to the next:

*P*: It's like . . . it's like this: my mood radically changes in one second. And I'm feeling fine. For example, today, up to now, I'm feeling great, eating great, I don't want to throw up or eat anything. If the thoughts don't come . . . if I behave, I have a positive attitude, I have projects, I plan to do this, I plan to do that . . . If I eat too much, binge and vomit . . . Now the same thing that had already happened with my eyes happened with my nose: I bled, my nose bled, and I don't know how it got to my nose, and then I start feeling I want to die, as if I couldn't handle things on my own, and I feel like saying, "Enough . . . I won't fight anymore; I don't give a damn about anything; I'll kill myself'. (nine months of treatment.)

Eighteen months later she asks me:

*P*: Are you asthmatic? I don't know where I got that; of course, I don't investigate you, well, only a little bit. My mother told me that you were fat because you took steroids because you were asthmatic. You know something? My mother is jealous of you, and I tell her, "You're competing with my analyst but my analyst isn't competing with you." My mother says that you would be happy if I studied psychoanalysis.

I don't admire you very much for your knowledge. Maybe what I'm going to say is a bit aggressive. I can't understand how you can be both happy and fat. I don't understand. In my opinion, that's impossible.

*A*: All this brings up the whole issue of the envy and rivalry that may develop among women.

*P*: Yes, maybe. It's very hard for me to go out with thin friends; I can't cope with it. I see myself as flawed.

*A*: How can we see here, in our relationship, the rivalry and envy that you're bringing to the session? Because you chose a fat psychoanalyst.

According to Irina's experience, in her family's view you have to be thin in order to exist.

*P*: It's important. Everybody is always paying attention to that. When you meet someone, it doesn't matter if you have good values or not, if you are intelligent or not; the first thing they mention is if you lost weight . . .

It is only through the transference that the patient allows herself to explore and see things in a different way by asking the analyst different questions. Her internal ideal, mingled with the family's ideals, has prevented her from regulating and handling her emotions better.

### *Internal and external communication: symbolisation*

The questions for this sub-dimension are as follows: how rich is the patient's dialogue with herself and others based on emotional experiences, bodily self, phantasies, dreams, sexuality, symbolic representations, and capacity for play and creativity?

As I mentioned before, Irina's dreams were repetitive and connected with her concern about food and thin figures. As the analytic process advances, we observe that she places her personal worth in her weight and figure. She has bulimic symptoms that make her feel ashamed and tries to hide them.

As the analysis developed, Irina started a dialogue with herself through her analysis. Furthermore, her dreams communicated her affective experiences. At that time, I considered changes in her dreams, in her association capacity, and in her link to her phantasies and childhood as a sign of improved mental functioning. At the beginning of the treatment, dreams were concrete. Moreover, not only were they repetitive, but also had few dream distortion and displacement mechanisms. I considered that the dreams and childhood experiences she started to bring to the session indicated progress in her symbolisation capacity. The patient showed a greater ability to engage in a dialogue with herself and with her analyst, which, in turn, allowed her to manage her affects and understand herself better.

### *Attachment to internal and external objects*

The group sought to observe these aspects in the clinical material: how deep, steady, and differentiated are the patient's relationships with internal and external objects? To what extent is she able to start and end relationships and tolerate separations? How does she handle relationships that imply the existence of a third person?

> *P*: I didn't tell you last week . . . I just covered it up with some other stuff. Like . . . Now I get tired, you know?
>
> Now the dance festival is coming up and I know I'll have to face things, because I'll be living with other people, and the food issue appears, the body issue appears, and I don't really want to go, to be honest. I'm going because it's the first time I'm dancing with a [female] partner. But I don't really feel like going, and I've brought this topic to therapy many times as something that scares me! Like, it's a matter of imposition, of quitting, of what other people expect of me, what I expect of myself, it's like, I don't know. Get it?

One clearly notices the difference in the way she talks; her ideas seem to be more fully developed and expressed.

Patients suffering from bulimia find themselves in a persisting oedipal conflict situation, often against a backdrop of extreme marital tension between the parents. The following constellation may be observed in the patient. For example, she becomes unapproachable or impenetrable.

Many interventions helped Irina to get in contact with her own mental states and her affective resources. The anguish of loss or fusion with the object that is observed at the first interviews changes into a better self-definition.

In the group discussion, the predominance of structural functions regarding mentalization, affect regulation, communication, symbolisation, and attachment were underlined as the main aspects to be worked. In the analytic work, conflicts that needed interpretation were mixed with structural limitations.

As she was gradually able to use the analyst as a containing external–internal object, she could enhance her reflecting function, which was stimulated by the analyst's interventions. Thus, she was able to better regulate her self-esteem and anxiety. Changes in self-image, differentiation of affects, and tolerance of affects allowed her to regulate affects and oral drives in a way that permitted her to anticipate certain reactions. This regulation was extremely important. It allowed a better communication, and communication led to increased processing and awareness of internal experiences. This makes a change in the interpersonal relationships. There was also a change in the quality of her dreams and her capacity to associate. Such strengthening of the patient's functions was achieved mostly through the transference–countertransference interventions and also with the analyst's non-interpretative interventions.

## *Conclusion*

This sixteen-year-old female came to treatment with complaints of anxiety and depression, binge/purge eating patterns and a distorted body image, and showed hints of conflictual grandiose exhibitionism and hysteric/hysteroid features. She displayed prominent oral and addictive tendencies, poor affect regulation, and frequent mood swings. Her interpersonal relations were relatively primitive, with stated disinterest in having a boyfriend, high separation anxiety, and an excessive, conflicting attachment to her mother. Nine months into the treatment, the material shows worry about her weight and maladaptive, destructive attempts to control it, major concerns with loss, death, and suicide, and signs of negative/critical/rejecting internal objects.

The group discussion focused on relationships. Irina could not take care of her body. When we analysed the changes she underwent, we observed that there were significant moments in the patient–analyst relationship. One of the topics that emerged in the analytic process was her fatness. This topic appears tied to her bond with her mother, father, and brother, and to her relationship with herself and the analyst.

We usually think of change in terms of the replacement of one structure by another, markedly different one in a way that may be properly called "revolutionary"—a sudden and qualitatively distinct occurrence. Yet, it is clear that change may also be the product of a gradual process of growth. The therapeutic outcome can be equally important, having resulted from an accumulation of small transitions that leads to new situations, but it does not correspond to the revolution metaphor. In this case, it would be appropriate to speak of a slowly evolving process that includes both progress and setbacks.

If we take this point of view into account, however, we should ask how many types of change there are. Certainly, much can be said about this topic. Ideas drawn from the field of mathematics may be of use here. What aspects of the material suggest the existence of positive changes, negative changes, or no change? Which kind of change predominates?

The major positive transformation observed by the group was that the way in which the patient expressed herself shifted from a kind of "video clip" narrative style to a dialogue with the analyst. Irina also showed an improved capacity to reflect on her feelings and actions as well as greater mentalization. Another important transformation was that her vomiting decreased (better digestion). At the same time, no change was observed in the patient's perception of her body as fat (which, from the analyst's point of view, was not so). Finally, no negative changes were detected.

Considering this description, we may identify two main transformations. One concerns her speech style, and the other her mental functioning with the analyst. The first one is the shift from an initial way of talking and sharing things in a "video clip" style to an ability to engage in a more open dialogue. I would say that Irina's symptoms got worse in a way, but were repeatedly displayed in different scenes that made it possible for the transference–countertransference relationship to change. The second one resulted in the improvement of her capacity to love and her sexuality. She showed less difficulty in relating to others. Furthermore, instead of changing from one boyfriend to the next, she was able to have a steady boyfriend for a certain period of time.

The group offered the following opinions:

- "I think there is a very significant change in relation to where the patient situates herself regarding her problems. There are some signs of this in the first interview: her body, how she attacks her body when she tries to commit suicide, her depression, the labile nature of her emotions, the grief caused by her grandfather's death, and the body issue, which has two different levels: body expansion and body destruction. All of the above may be considered part of the transference. They may be found in the dyadic relationship with her mother, in the relationship with her father and her reaction to physical contact, and also in her relationship with the analyst, that happy fat lady."

- "It's clear from the very beginning that she's asking for help, and this appeal is sustained; she asks for more sessions and gets closer to the analyst."
- "There is also something important about physical contact (with the audience, with the body) and about her relationship with her own body and the analyst's. Moreover, in the second interview appears this body that she cannot look after; her friend serves as her double."
- "After a year and a half of treatment there is a clear capacity to interiorise."

Was it possible to change this patient's mood, or do we have to think that there are certain aspects associated with adolescents' basic temperament that cannot be changed? It is worth noting that in the first interview I learnt that the patient had a somatic illness—hyperthyroidism. She had a hypomanic way of speaking. In addition, she was taking medication for her hyperthyroidism and an antidepressant. It was not the psychiatrist, but the general practitioner who had prescribed it. I did not tell her that she should consult a psychiatrist. It was the patient's own decision. It was hard for her to face these unchangeable physical realities and life circumstances; at that time, her father had lost his job.

One of the comments made by the group was that analysts tend to minimise physical or medical conditions. In our first interviews with a patient, we often overlook the possibility that psychological problems might be the expression of physical illness. For this reason, we must formulate the case very carefully, paying special attention to the patient's developmental history (McWilliams, 1999). In this particular case, I did not take into consideration how Irina's physical or medical conditions (such as her hyperthyroidism) might have influenced, for example, her communication style or her bulimic symptoms (McWilliams, 1999).

Another aspect that was considered "absent" by the group was the patient's adolescence. Even though I feel I did not make much progress in this area, I believe that it is a stage that requires and deserves further attention in order to follow the path towards discovery and conceptualisation.

The model allowed me to have a better and clearer picture of the different dimensions of change, both internal and external. The context of the clinical material was that of adolescent life in a country where young people do not have to leave home to go to college. We learnt what had changed and what had not, but also what could not be modified—the patient's unchangeable physical realities and life circumstances.

Our group studied Irina's case years after her treatment had ended. While I suspected she might have changed, I did not know in what specific areas. The model helped me to realise the manner and dimensions of the changes she had undergone.

At the beginning, the patient was unable to perceive her own internal states or those of others. She did not have an integrated sense of her own identity. She could empathise with her friends and understand them, but established no connection between them and her own problems. She had a conflict with her feminine identity that was rooted in her relationship with her mother and grandmother, and experienced difficulties in perceiving herself and others.

Her capacity for internal communication was very poor. She would jump from one topic to the next and had very little capacity for association. This feature really changed throughout the treatment. Dialogue with herself and others developed further thanks to her ability to come into contact with emotional childhood experiences, symbolic representation increased, and her handling or control of her body improved. At the very beginning, she could not forge deep, steady relationships and showed poor tolerance for separation. This trait was also modified.

This model allowed me to see in a more explicit way the importance of the structural problems of this patient. While I had implicitly worked on this patient's structural problems during the entire treatment, the 3-LM allowed me to see their significance more explicitly. The analysis aimed to work on her very foundations from a structural perspective; structural changes were identified in her relationship with the analyst. Yet, Irina was also able to work on her internal and external bonds. The model was crucial in recognising these transformations. Moreover, though I had been able to work without the model while I was treating her, further analysing the clinical material made me see the patient through a whole new lens; I could look into the case in greater depth.

I realised that transformations had occurred because I had tackled her self-esteem and ego functions, focusing on her body. I had dealt with her perception of herself and others and her conflict between dependence and independence. I had also worked on her differentiation from her mother and how it related to food. In a subsequent analysis of my interventions and interpretations, I could infer that most of them had aimed to structure the image Irina had of herself—so fragmented, lacking unity. I had addressed the many ways in which she experienced her body. I had worked from her body towards her psyche. Through organisation and systematisation, the model allowed me to identify the areas where changes had developed, and even made it possible for me to see aspects that had remained unseen.

One of the strengths of the model is that it adopted the *OPD-2*'s distinction between conflict and structure. In the structural dimension, the categories provided allowed me to detect this patient's considerable self-image problems, which posed obstacles to identity development and to her capacity for self-reflection, self-regulation, and affect differentiation (*OPD*, p. 136).

The *PDM* states that

> for children, the assessment of personality disorder is more difficult than with adults because we must take into account the child's age and developmental stage, the enormous flexibility children have to change, the sensitivity of children to changing family and environmental patterns, and the need for more research on the relationship between early personality patterns and late ones. (*PDM*, p. 210)

> Personality patterns form during childhood and continue to develop throughout the course of life. Depending on a number of factors, including biological dispositions, age and developmental stage of the child, the nature of the family and broader cultural influence, life events, and other factors, they may continually change or remain relatively stable. (*PDM*, p. 209)

The patient developed her capacity for love and sexual intimacy. She improved her social and family relationships. She took different jobs and had the ability to maintain her vocation despite parental opposition. She decided to pursue her project abroad. She still perceives herself as fat, but throws up much less frequently. The other dimension that showed many changes refers to the patient's ability both to perceive others and to perceive herself in relation to others. This dimension was displayed in the transference–countertransference relationship as well as in other meaningful bonds.

### *The model's contribution to the observation of clinical material*

One of the strengths of the 3-LM for observing patient transformations is that the patient is observed globally, with a focus on several dimensions. All these dimensions are taken into account in every clinical material. This procedure assures a comprehensive approach.

Questions always take the patient's perspective—her internal and external worlds, and changes, or the lack thereof, taking place inside her and in her life. They also consider the patient's physical and organic functioning.

Working in a small group helps curb prejudices and gives us confidence to voice our ideas. Eventually, it helps us to think better.

Participants offered very positive feedback. They highlighted that this method gave them the possibility of looking at the patient from a different perspective and to pose questions regarding how and with what therapeutic goals analysts work with a specific patient.

They considered that it was appropriate to work on three levels that study the material in increasingly greater depth.

Group members valued the fact that everyone talked in descriptive terms, even using everyday life metaphors. This speech style helps participants develop a more clinical perspective and enables them to get a better picture of the patient and his or her emotional functioning, while avoiding the risk of using more theoretically saturated approaches. In the unconscious construction of meaning, metaphor plays a salient role. Modell (2005) suggests that metaphor functions unconsciously as a pattern detector and, thus, is pivotal to the organisation and categorisation of emotional memory.

The role of reporters proved to be very important. They summarised insights gained, alternative hypotheses, and criticisms at the end of each level, and in certain moments helped to guide the dialogue.

Group members suggested working more actively on the aspects related to the analytic field, such as the emotional atmosphere of an interview or session, moments of strong interaction between analyst and patient that make it possible to talk about a transference scene, and role playing.

Some participants noted the need for, and obstacles to, systematisation (regarding the analytic method and the theory of technique), as well as its usefulness for analytic training. With the 3-LM, we get a more accurate, systematic observation. We re-observe our work field.

There is an implicit idea of what psychoanalysis and psychoanalytic changes are. External aspects are not the focus, but there must be a connection between the internal and external worlds.

The 3-LM allowed me to understand, through careful and systematic observation, the areas where changes had been achieved, and even made it possible for me to see aspects that had remained unnoticed. For all these reasons, we found the model very useful and deemed it ready to be implemented with other patients.

## *References*

Altmann, M. (2008). *Cómo se da el nacimiento del paciente en la mente del analista. XVI Jornadas de Psicoanálisis de APU. Desafíos del psicoanálisis contemporáneo.* Montevideo, Uruguay: Asociación Psicoanalítica del Uruguay (APU).

Altmann, M., Fitzpatrick-Hanly, M. A., & Leuzinger-Bohleber, M. (2012). Project Committee on Clinical Observation Panels. *International Journal of Psychoanalysis, 93*(3): 748–750.

Atwood, G. E., & Stolorow, R. D. (1984). *Structures of Subjectivity: Explorations in Psychoanalytic Phenomenology.* Hillsdale, NJ: Analytic Press.

Baranger, M., & Baranger, W. (1961–1962). La situación analítica como campo dinámico. *Revista Uruguaya de Psicoanálisis, IV*(1): 3–54.

Bick, E. (1986). Further considerations on the function of the skin on early object relations. *British Journal of Psychotherapy,* 2: 292–299.

Blatt, S., & Ford, R. Q. (1994). *Therapeutic Change. An Object Relations Perspective.* New York: Plenum Press.

Bucci, W. (1997). *Psychoanalysis and Cognitive Science.* New York: Guilford Press.

De León de Bernardi, B. (2013). Field theory as a metaphor and metaphors in the analytic field and process. *Psychoanalytic Inquiry, 33*(3): 247–266.

Dührssen, A. (1981). *Die biographische Anamnese unter tiefenpsychologischen Aspekten*. Göttingen: Vandenhoeck & Ruprecht.

Fonagy, P. (1998). Moments of change in psychoanalytic theory. *Infant Mental Health Journal, 19*(3): 348–352.

Fosshage, J. L. (2005). The explicit and implicit domains in psychoanalytic change. *Psychoanalytic Inquiry, 25*: 516–539.

Goldfried, M. (1980). Toward the delineation of therapeutic change principles. *American Psychologist, 35*(11): 991–999.

Greenberg, J. R., & Mitchell, S. A. (1983). *Object Relations in Psychoanalytic Theory*. Cambridge, MA: Harvard University Press.

Klimovsky, G., Vainer, S. B., De Goldberg, D. B., De Kuitca, M. K., De Liberman, J. F., & Siniavsky, M. (1994). Change in psychoanalysis: epistemological aspects. *International Journal of Psychoanalysis, 75*: 51–58.

Luborsky, L., Singer, B., & Luborsky, L. (1975). Comparative studies of psychotherapies. Is it true that "Everyone has won and all must have prizes"? *Archives of General Psychiatry, 32*(8): 995–1008.

Marty, P., & Parat, C. (1974). De l'utilsation des rêves et du matériel onirique dans certain types de psychothérapies d'adultes. *Revue Française de Psychanalyse, XXXVIII*: 1069–1077.

McWilliams, N. (1999). *Psychoanalytic Case Formulation*. New York: Guilford Press.

Messer, S. B. (1994). Adapting psychotherapy outcome research to clinical reality. *Journal of Psychotherapy Integration, 4*: 280–282.

Mitchell, S. (1988). *Relational Concepts in Psychoanalysis: An Integration*. Cambridge, MA: Harvard University Press.

Modell, A. (2005). Emotional memory, metaphor and meaning. *Psychoanalytic Inquiry, 25*: 555–368.

Nieto, M. (1965). Algunos problemas del analista como investigador. *Revista de la Asociación Psicoanalítica del Uruguay, 1*(VII): 5–27.

*OPD Gdt. Diagnóstico Psicodinámico Operacionalizado (OPD-2)* (2008). Barcelona: Herder.

*Psychodynamic Diagnostic Manual* (*PDM*) (2006). Silver Spring: Alliance of Psychoanalytic Organizations.

Reich, G., & Cierpka, M. (1998). Identity conflicts in bulimia nervosa: psychodynamic patterns and psychoanalytic treatment. *Psychoanalytic Inquiry, 18*: 383–402.

Reilly, E. A. (2004a). Skin deep. *Free Associations, 11*: 134–174.

Reilly, E. A. (2004b). The case of the bulimic Mafia and the tools of their trade. *Psychoanalytic Psychotherapy, 18*: 374–389.

Safran, J. D., & Greenberg, L. S. (1991). *Emotion, Psychotherapy and Change.* New York: Guilford Press.

Stern, D. N., Sander, L. W., Nahum, J. P., Harrison, A. M., Lyons-Ruth, K., Morgan, A. C., Bruschweilerstern, N., & Tronick, E. Z. (1998). Non-interpretive mechanisms in psychoanalytic therapy: the 'something more' than interpretation. *International Journal of Psychoanalysis, 79*: 903–921.

Stolorow, R. D., Brandchaft, B., & Atwood, G. E. (1987). *Psychoanalytic Treatment: An Intersubjective Approach.* Hillsdale, NJ: Analytic Press.

Vygotsky, L. (1966). Development of the higher mental functions. In: A. N. Leontiev, A. R. Luria, & A. A. Smirnov (Eds.), *Psychological Research in the USSR* (Vol. 1), (pp. 11–46). Moscow: Progress.

Widlöcher, D. (1970). *Freud et le problem du changement.* Paris: Presses Universitaires de France.

Wurmser, L. (1977). A defense of the use of metaphor in analytic theory formation. *Psychoanalytic Quarterly, 46*: 466–498.

# PART II

# OBSERVING AND WORKING WITH THE 3-LM

CHAPTER FOUR

# Tracking patient transformations: the function of observation in psychoanalysis

*Virginia Ungar*

## *Introduction: observation in psychoanalysis*

The function of observation in clinical work with patients is both important and controversial. It is commonly held that the act of observing entails paying careful attention to, and engaging all our senses with, objects or phenomena (regarded as external) in order to study them "as presented in reality" (though we are well aware of the difficulties implied in this statement).

To observe should not only mean to "watch" or to "look at", since good observation requires the concerted action of all senses. Precisely on this point, Bion tells us in his *Cogitations* (1992) that "private to the individual himself, the term 'common sense' is felt to be an adequate description covering an experience felt to be supported by all the senses without disharmony" (p. 10).

Traditionally, the concept of psychoanalytic *observation* has been favoured by the English school of psychoanalysis, in whose writings the notion of unconscious fantasy may be permeated with an emphasis on the perceptual and the visual. I think it important to call our attention at this point to the fact that, when referring to *blind spots,* Freud employed a *visual* metaphor.

On the other hand, French psychoanalysis, coherent with the notion of structure and the Lacanian proposition that the unconscious is structured as language, has preferred the idea of the analyst focused on "listening" to the unconscious.

Set side by side, and at first glance, these two positions appear to be in conflict, or with a possible pre-eminence of one sensorial mechanism over another: sight or hearing. Nevertheless, the closer we get to the clinical facts, the more difficult it is to sustain this polarisation.

Continuing this line of investigation, we can ask ourselves: is an analyst in the act of listening to what his patient is saying not also registering at the same time the tone and the music of his voice, the silence, the language without words of the body, the noises coming from outside the consulting room, or even his own thoughts, corporal sensations, anxieties, etc.? When the patient receives the analyst's interventions, is he not perhaps impressed by a multitude of subtle non-verbal perceptions that he himself "observes"?

Moreover, would an analyst observing and imagining, even *dreaming* with the information presented to him, not be including in his registration a shadow of complaint, a semitone of pain, genuine joy, a slip of the tongue, a game of words, a symptom somehow "speaking out" (Freud, 1895d, p. 296), or a pain that appears to be *joining the conversation* in a session?

In working as a child analyst (also seeing adolescent and adult patients), I have found the Esther Bick infant observation method has added to my experience, enhancing my capacity to observe while, at the same time, increasing my capacity to listen. The analytic encounter with small children deprived of language communicates much to us and forces us to attempt to understand what we are observing in order to be able to arrive at a hypothesis that can be either confirmed by recurrent patterns which arise or else be discarded, if we find that it does not relate to new elements.

In his brilliant paper, "Cognitive development", Money-Kyrle (1968) holds that the child is innately prepared to discover truth, and what hinders this process is to be found in the realm of the emotions. I dare to extend this idea further, based on my experience in longitudinal observation of babies and in the psychoanalytic treatment of patients of all ages. I believe that the human being has the power from very early on to observe, but, on accessing culture—into the realms of the rational logos—a very high price indeed is paid, and this can be evidenced in the diminishing capacity for observation due to neurosis or psychosis.

Observation has undoubtedly been the basis of central theoretical developments in psychoanalysis. We only need to remember Freud's fort-da or Klein's observations of her own son, later referred to as Fritz in her papers.

The quality of the phenomena encountered in our psychoanalytic practice, according to Bion, is not grasped by our sensory organs. In this way, his thought coincides with current philosophical trends which say that perception does not guarantee the comprehension of reality.

* * *

With respect to clinical observation, we notice that the patient, at some point after starting his treatment, through identification with his analyst, will "learn" to observe not just the events of the external world, but also those that are taking place in his internal world, those of his "psychic reality": his feelings, thoughts, activities, and, most fundamentally, his dreams. He realises to a certain extent that he is going to work together with his analyst on the material observed; he is going to collaborate with the task of transforming the elements from the sensorial data into thoughts, in Bion's terms.

The central focus of this chapter is to study the possibility of using the function of observation to track the transformations in a patient during a psychoanalytic or psychotherapeutic treatment.

First, the three-level model developed by the IPA Project Committee on Clinical Observation and Testing Group will be introduced as a helpful instrument for following transformations in a patient in the course of treatment. Next, clinical material with sessions from different phases of the treatment will be presented. Then, the three-level model will be applied to the clinical material. Finally, there will be a discussion of the dimensions of change.

## *Method of analysis of clinical observation: three-level model for observing patient transformations (3-LM)*

This method is part of the programme of the IPA Project Committee on Clinical Observation and Testing aimed at developing systematic clinical observation of the transformations of patients undergoing psychoanalytic treatment. The objective of the Committee is to promote a more accurate and systematic clinical observation, one that would be useful in the building and testing of theory in the field.

The 3-LM itself is more thoroughly presented in another chapter. In this chapter, I want to focus on the practical application of the method using one of my analytical cases.

As with all methods, it is possible to use part of the whole and, in this case, I chose a specific part to be applied and the questions to be used in the group discussion.

The model is a *guide* for *enriching, refining, conceptualising, and systematising clinical observations* focused on the transformations that occur in the patient during treatment. It was designed to be used at different levels of clinical practice and was conceptualised specifically with the group work context in mind.

The term "transformation" is used in the usual sense of "modification". The model prioritises the transformations in the patient, but it is accepted that this only happens in the course of the bi-directional relationship with the analyst.

The transformations that occur during analysis have multiple aspects pertaining to them and undoubtedly raise a wide range of questions. What changes? How does change occur? When? Why? Etc. The aim of the model is not only to try to answer these questions, but also to study ways in which a better clinical observation can contribute to advances in the study of their answers.

The three levels or steps considered in the model are the following.

## *Level 1: phenomenological description of the transformations*

This level comprises the discussion of the phenomenological description of two or more points of reference. The first point of reference (or what is termed the *anchor point*) is the manifestation in the first interviews of certain dimensions of psychic functioning. Points can be found in subsequent sessions that show the presence of change—positive *or* negative—or even the absence of change.

### *Questions for group discussion*

1. Do changes occur? What are the characteristics of these changes seen from the perspective of the analytic process?

2. If present, are these changes perceptible in the session? And between sessions? In what areas?
3. What is the patient's perspective regarding his/her changes?
4. Are there changes in the way the patient uses the analyst, the analyst's interpretations, and his/her own mind and body during sessions?

### *Level 2: identification of the main diagnostic dimensions of change*

The aim of discussions at this level is to analyse any changes that have occurred to the patient according to diagnostic dimensions described in a language close to that of experience.

Current psychodynamic diagnostic systems (*OPD-2, PDM, DSM-5*) offer a useful description of these dimensions. This level should prepare the observational basis for the discussion at Level 3, when the understanding of transformations will be deepened from different theoretical perspectives.

#### *Questions for group discussion*

1. What is the patient's subjective experience of his/her symptoms, his/her beliefs, and expectations about his/her problems and treatment?
2. Are there context-dependent factors that affect the therapeutic process (crises, traumatic situations, somatic illnesses, etc.)?
3. How does the patient experience others, and him-/herself in relation to others?
4. What are the main conflicts involved?
5. Are defences adequate and flexible, or predominantly dysfunctional?
6. How capable is the patient of adequately perceiving his/her own internal states and those of others? Up to where is he/she able to recognise and represent his/her own affects? Does he/she empathise with others, tolerating and understanding the existence of different points of view?
7. Is the patient able to adequately regulate his/her impulses, affects, and self-esteem?

8. How deep and stable is the bond or attachment with internal and external objects? How capable is the patient of starting relationships and tolerating separations? How capable is the patient of intimacy and reciprocity?
9. Is it possible to identify a type of personality disorder or other kinds of disorder?

*For all the previous questions*: How have these aspects changed in the course of treatment?

## *Level 3: explanatory hypotheses of transformations*

Transformations occurring during an analysis can be understood according to different explanatory theoretical models.

The discussion will be focused on the relationship between these hypotheses and clinical observation. The aim of the discussion is not to choose between hypotheses, but to examine the clinical support for each.

### *Questions for group discussion*

1. Where does the analyst centre most interventions?
2. What explicit and implicit hypotheses of change do we infer as present in the work of the analyst?
3. What are the more convincing and less convincing aspects of these different hypotheses and how could they be refined to better match the clinical material presented?

## *Clinical material*

The patient, whom I will call Andres and who is in his mid-forties, first came to see me in the last week of January ten years ago, a few days before my summer holidays.

At that time, we had two consultations and then a further one at the beginning of March, when we agreed to start analysis with a frequency of four times a week. He accepted my fees, adding that he "would never argue about the fees charged by a professional".

At the beginning of our first meeting in January, Andres stated that for a long time he had thought he did not need to have, as he put it, "an analytical situation". That position, however, changed, and about a year before we first met he had begun to think about having a consultation. He realised in the first interview that this change of mind coincided with having formed a close friendship with another man who, at that time, had been going through a course of treatment for two years with the analyst who had referred Andres to me.

In the same interview, he said, "I want to start a treatment for two reasons. The first is that I feel it is necessary to put some sort of order in my life, something that I think I cannot do on my own. Second, I'm interested in a course of treatment as it would be like 'working-out intellectually'." He went on to say that he had not undertaken any "intellectual exercise" since he had abandoned his studies in Law some years previously, just five subjects short of finishing his degree. He also expressed the opinion that he made a mistake in his choice of degree when he first started at university at the age of eighteen.

He met Emilia at university and they married nearly twenty years ago. She, in contrast, did finish her degree and, at the time of the start of his course of treatment, had an important technical post in a public institution; she works there to this day.

Andres, after referring to his wife, went on to tell me that he owned three shops in a fashionable neighbourhood of Buenos Aires, having also opened branches elsewhere in the city, two of them in the same year. In all three shops he sells wine, a sector that has experienced a boom in recent years. He continued, "I'm doing very well, taking into account the present economic climate. I opened my first shop soon after getting married. I have put in a lot of effort into the business, and it has been growing ever since. Today, I own five stores."

In this first interview, he went back to his time studying and reflected on the fact that he left his studies when he was near the end of his course, saying, "I think that one aspect of my personality is that I get bored very quickly. I shut the door and reopening it is very difficult for me. I like *doing* things. In business, if I get bored, I start something else."

With a view to giving some background to the case, in so far as his personal history goes, I shall offer here a summary of what came up in the second and third interviews.

Andres was born in the city of Buenos Aires but then, after a short while, the family moved to another city not far from there. His parents are both alive; they separated when Andres was one year old. They both live in a village in the province of Buenos Aires and have both remarried. He has two half-brothers on his father's side—both in their mid-thirties-and a half-sister on his mother's side, also in her mid-thirties.

The picture that he paints of his father is that of a bohemian type, a man who is very seductive; he was relatively present during Andres' upbringing, but never took financial responsibility. When Andres spoke about his mother, he said, "She always worked to support me. I have to tell you that, between the ages of two and six, I lived with my maternal grandparents in the village while my mother went to work in the city of Buenos Aires and travelled back to the village to be with me at weekends."

Then, at the age of six, and just one day before starting primary school, Andres and his mother moved back to the city where he attended good, private primary and secondary schools. It was then that Andres' mother met a man and they began a relationship. They eventually had a daughter when Andres was eleven, but they never lived together. In the same year, a half-brother was born to his father, followed by a half-sister the following year.

Smiling, he told me that he has to this day a group of friends from that time, particularly from his secondary school, people who before were better off than he was, and with whom he went on holiday to rather posh resorts. When he talks about them, he says in the interviews that he used to see them as "poor little rich kids".

In the March interview before analysis started, referring to his comment on those friends, I said it seemed to me that, to some extent, it was *he* who was feeling like a poor little rich kid now and that this might have been one of the reasons which brought him to analysis in the first place. This seems to have made quite an impression on him.

## *Early days in the treatment*

Andres is the kind of patient who turns up punctually for his four weekly sessions. He has used childishly seductive attitudes from the very beginning: he offers me sweets and asks my advice on everyday matters to do with his work, or information about doctors for him or his relatives.

That childish attitude is also reflected in his gestures, like his handshake on coming in as he says, rather pompously and with a somewhat mischievous smile, "And how are we today, doctor?"

The way he dresses, in my opinion, also reflects that attitude. He sports a "careful" untidiness. He wears the fashions of the young, combining 1950's clothes with large baggy jeans, and sometimes he carries a cool shoulder bag slung over his shoulder.

A subject that came up in the analysis, but not mentioned in the interviews, is that as well as smoking a packet of cigarettes per day, he smokes marijuana. At the beginning, he said that he does it only from time to time, but later on he explained that he does it nearly every day to relax when he gets home or when he has a work meeting that he finds particularly stressful.

Over time, the payment of fees became a core of resistance. In the first few months, he paid punctually at the end of the month, but then he began to space payments out without mentioning anything. His position centred on the fact that he did not understand how, in the economic situation in Argentina at that time, I could have anything to say to somebody who, albeit late, paid me. I said that, on that occasion, I would accept his system of payment but that we would have to discuss the matter. I interpreted to him that he wanted me to adapt to his way of working so as not to enter into the work of analysis.

Andres' sessions are on Monday, Wednesday, Thursday, and Friday.

### *A Thursday session in December from the second year of treatment (at that moment he owed the fees for October and November)*

He arrives on time and, as always, he empties his pockets, leaving his mobile phone (switched off), some bank notes, coins, and papers on my desk.

He lies on the couch, sighs, places his left hand on his forehead, remains silent for a short while, takes a packet of sweets out of his shirt pocket and, smiling, he turns round and stretches his hand to offer me one.

*P*: No sweets for you, right? The day you say "Yes" will be a hint to me that we are about to end, don't you think? Yesterday I remembered something you said once about my negative aspects and my aggression, which I cannot show here. But you see, I don't feel that I am in a hostile environment. When I do get aggressive it is as a response to certain stimuli. I think that would be a logical explanation. There must be negative things and it is not easy to admit them. Where I did see my aggression was in my relationship with Bernardo.

I was hoping he would give me a hand in my new business. And now that I have bought out my partners, he talks about bringing in a new partner, but he is too busy with his own concerns. This is an example of where when I need him he makes me wait, but when he needs me I to go him immediately. If I think about it calmly, I understand it and don't feel negative, but my first impulse is a feeling of rage.

*A*: I think you were angry because I didn't accept your offer of a sweet. In the same way, you get angry with Bernardo when he doesn't help you. You get very angry when things or people don't work the way you expected. I should respond to your expectations of how I should operate to avoid rage or anxiety building up in you.

*P*: I want to understand. If I talk about it, it's because I'm thinking that I must bring out that nasty dwarf inside me here.

*A*: I think the nastiness is not so apparent here and it has found a place in other areas, such as being behind with your payments.

*P*: Discovering that feeling with regard to Bernardo was important. I had never got annoyed with him before. I ask myself—maybe I shouldn't —Why?

I try to think why there is this question about payment here. The first explanation I can find is the most real one: it has to do with my lack of organisation, and part of that is my management of money. I have a strange list of priorities that has no real logic about it.

I am in charge of the money in my business. The first thing I always do is make the deposits in my current account so as not to have problems. That would lead to a real mess and telephone calls to banks to cover a cheque at the last minute. On the other hand, I can leave a telephone bill unpaid when I have $30,000 in my account. I don't even spend the money. While I am on the subject, let me see, when was it? Yesterday, no, Tuesday, oh well, I had decided that this year I was going to buy works from two artists: Martin and Lucia. I agreed with both of them to pay in instalments, which is current practice these days. On 14 November I was burgled, and a few days later a client called a creditors' meeting and I had to pay $50,000. Those two things together caused an imbalance.

I felt that I was being conflated with the two "poor artists": we could offer our work as artisans but there was no recognition from the patient of either our effort or our needs.

*A*: Here, in the analysis, so long as I don't say anything with regard to your lateness in paying, it would seem that I am accepting your conditions. I didn't take the sweet you offered me at the beginning of the session, but, by not raising the subject, I am accepting your terms of payment.

*P*: It isn't easy for me to recognise that. I don't even get to mentioning payment here. I understand what you are saying about the sweet; however, in wanting to see progress I see progress in the matter. For example: telephone, gas, electricity, all the services, used to be a taboo for me.

I think it is somehow related to the question of power. Now that they have been privatised, telephone companies are swimming in money; well I'm not paying! To hell with Telecom! They now send out monthly bills, and if you need to speak to someone a machine answers.

I admit these are rationalisations. What I did in my business was to take myself out of the administrative circuit and give it to my sister, who now takes care of that. A monthly telephone bill in one of the shops, for example, is $3,000. I am going to try to organise the question of payments with her. I don't consider myself a greedy person.

It took me some minutes to recover from the feeling of being mistreated. Once I felt that I had put the necessary space between me and my countertransferential feelings, I said,

*A*: It doesn't seem to be a question that can be defined as greediness. What you said about service companies showed how you see power relationships. Why should you pay me if, by withholding the money you owe me, you feel you have the power to decide how the relationship with me works? You must feel that otherwise you wouldn't have me instantly—if you needed me, a machine would answer.

*P*: I move in real life, you see, and where there is a space I take it.

*A*: That is precisely it; you take it without asking.

*P*: I feel that I have a right to do so, I have a right not to have to ask for or to question things. I pay the bank, obviously, and as from this year, having hired new accountants, I'll pay my taxes. On the other hand, I pay my suppliers under my own conditions.

I feel uneasy talking like this. It must give the impression that nothing is going to change. Here, in the analysis, at the beginning I was attentive to payment dates, but now I think I was trying at that time to be a good boy. Later on, as the relationship develops, one shows one's true nature, isn't that true?

Even though he seems to be aware of the way he behaved both with me in sessions and in his everyday life with his employees or with the people who worked with him, my feeling was that they were only words. What was predominant in him, in fact, was his feeling of being powerful, and this was shown in the way he spoke, the tone of his voice, and the attitude he displayed, which was one of arrogance and contemptuousness. At the same time, some modest change in the analysis could be seen in his uneasiness and in his idea that he was starting to show his own true nature.

*A*: Now we can see the more genuine aspects of your relationship with me, and probably outside here, too; that it is necessary for you to be the one who sets the conditions that I have to accept. If you need something immediately, you don't seem to be prepared to accept someone else's conditions or to wait and see.

*P*: Is it perhaps possible that I want to have my anxieties calmed immediately? Look, I don't know what is likely to happen later on, but at the moment I have no space for that sort of thing. I am only interested in the positive side. In time I will be able to see what is wrong. I am not discounting the fact that when I talk about Bernardo, I know that I am also projecting things that are mine into him, for example. We saw here on other occasions that we project our ambitions into other people, particularly if they managed to achieve things that we're not able to achieve. I don't know if the feeling is one of jealousy, but it is strongly charged.

I like talking about these things; I see things about myself that I didn't know. It is as if I am just beginning to open a door.

*A*: You might be opening a door but I am under the impression that you close it immediately. I don't think you give yourself the time to think about what I say.

## *A vignette from the fourth year of analysis*

Andres comes to a Monday session saying that he had a very good weekend. He went with his wife in his new car to visit his mother, who lives in the suburbs. Before his hour, he had a meeting with his company's accountant, and the figures are very good—compared to the previous year, the business has improved its sales by twenty per cent. As he speaks, his mobile phone falls from his trouser pocket and slides on to the couch. I notice it, but say nothing. While Andres speaks with vehemence, enthusiastically, the phone slides further and falls on the floor. He jokes about it, and picks it up.

Andres keeps talking, and I listen and watch. Coins start falling from his pocket, and two of them roll off the couch and on to the floor. He picks them up and says:

*P*: I don't know what's going on with me today, I'm losing everything. Could it be that I'm losing it? And just when I was talking about a successful end-of-year: I feel better, it's been two years since I stopped smoking, and I gave up pot . . .

*A*: You are telling me that you are happy about how you have felt these last few days, and about how things are turning out for you, but that you lose things—your phone, your money—because in a way you know that, even though you have improved in many respects, something remains unsolved: you are always behind in your payments to me, you frequently owe me money.

*P*: It's true. Before coming here I thought of bringing the cheque-book and paying you what I owe you once and for all, but in the end I forgot.

## *3-LM and the clinical material*

While the 3-LM intends to study the changes in a sequence of sessions, inferring the unconscious configurations, we can start by asking some questions from a conscious level, taking into account clinical material from the first interviews (an approach used in working with the groups).

How much does he really suffer?

What kind of "intellectual work" and "order in his life" is he looking for?

What expectation does he have of change through treatment?

What is the role of addictive habits (marijuana, etc.) in his wish for well-being?

How strong is his motivation for change in relation to the secondary gain of being a seductive "poor little rich kid"?

In the first interview how capable is the patient of:

- productively reflecting about himself?
- differentiating affects and having an integrated feeling of his identity and personal history? Can the patient adequately discriminate himself from others?
- perceiving others adequately, and empathising with them, tolerating and understanding different perspectives?

Of course, there are many other perspectives from which we could explore the patient's material. Several theoretical, psychopathological, and even technical points are implicated in the clinical situation with the patient. In order to appreciate the utility of the three-level model, and as an exercise, I shall select some anchor points significant for this specific treatment. I indicate some possible transformations from three anchor points that I have selected. In her discussion (below), Margaret Ann Fitzpatrick-Hanly will further explore the observations of change and no change in these anchoring diagnostic dimensions and bring in two other points from which to assess change and absence of change in the patient's functioning.

*The first anchor point* I select is in the first interview, when Andres accepted my fees, stating that he "would never argue about the fees charged by a professional".

While the phenomenological aspect (Level 1) shows the patient's agreement regarding the fees, we might be prompted to think of a defensive–compliant attitude, which becomes abundantly clear later in the material when the patient is persistently late with his payments and the analyst centres her interpretations on this issue.

If we take Level 3, the patient's lateness in paying can be understood as an enactment within the transference relationship of his resistance to psychic change. In spite of the effort made by the analyst to work on the subject, there is still no transformation of this situation in the fourth year of his treatment.

From the dynamic point of view (Level 3), we could make the hypothesis that the withholding enactment reflects a retaliatory response in the transference: "I will deprive you of me just as my parents deprived me of what I needed from them". This configuration leads to the patient's interpersonal tendency to coerce others into adopting his way rather than accepting theirs. Regarding Level 3, one compatible hypothesis could be that a pattern of fear of abandonment is acted out in the transference and in the interpersonal relations as an anticipated repetition of the early parental abandonment suffered.

The session seems to show that the analytic work with this patient has progressed quite a bit, but not enough to establish a relationship of true concern for the object (Level 3). Even though Andres acknowledges that he has improved, especially regarding the addictive aspect of his personality, delaying payment enables him to control his analyst, whom he renders exhausted and, from his perspective, "impoverished". There is then in his inner world a persecutory object that threatens him, his analyst, an object which he must struggle with, so much so that he is "losing it".

The *second anchor point,* closely related to the first, can be found in his ritual of emptying his pockets and leaving their contents on my desk. From a phenomenological description (Level 1), we could infer that the patient is not aware of a possible meaning of his behaviour: there is, however, another possible inference: (Level 2) this behaviour could involve a denial of his withholding tendencies which will appear very soon in the treatment. "I show everything I have in my pockets, I am not hiding anything". This could also be seen as part of his "seductive" tendencies.

If we go back for a moment to the questions corresponding to Level 2, it would be reasonable to think that conflicts of power (submission *vs.* control; need for care *vs.* self-sufficiency) and guilt are dominant.

Now, we proceed to the session from the fourth year of analysis in an attempt to track transformations at Level 3.

In the last vignette presented from the fourth year of analysis, the patient has stopped the ritual of emptying his pockets on the analyst's desk. He then, however, notices the inadvertent spilling of the contents out of his pocket as he lies on the couch. He immediately picks up the coins, and says, "I don't know what's going on with me today, I'm losing everything. Could it be that I'm losing it?"

At this stage of the analysis, he shows an awareness of the possibility that this event might have a psychological meaning and this pattern goes even further when he specifies that he is losing everything and, moreover, when he says, "I am losing it", even if, in the context, this is primarily a question.

The absence of the earlier denial of his behaviour regarding the emptying of pockets and the presence of a quite sophisticated awareness of the possible symbolic meaning of the falling out of coins, linked with his feeling of *losing it*, speaks in itself of a transformation in his capacity for a deeper self- and interpersonal communication. Furthermore, he exhibits a growing capacity to productively reflect about himself and an integrated feeling of his own identity that could be linked to his early history of losses.

The *third anchor point* selected was the patient's revelation, early on in the analysis, that he smoked marijuana daily. At Level 2, we could make the hypothesis that he has formed this habit as a way to "self-medicate" to deal with persecutory and depressive anxieties. At Level 2, the underlying basis of the practice could be seen as related to the attachment disruptions suffered by the patient during the first six years of his life.

The transformation point in the fourth year of analysis was the fact that he was no longer engaged in daily marijuana use. This implies (Level 2) that the patient no longer needs that particular external support to cope with persecutory or depressive anxieties. An additional hypothesis (Level 3) would be that an improvement in the attachment to the analyst and her capacity to receive and contain his anxieties made this transformation possible.

This commentary has been a brief application of the three-level model to a history and sessions from different points in the analysis of one patient. This model is usually implemented in group work and normally lasts between a day and a day-and-a-half. However, the model is sufficiently flexible to be used in different contexts. The importance of working in groups is that, during the time given and working with the same text of selected sessions, members of the group can bring different points of view to improve the overall understanding of the work with the patient.

In this chapter, I have set out to address both the importance of observation in our clinical practice and the utility of the 3-LM as a tool for studying transformations within a treatment. The model is a tool to be used in different contexts, but is primarily aimed at enhancing our ability to observe through the invaluable contribution of work in groups, where several minds are working together to convey simultaneous and varied points of view.

# Discussion: further reflections on the clinical narrative of Virginia Ungar, and the use of anchor points to track transformations

*Margaret Ann Fitzpatrick-Hanly*

## *Introduction*

Dr Ungar has applied the three-level model to a four-year psychoanalysis with her patient, Andres. She has composed a clinical "text" with a brief history and verbatim sessions, which provides a shared object for observation. A group of psychoanalysts or discussants can then reflect on the patient's associations and the analyst's interventions to review the data that led to her hypotheses on change and no change. The selection of sessions at intervals of time, from the beginning and from two later phases of the analysis, facilitates attention to change and no change over a specified period of time, and takes into account the nature and severity of the problems suffered by a particular patient on entering treatment. A group of psychoanalysts can then refine or reselect anchor points when core diagnostic dimensions in the patient's psychic functioning become clarified through discussion and re-reading of the sessions.

The concept of the "anchor point" (which we see used in Dr Ungar's chapter) is important in creating a method for developing a new kind of "clinical narrative" through work with the three-level model. Anchor points can be thought of as "starting points" (often presented in the words of the patient), which condense complex problems in the patient's psychic functioning. When absence of change is observed, these anchor points (symptoms, inhibitions, or anxieties) can reflect what is most difficult to change in the patient's dynamics and in the analytic process. The analysts in the work groups can return to the hypotheses about core problems explicit and implicit in the anchor points, moving back and forth between the early and later sessions. The groups will use the ordinary language of the sessions to become sensitive to resonances, repetitions, and developments in the material (Level 1), and then refine the clinical narrative, applying psychoanalytic concepts to the developing narrative (Level 2).

## *Discussion*

This discussion reflects on two anchor points selected by Dr Ungar in order to further understand their dynamic meanings and their vicissitudes in the later phases of the analysis. Reflections on links between the traumas of childhood and the enactments and associations in the analysis will be made to elaborate the clinical narrative about the patient's transformations. Two additional anchor points from the early sessions are selected and explored, which deepen the ideas about the specific changes and absence of change in the patient, confirming Dr Ungar's hypotheses.

### *The patient and two anchor points*

Dr Ungar presents her patient, Andres, to us through the vivid expressions and symptomatic acts that she selected as anchor points to use in her observations on change. Andres is a married male businessman in his mid-forties.

This discussion will first take up two anchor points: "he accepted my fees, adding that he would never argue about the fees charged by a professional" and "at the beginning of his sessions, Andres emptied his pockets, leaving all the contents on my desk: mobile phone, money, papers . . ."

One aspect of the depth and resonance of the presenting complaints and symptoms (used as anchor points) lies in the repetition of childhood attitudes and defences (adaptations made partly under the stress of traumatic loss), which come to life and then into language in the analytic couple's interchanges.

Let us recall a few details of the patient's history, so that we can reconstruct their likely impact on his infantile sexuality, aggression, and narcissistic vulnerability, as we continue to track change and no change. Andres' parents separated when he was one. His father moved out. Between the ages of two and six he lived with his maternal grandparents, while his mother worked in Buenos Aires (some miles away from their village) and came home at the weekends. His mother met a man, and had a baby girl when Andres was eleven, although she never lived with this man. Andres felt his mother always worked to make a living for him. His father remarried, and had two sons, his half-brothers, now twenty-six and twenty-seven, born when he was aged eleven and twelve. His father is a kind of bohemian, not taking financial responsibility.

*First anchor point*: the patient "would never argue about fees charged by a professional".

What are the hidden depths in this statement with its strong denial? The patient's history suggests that, given the divorce and separations, Andres might have had to show "acceptance" on the surface, when the situation was too painful or disruptive for him to process: his parents' divorce at one, his mother's going away all week to work at two, his grandparents' being his care-takers, his parents' having new sexual partners with three baby siblings born when he was eleven and twelve. To accept and never to argue might have seemed necessary, especially with respect to the mother/care-taker/analyst making a living, but aggressive feelings and impulses lurk just beneath the surface.

### *Power, money, survival*

Dr Ungar asked where was Andres' psychic pain when he came to the analysis. What experiences were split off or repressed? How would they come into the analysis? We can see, in exploring the vicissitudes of the anchor points, that much of what goes on in the sessions allows the patient to bring what has been unconscious and split off about power, money, and survival into the analysis, first in defiance and then with greater reflection and the beginnings of ownership.

Andres says that in business "he is doing very well, given the present economic climate". Difficulties in the economic climate in Argentina at that time were real, but serving also to hide fixations and conflicts at the oral and anal phases in the one- and two-year-old Andres during the divorce and the week-long separations from his mother.

At first, the patient paid punctually, and then there were intervals of two months when he did not pay, acting in direct contradiction to his statement that he "would never argue about . . . fees". He protested that how could his analyst take this up, when the real economy was so troubled, but, in fact, he makes his analyst work for him for nothing; his infantile longings and his impulses to turn the tables on his mother are enacted in the analysis, not yet expressed in words and affects.

In the second year of treatment, in a Thursday session, we hear that Andres owed fees for all of October and November. He offers the analyst a sweet, not the money he owes her, and, part way through the session, he says about his friend, "When I need him he makes me wait, but when he needs me I go to him immediately." The analyst says, "I think you were angry that I didn't accept your sweet", and adds that Andres believes she should help him manage his anxiety and rage. He says "there is an angry dwarf in me". Now observations of some change can be made, in that the patient can use the analyst's intervention to portray more vividly the nature of his inner world. The dwarf is a classic image for the enraged, troublemaking, envious child in the adult, who wants to spin gold out of straw, a Rumpelstiltskin from Grimm's fairy tales.

The patient talks about his anger with his friend, Bernardo, who makes him wait (as his mother made him wait all week long when he was two, in the anal toddler stage), and he comes back indirectly to the question about payment in the analytic treatment. He says, "I'm in charge of the money in my business."

Contrary to this statement, disorganisation about his money has been a serious liability for the patient in his business. He leaves bills unpaid, including his analyst's bill, while he buys art. He leaves bills unpaid in a way that threatens the survival of his reputation in business even when he has money in the bank.

The analyst interprets, "If I don't raise the subject of payment, it would seem that I am accepting your terms." She notes the win/lose idea in his mind, that when one of them is in charge the other is not in charge. He is now able to think in a new more cogent way, "that all this is related to power". But still he does not want to pay "the rich utility companies".

In relation to his outside life, we note a modest change at this stage of the analysis: the patient makes a constructive practical decision to put his sister in charge of his business payments, because he can see that withholding payments endangers his own interests. The analyst says that he wants the power to decide how their relationship works, because otherwise he would feel that she was just a machine, and that there was no one really receiving his messages and responding. He says he has a "right to pay his suppliers, under his own conditions". His messages about control and defiance, expressing his one- and two-year-old child's split off demands are now in the analysis, received by the analyst, and removed from harming his interests in his business.

The anchor point, "I would never argue about a professional's fees", has revealed more of its dynamic meaning in the analysis, its relationship to the patient's childhood trauma, to ways he has repeated maladaptive dynamics in his work life and friendships. He makes others wait, forcing them to feel financial insecurity. We are able to observe some change in the patient's use of the analysis, and in his functioning in business by the second year. However, Dr Ungar also gives feedback to her patient on what has not changed, noting the continuing repetitions in the analysis, in his not paying her on time. She says, "You may be opening a door but you close it right away." She alerts the patient to what still lies ahead in their work. His lateness in paying for the analysis has not changed. The resistance continues to communicate that important infantile forces are still in play, and that overwhelming experiences and fantasies of childhood remain yet to be processed.

The value of thinking about where there is no change yet, in using the three-level model, is that it clarifies for the analyst the most powerful psychic forces at work defending against unbearable anxiety in the patient. The reader of Dr Ungar's clinical narrative wonders, what happened when Andres was one, and two years old? What depression might the mother have suffered after the divorce when she had to go away to work, with what effect on the patient? What were his longings for a financially responsible father? What Dr Ungar appreciated as a defensive compliance in the early sessions—he would "never argue about the fees"—became an acting in, with the patient protesting, "you will have to wait till I decide to feed you or give to you". By the second year, the patient had turned the tables.

In working with Level 2 of the model, bringing analytic concepts to review observation of change from the session material, Dr Ungar states, "It would be reasonable to think that conflicts of power (submission *vs.* control; need for care *vs.* self-sufficiency) and guilt are dominant." My discussion confirms her thinking on these major dimensions of psychic functioning along which to assess change and no change.

*The second anchor point.* The patient empties his pockets and leaves all the contents on the analyst's desk, money, mobile phone, etc.

Dr Ungar tracks transformations in the patient from the anchor point of his emptying his pockets of his mobile phone and money on to her desk, a gesture made with no comment and no psychological self-questioning in the first sessions. By the fourth year session, the analyst hears the patient's associations in relation to losing his things as showing a new capacity for self-reflection.

In the fourth year, the patient stopped emptying his pockets on to the analyst's desk, but one day his mobile phone and his coins slipped slowly on to the floor. He says, "I'm losing everything. Could it be that I'm losing it?"

Dr Ungar notes in his tone a new capacity to feel anxiety about loss. We have underlined that Andres suffered many losses in childhood at key developmental stages: his father at one, his mother's presence during the week when he was two, and financial stability. Just as he entered puberty, both his mother and father had babies, and he lost his place as only child, however insecure it had been. The patient's contact with a broader range of affects, and especially with his anxiety about loss, represents a significant gain in the analysis, implicit in his wondering about the symbolic meaning of the falling coins.

### *A third anchor point (selected by the discussant)*

This discussion will continue to explore Dr Ungar's observations of change in the patient's growing capacity for symbolisation by selecting an anchor point from the second year of the analysis: a story about loss. In comparing the narrative of loss in the fourth year of analysis, we can observe that Andres' habitual disavowal of affect (and the consequent blocking of intrapsychic communication) was giving way to more tolerance for difficult affects.

Andres brings a brief narrative of loss in the second year: "On 14 November I was burgled, and a few days later a client called a creditors' meeting and I had to pay $50,000. Those two things together caused an imbalance."

The patient has been robbed, but he expresses no anger in his narrative, no distress or worry. He has suddenly been asked to pay $50,000, and his response is that "It caused an imbalance". The defensiveness of the patient's intellectual style, drained of all affect, is striking. By the fourth year of the analysis, he tells the narrative about loss, discussed by Dr Ungar, as his money and mobile phone slide to the floor in the analyst's office: "I'm losing everything. Could it be that I'm losing it? And just when I was talking about a successful end-of-year." The change from intellectual assertion about "an imbalance" to the meaningful question about "losing it" and the change in tone and the narrative style could have been used in a theatre production to dramatise character development in a protagonist. When we compare these two brief narratives about loss, using the verbatim of the sessions, we can hear the change from intellectualisation to the expression of complex affects of chagrin, worry, and self-doubt. Andres asks implicitly, "What *am* I doing? What is going on in me?"

The use of the narrative of loss from the second year as an anchor point confirms Dr Ungar's conclusion that the patient exhibits "a growing capacity to productively reflect about himself and an integrated feeling of his own identity that could be linked to his early history of losses."

*A fourth anchor point*: "I have a right."

In the second year of the analysis, the patient responded with defensive defiance to an important and challenging intervention by the analyst, in which she linked many counterproductive activities in his life and in the analysis.

*P*: I move in real life, you see, and where there is a space I take it.

*A*: That is precisely it; you take it without asking.

*P*: I feel that I have a right to do so; I have a right not to have to ask for or to question things.

The patient's response to his analyst's intervention is expressive and defiant (showing the impulses of the one- and two-year-old). But, although he is unable to take in and reflect on the intervention more effectively for himself at this stage, he does elaborate Dr Ungar's understanding of his basic stance in life, which clarifies for both of them that he feels (in a way linked to his traumatic experiences) entitled to take without asking.

In the fourth year of the analysis, the patient's response to an intervention allows us to compare his internal position with what he expressed implicitly at the beginning of the analysis. Here, the analyst acknowledges change, but keeps in the open the unresolved symptom of the late payments.

*P*: I feel better, it's been two years since I stopped smoking, and I gave up pot . . .

*A*: . . . even though you have improved in many respects, something remains unsolved: you are always behind in your payments to me; you frequently owe me money.

*P*: It's true. Before coming here I thought of bringing the cheque-book and paying you what I owe you once and for all, but in the end I forgot.

The analyst has noted in her discussion that the patient continues to decide when he will pay. However, I think that he also takes in and uses the analyst's interpretation in a way that expresses more fairness to her. "I thought of paying you what I owe you." In the second year, he used a very entitled expression, affirming his "right to pay his suppliers under his own conditions" (as well as the analyst, the artists, etc.). Here, in the fourth year session, he acknowledges that he "owes" his analyst money, and would feel some relief at paying once and for all. To admit this much, the patient must be less hungry, enraged, and entitled, with a positive attachment to the analyst creating space in his mind. "But in the end I forgot." He can state that he is at fault, "I forgot", in a way that is not so defiant or entitled, but also still provocative in a childish way.

Andres started the analysis expressing compliance: he "would never argue about . . . fees". But the part of him that wanted to "argue" about having to give something of his to another was alive under the negation, and needed expression. His conflicts about power, money, and survival, originating in traumatic losses at early stages of childhood, have entered fully into the analysis. His narrative shows he is closer to recognising the needs of the other.

## *Conclusion*

It is remarkable that, with three sessions from different points in an analytic treatment, we can observe so precisely both repetition and change in the patient. I thank Dr Ungar for providing this excellent work in clinical observation. Her presentation was a pleasure to discuss and her clear observations on change and absence of change using the three-level model show that it is possible to track transformations in a way that provides confidence in the work of psychoanalysis.

## *References*

Bion, W. R. (1992). *Cogitations*. London: Karnac.

Freud, S. (1895d). *Studies on Hysteria. S.E., 2*: 253–306. London: Hogarth.

Money-Kyrle, R. (1968). Cognitive development. *International Journal of Psychoanalysis, 37*: 300–306.

CHAPTER FIVE

# Depression and trauma: the psychoanalysis of a patient suffering from chronic depression

## An exemplary case study based on the three levels of clinical observation

*Marianne Leuzinger-Bohleber*

### *Preliminary remarks*

#### *From focusing the analyst's mind on the transformations of the patients*

At the EPF Conference in Copenhagen in April 2010, I was asked to participate in a panel devoted to reflections concerning the achievements of the ten years of Working Parties within the EPF. To summarise: in my perspective, one of the great achievements of the Clinical Working Parties, initiated by David Tuckett in 2000, is that the endless feuds between different psychoanalytical schools have become subdued. Particularly in the Clinical Working Parties (CCM, see Tuckett, 2008), but also in the other groups of the EPF initiatives, who regularly met and worked together for nearly ten years, a new culture of curiosity and respect was created for the Others, for different clinical and conceptual thoughts of colleagues from many different regions within the EPF and from different "schools" (Kleinans, contemporary Freudians, "object relationalists", Kohutians, intersubjectivists, etc.). This culture helped to overcome the unproductive competition for the "right" or "wrong" theoretical point of view, the "right" or "wrong" interpretation, clinical attitude, etc. A new appreciation for the richness of contemporary pluralism within European psychoanalysis developed. In my eyes, this is an immense liberation from narrow-mindedness or even pseudo-religious structures, which have proved to be so destructive for psychoanalysis as a scientific discipline in the past (see, e.g., Makari, 2008; Zaretsky, 2004).

In my statement in Copenhagen, I made a plea to use this new culture of curiosity and appreciation for the pluralism of clinical and conceptual approaches involving the complexity of clinical psychoanalytic observation once again for the central task of all psychoanalysts: to understand unconscious fantasies and conflicts of our patients and to help them to change their inner psychic worlds. It is important to reflect on our own professional tools, on the minds of the analysts, transference and countertransference etc., but, seen from the outside perspective of our patients or the mental health system, they are only instruments, "professional tools" in the basic sense of the word, that serve the central aim of helping the patient suffering from psychic pain to change his inner pathological world in order to regain his capability to "to make him as efficient and as capable of enjoyment as is possible", as Freud put it long ago (Freud, 1923a, p. 251).

The Project Committee on Clinical Observation and Testing thus tries to offer some steps in this direction: to improve our clinical observations and communication. We developed the three levels of clinical observation, which are presented in this volume in great detail by Ricardo Bernardi. The model can be applied to different settings, as we have discussed in several international congresses during the past few years: for an intensive exchange on transformational processes of patients in local groups of colleagues or in groups from different regions of the IPA with different theoretical orientations, for training purposes, and, as I shall illustrate in this chapter, as one possibility of writing up clinical cases, one outcome of what we in Germany call "clinical psychoanalytic research" (*klinisch-psychoanalytische Forschung*). We are taking up the original idea of the "*Junktim-Forschung*" by Freud[1] and trying to rediscover the clinical treasures of our intensive, unique, clinical psychoanalytical work with analysands.

### *Improving the writing of psychoanalytic case narratives: one application of the three-level model for observing patient transformations*

Established by Freud, the psychoanalytic extended case report continues to be one of the most important forms of communication in international psychoanalysis, albeit in more recent years such reports have rarely been published in international journals of psychoanalysis. Among other reasons, the partial disappearance of this erstwhile tradition in psychoanalysis as "clinical science" might be linked to the heated controversies in which various authors have questioned the very validity of such case reports for science (cf., e.g., Meyer, 1993; Thomä & Kächele, 1985). A discussion of these controversies would exceed the constraints of the present contribution (cf. also Leuzinger-Bohleber, 1995, 2010a; Leuzinger-Bohleber, Rüger, Stuhr, & Beutel, 2002, 2003). I contend that, to date, no credible alternative to the case reports has been developed for adequately and "legibly" presenting the "narrative truths",[2] as acquired over the course of lengthy psychoanalysis, to the psychoanalytic and non-psychoanalytic communities. Indeed, while precise reports of sessions (either verbatim, or based on analyst's notes) may be indispensable for many clinical and conceptual discussions, they remain, nevertheless, insufficient for conveying the total impression of a treatment and its results. By contrast, and naturally as best exemplified in Freud's own extensive literary case studies, the comprehensive case report succeeds in conveying both to students and to a broad public "what psychoanalysis is", the goals it pursues, and the types of transformations it effects in patients,[3] etc. Hence, as an empirical and clinical psychoanalytic researcher, my admiration is not exclusively confined to the work and legacy of Freud: it also encompasses writers and poets as a whole, to the extent that the latter succeed in giving masterful articulation to their insights in complex, psychic processes of transformation, and in conveying the results to their readers. For these reasons, I concur with leading narrative researchers who postulate that many "truths can only be told and not be measured".

It is precisely because of this esteem for clinical case reports—along with the knowledge that but a handful of psychoanalysts are endowed with the literary gift of Freud—that I decided to engage in the Project Group for Clinical Observation (as initiated by the former

President of the IPA, Charles Hanly) in their endeavour to improve the quality of clinical research. The drawbacks associated with this tradition are well known. These range from the arbitrary status of clinical observations for buttressing a given theoretical stance or hypothesis; the hazard of hermetically closed viewpoints; narcissistic confirmation, in lieu of the (self) critical reflection of an observation; a gravitation towards "positively resolved" star cases, in contrast to the absence of poorly performed treatments; the danger of (unconscious) "fabrication" (especially in cases during training); repetition or conformity to mainstream discussions within the psychoanalytic community and, as a consequence, the disappearance of innovative, unconventional ideas, and much else. The various methods elaborated for dealing with such drawbacks of clinical research also comprise the object of critical discussion. One such drawback will be presented for discussion in the following: it is an attempt to critically approach the arbitrariness and condensation in the presentation of clinical material, in theoretical assessment as well as in the interpretation of clinical observations with the aid of so-called *psychoanalytic expert validation* (cf., among others, Leuzinger-Bohleber, Rüger, Stuhr, & Beutel, 2003; Leuzinger-Bohleber et al., 2008, pp. 153ff.).

### *Psychoanalytic expert validation: one form of clinical research in psychoanalysis*

The method of "psychoanalytic expert validation" proposed here is very close to clinical practice. Supervision and intervision groups, as well as courses with candidates or IPA members, could be systematically used to expertly validate ongoing psychoanalyses and document the knowledge gained in extended case reports with different theoretical foci. In my view, this would be a contribution to improving clinical psychoanalytic research in contemporary psychoanalysis.

The method has been developed in the frame of a large retrospective study on the long-term outcomes of psychoanalyses and long-term psychoanalytic psychotherapies, the so-called "DPV Katamnese-studie" [Follow-up study of the German Psychoanalytic Association]. In this study, we investigated a representative sample of all the patients who had terminated their psychoanalyses and psychoanalytic long-term psychotherapies with members of the DPV between 1990 and 1993 ($n = 402$ patients). We applied a large variety of different instruments, questionnaires, psychological tests, analyses of "objective data" from the health insurance companies, and intensive psychoanalytic follow-up interviews. The study led to important results: for example, around 80% of all the treatments showed—on average six years after termination—a good outcome according to the evaluations of the former patients, their analysts, independent analysts, and non-analysts, as well as "objective information" concerning mental health data (significant reduction of costs by a significant reduction of days off work, days spent in hospitals, etc.; see Leuzinger-Bohleber, Rüger, Stuhr, & Beutel, 2002, 2003). But the most important, often unexpected insights were gained through the 200 intensive, psychoanalytic follow-up interviews with the former patients and with their former psychoanalysts by independent psychoanalytic interviewers. The interviews were mostly tape-recorded or, if patient or analyst did not consent, carefully documented directly after the interview. This documentation proved to be a unique and rich source for psychoanalytic and non-psychoanalytic insights (particularly concerning the tragic findings of the 4% of the psychoanalyses with negative outcomes). The richness of the interview material confronted us with the methodological challenge of how to summarise and communicate the complexity of the conscious and unconscious discoveries of these interviews in a critical way that would be transparent, reliable, and acceptable by members of the psychoanalytic, as well as the non-psychoanalytic, community. In this context, we developed the so-called psychoanalytic expert validation, which proved to be a very helpful and convincing method to summarise the psychoanalytic findings of the follow-up interviews. I shall briefly describe the method.

1. An expert group of psychoanalysts (6–8 members) was constituted and met regularly for two hours a week. It was important that we had a good mixture of very experienced and relatively young psychoanalysts who also had different theoretical preferences (Kleinian, British or American object relational theories, modern ego psychology, self psychology, etc.)
2. One psychoanalyst (A) of the group met a former analysand for two psychoanalytic interviews (following an open psychoanalytic technique, with certain questions to be asked at the end of

the second interview). Between the two interviews, he had a supervision with another member of the group (C) in order to understand his transference–countertransference reactions, associations, psychodynamic hypotheses, etc., and "test" them by mean of a psychoanalytic interpretation, if possible, in the second interview. Because of confidentiality reasons, it was important that the former patient lived in another city and that his analyst was not known to the interviewer and the supervisor.

3. Independent of these interviews with the former patients, another member of the group (B) interviewed the former psychoanalysts (mostly by telephone in order to guarantee the confidentiality and the anonymity of the analyst).
4. The group met for a two-hour session (close to the dates of the interviews), adhering to a clear procedure:
    (a) interviewer A summarised the two follow-up interviews with the former patient (approximately twenty minutes);
    (b) the group listened to five minutes of the tape-recorded interview (if possible);
    (c) free association in the group about the unconscious and conscious communication of the former patient to the interviewer, and of the interviewer to the group (by carefully observing one's own transference–countertransference reactions, association, etc.). Analysts A, B, and C did not participate in this round of "free associations" (about 10–15 minutes);
    (d) analyst B summarised his telephone interview with the former analyst of the patient (about ten minutes);
    (e) each member of the group filled out questionnaires focusing on the outcome of the treatment (Scales of Psychological Capacities, by Wallerstein et al., and some other short questionnaires) (about five minutes);
    (f) the group associated further about the clinical material, focusing on questions concerning the outcome of the psychoanalysis or the psychoanalytic long-term treatment (thirty minutes). Possible controversial clinical aspects were registered, discussed, and not harmonised;
    (g) one member of the group summarised the group discussions and the different positions after the session and sent it to the members of the group;

(h) at the beginning of the next group meeting, this summary was briefly discussed. Statements of agreement and disagreement were documented;

(i) The summary of the "case history" based on the follow-up interviews with the former patient and his analyst, as well as the group discussion and the questionnaires, were written up by one of the group members and given to the other members of the group for correction, modification, etc. Still open controversial perspectives were discussed and again documented instead of being harmonised.

The psychoanalytical expert validation proved to be very helpful for the publication of the many follow-up interviews (see, e.g., Leuzinger-Bohleber, Rüger, Stuhr, & Beutel, 2002). Compared with other methods (e.g., content analyses of the interviews, linguistic analyses, method of "Typenbildung", by Stuhr, Leuzinger-Bohleber, & Beutel, 2001), the method was relatively time saving and economical. It helped to condense the complexity of the clinical material in a functional way, taking into account possible "blind spots" of the interviewer. Because the method takes up the genuine psychoanalytic tradition of supervision and intervision, it was well accepted by the psychoanalytic colleagues. Many of them told us how fruitful and interesting the group sessions and the joint endeavour had been for them, being able to understand the retrospective view of former patients and their analysts of their psychoanalyses as well as their outcomes (and limitations), and how much they had learnt by carefully listening to former patients and colleagues.

This was one of the reasons why we further developed the method of psychoanalytical expert validation and applied it in several large studies, for example, EDIG (Ethical Dilemma due to Prenatal and Genetic Diagnostics) (see, e.g., Fischmann, Russ, & Leuzinger-Bohleber, 2013; Leuzinger-Bohleber & Teising, 2012; Leuzinger-Bohleber, Engels, & Tsiantis, 2008) and in the ongoing LAC Depression Study[4] as illustrated later in this chapter.

In summary: in weekly clinical conferences, ongoing psychoanalytic treatments of chronic depressed patients have been presented—carried out as part of the LAC-study on depression—so that colleagues were already familiar with the course of the treatment. The course of the treatment was documented systematically and in detail, as well as the different group supervisions. Case studies, based on these supervisions, were presented to the supervision group several times, requesting their agreement or disagreement on the condensation of the clinical material, the theoretical perspectives, and interpretations. The feedback of the group members was recorded by the author of the paper and considered in new versions of the paper, which was again read by the group members.

We also offered the opportunity to apply the three levels of clinical observation to our colleagues as one aid to reflecting on the transformation processes of the analysand, to concentrating on one specific focus for writing up the case, and for using the members of the group, in the sense of the psychoanalytic expert validation, to productively cope with one's own blind spots. This offer has proved to be a great help for improving the case studies of the chronically depressed patients which have been published already or are in the process of being published (see, e.g., Goebel-Ahnert, 2013; Leuzinger-Bohleber, 2010c; Westenberger-Breuer & Maccarrone Erhardt, 2010).

To illustrate this application of the three-level model for observing patient transformations in combination with the method of psychoanalytical expert validation, I shall summarise one of the psychoanalyses with a chronically depressed patient in the following section. The "truth content" of the following summary is, thus, based on the above procedure, which, in our view, may be considered as one helpful step in improving the quality of extensive psychoanalytic case reports.

## *Depression and trauma*

### *The psychoanalysis with a chronically depressed patient: an exemplary, expert-validated case study*

The following case vignette presents an exemplary document of an attempt at such an "expert-validated" summary of a psychoanalysis with a specific focus, entitled "Depression and trauma". Using this case report, I hope to demonstrate the way in which we can improve such case studies as a useful supplement to the no less necessary micro-analyses of analytical interaction in single sessions.

Dreams have long been considered the "via regia" to the unconscious. Hence, considerable importance has been, and continues to be, attributed to them in clinical practice and in the special clinical research in psychoanalysis. In the following case, the transformation of manifest dream content, as well as the analytic work with dreams, serves as an indicator for the unconscious reactions of the analysand to the therapeutic process. In the following narrative, all relevant clinical observations are compressed, summarised, and "recounted" by "validated experts" with the greatest possible precision. Here, a compromise is sought when summarising the entire treatment "narratively": to mediate, on the one hand, the above-mentioned, total impression of the psychoanalytic process as it occurs, along with the transformations in the object world of the analysand, while, at the same time, the selection of central sequences of consecutive sessions is to be reproduced verbatim, at least in part (as based on the three-level model for observing patient transformations), though without thereby disrupting the narrative structure of the summary.

### *Thematic introduction to the case study*

In psychoanalytic literature, reference is not frequently made to the connection between depression and trauma (Blum, 2007; Bohleber, 2005, 210b; Bokanowski, 1996; Bose, 1995; Bremner, 2002; Denis, 1992; Katz, 2003; Kernberg, 2000). Therefore, we found it astonishing to have discovered in the LAC study on depression currently being conducted that almost all of the patients suffering from chronic depression had also experienced cumulative traumatisation. The first systematic analysis shows that 84% of chronically depressive analysands indicate a severe history of trauma. For this reason, one of the results of this extensive, comparative psychotherapeutic study will be to provide a detailed empirical, as well as analytic, reappraisal of this connection (see, e.g., Leuzinger-Bohleber, 2013). As mentioned above, the Frankfurt Group of the LAC Depression Study is working on a publication with comprehensive case reports illustrating both the influence of early traumatisation on the emergence of chronic depression and a range of consequences relevant to treatment of these findings. The following case study represents one of these narrative summaries of a lengthy psychoanalysis with a chronically depressed patient. The following observations are presented for discussion here:

- unresolved traumatic experiences may lead to chronic depression;
- the traumatic experiences are buried in the body as "embodied memories"[5] (Leuzinger-Bohleber & Pfeifer, 2002, 2013), and unconsciously determine present thinking, feeling, and action;
- a sustained transformation of a depressive complex of problems can only be introduced to the analyst by an understanding of the enactment of the specific trauma within the transference situation;
- the "historic reality" of the trauma must be acknowledged. To this also belongs the fact that although the effects of traumatisation may be alleviated in the process of working through the analytic relationship, they cannot be erased. Recognition of the destruction of the basic sense of trust in good, helpful inner objects through the traumatic experience appears to be a prerequisite for recognising the enactment of the trauma, and, thus, for containing its effects;
- the traumatic experience may also manifest itself in dreams. For this reason, psychoanalytic work with dreams may contribute to the symbolisation and mentalization of the trauma.

In that this contribution places emphasis on the communication of clinical observation, the following theoretical deliberations must remain fragmentary.

### *"There is no unitary concept of depression . . . " Psychoanalytic remarks on the genesis of depression*

Modern depression research postulates a multi-factorial model of explanation: genetic vulnerability, early object relations, environmental factors, traumatisation, and acute individual, institutional, and social stress situations all intertwine in the development of a severe depressive dysfunction (also, see Bleichmar, 2013; Leuzinger-Bohleber, Bahrke, & Negele, 2013; Schulte-Körne & Allgaier, 2008; Taylor, 2010). Within this multi-factorial explanation model, psychoanalysis contributes specific knowledge about the unconscious, individual roots of the depressive dysfunction: with each analysand, we find complex idiosyncratic, unconscious, determining factors resolving into a specific form of depression at a specific point in life: *Every depression shows its unmistakable, individual face.* "There is no unitary concept of depression . . ." (McQueen, 2009, p. 225).

Depression is not a confined, restricted, and static category, it is more a highly personal, individual process. Therefore, psychoanalytic literature features a rich abundance of conceptual work on the development and therapy of depression.

In order to provide you with a short outline on recent psychoanalytic models of explanation of depression across various psychoanalytic schools, we have chosen a graphic by Hugo Bleichmar (2013) (Figure 5.1). Herein, he summarises a model representing the multiple, yet not exclusive, developmental pathways that can lead to a chronic depression.

Hence, various paths can lead to a centrally depressive feeling of hopelessness and helplessness: not one of these pathways is an obligatory factor. Every path leading to depression is determined by different factors or areas, according to their pathology.

It seems highly relevant within our context that Bleichmar (1996, 2013) also considers traumatic, external reality to play a role in the development of depression (also, see Balint, 1968; Baranger, Baranger, & Mom, 1988; Brown & Harris, 1978; Winnicott, 1965). Yet, as we have argued in detail in other works, the link between trauma and depression appears to be much more dramatic and causal than depicted throughout psychoanalytic literature on depression until now

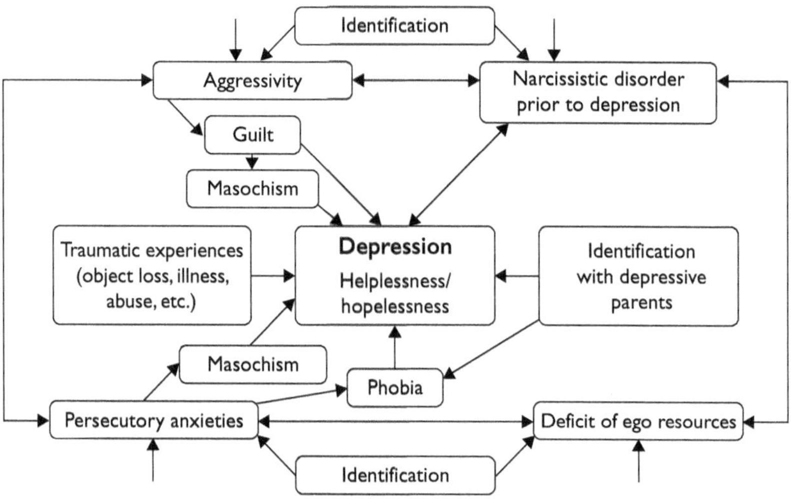


*Figure 5.1.* Model representing the developmental pathways that can lead to depression (Bleichmar, 2013).

(Leuzinger-Bohleber, 2014). Although a few authors have recently addressed this fact, to this very day we consider the central role of traumatisation in generating severe depressions to be underestimated (Blum, 2007; Bohleber, 2005, 2010a; Bokanowski, 2005; Bose, 1995; Bremer, 2002; Denis, 1992; Leuzinger-Bohleber, 2010b, 2013; Leuzinger-Bohleber, Bahrke, & Negele, 2013; Skalew, 2006; Taylor, 2010; Varvin, 2003).

Interestingly, a growing body of interdisciplinary literature has come out in favour of this position. Just to mention a few such authors: Hill (2009) summarised developmental perspectives on adult depression in a general paper. Numerous studies showed the increasing probability of developing adult depression after early neglect or the loss of a parent (Bifulco, Brown, & Harris, 1987; Hill, 2009, pp. 202–212; Hill et al., 2001). Fergusson and Woodward (2002) reviewed the literature regarding the role of childhood sexual abuse, and showed that the association with depression in adulthood was substantial: a history of childhood sexual abuse increased the risk of depression by approximately four times.[6] Twin studies have established that unipolar depression is moderately heritable (Kendler, Gatz, Gardner, & Pederson, 2006; Hill, 2009, p. 202–212.). New research in epigenetics, however, shows that even genetic vulnerability leads into depression only when the person also undergoes severe early traumatisation. Caspi et al. (2003) have been able to show that only severely negative environmental factors, such as early trauma, trigger the short allele of the 5-HHT gene which regulates relevant neurotransmitters and might afterwards cause depression. If no such trauma occurs, then no subsequent depression is observed.

These findings are of extreme importance for psychoanalysts, and support our clinical findings that early prevention and intervention programmes for depressed children, adolescents, and adults—even those from genetically vulnerable families—may be helpful and effective in strengthening the resilience of those individuals at risk.

Epigenetic and neurobiological studies also give new relevance to the famous studies of René Spitz on anaclitic depression and hospitalism in the 1940s, which showed impressively how early separation trauma can determine severe depression as early as in infancy. Robertson and Robertson have replicated his findings in the 1970s with their impressive studies on early separation. Their observations correspond significantly with Harlow's famous experiments on monkeys. Thanks to modern research instruments, one of Harlow's successors, Suomi (2010), was even able to demonstrate that early separation trauma has an enormous influence on neurobiological factors that determine the development of aggression, anxiety, and social integration, and, thus, the survival of genetically vulnerable Rhesus monkeys. These findings are highly relevant for the following case study.

These influences of early trauma are transmitted to the next generation, a finding which corresponds in detail to numerous clinical psychoanalytic observations by many authors, including ours in the above mentioned LAC depression study. Goldberg (2009) concludes his overview of more recent studies in these fields thus:

> These interactions between gene and environment, between behavior and genotype are important for the manner in which they provide explanations of how the many different features constituting the '*depressive diathesis*' arise. However, they have a much wider significance. They provide a possible pathway by which *changing interpersonal and cultural factors across the generations* can be both cause and effect of genotype, and through which changes in human culture might possibly operate as an accelerator of evolutionary processes.
>
> To sum up, we see that adverse environmental conditions are especially harmful to some particular genotypes, leaving the remainder of the population relatively resilient. Research in this area is expanding very fast—and we may expect many more advances in the years to come . . . (Goldberg, 2009, pp. 244–245)[7]

Another finding is especially relevant for us as psychoanalysts. Suomi (2010) has shown that undoing the separation trauma in baby monkeys might "undo" the neurobiological and behavioural damages once again—clearly, a revolutionary finding for all forms of early prevention and for psychoanalytic treatment. As the following summary seeks to illustrate in the psychoanalysis of chronically depressed Mr W, the understanding of the enactment of traumatic experience in the transference enables the analysand to recognise the continual repetition of the trauma, and, thus, to counteract it with a new and different psychic reality. The horror of the original experience of helplessness and of inundation through the trauma can be countered by an adult psychic reality, an active approach to the trauma. In this sense, while the memory of the trauma is not erased, its automatic, retraumatising effect in the present can be "undone".

*". . . being alone without any protection, love and security, makes it impossible for me to survive in this world . . ." (Mr W)*

*Summary of a psychoanalysis*

"It is like a deeply engraved, though entirely irrational programme: that alone and without protection, love and security I am unable to survive in this world . . ." (Mr W)

### *Assessment interviews*[8]

Meeting him for the first interview, Mr W at once reminded me of Little John, a child in the famous 1970s film series by the Robertsons.[9] I was puzzled about why these countertransference phantasies occurred at all to me, since Mr W is in his early fifties; a well-built, handsome man, though with a somewhat severe facial expression, melancholy eyes, and heavy facial neurodermatitis. He explained that he had been suffering from severe depression for the past twenty-five years, and that he is coming to us because, after the last depressive breakdown, he had submitted an application for a retirement pension. The doctor who assessed his application concluded that he did not require a pension, but an "intelligent psychoanalysis"—initially a response Mr W found highly insulting. He felt that he had not been taken seriously, especially his severe physical symptoms, the unbearable pain in his entire body, his acute eating disorders, as well as his acute suicidal tendencies. Furthermore, the patient suffered from acute sleep disorders. Often, he is unable to sleep at all. As a rule, he wakes up after one and a half hours, or after three hours at the most. He feels physically exhausted and is barely able to concentrate his thoughts on anything. He describes his situation thus.

> "Thinking about what it is that tortures me so, I would say it is a deep-seated and monstrously pervasive sense of anxiety and panic. It is the absence of trust. I feel anxious about life, about the world in which I live, about being alone and isolated, but also and especially about other people. The only persons about whom I do not experience any anxiety are my own closely related persons (parents and partners—when I find the relationship harmonious). It is like a very deeply engraved, though entirely irrational programme, that I am unable to survive in this world because I am alone and without protection, love, and security. I then fall into states of bottomless anxiety, desperation, and depression. When I am able to

function, I have many abilities and talents. I am like a fine house without foundations, and which consequently collapses into a heap of ruins when the loaned, stabilising scaffolding can no longer bear the weight.

"All attempts and struggles to rewrite this programme—the many tears through which I sought to weep away my anxieties, the many endeavours to subject myself more intensely to this anxiety so as to habituate myself to it and to do without security—have only drawn me more deeply into depression . . ."

Mr W had already undergone several unsuccessful attempts at therapy, including behavioural therapy, Gestalt therapy, and "body therapy", as well as several inpatient treatments in psychiatric and psychosomatic clinics. He is among that group of patients who, for the most part, are apparently unable to respond to psychotropic drugs, and whose relapses occur at even shorter intervals and with increasing intensity. After many consultations with various psychiatrists and neurologists, he then discovered that only lyrica[10] helped him to more or less deal with his states of physical stress and anxiety attacks.

Although psychoanalysis involving four sessions per week is indicated, due to the distance from his place of residence, Mr W has only been able to manage three sessions per week throughout most phases of the treatment. Due to his extreme sleeping disorders, the thirty-minute car journeys are often a cause of concern.

### *Biography and trauma history*[11]

The patient is an only child. One of the known details about his early history is that he was a "cry-baby". Clearly, his parents most often felt helpless, and sought out a paediatrician who advised them to ignore the infant as much as possible, and to "let it cry itself to sleep . . . this helps strengthen the lungs". Over the course of the first three months of psychoanalysis, the patient characterised his parents as being loving, who showed him considerable care and attention. Yet, over the course of time, what increasingly became clear was that both parents showed a severely disturbed sense of empathy: the mother, moreover, suffered from migraines and from a pronounced compulsion to clean. The father also complained of a series of psychosomatic symptoms. Like Mr W, he also suffered a "nervous breakdown" in a situation of professional stress. Both parents had experienced the Second World

War as adolescents and still retain vivid memories of how they had suffered as children under the straightjacket of National Socialist educational ideology (the children were to be as "hard as Krupp steel", etc.). The grandfather had lost an arm in the First World War. He was violent-tempered and would frequently thrash his children.

When he was four years old, Mr W's mother had to undergo an operation. Mr W was admitted to a children's foster home evidently founded on authoritarian, inhumane educational principles reminiscent of National Socialist ethos. Just how traumatic an experience this stay in the home was is something that became absolutely clear during psychoanalysis. After a courageous aunt literally battled for, and finally gained, access to her nephew, she found him in a state of utter apathy, seriously ill and in an isolation room. The official version, as conveyed to the parents, was that the boy was cheerful, that he played, and that he was in general doing well. The aunt sounded the alarm, and the father collected Mr W immediately. Mr W's first childhood memories revolve around the following event: he recalls how his father took him by the hand and led him out of the home. He also recalls how a girl had been forced to eat her own vomit.

When asked, the mother recounted that after his stay at the home, Mr W had completely changed: he had become silent; he did not wish to go to kindergarten and was a shy, day-dreaming boy who felt best in the countryside. Over the course of psychoanalysis, it became clearer that through the traumatic separation from the primary objects, he lost his basic trust in his inner objects, and that he has subsequently been living in a state of dissociation for years.[12] In many of his dreams he feels that he is in mortal danger after having been left alone and full of panic-ridden anxieties and desperation (cf. below). Mr W experienced two further separations from his ill mother, but these incidents had proved less traumatic because he had been taken in by relatives. The family moved when he was eleven years old. He recalls how he had protested against this move with everything he could rally, and his parents found his panic-ridden anxiety connected with the move incomprehensible. They perceived him as being tyrannical and strange.

In spite of the dissociative states and his social isolation, Mr W was a good pupil who went on to complete his first apprenticeship training and, later, his university studies. During adolescence, he had a psychosomatic breakdown, which his parents diagnosed as a "crisis in growing up", and sought to help him by means of a vitamin cure. At the age of fifteen years, he met his first girlfriend. His condition improved. At the age of twenty-two, he separated from his first girlfriend because he fell in love with another woman. Although the separation ran in his favour, he reacted very severely to it. A few weeks later, he could barely eat and suffered intestinal complaints. After enduring horrendous diarrhoea, he then suddenly felt better. He also initiated the separation from his second girlfriend, though he suffered for weeks due to the separation. After entering another relationship, he was dramatically overcome by a nervous breakdown during a party held by his new girlfriend: he had to be taken to hospital due to hyperventilation (panic attack). "I have been unable to trust my body ever since that experience. I experienced repeated panic attacks and a sense of being unable to breathe." He experienced another severe depressive collapse when this third girlfriend betrayed him with another man. He was unable to defend himself, and instead pleaded with her, in what he then felt to be a humiliating manner, to stay with him. Although all his therapies alleviated his symptoms, "none of them cured me".

He is married to a woman from a non-European country, and has a son, who was three and a half years of age at the beginning of treatment. The last severe depression (one and a half years ago) was first triggered when his wife coldly, and lacking all empathy, attacked him while he was in a state of exhaustion after a month-long, twofold burden in connection with the building of a house. Without any grounds, his wife accused him of endangering the life of his son because he had failed to stop the infant from crawling around dangerous objects. Mr W was incapable of defending himself against this unfounded attack. He awoke the next morning in a state of unbearable depression.

In spite of this, after a few weeks, he attempted to start work again for the sake of securing the well-being of his family. However, after some time, he felt himself unable to persevere with his profession. He took a vacation. He then fell ill with acute bronchitis, which developed into pneumonia. During his stay in hospital, a tumour was discovered which had to be operated on. During the first interview, he gave an impressive description of how he had wished to die during the operation "to escape the misery". At the same time, he hoped the tumour was a contributory cause of his depressions, something that proved to be an illusion. It was for this reason that, several weeks after the operation, he very unexpectedly submitted his application for a pension.

### *On the course of the treatment: changes of the manifest dream content: an indicator for the enactment of the trauma in the analytical relationship?*[13]

An intensive relationship between Mr W and me began to show itself already during the assessment interviews; I began struggling with the fantasy that it would no longer be possible for me to transfer him to a colleague so that the patient would have a choice as to with which analyst he would wish to begin a treatment, as is my common assessment practice. During supervision, it became evident that, in my countertransference, I would most usually experience myself as the "saving father", who took the patient away from the home: that is, an irreplaceable primary object. Mr W established an apparently almost symbiotic proximity to the object of love and experienced a separation from it as a life-threatening danger: this world of inner fantasies corresponded to my countertransference fantasies, being strongly absorbed from the outset of the treatment with the question as to whether or not we would manage to draw near to the core of the chronic depression. It seemed almost a fantasy of omnipotence to me, such that, in contrast to many of Mr W's previous therapists, I could be successful in such an attempt.

### *". . . it was war . . ." (Mr W)*

To my surprise, the first therapy sessions were filled by the most ferocious affects: Mr W was full of rage towards his wife and described the most terrible marriage scenes. His wife attacked him verbally and physically in front of his small son, with whom she would also become involved in the most heated affective confrontations. His child suffers from selective mutism: he talks only with his parents. Moreover, he continues to wear nappies.

It soon became evident during the sessions that, due to his fear of being abandoned by his wife, Mr W is incapable of defending himself against her onslaughts. He lives in an inner world of panic, desperation, and profound loneliness. When I sought to suggest a link between the affects and the trauma of separation he had experienced, Mr W rejected this vehemently. "Other therapists had repeatedly made reference to my stay in the children's home. I simply cannot believe that a three-week stay in home at the age of four could exert such a long-term influence on me . . . this just all seems very contrived . . ." Another initial fierce conflict emerged after I cautiously enquired about whether he might not be inclined to seek solace from the present intolerable marital conflicts, and the demands of his work, in depression. Mr W erupted in fury and went on to explain just how offended he had been when the doctor, who made the original assessment, had described him as "a sort of hypochondriac who had no desire to work and who wished to escape into illness". "He had no idea or conception of the existential dimension of my anxiety and depression. I am not a shammer!" These scenes revealed to me how important it was for Mr W, during psychoanalysis, that I grasp his unbearable psychological suffering and take it seriously. Furthermore, in retrospect, I came to understand these scenes as an indication that in the transference he was struggling with the reactivation of the traumatic experience he had had with his non-empathetic primary objects. As mentioned, both parents had suffered from a seriously disturbed sense of empathy and were incapable of understanding, supporting, and containing Mr W's affect outbreaks during both the latter's infancy and early childhood in "good enough ways"—experiences of relationships which, in all likelihood, possessed a traumatic quality for Mr W (attachment trauma according to Fonagy, 2007, trauma type II according to Terr, 1994). For this reason, he appeared to carry within him an archaic, yet unappeased, need for a (anaclitic) melting with a (symbiotic) primary object (cf. Blatt & Luyten, 2009).

After the scenes sketched in the above description, Mr W recounted his initial dream in the tenth session:

> "The context was war. I was in a concentration camp with my wife because she is a foreigner. I tried to protect her, but was overcome by a sense of panic."

The associations led to a present, though helpless and threatened, object of love, which the self is unable to protect, a self which, in a state of panic and powerlessness, is subject to a situation of inner war and persecution. Later in the night, Mr W had a further dream:

> "Several people had barged their way into the courtyard of our house. I flew into a terrible rage and yelled out: what the hell do you want here! Go away . . . They actually did vacate the garden. My wife remarked how well I managed the situation."

Among other interpretations, we understand the second dream as an investment of hope in psychoanalysis: he wishes to acquire the ability to apply his aggressive impulses for the protection of his "house", of himself and the objects of his love, so as to actively encounter danger rather than being passively subjected to it and inundated by anxiety and panic. This would empower his sense of autonomy and masculine identity and, also, so he hoped, win the acceptance and love of his wife, who, in reality, would scorn and degrade him due to his depression.

### *The staging of the traumatic loss of the object of love and "embodied memories" in the existentially threatening physical state during the stay at the home . . .*

The subsequent weeks witnessed a dramatic escalation in the external realities of the analysand: his wife had fallen in love with someone else. Terrible scenes erupted in which, among other things, his wife revealed to the patient that she had never actually loved him, and was presently experiencing for the first time what a fulfilling sexuality really means.

For Mr W, everything collapsed: he was flooded by a sense of panic and desperation, and could barely sleep. He felt completely degraded by the rival. It was shocking to observe the sheer extent to which he identified with the degradation heaped upon him by his wife. The sessions were filled by depressive self-accusations and ferocious self-loathing, such that I finally confronted him by saying, "You experience this terrible slight and this abandonment probably in the same way you experienced it then during the stay at the home as a young child, and that you now see everything through the depressive eyeglasses you have since been wearing. Instead of defending yourself, as you do in your second dream, you inwardly leave the house and home to your rival without even putting up a fight. Clearly, your wife then confirms your depressive self-image which you carry within yourself."

Thus, during this phase the sessions frequently took on the character of a crisis intervention: the traumatic separation anxieties shifted to the core of the work and disclosed their existential attributes. The massive rage and destructive aggression towards the object of love or the primary object were discussed. The perpetually recurring attempt during the sessions to distinguish the inner objects from the painful experiences of loss and betrayal in the present reality in the end enabled Mr W to overcome the paralysing passivity and sheer desperation. He booked a plane ticket for him and his son for a summer vacation in his wife's distant homeland. He left his wife behind with her lover. In spite of feelings of guilt, he then had a surprising and fulfilling sexual encounter with an acquaintance, which he experienced as reconfirmation of his adult masculinity and, to a certain extent, as a narcissistic restitution.

Yet, the subsequent months signified a dire period for Mr W, marked by dreadful wounds and humiliation: his wife lived with her lover and left the son with the patient. Mr W manages to care for his child with the support of his parents. His general body pain has increased substantially, to the extent that he often feels like an "open wound". We suspect that, what for him represents an almost life-threatening physical condition, is related to the "embodied memories" of the life-threatening illness experienced during his stay at the home. A certain amelioration of the symptoms as an answer to the corresponding interpretations apparently confirms this hypothesis.

Mr W refers to gruelling nightmares: for example, that in the woods he observes at a distance how a blazing helicopter plunges to the ground. In addition, during the sessions his existential anxieties about being abandoned become clearly evident, as well as his pathological bond to his parents.

Astonishingly enough, during these months, his child displayed a relatively calm disposition and, in the words of the kindergarten nurse, was presently developing positively, gradually overcoming his selective mutism, now being able to visit the toilet alone, and cautiously beginning to find his way out of his social isolation.

The extent to which the patient continues to be tied to his wife was revealed when the wife demanded to have the child returned to her custody: against the advice of his parents and his friends, he was unable to use the situation to separate from her and to apply for custody of the child himself. He persistently reacted with panic at the thought of divorcing his wife, hoping, thereby, that in spite of the injuries, the marriage can be upheld. Similar fantasies appear in connection with the treatment: Mr W expresses anxiety about becoming so dependent on me as an analyst that he will not be able to bear it when the treatment finally comes to a close. Here, we encounter his unconscious conviction that "nothing and nobody can really help me . . ."

In the subsequent session, Mr W recounted the following dream:

> "I am in the woods close to X, and crawl through a long, dark tunnel. I then come to a hotel with a capacious terrace looking out across the Swiss Alps.[14] It is very pleasant and yet I am still gripped by the anxiety that I might topple from the terrace into the abyss. Thus, I do not dare stay on the terrace, and rather turn back, even though I know that at the other end of the tunnel, in my home village, things are no longer the way they were."

His associations prompt a deep-seated doubt within him as to the value of embarking on a course of psychoanalysis—to crawl through the dark tunnel of depression so as to be able to behold the light, distant Alps of Switzerland and to orientate himself on them, but also to gaze into the abyss without falling into it, or whether it is preferable to return to the familiar, albeit gloomy, "security" of depression, the home village. Most probably attached to the additional, secondary illness is also the fact that Mr W flees into depression instead of once again resolving to venture into a relationship with the attendant risk of being abandoned and rejected by the object of love. A further aspect is vehemently rejected by the patient during this period: the conflict of loyalty connected with distancing himself from the home village, the inner world of representation of the depressive primary objects, of leaving this behind him, and of divorce. The existential dimension of divorce triggers thoughts of an early conflict in individuation and autonomy.

### *"The revenge on the traumatising primary object"*

By this stage in the treatment, it became clear what severe consequences the reactivating of the separation trauma—of being directed by the panic-ridden anxiety of being abandoned—was capable of exerting on the narcissistic regulation of his sense of the regulation of his basic self-esteem: towards his wife he feels akin to a helpless, dependent child permitting itself to be humiliated, wounded, and attacked. In this connection, he recalled the following dream:

> "I catch sight of a man lying at the side of the road severely wounded—his intestines are spewing out, and everything is saturated in blood . . . A helicopter appears. It is unclear as to whether the man is still being shot at, or whether one should go to his aid. Someone appears, claiming that the man has now passed away. I notice that the man is still alive and he really does open his eyes and enquires "Why is nobody helping me?" The woman hands him a saucepan lid, which he should hold over the open wound . . . I then wake up, riveted by panic . . ."

In the manifest dream, I see in the figure of the woman, who, in a cold, unsympathetic and helpless manner, hands a saucepan lid to the man suffering from life-threatening wounds so that he may cover them, an indicator that in the transference Mr W now experiences me as an unsympathetic, helpless, indeed perhaps even sadistic, primary object. Approached cautiously, it then also becomes possible to address his debasing aggressive fantasies towards me. He observes his massive anxieties; like his mother, I was not able to bear his massive anxieties, such aggressive impulses: even today, his mother responds fiercely to criticism most often in the form of a migraine.

### *Recognition and working through aspects of negative transference*

Only once it had become possible to directly address his mistrust and his aggressive fantasies, also towards the analyst, did it appear—gradually, into the second year of the treatment—that changes were occurring. Mr W became somewhat more self-confident. He began a new love relationship with a woman clearly disposed to a greater degree of sensitivity. More secure self and object boundaries began establishing themselves. Furthermore, it was now that archaic feelings of guilt became accessible to therapeutic work: in one session, he discovered the fantasy in being unable to leave his wife since he is somehow convinced that, by doing so, he would destroy her. The analyst offered him an explanation based on developmental psychology:

> *A*: If parents are not in a position to calm a crying baby, the baby then becomes subject to a condition of acute desperation. Psychoanalysts

assume that this can stimulate early fantasies, which contain within them untamable destructive impulses, since the extremely aggressive fantasies that a child perceives in such a situation of desperation cannot be absorbed and, thereby, alleviated by the parents. The child then experiences his parents as powerless and impotent (indeed, in much the same way as you experience me in relation to your depression). A further consequence is that the aggressive–destructive fantasies remain excluded by other psychological developments. They then occasionally appear in such unreal convictions as those you have just mentioned.

In the next session, Mr W reported the following dream:

"I dreamt that, full of anxiety, I was suspended over a deep chasm. Two women are above me; they do not come to my assistance, but instead proceed to cast a white ribbon across the chasm in a strange way. Clasping the ribbon, they then attempt to cross to the other side of the chasm. I cannot help but being astonished about this stupid idea, and then witness how they really do fall into the chasm . . . I wake up in a state of utter panic."

*A*: You often complain of the "stupidity" of your wife, and the previous session focused on your sometimes having the impression that I, too, am limited and helpless to build a bridge across the chasm of depression. Do you think this was to some extent taken over into the dream? The women were unable to help you out of your life-threatening situation, but then also finally plummeted to their deaths due to their own idiocy.

Technically, it is not easy to express the fact that these catastrophic dream images probably encapsulate his enormous rage towards women (and the analyst!). Often, humour proves helpful in such contexts. When, after the above-mentioned session, Mr W, by chance, discovered that I had a technical problem with my car, I then intuitively said, "Yes, perhaps I really am a stupid woman." Mr W responded with an outburst of laughter at this remark, most probably an indication that I had just hit the nail on the head.

The subsequent months centred over and again on his wrath towards women. Working through the unconscious fantasies and conflicts connected with this led to further transformations: the slack attitude improved substantially, to such an extent that the patient then dared to reduce his medication (dosage of Lyrica). He rediscovered an increased sense of joy in life, and developed more creativity in his work. Despite massive anxieties about failure, he took on an important private work contract, which, in his financial situation, was a ray of light, and which offered important narcissistic fulfilment.

### *"Taking the black dog out on a lead"*[15]

Over the following months, his struggles increased in dealing with his panic-driven anxieties of abandonment, and with not allowing the self to be passively inundated. Occasionally, he succeeded in putting a leash on the "black dog", as he would refer to it. The content of his manifest dreams also visibly changed: the dream self became more active and less susceptible to passive catastrophes and mortal dangers, but was often aggressive and involved in conflicts important for survival. We understand the following dream to be a key dream for this inner transformation.

> "I am in the car with my father, but am barely able to control the vehicle. It drives faster and faster. Suddenly, a high tower stands in the middle of the road. The car drives wildly up the wall of the tower and down the other side again. Although I am terribly anxious, nothing happens to us. We are able to continue driving. We then notice how another man likewise races up the tower and, similarly, slumps down the other side again. Nothing happens to him, either . . . We follow this man and then get out. He is then transformed into a man with a slippery surface, like Delta in *Startrek Enterprise*. I do not know whether he is man or robot. He had a black dog. It becomes bigger and bigger, rests its paws on my shoulders. I begin panicking; the dog could bite through my throat. And then I suddenly see that the dog has the face of a woman, who also appears to be frightened. I then say to it that it is not as dangerous as I had thought and compliment it, which it clearly finds pleasing."

The associations to the dream lead to several references which Mr W takes up and pursues in the subsequent sessions, for example, in the identification with the father, the attempt to regain a piece of his masculine phallicity (cf. dream pictures with the tower), the experience of dissociation and of not being quite anchored in this world (cf. the robot man in the dream), his existential anxiety when in front of an affectionate object of love (dog–woman), etc. However, above all, it has to do with the active overcoming of his panic and anxiety. In the dream, he does not disavow the dangers and the extreme feelings that are consequently released, but instead dares to look the dog straight in the eye. He discovers the anxiety of the other by way of his own activity, and is no longer flooded by his own panic: that is, while the ego is unable to inhibit the reactivation of death anxiety and panic, it is able to actively counter it somewhat by looking at it and by understanding. What I found interesting was that Mr W had been processing my own feelings of insufficiency in his dream (dog with woman's face, which is itself in need and is anxious): during this period, I was often gripped by doubt as to whether it really would be possible to modify the depression by means of our psychoanalysis: the "Black Dog" often assumed disproportionately large proportions and was barely possible to subdue.

To each of us, this dream thus assumes a symbolic function for the presently occurring therapeutic work, an attempt, together, within the psychoanalytic relationship, to look the terror of traumatisation in the eye, to not repudiate its reality, or dismiss it, but, rather, to psychically accept its existence: to actively counter it with something so as not to be flooded by panic, desperation, and anxiety, and, hence, to allow oneself to be unconsciously determined by it.

After the reactivation of the trauma could be discussed, above all in outer reality (in relation to his wife, for example), it then become more possible for Mr W to experience and comprehend the traumatic separation anxiety directly in the transference during the third year of psychoanalysis.

### *"The reactivation of the trauma in the transference"*[16]

Mr W reacted with increasing vehemence to situations of separation from the analyst. During a vacation, he underwent a problematic orthodontic operation, which led to intolerable headaches. He was unfit for work for over two months, and unable to come to the analytic sessions. Finally, I telephoned him. Several crisis interventions then ensue per telephone, which see him gradually emerging from "the black hole". Evidently, Mr W was acting out his early separation trauma and brought me, as analyst, into the situation of the "rescuing father object" (who took him away from the home). When I referred to this fantasy directly, in the next telephone call Mr W then recounted the following dream.

> "I am gazing at a group of people all smeared with clay and who are working together on the shell of a house. A cold wind blows—the work is torturous, arduous, and barely tolerable. And yet, in the dream I have the certain sense that the men will succeed: at some point the house will be built and provide them with a warm home. I then turn to my wife and say, "You see, one can do it—one just has to stay together . . ."

The associations led to a fundamental sense that "my house cannot be repaired: it will always remain a draughty, dangerous shell . . . but, perhaps a spark of hope remains in the dream: I am convinced that the building of the house will finally be completed". We draw a comparison to the way he depicted himself at the beginning: "I am like a fine house, though without a foundation."

Six months later, just before a one-week vacation, he seemed really confident. Yet, afterwards, he appeared at an analytic session in a state of complete desperation.[17] He was convulsed with sobbing on the couch. "I am completely finished—my overall bodily symptoms are unbearable. I can't take it any more, I cannot live any more." He had overlooked taking his medication one evening, and broke down the next morning. "I noticed just how dependent I still am on medications—without them I am simply unable to live." The analyst also felt distressed, powerless, and helpless, and once again doubted her ability to really help Mr W.

*A*: This relapse was certainly a bitter disappointment to you—and I was once again not available to you. Were you also tortured by thoughts that the psychoanalysis also amounted to nothing?

*Mr W*: Yes, that's right: everything that we covered here in discussion seemed to me to be so far away, so theoretical . . .

*A*: Did you lose the inner connection to me?

*Mr W*: Yes, I felt utterly alone—I was unable to imagine you any more: you were foreign to me and in some sense entirely unreal . . .

*A*: Probably similar to how Little John felt when his parents left him for several weeks in the home.[18]

At this point, Mr W wept uninhibitedly and was in great distress throughout the duration of the session. The psychoanalyst also felt herself inundated by powerful emotions and a sense of helplessness and powerlessness.

The next day, Mr W came to the session with greater composure.

*Mr W*: In some way it did me some good to be able to weep here, in spite of the fact that I continue to feel very distressed. In the days before this incident, I felt myself as if in a cage—I felt absolutely nothing, everything was dead within me. At night, my body began reacting chaotically—everything was painful and I was unable to sleep at all. [After a pause]

*A*: We frequently return to the thought that your body remembers the unbearable pains and fear of death, which you had most probably experienced during the stay at the home.

*Mr W*: I am really unable to say whether this is true . . . in any case, the pain is utterly intolerable.

After a lengthy pause, during which I sense the analysand's distress and hopelessness, as well as my own perplexity, I then say:

*A*: Perhaps, it is very important for you to show me here the full extent of your distress and sense of panic. Quite some time ago, you once said to me that you are convinced that nobody, nobody at all, is capable of understanding you in your misery, and, consequently, you feel profoundly alone. You were also unable to really show your distress to your parents after the stay at the home—you simply went silent. As a result, your body was unable to relax; it could not be calmed. You remained alone.

Mr W silently wept for a long time.

During the next session, Mr W still seemed distressed and in a state of panic.

*Mr W*: I really have no idea. Last night I must have briefly dropped off to sleep. I had two dreams, which bear no relation to my present state. I first dreamt that a woman fell in love with me. I wondered, and I was unsure about whether or not I felt attracted to her. And yet she said that this was not important and that everything would turn out well. . . . I then dozed off again and continued to dream. I was seated in a lecture hall. An especially desirable looking woman began caressing my thigh. This I found extremely agreeable. She revealed to me that she was in love with me, that I am so charming and so calm. I was very fond of this woman. However, in the dream, I then thought that I ought to tell her that I am not calm, but rather depressive and that she ought to know this.

*A*: Yes, here you have often mentioned that you no longer wish to act a part—neither in a love relationship nor here during psychoanalysis.

*Mr W*: Yes, this is true. Do you really think that the dream might contain a spark of hope?

Mr W now remains silent for quite some time and appears relaxed.

Over the following ten days, he appeared visibly relaxed, though to some extent particularly ill at ease. Mr W oscillates between hope and profound desperation also during the sessions.

*A*: The depressive dog seems to defending itself against any form of change, attempting to make the spark of hope disappear again.

*Mr W*: And then the depressive holes and the bodily pain seem to become far more difficult to endure.

After the weekend, Mr W explained that he had had two anxiety dreams, but that he could only recollect one, since his wife had woken him up owing to his terribly loud yelling.

*Mr W*: The dream resembled a horror film. Strangely, I had a brother who mutated into a dangerous and ominous entity that would kill other people. I observed all this aghast, thinking, to begin with, that since he was my brother I would be spared the same fate. But I then discovered that my execution had, indeed, not been overlooked. I was filled by terrible anxiety, and ran away as fast as possible, finding myself in a square. I then gazed upwards into a building to my mother's window. I yelled and yelled, but she still did not hear me. The dream was interrupted at this point by my wife awakening me.

After a lengthy silence, Mr W made the following associations:

*Mr W*: The first thing that occurred to me was the home and the yearning I felt for my mother, who was unable to hear me when I yelled out and felt distraught. . . . Strange that I had a brother here.

*A*: Who mutated into a dangerous, ominous entity.

*Mr W*: And triggered a fear of death.

*A*: And as you noticed in the case of John, the inner picture of your parents also changed during the stay at the home—they probably became dangerous and threatening; Little John could no longer keep hold of the loving inner image of his parents, which, now shattered, revealed itself as a "murderous", persecuted inner image—a terrifying, life-threatening experience.

*Mr W*: Yes, and afterwards nothing was what it once was.

*A*: The trust in your parents was repeatedly broken—although you apparently seemed to be normal again.

*Mr W*: Though nothing was normal again . . . like with my body—nothing was right, everything hurt.

In the next session, Mr W reported, almost amused, that he had dreamed of his neighbours and a concrete mixer.

*Mr W*: Like me, my neighbour had also been extending his house, and I would often hear the noise of his cement mixer during the summer. I had often had occasion to admire him, since he appeared to have an abundance of energy, and that he was somehow successful in his family life. Perhaps, I do have a spark of hope after all, and I'll be able to get my cement mixer working again.

This sequence in the psychoanalysis could mark a turning point in the treatment: had Mr W re-experienced his trauma in the transference, and, consequently, been able to, at least in part, understand and psychically accept it?

In any case, after the Christmas break, he returned and in the first session reported that during the separation he had struggled fiercely against the "Black Dog", and with varying degrees of success. He had had, he found, an astonishing dream:

"I dreamt of a couple—they were most probably not lovers, and yet their relationship was genial. They had a business with flowers in Africa . . . (it then occurred to me that the day before I had watched a television programme about a couple in Africa who planted and cultivated Christmas poinsettia and had established a successful business from this). I felt particularly attracted towards the two people and their charming

> manner and asked them fervently to allow me to take a share in their business. They accepted me—and the woman even embraced me. I sold my house and dared to make a new beginning . . . I was so happy when I awoke that all I wanted to do was to go back to sleep and continue the dream . . . Perhaps something is changing in me after all."

### *Discussion*

The close connection between early traumatisation and severe, chronic depression became clear in the course of psychoanalysis with Mr W. It was especially the separation trauma suffered at the age of four years during his stay at a children's home without an empathetic substitute relationship that, to a large extent, remained unresolved, and which then triggered depressive reactions after the separation from his close relationships. These reactions were significantly exacerbated following the separation: the depression became increasingly chronic. It was striking to note, during treatment, how the traumatic experiences had been retained within the body: decoding these "embodied memories" led to a certain alleviation of the symptoms through which Mr W was able to actively approach his condition without making them disappear altogether. For quite some time, Mr W refused to acknowledge the "historical reality of the trauma" as a part of his own biography: that this exerted a sustained effect on his depression, as well inducing a fundamental mistrust towards close persons due to the traumatic collapse of his basic trust (*Urvertrauen*) in "good, helping, inner objects". Only once this profound mistrust and the unconscious truth that "nobody, but nobody, can really understand and reach me in my psychic misery and so contribute to alleviating my intolerable condition" had become tangible and, to some extent, understandable in the transference to the analyst, was the "power of the trauma" relativised and no longer determined his present thinking, feeling, and action as a dominating, unconscious belief system. This initially revealed itself in the transformation of the manifest dream content, which, as indicated, constituted a key for successively understanding the unconscious fantasies and conflicts as a reaction to the analytic work.

The transformations in the manifest dream content and their latent (unconscious) thoughts in the dreams were selected as the Ariadne's thread for this case report, since, in my view (as also of other indicators in the case), they are able to provide clues about whether the work of analytic interpretation was unconsciously understood by the analysand and experienced as "true". This was illustrated both in the narrative summary of the treatment and by way of the detailed sequences from four consecutive sessions.

As touched upon in the preliminary remarks, with this case report, I sought to formulate a defence for the revaluation of the narrative tradition of psychoanalysis as a unique, valuable form for communicating the results of clinical–psychoanalytic research. With the aid of the method of psychoanalytic expert validation, the quality of such narrations can be enhanced, thus making it possible to systematically encounter the danger of subjective distortion in clinical observations, as indicated at the outset. This can be achieved, moreover, without destroying the advantages of the clinical case report (the compression of observations and "truths", the communication of unconscious semantic structures by readable "histories", as well as the proximity to metaphor, literature, and art).

However, in the contemporary age of the Internet, the difficulties concerning attitudes of discretion and the protection of privacy—something that has always been connected with comprehensive case summaries—are tending to become greater. As is often the case in the context of the LAC depression study, the analysand is able to sufficiently identify with the analyst's research interests such that, through the codified summary of his treatment, he has the impression of being valued and taken seriously. Several of the analysands declared themselves prepared to read and comment on the case report. This is a unique opportunity for (externally) validating the "truths" by the analysand himself.

However, owing to ethical and psychoanalytic considerations, it is not always possible to acquire former analysands for this co-operation. In such cases, one might attempt casting the summary of the treatment report in relatively abstract terms and with active codification, and assign greater weight to the depiction of sequences of sessions (cf. the last section of this case report). Often, adding additional biographical data that does not distort the "narrative truth" (e.g., number of siblings, similar but not "real" professional positions, etc.) may help to protect the anonymity of the analysand. Naturally, the reader must be adequately informed of this attempt in order to be convinced of the author's wish that, while protecting the intimacy of the psychoanalytic treatment belongs to the specific professional ethics of the analyst, it is also one of the outstanding characteristics of psychoanalysis as a clinical science to convey experience and knowledge to the scientific community, the essential aspects of which "can only be narrated and not measured".

## *Notes*

1. "In psycho-analysis there has existed from the very first an inseparable bond between cure and research" (Freud, 1926e, p. 256).
2. There is an extensive discussion on "narrative", "historical", and "empirical" truth in psychoanalytical literature (see, e.g., Leuzinger-Bohleber, 1989, 2001, 2010a,b,c; Spence, 1982; Thomä & Kächele, 1985).
3. Freud's and other psychoanalysts' major case vignettes (e.g., Argelander, 1972) continue to form an indispensable building block in psychoanalytic training and also in university teaching.
4. LAC stands for the short- and long-term results of psychoanalytic as compared to cognitive–behavioural long-term therapy among sufferers of chronic depression: a prospective, multi-centric therapy effectiveness study which is currently being conducted (project directors: M. Leuzinger-Bohleber, M. Beutel, M. Hautzinger, & U. Stuhr, supported by the DGPT, the Heidehofstiftung, and the Research Advisory Board of the International Psychoanalytical Association).
5. Embodiment has been widely studied in the past decades. "Embodied memories" is a concept based on a new understanding of memory functions in the sense of embodiment. Inspired by biology and the life sciences, embodied cognitive science currently understands memory as being a function of the entire organism, the product of complex dynamic recategorisation and interactive processes that are always "embodied" (see, among others, Leuzinger-Bohleber & Pfeifer, 2002, 2013). The human organism—and the human psyche—is in an ongoing (embodied) state of change involved in constant dynamic processes of interaction with the environment in which a continuous process of recategorising experiences occurs. Memories of earlier situations unconsciously determine present thought, feelings, and action, but not in the sense of "stored knowledge", analogous with a computer, or "static memory traces". In contrast, memories are the products of dynamic, complex "constructions" in the here and now. Embodiment—sensorimotor coordination—in the present always operates in an analogue manner, as was the case in earlier situations. The similarities between a current and a past situation are not perceived cognitively, for example, by pattern matching, but by means of

similar complex information gained through different senses (auditory, olfactory, touch, smell, etc.) and actions of the body (characterised as "sensorimotor coordinations" in embodied cognitive science). Through these sensorimotor coordinations, memories and categories are constructed automatically in the sense of a self-regulating process by "learning by doing" (Dewey), which means coordinating information from sensory channels and connected (motor) actions of the body. Thus, memories due to sensorimotor coordination offer an orientation in a new situation.

6. Although it is fascinating to note how new epigenetic research adds a new dimension to this knowledge, the results of the epigenetic studies remain controversial. "In sum, we conclude that the totality of the evidence on G x E is supportive of its reality, though more work is needed to properly understand how 5-HTT allelic variations affect response to stressors and to maltreatment" (Rutter, 2009, p. 1288).
7. Thus, I agree with Goldberg's formulation:

> It is time that the dialogue of the deaf between psychiatric geneticists and psychotherapists came to an end: exiting progress has been made in understanding the interaction between our genetic constitution and social environment that either allow genes to manifest themselves in the phenotype, or suppress them altogether. (Goldberg, 2009, p. 236).

His conclusions, after having provided an overview of the contemporary state of research in this field, are highly relevant:

> In humans, the effect of maternal care on hippocampal developments have so far been demonstrated (in females, but not in males). The effects of the environment in promoting gene expression appear to be supported by work showing that the extent of abnormalities in a particular gene responsible for the metabolism of an important inhibitory neurotransmitter (serotonin), can be shown to be responsible for the sensitivity of the adult to external stress. This gene is also related to the likelihood of secure attachment. Thus the abnormalities observed in the rat also appear to apply to the human.
>
> Similarly, abnormalities in another gene responsible for the neurotransmitter monoamine oxidase A are associated with the sensitivity of the infant to the harmful effects of physical punishment: with the normal gene, the relationship is fairly weak, though when abnormal anti-social behaviour results . . . (Goldberg, 2009, pp. 244–245)

8. Following the Hampstead profile, staged observations and important scenes drawn from the first interview, transference–countertransference reactions, as well as the symptoms, the motivation behind treatment, and the socio-economic context examination are presented here. A short and different version of this case report will also be published in Leuzinger-Bohleber (in press).
9. Robertson and Robertson published films observing children during early separation, for example, John during a ten-day stay in a children's home due to the birth of his sibling.
10. Lyrica (generic name: Pregabalin) is an anticonvulsant drug used for neurotic pain, also effective for generalised anxiety disorder (approved for this use in the European Union since 2007).
11. Again following the Hampstead Profile, important information on early object relationships, important biographical events, the socio-economic background on the dynamic structural assessment of the conflict, the developmental level, etc., are summarised in narrative form.
12. I am using a narrow definition of trauma, following Bohleber (2010):

    > Psychoanalytic trauma theories have evolved on the basis of two models, one psychoeconomic, the other hermeneutic and based on object relations theory. To grasp the phenomenology and long-term consequences of trauma, we need both models. The psycho-economic model focuses on excessive arousal and on anxiety that cannot be contained by the psyche and that breaks through the shield against stimuli. The model based on object relations and the breakdown of internal communication produces an experience of total abandonment, precluding the integration of trauma by narrative means. (p. xxi)

13. In the case vignette, the attempt is made to provide in narrative form a highly plastic impression of the analytic process and the course of treatment, and yet also to depict as closely as possible several clinical key scenes of the concrete interaction in the analytic session. In these narrative summaries, the clinicians of the LAC survey select various foci (e.g., handling suicidality of the patients, the role of medication, the "psychic retreat" of the analysands, etc.). Here, emphasis is placed on the transformations in the dream content or the acquisition of knowledge by way of the analytic work with dreams in the transference to the analyst.
14. I am a Swiss national!
15. Mr W caught sight of the impressively illustrated book by Matthew Johnstone (2006) entitled *Living with a Black Dog: His Name is Depression*

lying in my office, and purchased a copy. Occasionally, reference is made to the book in the psychoanalysis.

16. As is known, in the specialist psychoanalytic literature of recent years, an interesting controversy is taking place on the question as to how the life-threatening truth of the trauma bears in on the analytic process (cf. Bohleber, 2010; Fonagy & Target, 1997; Leuzinger-Bohleber, 2013; Leuzinger-Bohleber et al., 2010).
17. The specific interactions between analyst and analysand in the following are, in part, recorded verbatim (based on model II of the Clinical Project Group).
18. Mr W has, meanwhile, watched the CD of John from the above-mentioned Robertson films, which we had discussed in earlier stages of the treatment.

## References

Argelander, H. (1972). *Der Flieger. Eine charakteranalytische Fallstudie.* Frankfurt: Suhrkamp.

Balint, M. (1968). *The Basic Fault: Therapeutic Aspects of Regression.* London: Tavistock/Routledge, 1989.

Baranger, M., Baranger, W., & Mom, J. M. (1988). The infantile psychic trauma from us to Freud: pure trauma, retroactivity and reconstruction. *International Journal of Psychoanalysis, 69*: 113–128.

Bifulco, A. T., Brown, G. W., & Harris, T. O. (1987). Childhood loss of parent, lack of adequate parental care and adult depression: a replication. *Journal of Affective Disorders, 12*: 115–28.

Blatt, S. J., & Luyten, P. (2009). Depression as an evolutionarily conserved mechanism to terminate separation distress: only part of the biopsychosocial story? *Neuro-Psychoanalysis, 11*: 52–61.

Bleichmar, H. B. (1996). Some subtypes of depression and their implications for psychoanalytic treatment. *International Journal of Psychoanalysis, 77*: 935–961.

Bleichmar, H. B. (2013). Verschiedene Pfade, die in die Depression führen. Implikationen für spezifische und gezielte Interventionen. In: M. Leuzinger-Bohleber, U. Bahrke, & A. Negele (Eds.), *Chronische Depression. Verstehen – Behandeln – Erforschen* (pp. 82–98). Göttingen: Vandenhoeck & Ruprecht.

Blum, H. P. (2007). Holocaust trauma reconstructed: individual, familial, and social trauma. *Psychoanalytic Psychology, 24*: 63–73.

Bohleber, W. (2005). Zur Psychoanalyse der Depression. *Psyche – Z Psychoanal, 59*: 781–788.

Bohleber, W. (2010a). Neue Ergebnisse der Depressionsforschung. Erklärungsansätze – Therapiemodelle – Behandlungstechnik. *Psyche – Z Psychoanal, 64*: 771–781.

Bohleber, W. (2010b). *Destructiveness, Intersubjectivity and Trauma: The Identity Crisis of Modern Psychoanalysis*. London: Karnac.

Bokanowski, T. (1996). Freud and Ferenczi: trauma and transference depression. *International Journal of Psychoanalysis, 77*: 519–536.

Bokanowski, T. (2005). Variations on the concept of traumatism: traumatism, traumatic, trauma. *International Journal of Psychoanalysis, 86*: 251–265.

Bose, J. (1995). Trauma, depression, and mourning. *Contemporary Psychoanalysis, 31*: 399–407.

Bremner, J. D. (2002). *Does Stress Damage the Brain? Understanding Trauma-related Disorders from a Mind–body Perspective*. New York: Norton.

Brown, G. W., & Harris, T. (1978). *Social Origins of Depression*. London: Tavistock.

Caspi, A., Sugden, K., Moffitt, T. E., Taylor, A., Craig, I. W., Harrington, H., McClay, J., Mill, J., Martin, J., Braithwaite, A., & Poulton, R. (2003). Influence of life stress on depression: moderation by a polymorphism of the 5-HTT gene. *Science, 301*: 386–389.

Denis, P. (1992). Depression and fixations. *International Journal of Psychoanalysis, 73*: 87–94.

Fergusson, D. M., & Woodward, L. J. (2002). Mental health, educational and social role outcomes of adolescents with depression. *Archives of General Psychiatry, 62*: 66–72.

Fischmann, T., Russ, M., & Leuzinger-Bohleber, M. (2013). Trauma, dream and psychic change in psychoanalysis. A dialogue between psychoanalysis and the neurosciences. *Frontiers in Human Neuroscience, 7*: 1–15.

Fonagy, P. (2007). Violent attachment. Lecture given at the conference "In Gewalt verstrickt – psychoanalytische, pädagogische und philosophische Erkundungen", Universität Kassel, 9–10 February.

Fonagy, P., & Target, M. (1997). Voraussagen über die Ergebnisse von Kinderanalysen: Eine retrospektive Studie von 763 Behandlungen am Anna Freud Centre. In: M. Leuzinger-Bohleber & U. Stuhr (Eds.), *Psychoanalysen im Rückblick* (pp. 366–406). Gießen: Psychosozial.

Freud, S. (1923a). Two encyclopaedia articles. *S.E., 18*: 233–260. London: Hogarth.

Freud, S. (1926e). The question of lay analysis. *S.E., 22*: 177–258. London: Hogarth.

Goebel-Ahnert, I. (2013). Die schlechten und die guten Phasen – Gesichter einer Depression. Bericht einer psychoanalytischen Behandlung mit Kommentar von Hugo Bleichmar. In: M. Leuzinger-Bohleber, U. Bahrke, & A. Negele (Eds.), *Chronische Depression. Verstehen – Behandeln – Erforschen* (pp. 168–179). Göttingen: Vandenhoeck & Ruprecht.

Goldberg, D. (2009). The interplay between biological and psychological factors in determining vulnerability to mental disorder. *Psychoanalytic Psychotherapy, 23*: 236–247.

Hill, J. (2009). Developmental perspectives on adult depression. *Psychoanalytic Psychotherapy, 23*: 200–212.

Hill, J., Pickles, A., Burnside, E., Byatt, M., Rollinson, L., Davis, R., & Harvey, K. (2001). Sexual abuse, poor parental care and adult depression: evidence for different mechanisms. *British Journal of Psychiatry, 179*: 104–109.

Johnstone, M. (2006). *Living with a Black Dog: His Name is Depression.* Kansas City: Andrews & Mcmeel.

Katz, C. L. (2003). Book review. Does Stress Damage the Brain? Understanding Trauma Related Disorders from a Mind–body Perspective, by J. Douglas Bremner, Norton/New York, 2002. *Journal of the American Academy of Psychoanalysis, 31*: 732–735.

Kendler, K. S., Gatz, M., Gardner, C. O., & Pederson, N. L. (2006). A Swedish national twin study of lifetime major depression. *American Journal of Psychiatry, 163*: 109–114.

Kernberg, O. F. (2000). Mourning and melancholia: eighty years later. In: H. Sandler, R. Michels, & P. Fonagy (Eds.), *Changing Ideas in a Changing World. The Revolution in Psychoanalysis. Essays in honour of Arnold Cooper* (pp. 95–102). London: Karnac.

Leuzinger-Bohleber, M. (1989). *Veränderung kognitiver Prozesse in Psychoanalysen. Bd.2.: Fünf aggregierte Einzelfallstudien.* Berlin: Springer.

Leuzinger-Bohleber, M. (1995). Die Einzelfallstudie als psychoanalytisches Forschungsinstrument. *Psyche, 49*: 434–481.

Leuzinger-Bohleber, M. (2001). The "Medea fantasy": an unconscious determinant of psychogenic sterility. *International Journal of Psychoanalysis, 82*: 323–345.

Leuzinger-Bohleber, M. (2010a). Psychoanalysis as a "science of the unconscious". Lecture to the IPA Anniversary Celebration: "Contemporary Perspectives on Psychoanalysis". London, 27 March.

Leuzinger-Bohleber, M. (2010b). Transgenerational trauma—an unexpected clinical observation in extra-clinical studies. Lecture given to the 36th annual meeting of the Canadian Psychoanalytic Society "100 years on the couch—psychoanalysts worldwide celebrate centenary of International Psychoanalytical Association". Toronto, 3–6 June.

Leuzinger-Bohleber, M. (2010c). Depression and trauma—a transgenerational psychoanalytical perspective. Lecture given to the 1st IPA Asian Conference 2010 "Freud and Asia. Evolution and Change: Psychoanalysis in the Asian Context". Peking, 23 October.

Leuzinger-Bohleber, M. (2013). Facing the pain in psychoanalyses with severely traumatized chronic depressed analysands—new ways in conceptualization and treatment. Lecture given to the IPA congress in Prague, 1 August. Submitted to the *International Journal of Psychoanalysis*.

Leuzinger-Bohleber, M. (2014). Working with severely traumatized analysands. *International Journal of Psychoanalysis* (in press).

Leuzinger-Bohleber, M., & Pfeifer, R. (2002). Remembering a depressive primary object? Memory in dialogue between psychoanalysis and cognitive science. *International Journal of Psychoanalysis, 83*: 3–33.

Leuzinger-Bohleber, M., & Pfeifer, R. (2013). Embodiment: Den Körper in der Seele entdecken. Ein altes Problem und ein revolutionäres Konzept. In: M. Leuzinger-Bohleber, R. Emde, & R. Pfeifer (Eds.), *Embodiment – ein innovatives Konzept für Entwicklungsforschung und Psychoanalyse* (pp. 14–38). Göttingen: Vandenhoeck & Ruprecht.

Leuzinger-Bohleber, M., & Teising, M. (2012). "Without being in psychoanalysis I would never have dared to become pregnant": psychoanalytical observations in a multidisciplinary study concerning a woman undergoing prenatal diagnostics. *International Journal of Psychoanalysis, 93*: 293–315.

Leuzinger-Bohleber, M., Bahrke, U., & Negele, A. (Eds.) (2013). *Chronische Depression. Verstehen – Behandeln – Erforschen*. Göttingen: Vandenhoeck & Ruprecht.

Leuzinger-Bohleber, M., Bahrke, U., Beutel, M., Deserno, H., Edinger, J., Fiedler, G., Haselbacher, A., Hautzinger, M., Kallenbach, L., Keller, W., Negele, A., Pfenning-Meerkötter, N., Prestele, H., Strecker-von Kannen, T., Stuhr, U., & Will, A. (2010). Psychoanalytische und kognitivverhaltenstherapeutische Langzeittherapien bei chronischer Depression: Die LAC-Depressionsstudie. *Psyche – Z Psychoanal, 64*: 782–832.

Leuzinger-Bohleber, M., Belz, A., Caverzasi, E., Fischmann, T., Hau, S., Tsiangtis, J., & Tzavaras, N. (2008). Interviewing women and couples after prenatal and genetic diagnostics. In: M. Leuzinger-Bohleber,

E. M. Engels, & J. Tsiantis (Eds.), *The Janus Face of Prenatal Diagnostics: A European Study Bridging Ethics, Psychoanalysis, and Medicine* (pp. 151–218). London: Karnac.

Leuzinger-Bohleber, M., Engels, E. M., & Tsiantis, J. (Eds.) (2008). *The Janus Face of Prenatal Diagnostics: A European Study Bridging Ethics, Psychoanalysis, and Medicine*. London: Karnac.

Leuzinger-Bohleber, M., Rüger, B., Stuhr, U., & Beutel, M. (2002). *"Forschen und Heilen" in der Psychoanalyse. Ergebnisse und Berichte aus Forschung und Praxis*. Stuttgart: Kohlhammer.

Leuzinger-Bohleber, M., Rüger, B., Stuhr, U., & Beutel, M. (2003). How to study the 'quality of psychoanalytic treatments' and their long-term effects on patients' well-being: a representative, multi-perspective follow-up study. *International Journal of Psychoanalysis, 84*: 263–290.

Makari, G. (2008). *Revolution in Mind: The Creation of Psychoanalysis*. London: Duckworth.

McQueen, D. (2009). Depression in adults: some basic facts. *Psychoanalytic Psychotherapy, 23*: 225–235.

Meyer, A.-E. (1993). Nieder mit der Novelle als Psychoanalysedarstellung – Hoch lebe die Interaktionsgeschichte. In: U. Stuhr & F. W. Deneke (Eds.), *Die Fallgeschichte. Beiträge zu ihrer Bedeutung als Forschungsinstrument* (pp. 61–84). Heidelberg: Asanger.

Rutter, M. (2009). Gene-environment interactions: biologically valid pathway or artifact? *Archives of General Psychiatry, 66*: 1287–1289.

Schulte-Körne, G., & Allgaier, A.-K. (2008). Genetik depressiver Störungen. *Zeitschrift für Kinder- und Jugendpsychiatrie und Psychotherapie, 36*: 27–43.

Skalew, B. (2006). Trauma and depression. *International Journal of Psychoanalysis, 87*: 859–861.

Spence, D. P. (1982). *Narrative Truth and Historical Truth: Meaning and Interpretation in Psychoanalysis*. New York: Norton.

Spitz, R. (1946). Anaclitic depression. *Psychoanalytic Study of the Child, 2*: 313–341.

Stuhr, U., Leuzinger-Bohleber, M., & Beutel, M. (Eds.) (2001). *Langzeit-Psychotherapie. Perspektiven für Therapeuten und Wissenschaftler*. Stuttgart: Kohlhammer.

Suomi, S. (2010). Trauma and epigenetics. Lecture given at the 11th Joseph Sandler Research Conference: Persisting shadows of early and later trauma. Frankfurt am Main, 7 February.

Taylor, D. (2010). Das Tavistock-Manual der psychoanalytischen Psychotherapie – unter besonderer Berücksichtigung der chronischen Depression. *Psyche – Z Psychoanal, 64*: 833–861.

Terr, L. C. (1994). *Unchained Memories: True Stories of Traumatic Memories, Lost and Found*. New York: Basic Books.

Thomä, H., & Kächele, H. (1985). *Lehrbuch der psychoanalytischen Therapie*. New York: Springer.

Tuckett, D. (Ed.) (2008). *Psychoanalysis Comparable and Incomparable: The Evolution of a Method to Describe and Compare Psychoanalytic Approaches*. London: Routledge.

Varvin, S. (2003). *Mental Survival Strategies after Extreme Traumatization*. Copenhagen: Multiverse.

Westenberger-Breuer, H., & Maccarrone Erhardt, R. (2010). Ich möchte vor allem meine Ruhe haben . . . Der depressive Rückzug. In: M. Leuzinger-Bohleber, K. Röckerath, & L. V. Strauss (Eds.), *Depression und Neuroplastizität. Psychoanalytische Klinik und Forschung* (pp. 186–197). Frankfurt: Brandes & Apsel.

Winnicott, D. W. (1965). *The Maturational Processes and the Facilitating Environment*. London: Hogarth Press.

Zaretsky, E. (2004). *Secrets of the Soul: A Social and Cultural History of Psychoanalysis*. New York: Knopf.

CHAPTER SIX

# Close to observation: some reflections on the value of the three-level-model for studying change

*Siri Erika Gullestad*

## *Observation and interpretation*

In his work "On narcissism", Freud discusses the differences between a speculative theory and a theory erected on empirical interpretation (Freud, 1914c). The latter will not envy speculation its "smooth, logically unassailable foundation", but will content itself with nebulous basic concepts

> which it hopes to apprehend more clearly in the course of its development, or which it is even prepared to replace by others. For these ideas are not the foundation of the science upon which everything rests. That foundation is observation alone. They are not at the bottom, but the top of the whole structure, and they can be replaced and discarded without damaging it. (Freud, 1914c, p. 77)

This formulation implies that: (1) psychoanalysis is fundamentally an empirical science; the starting point for its concepts is clinical observation; (2) psychoanalytical science is aware of the fact that its concepts are tentative and imperfect and in continuous development towards greater precision. At the same time, it is prepared to replace existing concepts with new ones, if necessary. With his dictum, Freud establishes an attitude of principle towards psychoanalysis as a discipline and demonstrates an approach to research characterised by openness, flexibility, and fundamental respect for the unbiased observation. To Freud, theory is the servant of clinical practice—not the other way round. Every psychoanalytic concept starts and ends in observation.

Of course, this does not mean that the clinician operates without theory, or that theory only comes afterwards. On the contrary, theory defines the listening perspective of the therapist; it is through theory that the observations become "psychoanalytical"—". . . there are no unconceptualised clinical facts" (Schafer, 1994, p. 1024), that is, there is no observation that in any absolute sense stands outside the theoretical framework within which it is perceived. The therapist is guided by a frame of reference containing hypotheses about development of personality, psychopathology, and change. In addition, the therapist's private theories and subjective *Weltanschauung* will also play a role. Clinical observation is always embedded in what hermeneutic science calls *Vorverständnis* (fore-understanding/pre-understanding) (Gadamer, 1960; Heidegger, 1927). Thus, it is also true that theory comes first. However, to emphasise the role of theory in observation is by no means the same as saying theory and observation are the same thing. On the contrary, this should guide us towards a much more careful attitude to what we regard as psychoanalytical data.

Such a careful attitude has often been lacking within the field of psychoanalysis. It seems warranted to say that psychoanalytic case presentations do not always heed the distinction between observation and interpretation. For example, therapeutic change may be described in terms of the patient having reached the "depressive position", without reference to what kind of observational data lies behind this assertion. In such cases, the reader is obliged to trust the presenter of the case, without the ability to form her own evaluation of what has happened. Arguments are too often wanting; we are impressed by the rhetoric of the "good case", accepting propositions backed by carefully selected clinical vignettes confirming the theoretical viewpoint of the author.

During the 1990s, this state of affairs was recognised as a major problem for the development of psychoanalysis as a science. In meetings commemorating the seventy-five years of the *International Journal of Psychoanalysis*, the problem was discussed under the heading "conceptualization and communication of clinical facts". David Tuckett, then editor of the journal, states that we have had a collective tendency to ignore questions of validity of our clinical understanding, and that our "standards of observation, of clarifying the distinction between observation and conceptualization, and our standards of discussing and debating our observations are extraordinarily low" (Tuckett, 1994, p. 865). As a consequence, the aim should be, for example, in case presentations, to distinguish between observation and interpretation, and to "collectively take steps to clarify our focus of observation and reporting, our standards of evidence and clinical illustration" (Tuckett, 1994, p. 869). Certainly, the creation of the Clinical Working Parties by Tuckett in 2000 (Tuckett et al., 2008) was a major step in this direction, as was his initiative to establish more rigorous criteria for reporting and publication of case studies.

## *Clinical observation method*

The formation of the Project Committee on Clinical Observation and Testing and the development of the three-level model for observing patient transformations (cf. Bernardi, Chapter One) represent a further important step in realising the aim of improving the observation, conceptualisation, and communication of clinical psychoanalytic data. A specific focus of this project's group work is the detailed study of therapeutic change, that is, the transformation processes of patients in psychoanalytic treatment. As stated by Leuzinger-Bohleber (Chapter Five), a superordinate aim is to demonstrate, to the outside world and to the mental health authorities, that our method is capable of helping patients suffering from psychic pain.

A clinical observation group will typically work with two complete analytic sessions (see Bernardi, Chapter One), one from an early stage of the treatment and one from a later stage, with the goal of assessing possible transformations. Four advantages of this working method should be emphasised, discussed under the following headings: opening the analytic room; dialogue material; a culture of argumentation; therapeutic change.

### *Opening the analytic room*

First, this way of presenting clinical material "opens up" the analytic room. Every participant is invited into the very private and intimate dialogue between patient and therapist. Psychoanalytic treatment is often surrounded by mystery, and psychoanalysis is often regarded by the outside world, as well as by colleagues of other theoretical orientations, as a "secret brotherhood". Presenting more comprehensive case reports of transformative processes permits a meticulous demonstration of what is actually going on. Obviously, this is also a prerequisite for clinical research. Needless to say, this way of exposing clinical material puts the analyst in a vulnerable position, revealing her "naked" professional self, thus potentially disclosing her own shortcomings. To do this presupposes a climate of respect. In my experience, one of the great achievements of clinical observation groups is to create an atmosphere of safety, enabling analysts to present authentic clinical material.

### *Dialogue material*

As stated before, all too often case studies are presented in the form of selected vignettes which do not allow the reader to form her *own* judgement of what is happening in the treatment—the reader/listener is at the mercy of the analyst's interpretation. In contrast, clinical observation groups deal with the raw material of the therapeutic dialogue, what is really said and expressed between the two parties.

### *A culture of argumentation*

Presented with the concrete material of the therapeutic dialogue, participants in a group, usually coming from different theoretical orientations, will "see" the material through diverse conceptual "glasses". Most importantly, when a participant states that she views a specific part of the dialogue as an expression of, for example, significant change, she will normally be asked to point out what is the observational basis of what she "sees", thus making it possible for other participants to disagree. In short, participants are asked to substantiate their interpretations—make explicit *why* they had the thought that they had. Thus, all participants have to try to work out why they agree or disagree about what they are seeing when making a judgement in a specific case, clarifying and clarifying again, thus creating a lively culture of argumentation and enquiry. This process is analogous to the psychoanalytic expert validation developed by Leuzinger-Bohleber in a seminal follow-up study of psychoanalytic treatment (Leuzinger-Bohleber, Rüger, Stuhr, & Beutel, 2003, also described in Chapter Five). The method was elaborated to deal with the drawbacks of case reports mentioned above (hermetically closed viewpoints, arguments from authority, etc.) and represents a major contribution to improving clinical research—so needed in the psychoanalytic field today.

### *Therapeutic change*

Certainly, to be relevant, therapeutic change has to be related to the aims of a specific treatment. As demonstrated by Sandler and Dreher (1996), psychoanalysis has never been able to formulate theoretically precise treatment goals that are generally agreed on, although several attempts to do so have been made: for example, "liberation of libido", "depressive position", "tolerance of ambiguity", "ability for self-observation", etc. Furthermore, it is a problem that aims are often articulated on an abstract theoretical level, without adequate operationalisation. In the daily clinical situation, however, the analyst's attention is directed towards transformations regarding the specific problems of the patient. For example, the presenting problem of a patient when starting treatment may be chronic insecurity. In social situations, he continuously searches for what is expected behaviour, and watches other people's reaction to him. The radar is always turned on—an extreme vigilance. In assessing transformations during the process, this vigilance will constitute a standard. The focus is changes at a *micro-level*: is the patient now less anxious to represent his *own* self more autonomously? Is his voice more vigorous, his look more direct? Changes at a micro-level, constituting the therapist's primary observational data, may be grouped into superordinate categories: for example, relationship to others, relationship to self, flexibility of defences (Gullestad & Killingmo, 2013). In my view, a specific asset of the three-level model is that the raw material of the dialogue makes possible such a micro-analysis of change—with the patient as his own standard.

## *Release of tears*

A rich illustration of how analytic change may be documented is provided by the case of Marianne Leuzinger-Bohleber presented in this book (Chapter Five). The case of Mr W demonstrates how a seriously traumatic self-state became reactivated, and subsequently transformed, in the transference to the analyst. Mr W was admitted to an authoritarian, inhumane foster home at the age of four, resulting in a state of utter apathy, serious illness, and desperation at being left alone. Dreams revealed an inner world of feeling in mortal danger. A significant phase of the analysis is when the patient is able to express his inner feelings of despair more openly. After a one-week vacation of the analyst, before which Mr W seemed quite confident, Mr W returns in a state of complete desperation: "I am completely finished—my overall bodily symptoms are unbearable. I can't take it any more, I cannot live any more." The analyst feels distressed, powerless, and helpless.

Then this dialogue follows (from Leuzinger-Bohleber, Chapter Five):

*A*: This relapse was certainly a bitter disappointment to you—and I was once again not available to you. Were you also tortured by thoughts that the psychoanalysis also amounted to nothing?

*Mr W*: Yes, that's right: everything that we covered here in discussion seemed to me to be so far away, so theoretical . . .

*A*: Did you lose the inner connection to me?

*Mr W*: Yes, I felt utterly alone—I was unable to imagine you any more: you were foreign to me and in some sense entirely unreal . . .

*A*: Probably similar to how Little John felt when his parents left him for several weeks in the home. ([Note:] Mr W has meanwhile watched the CD of John from the above-mentioned Robertson films, which we had discussed in earlier stages of the treatment.)

To me, this seems a most significant moment. Here, the analyst comes forward as an object not only able to contain Mr W's despair, thus facing his pain, but also his disappointment about the analyst's lack of availability (I was once again not available to you), that is, feelings directed towards the analyst herself. When Mr W says "Yes, I felt utterly alone", it seems that he, for the first time in his life, is able to express how he feels, not through bodily symptoms but directly through exact words. Tears are released, in the presence of an object capable of containing them. Paradoxically, when Mr W can tell the analyst about his feeling of being alone and this feeling is met with an affirmative intervention (Killingmo, 2006) aiming at establishing relatedness, he is no longer alone. Mr W has come in from the cold.

Certainly, a value of this case report is the inclusive documentation of the process of transformation through comprehensive dialogue material. Leuzinger-Bohleber focuses specifically on changes in Mr W's dreams as a criterion of the transformation that has taken place. However, the case also may serve to demonstrate crucially important curative factors of psychoanalytic treatment. The above-mentioned dialogue gives a vivid account of how central feelings of despair and utter loneliness, actualised here-and-now, by being contained and analysed by the analyst, could subsequently be contained by Mr W himself. Changes in ways of being with the other, as expressed in the relationship to the analyst, precede changes in dreams. Thus, the case provides a rich picture of what analysis is all about and what kind of healing dynamics are at work in the therapeutic process. Arguably, at the heart of the process lies increased integration of previously split-off affects.

Indeed, it would seem that this case also might serve to illustrate a difference between psychoanalysis and other methods, such as CBT, with regard to treatment aims. Whereas cognitive therapy models aim at correcting negative ways of thinking, psychoanalytic treatment aims at greater tolerance and integration of affective self-states. By demonstrating that containment of dysphoric affect is adaptive, the case report elucidates a specific contribution of psychoanalysis to the treatment of depression.

## *References*

Freud, S. (1914c). On narcissism. An introduction. *S.E.*, *14*: 67–102. London: Hogarth.

Gadamer, H. G. (1960). *Wahrheit und Methode.* Tübingen: J. C. B. Mohr.

Gullestad, S., & Killingmo, B. (2013). *Underteksten. Psykoanalytisk terapi i praksis.* (The Subtext. Psychoanalytic Therapy in Practice). Oslo: Universitetsforlaget.

Heidegger, M. (1927). *Sein und Zeit.* Tübingen: Max Niemayer.

Killingmo, B. (2006). A plea for affirmation. Relating to unmentalised affects. *Scandinavian Psychoanalytic Review*, *29*: 13–21.

Leuzinger-Bohleber, M., Rüger, B. Stuhr, U., & Beutel, M. (2003). How to study the "quality of psychoanalytic treatments" and their long-term effects on patients' well-being: a representative, multi-perspective follow-up study. *International Journal of Psychoanalysis, 84*: 263–290.

Sandler, J., & Dreher, A. U. (1996). *What Do Analysts Want? The Problem of Aims in Psychoanalytic Therapy.* London: Routledge.

Schafer, R. (1994). The conceptualisation of clinical facts. *International Journal of Psychoanalysis, 75*: 1023–1030.

Tuckett, D. (1994). The conceptualisation and communication of clinical fact in psychoanalysis. *International Journal of Psychoanalysis, 75*: 865–870.

Tuckett, D. Basil, R., Birksted-Breen, D., Bohm, T., Denis, P., Ferro, A., Hinz, H., Jemstedt, A., Mariotti, P., & Schubert, J. (2008). *Psychoanalysis Comparable and Incomparable: The Evolution of a Method to Describe and Compare Psychoanalytic Approaches.* London: Routledge.

CHAPTER SEVEN

# Working with the third level of the three-level model: the incidence of our theoretical model on our clinical thinking*

*Adela Leibovich de Duarte*

The Scottish philosopher, David Hume, affirmed in the *Treatise of Human Nature* (1739) that people have a need to understand and explain everything they observe because that makes the world more meaningful.

This intrinsic need to understand and explain the world that surrounds us includes our need to recognise and try to make sense of the others with whom we share, or do not share, perceptions and conceptions about it. The recognition of otherness is intrinsically interwoven in our general understanding of the world. According to Bowlby (1969, 1973), the processing of that information takes place in the context of our "internal working model" that helps us to perceive events and construct our plans for the future.

Our subjectivity exists in an intersubjective space, and, as Mitchell (2000) states, one mind presumes other minds. It is precisely in an intersubjective space that the analytic encounter takes place, as it is the encounter between two different subjectivities who usually share a

* A shorter version of this chapter was originally presented to the Panel: "Clinical observation projects for sustained enquiry into analytic sessions and therapeutic actions". 47th Congress, International Psychoanalytic Association, Mexico, 5 August 2011.

general common cultural background and the same language. The recognition of otherness is intrinsically interwoven in our clinical work.

As Bruner and Tagiuri expressed in their classic paper, "The perception of people" (1954), we, as members of a community that share a general common cultural background and language, have constructed during our lives "implicit theories of personality". On the basis of these theories, we make inferences, attribute intentions, anticipate and predict future behaviours, especially from those belonging to the same culture. These theories include a relatively stable set of suppositions and predictions regarding what to expect from people.

We make value judgements, establish motives, and compare and contrast ourselves with others in order to discover constants, similarities, or differences. We attach meaning to the behaviour of others, especially when that behaviour is perceived as atypical or unexpected.

It should be kept in mind, then, that we analysts, owing to our prior socialisation, begin our training holding a set of beliefs and presuppositions that are reviewed, reconsidered, or modified in our personal analysis, supervisions, and systematic psychoanalytic education.

We have learnt during our psychoanalytic training to listen to our patients "going beyond the information given", to use Bruner words (1957); that is, we take into account more information involved in the psychoanalytic process than that which is provided by the patient's verbal discourse (Leibovich de Duarte, 2006, 2010). In this regard, Freud was the first to develop the idea that more was said and shown than patients intended to say while talking about themselves.

As Jiménez (2008) states, our clinical work is constructivist in its nature. A set of conscious and preconscious assumptions and theoretical considerations that are part of our implicit knowledge help us to understand and organise what goes on in the analytic situation, and to recognise and evaluate transformations along the process.

Different factors come into play in our analytic work: personality factors, training, professional experience, the knowledge integrated into our general background, the transference and countertransference balance with the patient, and our theoretical orientation, to mention the most relevant.

In the clinical situation, with the help of the theoretical and technical resources at our disposal, we psychoanalysts try to understand and account for—or discover—the reasons behind another person's behaviour. In the end, we attempt to substantiate our hypotheses through the iteration of significant data that reinforces them or through the convergence of data that makes them meaningful. By the same token, we record everything that appears relevant, serving either to confirm our conjectures or to send them off on a new track (Leibovich de Duarte, 1996).

Canestri considers that:

> the quantity of elements of every type and origin that contribute to the construction of these [personal] 'theories' or partial models are not to be underestimated. Among these elements are the specific contents of the analyst's unconscious and preconscious, his *Weltanschaung*, the psychology of common sense, his connection to a psychoanalytical group or school, the quality of this connection and the relationship he has with the psychoanalytic 'authorities', his scientific and pre-scientific beliefs, his personal re-elaboration of the concepts of the discipline, counter-transference, etc. . . . If due account is taken of the specificity of clinical practice, it can be seen that concepts in psychoanalysis are never formed once and for all, but are in continuous transformation and re-elaboration. (2006, pp. 13–14)

Our theoretical model operates as a "scaffolding" (Schwaber, 1990), as a referential framework. It functions as an organiser of our clinical work, guiding our listening and contributing to the intelligibility of our patients' material, and to the selection of the narratives we highlight and privilege to elaborate our hypotheses and interventions. It facilitates our comprehension and offers consistency and coherence to our reading of the patients' materials on which we base our interpretations.

Psychoanalytic theories provide us with cognitive structures for perceiving, apprehending, decoding, and organising the intersubjective experience in the clinical setting. They supply us with mediating categories that facilitate our comprehension of the patient's inner world, and with technical resources that, in turn, make interpretations possible.

Where we place ourselves to make our interventions and to foresee possible transformations in the psychoanalytic process will depend, in part, on these theoretical–technical co-ordinates.

A fluent psychoanalytic process requires on our part a permanent dialectical movement between our clinical work and our "free-floating theorisation" (Aulagnier, 1979).

Our implicit and explicit theoretical–technical model functions as an active referential support upon which we base our clinical observations and construct our clinical hypotheses. It is an intrinsic part of our professional identity (Leibovich de Duarte, 2006).

In this regard, Bohleber (2012) considers that "The striving to learn and apply consensually validated technical principles and procedures is accompanied by the wish to belong to a psychoanalytic group or school of thought" (p. 2).

Sandler (1983) has shown us that the analyst is the "implicit" bearer of "private theories" that affect what he/she hears and chooses from the material provided during a session by the patient, who, naturally enough, also has his/her own private theories. He wrote,

> With increasing experience the analyst, as he grows more competent, will pre-consciously (descriptively speaking, unconsciously) construct a whole variety of theoretical segments which relate directly to his clinical work. They are the products of unconscious thinking, very partial theories, models or schemata, which has a quality of being available in reserve, so to speak, to be called upon whenever necessary. That they contradict one another is no problem. They coexist happily as long as they are unconscious. (p. 38)

Our theoretical identity functions as an organiser of our clinical work, as Freud expressed clearly in the following paragraph of his 27th Lecture "Transference" (1916–1917, pp. 431–447):

> If I say to you: 'Look up at the sky! There is a balloon there!' you will discover it much easier than if I simply tell you to look up and see if you can see anything. In the same way, a student who is looking through a microscope for the first time is instructed by his teacher as to what he will see; otherwise he does not see it at all, though it is there and visible. (p. 437)

Freud's permanent preoccupation was to keep psychoanalysis protected from external attacks and internal splitting. His aspiration was the development and growth of the "psychoanalytic movement", enriched with the contributions of loyal, dedicated, and disciplined followers who would expand psychoanalytic theory and technique without deviating from the mainstream.

Wallerstein (1988) claimed that, despite the existence of multiple theoretical perspectives, psychoanalysis is unified by having a common ground in clinical theory shared by all metapsychologies.

However, one question that must be posed is whether psychoanalysts using the same concept, even psychoanalysts belonging to the same school, mean the same thing when applying it? In other words, does intersubjective confirmation exist in psychoanalysis? Clarifying the link between theoretical postulates and what they are taken to mean in the course of a psychoanalytic session can be difficult. A psychoanalyst handles what is basically semiotic data, which brings up the problem of the coexistence of private and shared codes, the latter of which may be shared to a greater or lesser degree. A review of psychoanalytic literature clearly shows that certain concepts from shared codes are not given the same meaning, even by members of the same theoretical group.

In relation to this issue, Bernardi (1989) wrote,

> It seems difficult to find a single term used by all three theories [Freudian, Kleinian, Lacanian] and with the same meaning in each, even though their authors might use the same word. For example: instinct, unconscious, repression, ego, id, Oedipus, etc. On passing from one theory to another, a modification of meaning takes place, the new meaning not being commensurable with the one it had in the previous context. Even clearer are cases of untranslatability. (p. 342)

There are several publications dedicated to showing how the same clinical material can be understood from different psychoanalytic theories.

* * *

In 1987, Sydney Pulver edited an entire issue of *Psychoanalytic Inquiry* focused on how theory shapes technique. Articles by seven well-known psychoanalysts belonging to different theoretical schools were included, in which they presented their perspective on the same clinical material. Pulver formulates as an "ineluctable conclusion" that: "an analyst's theoretical orientation has a marked impact on the way he thinks about patients and the way he works with them" (p. 289).

In the same direction, in 1994 Virginia Hunter edited the book *Psychoanalysts Talk*, in which eleven well-known psychoanalysts from different theoretical orientations take on the task of understanding from their own perspective the same clinical material.

In a study on the similarities and differences in the production of clinical inferences on the same clinical material by psychoanalysts and cognitive therapists, it was found that adherence to a particular theoretical school of thought was not reflected in the nature of the clues psychotherapists selected, but theoretical differences did appear in the way those clues were organised and explained. Their clinical inferences were different, essentially based on their different theoretical frameworks (Leibovich de Duarte, 2010; Leibovich de Duarte, Huerín, Roussos, Rutsztein, & Torricelli, 2002). The theoretical framework colours the way in which the clinical material is interpreted, allowing the configuration of the data and attributing sense to them (Roussos & Leibovich de Duarte, 2002; Roussos, Boffi Lissin, & Leibovich de Duarte, 2007).

Since there are no established formulas or specific rules for making inferences in psychoanalysis, ample space exists for psychoanalysts to display their cognitive style or way of perceiving and processing information in their clinical work. Moreover, evidence indicates that psychoanalysts who share the same theoretical framework often fail to agree in their clinical judgements on the same clinical material. Interpreting clinical material is not a question of mechanically applying rules; instead, it depends, above all, on the analyst's skill in discovering, integrating, and explaining significant cues. An inferential step is necessary to organise in a new way the evidence gathered.

We psychoanalysts bring into play our clinical inferential process to decode our patients' production and elaborate hypotheses on it. It is a cognitive–affective process that involves linking, reorganising, and possibly enunciating something unspoken, by means of which data start to make sense. During a session, we analysts listen and observe, decoding, selecting, prioritising, classifying, comparing, relating, and retaining linguistic and paralinguistic messages; we associate, note recurrences and discrepancies, integrate, anticipate, and, attentive to the polysemic richness and multiple levels of the patient's text, enter into diverse associative chains. The patient's verbal and non-verbal messages are complemented by our own impressions, reflections, and insights. Thus, our hypotheses can be confirmed, rejected, or modified in the course of the analysis. Certain data only become relevant over time, while new details appear that shed fresh light on prior material; some information combines with and enriches the patient's material, while other data become irrelevant and fade away.

In this way, a psychoanalyst is able to constantly update his/her account of what the patient says during the session. When certain indicators and clues become significant, the patient's intrapsychic and interpersonal functioning are seen from a new perspective; former meanings are reorganised, and the patient is seen in a new light. The analyst's digressions do not always take the form of verbal interpretations voiced to the patient.

Bion (1992) expressed how his inferential process worked with this clear metaphor:

> I have found it important to regard every session, no matter how familiar it may seem to be, as if one were scrutinizing the elements in a kaleidoscope before they shake into a definable pattern. The temptation is always to terminate prematurely the state of uncertainty and doubt about what the patient is saying. (p. 290)

* * *

The pluralistic theoretical panorama is a fact on which Bernardi (1992) has written,

> Pluralism in psychoanalysis must be accepted as a fact that can be perceived in three different ways, institutional, epistemological, and mental. The main challenge it poses refers not to the possibility of limiting or reducing differences, but of transforming them into an object of study and learning from them. I believe a better understanding and acceptance of the differences in theories and of the phenomena that occur when these, each belonging to the psychic reality of each analyst, collide would signify an advance for psychoanalytical knowledge. (p. 524)

Now I shall present an example of how theories have been used to understand and explain transformations during a psychoanalytic process using the three-level model.

Regarding the three-level model for observing patient transformations, Bernardi (2011) clearly explains:

> The transformations that occur during analysis have multiple aspects and raise a wide range of questions: What changes? How does change occur? When? Why? These problems have been extensively discussed in literature. The aim here is not to answer these questions themselves

> but to study ways in which a better clinical observation can contribute to advance in the study of their answers.
>
> The model is basically a heuristic for refining, systematizing and conceptualizing clinical observations. It can be used in personal reflection or deliberation processes, when the analyst feels necessary to have a "second look" (Baranger) over the material. It could also be used as an open guide for discussion groups who want to enhance clinical observation through the systematic analysis of a clinical material.

In June 2011, in Montevideo, I had the privilege to be part of a focus group organised by the Chair of the Clinical Observation Committee. It was a group of experienced psychoanalysts who worked during a whole day on three sessions of Irina, a patient presented by a member of the group.

The analyst presented her adolescent patient, Irina, and in different moments of the encounter she read four sessions: the first two sessions, one at nine months later and one at a year and a half later. In her clear and sensitive report of Irina's analysis, the analyst shared with us the patient's problems and concerns, her non-verbal and emotional expressions as well as her transferential responses. The analyst also showed her personal thoughts, insights, and interpretations.

The patient's sessions were analysed going through levels one and two of the three-level model of patient transformations (see Bernardi, Chapter One) and the last part of the meeting was devoted to trying to understand Irina's changes, using psychoanalytic concepts to explain them focusing on level three of the three-level model.

As Bernardi states in this book (see Chapter One) "While the two previous levels intend to describe what has changed, the aim of the third level is to understand how and why changes occurred (or did not occur) . . .", and he adds,

> Participants are asked to propose alternative hypotheses or points of view that come from their own theoretical and technical frames. The different approaches themselves are not under discussion, but their contribution to proposing alternative ways to interpret the material is considered. From the heuristic point of view, these new hypotheses may suggest revising the discussion of previous levels, checking how convincing and fruitful the diverse hypotheses are. (See p. 18)

How did the group understand and explain Irina's changes?

The group focused on the patient's evolution, trying to understand and explain the transformations during the analytic process. Different clinical inferences on Irina´s sessions were formulated.

I will present only briefly some of the explanatory clinical inferences produced by members of the group.

What the participants said regarding the patient (see Levels 1 and 2) I quote, as I said, only some of the considerations made.

One analyst considered that:

> "Related to the theme of change, I think it was possible because the analyst functions as a container, in Bion´s terms. This makes the affective regulation possible. The patient has ups and downs and the analyst helps her to contain her positive and negative affects, using Bion and the English school's ideas. Thinking in terms of the French school, I thought about the patient's narcissistic identification with her mother. I can see it from the imaginary side, with an emphasis on that narcissistic figure, all brightness, with no deficiencies."

Another analyst expressed,

> "I have no doubts that the mother is part of the problem. But I think that her wish for autonomy is very strong. It is her search. One can say, in a French style, that she was prisoner of her mother's Imaginary and is trying to fly away."

Another analyst had recourse to Erik Erikson´s ideas and said,

> "Erikson would have said that this girl is in the process of searching for her identity. She is building her identity with some difficulties. The body area is the most difficult for her and it is where she feels she fails. "'Who am I?' for others, which is the first impressions other people get from me." And this is central for her. The problem is not only whether she is fat or she perceives herself as fat, but how others perceive her and how this is a basic part of her relational difficulties with boys. What she considers her fatness prevents her from relating to others, from accepting any physical approach. "Don't touch me'" are her words. I think that during her psychoanalytic treatment she is able to regulate her self-esteem and slowly build a more realistic identity."

Afterwards, the group carried out the exercise of reading, one after the other, all the interpretations made by the analyst. Then, they observed that the analyst was exploring the field little by little and it was in the session a year and a half after starting therapy that she interpreted the patient´s rivalry when she talked about the "fat analyst". The group considered it as a displacement of the figure of the mother to the analyst.

One participant said,

> "The patient needed to build in the analysis an image of herself in which she could recognise herself in order to be able to have a more coherent relationship with her own body. All these are related to her libidinal body and not to the cut body present in "her dream of the cut arms". She needs to find another way of dealing with her body and with herself, another way that allows her to work better with her primary and secondary identifications. All these have to do with narcissism and Oedipus."

Regarding the very important issue of how the patient regulates her impulses, the following was said:

> "She has preconscious representations with no possibility of internal communication.'

> "She needs to stop functioning as a "leaf in the wind' and as a 'video clip'. The patient has a non-integrated self, this is her pathology."

The group considered that the analyst was a good container figure who was able to offer a solid support for the patient. One analyst described her role in the following terms:

> "Using Winnicott and Green's notions, I consider that the analyst was *able to tolerate this girl´s attacks* on her narcissism. That made the continuity of the analysis possible."

According to the group, which were the ideas that guided the analyst's work during the sessions? These were some of the interventions made by the group participants regarding this point:

> "Her hypotheses of change were based on the Barangers' field theory (Baranger & Baranger, 1961–1962)."

> "When one analyses the different interventions and interpretations of the analyst, one can see her hypotheses about change. The patient is searching for valid identifications."

> "The analyst's hypotheses: to work from the body in order to find the real foundation inside the patient: her femininity, her identity conflict. Identification with the feminine body."

Regarding the hypotheses of change upon which the analyst worked with the patient, the group inferred that they were based on ideas of Willy and Madelaine Baranger, Donald Winnicott, Wilfred Bion, and Pierre Marty.

* * *

As the previous examples illustrate, the participants' interventions reflected their diverse implicit or explicit theoretical approaches. Wilfred Bion, André Green, Erik Erikson, and Donald Winnicott were the authors mainly mentioned as references.

An analyst from North America, a member of our committee (Professor Margaret Ann Fitzpatrick-Hanly), after reading Irina's sessions, produced the following explanatory hypotheses regarding Irina´s changes.

1. The importance of the analyst's interpretation of transference and containment of the attacks on her narcissism are linked to Irina's being the prisoner of her mother's imaginary.
2. The analyst's containment of attacks helped the patient to regulate her affects and allowed darker thoughts to emerge.
3. Irina's growing ability to tolerate a wider range of affect created a shift in her dreams and allowed them to be reported and associated to.
4. Irina was helped to regulate her self-esteem (related to Erikson's identity question, "who am I?") by the analyst's helping Irina to understand her entrapped focus on what others think.

These examples of explanatory hypotheses produced by expert psychoanalysts illustrate the incidence of our implicit and explicit theoretical–technical model in shaping our clinical observation. The clinical inferences produced by the participants expressed diverse perspectives and theoretical approaches that, in the end, enriched the comprehension of the clinical material presented by the analyst.

Our theoretical–technical model functions as an active referential support that helps us to highlight, understand, and organise the significant bits and pieces of the patient's material in order to produce an intervention.

The existence of different theories, the development of alternative new ones, and the interchange and cross-fertilisation among them is an incentive for the improvement of psychoanalysis. In this regard, Bernardi (2002) wrote "controversies are also good for developing better substantiated theories, encouraging more careful examination of our clinical evidence" (p. 870).

## *References*

Aulagnier, P. (1979). *Les destins du plaisir, alienation, amour, passion*. Paris: PUF.

Baranger, M., & Baranger, W. (1961–1962). La situación analítica como campo dinámico. *Revista Uruguaya de Psicoanálisis, IV*(1): 3–54.

Bernardi, R. (1989). The role of paradigmatic determinants in psychoanalytic understanding. *International Journal Psychoanalysis, 70*: 341–357.

Bernardi, R. (1992). On pluralism in psychoanalysis. *Psychoanalytic Inquiry, 12*: 506–525.

Bernardi, R. (2002). The need for true controversies in psychoanalysis. *International Journal of Psychoanalysis, 83*: 851–873.

Bernardi, R. (2011, internal document). Method of analysis of clinical observation: three-level model.

Bion, W. R. (1992). *Cogitations*. London: Karnac.

Bohleber, W. (2012). The use of public and of private implicit theories in the clinical situation. In: J. Canestri (Ed.), *Putting Theory to Work. How Are Theories Used in Practice?* London: Karnac.

Bowlby, J. (1969, 1973). *Attachment and Loss. Vol.1. Attachment. Vol. 2. Separation: Anxiety and Anger*. London: Hogarth Press.

Bruner, J. (1957). Going beyond the information given. In: *Contemporary Approaches to Cognition* (pp. 41–69). Cambridge, MA: Harvard University Press.

Bruner, J. S., & Tagiuri, R. (1954). The perception of people. In: D. T. Gilbert, S. T. Fiske, & G. Lindzey (Eds.), *Handbook of Social Psychology* (Vol. 2) (pp. 634–654). Cambridge: Addison-Wesley.

Canestri, J. (2006). Implicit understanding of clinical material beyond theory. In: J. Canestri (Ed.), *Psychoanalysis: From Practice to Theory* (pp. 13–28). London: Wiley.

Freud, S. (1916–1917). *Introductory Lectures in Psycho-analysis. S.E., 16*. London: Hogarth Press.

Hume, D. (1739). *A Treatise of Human Nature*. New York: Dover, 2003.

Hunter, V. (Ed.) (1994). *Psychoanalysts Talk*. New York: Guilford Press.

Jiménez J. P. (2008). Theoretical plurality and pluralism in psychoanalytic practice. *International Journal of Psychoanalysis, 89*: 579–599.

Leibovich de Duarte, A. (1996). Variaciones entre psicoanalistas en el proceso inferencial clínico [Variations among psychoanalysts in the inferential clinical process]. *Investigaciones en Psicología. Revista del Instituto de Investigaciones. Facultad de Psicología, UBA, 1*: 27–38.

Leibovich de Duarte, A. (2006). "Going beyond the information given": constructing our clinical hypotheses. *Bulletin of the European Psycho-analytic Federation*. Electronic publication No. 60, January. www.epf-eu.org/pub/bullettin.

Leibovich de Duarte, A. (2010). Psychotherapists at work: exploring the construction of clinical inferences. In: R. Schwarzer & P. A. Frensch (Eds.), *Personality, Human Development, and Culture: International Perspectives on Psychological Science* (Vol. 2) (pp. 29–43). Hove: Psychology Press.

Leibovich de Duarte, A., Huerín, V., Roussos, A., Rutsztein, G., & Torricelli, F. (2002). Empirical studies on clinical inference: similarities and differences in the clinical work of psychotherapists with different theoretical approaches and levels of experience. In: *IPA An Open Door Review of Outcome Studies in Psychoanalysis* (2nd rev. edn) (pp. 201–204.) London: International Psychoanalytic Association.

Mitchell, S. A. (2000). *Relationality: From Attachment to Intersubjectivity*. Hillsdale, NJ: Analytic Press.

Pulver, S. (Ed.) (1987). How theory shapes technique: perspectives on a clinical study. *Psychoanalytic Inquiry, 7*(2): (whole).

Roussos, A., & Leibovich de Duarte, A. (2002). La incidencia de la Actividad Referencial en el proceso de formulaciones clínicas. La importancia del marco teórico en la formulación de las inferencias clínicas en psicoterapia [The impact of the referential activity in the process of clinical formulations. The importance of the theoretical framework in the formulation of the clinical inferences in psychotherapy]. *Intersubjetivo, 1*: 45–63.

Roussos, A., Boffi Lissin, L., & Leibovich de Duarte, A. (2007). The importance of the theoretical framework in the formulation of clinical inferences in psychotherapy. A comparative study of clinical inferences of psychoanalysts and cognitive therapists using the Psychotherapy Q Sort. *Psychotherapy Research, 17*(5): 535–543.

Sandler, J. (1983). Reflections on some relations between psychoanalytic concepts and psychoanalyticv practice. *International Journal of Psycho-analysis*, *64*: 35–45.

Schwaber, E. A. (1990). Interpretation and the therapeutic action of psychoanalysis. *International Journal of Psychoanalysis*, *71*: 229–240.

Wallerstein, R. S. (1988). One psychoanalysis or many? *International Journal of Psychoanalysis*, *69*: 5–21.

# PART III

# A PATIENT, A CONCEPT, AND A CASE

CHAPTER EIGHT

# A traumatised patient in analysis: observing patients' transformations

*Margaret Ann Fitzpatrick-Hanly*

## Introduction

The transformations that occur during analysis have multiple aspects and raise a wide range of questions. What changes? How does change occur? When? Why? These problems have been extensively discussed in literature. The aim here is not to answer these questions themselves, but to study ways in which a better clinical observation can contribute to advance in the study of their answers (Guidelines, three-level model, Appendix I).

The three-level model for observing patient transformations was developed by the IPA Committee on Clinical Observation to guide groups of psychoanalysts in observing change and no change in a patient in psychoanalysis, using a brief history and the verbatim records of selected psychoanalytic sessions. Several kinds of observation come into play in an analytic process, as well as in writing clinical reports and clinical papers, and a rich language for observational functions exists in all psychoanalytic cultures. Grinberg (1990) quotes Fleming and Benedek (1964) on a range of observational abilities to be transmitted in the education of psychoanalysts: "listening with floating attention (the self acts as an instrument of reception and perception, with a synthetical function)"; inferring "interpretations from latent material, but without formulating them yet"; estimating "the degree of resistance and anxiety in the patient, and developing empathy with the patient's regressive state (function of sensitivity)"; "judging the moment and distribution of responses and interventions"; "grasping, at the greatest possible depth, reactions of transference and countertransference"; "recognizing the dynamic trends and changes session to session" (Grinberg, 1990, p. 294).

In the groups, which set out to "observe" transformations in an analytic patient, these listening abilities are important. While reading and re-reading the selected sessions and thinking about change and no change in the patient, the groups pay attention to these psychoanalytic functions and also take a "second look" (Baranger, Baranger, & Mom, 1983) at any parallel process that develops in the course of the group work.

## *Clinical observation groups*

The three-level model for observing patients' transformations adopted the idea of using a "text" with brief history and selected sessions (typed and distributed to the group) developed by Haydee Faimberg for her method based on "Listening to the listening" (1996). "By listening to the patient's reassignment of meaning to his interpretations, the analyst can discover the patient's unconscious identifications and, together with the patient, thereby facilitate the process of psychic change" (p. 667). The "text" of a series of typed analytic sessions was used in other working party methods developed by Tuckett (1993, 2008), Reith (2011), Norman and Salomonsson (2006), and many EPF chairs and moderators over the past dozen years. The three-level model has adopted the text of clinical material with a specified sequence of sessions, a flexible setting for groups, and a focus on change in the patient. The sessions are to be selected by the analyst *from the beginning of the analysis and from two later phases*; the method is to focus on observing *transformations in psychoanalytic patients and the process*; and the context is to be small groups formed in local IPA societies.

Two IPA work groups were formed in Toronto (and worked without knowledge of each other) to explore a text with a history and six psychoanalytic sessions, over fourteen hours. A group of six training analysts and a senior analyst met with the analyst present for seven two-hour evening meetings once a month. A group of recently graduated analysts and senior candidates met for twelve hours over a Saturday and Sunday and two subsequent two-hour evenings, also with the analyst present. In their reports, the psychoanalysts focused on explicit and implicit dynamics in the patient and in the analytic process. Members of these two IPA work groups using the three-level model came independently to very similar conclusions about kinds of change and absence of change in the patient and in the analytic process. They listened to the session material to infer the workings of the unconscious mind, and to make subtle judgements about how interpretations had been heard, taken in, or rejected. They recognised the dynamic trends and changes session to session, and over the two years of the analysis, looking from starting points to the later sessions. They attended to particular resonances in their groups as members read, re-read, and discussed the sessions.

The final task in the group project is the creation of a clinical narrative. Classic narratives move from "scene" to "summary" and the opening paragraphs are replete with hints of later developments. Using this idea to shape the clinical narrative, the groups progressively refine a selection of "anchor points", or starting points, which emerge from among the patient's "presenting problems" as key aspects of his or her psychic functioning. Good anchor points will offer highly condensed depictions of the patient's core dynamics on entering the analysis. The condensations will become apparent as meanings of greater depth and complexity are revealed in the later sessions of the analysis. Unconscious infantile fantasies and hints of traumatic memories in the first sessions will be returned to again and again in the later associations and enactments, making change and absence of change accessible to observation. Psychoanalytic narratives emerge from the work of the group, as they select brief "scenes" of the analysis (session verbatim) and formulate "summaries" about what could be observed and conceptualised in relation to repetition and change.

What follows in this chapter is a set of clinical narratives on transformation (each starting from a question in the model) written by me, who acted as moderator for the two groups. The narratives draw on the highlights and conclusions from several reports, composed during the course of the groups' discussions. The first "narrative" opens with reflections from Level 1 on change and no change seen in the patient's way of responding to the analyst's interpretations over the two years of analysis. A second narrative adds conceptual depth, using Level 2 questions, adopted into the model from the current psychodynamic diagnostic systems (*OPD-2, PDM*). The questions rendered into ordinary language can open up discussion, as the groups try to "unpack" concepts and to clarify meanings in relation to the clinical material. Finally, at Level 3, the discussions take up ideas on how the transformations might be understood according to different psychoanalytic theories of change. The aim of the discussion is not to choose among hypotheses on therapeutic action, but to examine the clinical support for each. The testing of hypotheses should then be understood as an attempt to explore and enhance the observational base of theoretical hypotheses, in order to develop the ability to link them critically with clinical observations and to make predictions or conjectures that can stimulate new clinical observations.

## *Brief history of the patient*

Mrs C began psychoanalysis at four times a week several years ago, after having been in once weekly psychotherapy for seven years. The session notes are from the first two years of the analysis. Mrs C was married with two adult daughters, who had both recently married. She was born and passed her childhood in a war-torn country. As an infant and young child, she often stayed with an extended family, for her parents, who both worked, saw her only in the evenings. Her mother left her, her brother, and father and went to live in a safer area of the country when the patient was ten. Mrs C's mother committed suicide in her eighties. In her late teens, the patient suffered from harassment at work, a rape followed by a depression, and briefly saw a psychotherapist. She developed cancer in her forties, became depressed, and suffered two psychotic episodes, hearing voices saying she was "not caring for the children". She was in hospital twice for a month, and entered psychotherapy shortly after. The patient works in industry, instructing classes in business organisation. She has a problem with an error of a date in an important legal document. The need to correct that error evokes in her a sense of being in the wrong and makes her feel in danger of letting her children down.

### *Brief review of presenting problems and the psychotherapy*

The analyst had written up some notes on how Mrs C had first presented herself in the psychotherapy seven years before the analysis began.

> Mrs C arrived ten minutes early and she walked into my office (I had not called her in yet); she called me by my first name, and announced who she was; she moved her chair away from the wall to the edge of my desk and sat down. She is a petite woman with short hair wearing no make-up and loose-fitting clothes; she appeared moderately anxious and seemed unaware of social protocol.

She felt her husband was "withholding and critical" and, therefore, she keeps secrets from him; she felt she needed "to become more assertive and wants their relationship to get better". During the course of psychotherapy, Mrs C's relationship with her own children (now married) had improved, and her work life had become more settled. She was on a low dosage of an antipsychotic medication when she began the analysis.

### *First anchor point: the patient's response to the analyst's interpretations*

A fruitful anchor point for observing change in this patient came in answering a question from Level 1 of the three-level model: "how does the patient use the analyst's interventions and are there changes or no changes in this dimension of the analytic process?" I studied the reports made during the group work and formulated anchor points according to the issues the analyst felt to be most important in the groups' discussions.

In working with the patient's responses to interventions, both groups were aware of Mrs C's harsh superego. In the early weeks of the psychoanalysis, Mrs C struggled with the new setting. The patient had reported that she was setting up a separate bank account for the analysis and keeping the treatment and new frequency a secret from her husband.

> (Mrs C arrived thirty minutes early and sat in the waiting room.)
>
> *P*: PK [her husband] and I had a very nice evening but I had to wait . . . we went to the restaurant. I didn't enjoy the ravioli very much, but enjoyed the evening . . .

[The analyst intervened at t his point, suggesting the patient was avoiding what made her most anxious.]

*P*: Symbolically, I'm not fully accepting the therapy, giving to myself. There is also a feeling that I'm doing something wrong because my husband won't accept it . . . sometimes I do think what I am doing is right, not wrong, but there is a big conflict around that.

*A*: Let's explore this conflict.

*P*: Like depriving myself, like since childhood . . . Because I'm not worth it; a coffee and an olive. I was depriving myself.

The patient's response to the analyst's intervention addressing the conflict about whether she was "right" or "wrong" to be in therapy was "Because I'm not worth it; a coffee and an olive. I was depriving myself." This response became an anchor point for looking at change and no change. Mrs C's self-deprivation linked to low self-esteem was a key aspect of her masochistic–depressive character (Level 2). Importantly, the action implicit in the way she responded to the analyst was simultaneously *a going along with the analyst's interpretation and a turning of insight into self-blame*. This dynamic, implicit in her complex response, indicated a core "presenting problem": was she in the right or in the wrong? The derivatives of oral fantasies could be heard in the material, her not liking the ravioli and having to wait suggesting a regression in the new setting and the emergence of core infantile situations and conflicts. Mrs C's mixed use of the analyst's interventions revealed a complicated defensive/adaptative strategy, as she used compliance, turning back on the self, and not knowing (Level 2), imagined by the groups to be a repetition of positions first adopted during early experiences of waiting, of danger, and of loss.

In this early analytic session, the groups could see the patient struggling openly with fears and doubts about deserving the analysis (at four times a week). Defending against her own feared ambivalence, she projected her rejection of the analysis on to her husband, whom she said "won't accept it".

(Later in the same session.)

*P*: Ya [sad tone]. I was punishing myself for my mother leaving. I had a dream a long time ago . . . I was in a washroom with a woman and we were sharing one piece of bread, like we were poor or something . . .

*A*: What comes to mind about the dream?

*P*: Sharing bread, Jesus cut the bread and shared it with many people [laughs] . . . As a child I always had food, but in some ways I felt poor. Mum and dad would hide the chocolate . . . Why was I stealing? Because I felt poor. [She stole from other children.]

*A*: At times you stole from them and at other times you gave something away to be liked.

*P*: Ya, I do that a lot, even now, giving up therapy in order that K [husband] will like me, or not giving a class honest feedback.

*A*: I think that is connected to paying me.

*P*: I pay you so you'll like me [pause]. Ya [sad voice]. Somewhere in my mind I know you'll give me unconditional positive regard, even if I'm not good, but maybe at some level I think if you don't like me you'll leave me. I was a little angry with you the other day—why open all these cans of worms?—and then I was more depressed. A cognitive therapist wouldn't open all these things, would just teach me to think more rationally [laughs]. I remember you said that I opened a can of worms myself when I became depressed with psychotic symptoms and that's true. . . .

References to stolen chocolate (the hungry guilty child) and then to opening of a can of worms (the bad child punished) were suggestive of the complex dynamics including a primitive guilt with fear of retaliation (Level 2). The analyst interprets to help her see that she both steals *and* gives away, wanting to be liked. The patient uses the analyst's next explicit transference interpretation ("I think that is connected to paying me") to associate further. She opens up: ". . . if you don't like me you'll leave me", elaborating her fears and her self-blame (I stole), but indirectly she begins to blame the analyst in the maternal transference (the analyst, like the mother, might leave her, not liking her). Mrs C can also express how afraid and angry she was that the psychoanalyst might lead her back into depression and psychosis. The mixture of compliance and guilty self-blame in the anchor point shows up again, as if she caused her own psychosis: ". . . you said that I opened a can of worms myself when I became depressed with psychotic symptoms and that's true."

*A*: I think you want this therapy, but are also concerned about what will come up if we open things up.

*P*: With a cognitive therapist you don't have to open up all the dust that's inside. I wonder if I'm ashamed of opening things up. Like the stealing,

> that was shameful . . . Recently I dreamt of the astronaut who drove all that way in a nappy. I dreamt of pooh. I think it's about being dirty or something . . . not resolving something. I don't know . . . being ashamed of being exposed, of having an accident or something.

In response to the transference intervention, "concerned about what will come up if we open things . . .", Mrs C elaborates her fear of "exposing" her inner world and showing her impulses and fears, which she displaces on to the astronaut, interjecting a denial: "I don't know", a phrase she uses to push away difficult feelings. There had been a newspaper report of the woman astronaut who actually drove to Florida in a nappy without stopping, in order to kill a rival who was having an affair with her lover. The details of this story in the patient's dream and in her associations were derivatives of unconscious anal and rivalrous fantasies projected on to the astronaut. Mrs C repeats "I don't know" in the face of unbearable anxieties connected to continuing fears of psychic fragmentation, "the dust inside", and fears of being dirty (too aggressive and unwanted?). The analyst's intervention stirred things up, which brought out an expression of the patient's defensive splitting, her "knowing and not knowing".

The groups thought that the patient was showing some *change within this session* early in the four times a week analysis, able to use the analyst's interventions, to reveal more about her inner world. Mrs C could acknowledge that she felt "a bit angry" with the analyst. Her ongoing difficulties, that is, absence of change, could also be seen in the repetition of the core dynamic (anchor point): compliance along with aggression turned back on the self in response to the analyst's interventions (Level 1).Discussion was also focused on her projections on to the husband and astronaut and her characteristic splitting and minimisation of affect (Level 2).

In reading a selected session, from eight months later in the psychoanalysis, the groups were struck by the fact that Mrs C was able to take in and reflect on an interpretation of projection by the analyst: Mrs C says, "I am disappointed in my husband; he did not accept our son-in-law." The analyst says, "But what did *you* feel?" The patient admits, "I didn't accept him either . . . I made my husband look bad, like a villain."

The analyst's interpretation allows the patient to admit her own initial rejection of her son-in-law, and her projection of what she saw as an unacceptable "bad" feeling on to her husband, suggesting a softening of her defensive strategies. However, again the patient takes in the analyst's interpretation in a way that generates self-blame, "I made my husband look . . . like a villain." Along with some change, the absence of change in the self-reproaches seemed to indicate a need to protect her primary objects from reproach and from her hostile impulses, which would take longer to shift in the analysis. The analyst's next intervention was aimed at helping the patient gain a more realistic and less self-reproaching perspective, "you *felt* dislike but you *did not act* on it" (confirming the group's ideas on the patient's core problem).

* * *

At the beginning of this session, eight months into the analysis, Mrs C tells the analyst of intense anger at her husband for taking her too close to a "dangerous intersection" where they were almost hit by a bus. She wondered if her husband had pushed her to save her or to kill her.

*P*: Something happened a few weeks ago that changed my mood. I didn't tell you because I thought it wasn't important. K and I were walking, thirty minutes away is a grocery store and there's a bad intersection there. We looked, no cars, a bus far away. As we were crossing, the bus went towards us, didn't see us. I felt K pushing me. We were almost hit by the bus . . . Days passed and after our Friday session we walked at the same place, crossed carefully, and since then I've been very unhappy, on an off sad or something, thinking what was it? We were close to death and it brought up a lot of stuff. I'm very worried about K. if he's late, if he has an accident, if he dies, if he got killed, then all the stuff in our relationship would come up, regrets, what we didn't work out. I've been very unhappy in the last few days.

*A*: Something is still stirring in you.

*P*: Ya, I hope it is not PTSD [post traumatic stress disorder]. I was close to death, thinking about all my unresolved issues. Sorry, I have to go to the washroom [she got up and left, clearing her throat].

Many saw the patient's way of telling the analyst about her experience of the bus at the dangerous intersection as a displaced elaboration of intense split-off anxieties, related to childhood experiences of danger in her home country. The analyst's intervention, "Something is stirring in you" brought out still more intense anxieties and attendant anger which then became conscious, "I was close to death". Ongoing difficulties could also be observed in her paranoid fear that her husband had wanted to kill her, which emerged in the session. The groups discussed the patient's enactment in having to go to the washroom, possibly flushing away her thoughts and feelings at the point in the session when she felt "close to death", although some analysts thought of the enactment as bringing her defence of splitting into the analytic setting, representing a deepening of the analytic process.

Later in the session, the analyst implicitly asked the patient to reflect on her feelings about the dangerous situation and her husband's act.

> *A*: He took you into a dangerous situation.
>
> *P*: Ya, maybe I'm angry at him. Yesterday I was thinking of him and crying, deep crying. He was close to being killed and I was close to being killed.

* * *

Re-reading the session eight months into the analysis, the groups began to hear the patient express difficult feelings in a new way. The transference interpretation allows Mrs C to name and feel previously projected affects, anger and fear of loss, ". . . maybe I'm angry . . . he was close to being killed". She conveyed to the analyst a deep anxiety about aggression ("I felt K pushing me") and about not being protected. The groups discussed the patient's inability to perceive her own internal states when she experienced annihilation anxiety or murderous impulses ("why did he push me?" or "take me [there]").

In summary, the way Mrs C responded to the analyst's interventions portrayed an oscillation between compliance, paranoia, and turning back on the self of aggressive impulses, in a context that further revealed the traumatic origins of the dynamics of the anchor point. The dangerous intersection presented a situation of danger and terror in her childhood, alive in a split-off section of her psyche (Level 2), during the war with intermittent presence of her parents. Her husband's perceived aggression or carelessness had evoked her rage at being unprotected. Some members of the groups who knew more about war were able imaginatively to reconstruct her experience in greater detail. The patient seemed to also be experiencing the analyst as leading her into a dangerous phase of the analysis, wherein she might relive fear, hunger, and loss. Mrs C makes a strong protest in regard to her need for safety. The analysis was deepening.

In a session selected by the analyst, twenty-two months into the analysis, the analyst interprets the patient's affects of frustration and anger when her husband was telling her not to buy her aeroplane ticket (to see her children during the vacation) because he wanted her to use points.

Mrs C says, "I'm dependent on him but frustrated with him . . . My anxiety about being punished, being caught, paperwork, can be so overwhelming . . . I say come on let's buy the ticket and he says, not yet. It triggers me." The analyst notes the deprivation and anxiety: "You feel he deprives you, and the deprivation triggers the urgency"; and the patient responds with emphasis, "Yes!!! I'm a little angry at him that he deprived me."

Mrs C begins to own and express anger with her husband. Two years into the analysis, the patient can affirm her husband's real tendency to withhold: "he deprived me". However, in her response to the analyst's intervention, we also saw the minimisation of anger ("a little angry at him"). Later in the session (after missing a Wednesday session for a specialist appointment), Mrs C is able to feel and express her dependency on the analyst but denies her annihilation anxiety: "I missed you, but I thought, I will not die."

In summary, Mrs C's ways of responding to the analyst's interventions were heard by the groups to be changing, with less turning back on the self, less compliance with her husband and analyst. The analyst was helping her to express her aggression and her wish to survive more directly (although often in displacement): "he deprived me"; "I was close to being killed". The patient was frightened about potentially disorganising feelings and impulses, but able to tolerate her disturbing thoughts and affects better, using the analyst's interventions.

After two years of analysis, an absence of change was still observable in the deeper layers of her defences against unbearable early experience. From the point of view of the anchoring dimension, the participants observed some continuing "turning back on the self" in her responses to the analyst. They noticed a minimal direct remembering of traumatic experiences, an inability to tolerate severe anxiety about object loss, or to own aggressive impulses towards the analyst without some disavowal and projection.

### *Second anchor point: "What were the patient's symptoms, beliefs, and expectations about her problems and treatment and did these aspects change?"*

This question led to an anchor point being formulated by the author about the patient's fear of psychosis, a central issue discussed by the groups: "I don't want to look like a bag lady . . . the bag lady is about psychosis." The groups listened for indicators of a shift in the patient's implicit beliefs about her ability to test reality, because any change in this difficulty would be an indicator of transformation. Early in the analysis, Mrs C was worried about whether she might have another breakdown. In the later sessions, her anxieties about loss of memory and loss of control could be somewhat differentiated from impending psychosis.

In one of the first analytic sessions, the patient asked the analyst if she actually did look like a bag lady. Did Mrs C have a momentary delusion that she looked like a bag lady, or was she asking for reassurance? Later in the session, the patient associated the "bag lady" explicitly with psychosis.

*A*: You asked me if you looked like a bag lady, what does one look like?

*P*: Very bad teeth, hair long, not combed, baggy clothes that don't fit, smokes, pushing a stroller that has bags in it, a cart that has things in it, I don't want to look like a bag lady . . .

[The patient then recounts a dream about college "maybe about therapy" and, in her associations, worries that her day-dreaming means that she is not doing her job well enough and she has "to compensate". Mrs C goes on to say she is doing her therapy for herself but against her husband.]

*A*: I think you are telling me that if you don't keep an eye on your mood, you can become depressed and the depression can lead to psychosis . . .

*P*: Ya, and the bag lady is about psychosis too, because bag ladies are often psychotic on the street.

The bag lady description also had elements suggesting the oral stage: teeth, smoking, a stroller. Her fear of a disintegrating effect of analysis was projected on to her husband as a refusal to accept the analysis.

Two years into analysis, the patient returns to her fears that she is not able to test reality. Mrs C had an irrational belief that she might be caught and punished while trying to fix an important legal document and stopped from seeing her children, who live in another country. She found it difficult to think clearly about the task of fixing the document (which the analyst felt would not, in fact, have been so difficult).

*P*: K is so difficult with times, even with minor things . . .

*A*: As you say this, you sound frustrated and exasperated.

*P*: Ya, but it's better than being depressed. I notice that in my mood I'm not depressed but a bit anxious, worried about this process of getting the legal document fixed.

Mrs C is not sure that she has the courage to try to resolve the document problem. She is worried about delusional states, and yet she shows a growing separation from her husband, and more trust in her own mind (indicating change).

*P*: Once I tell K I want to fix it, he'll put a resistance . . . if I insist he'll say I'm sick.

*A*: He'll think there is something wrong with your mind.

*P*: Ya, where in fact the opposite is true.

Mrs C replies with more self-definition and distances herself from her husband's views of her. But, later in this session, Mrs C worries again about losing control of her mind:

*P*: "It's kind of on my mind, Alzheimer's. I know I don't have it but it did bother me . . .

*A*: Your concern about being forgetful has come up many times . . .

*P*: Yes! And here too, it drives me crazy when I forget things. I must remember! I need to be organised. I need to be in control. To forget is unacceptable. If I forget something I try so hard to remember it . . . My father was forgetful, even before he had Alzheimer's.

*A*: Being forgetful has many meanings.

*P*: Ya, like not being like my father, not being in control.

*A*: And the fear of losing your mind.

*P*: Oh ya! I think that's what it is! It has to do with me being sick.

As the analyst clarifies the patient's anxiety about forgetting things ("here too, it drives me crazy when I forget things") and names her fear that forgetting is the same as psychosis, Mrs C begins to differentiate between forgetting, having Alzheimer's, and having a psychotic breakdown. Both groups discussed the patient's fear of another psychotic breakdown and the pressure on the analytic couple given the patient's history, and they paid close attention to any signs of loss of contact with reality in the session material.

In summary, the traumatic elements of Mrs C's experiences came to be appreciated as critical to the genesis of her psychotic symptoms (Level 2). The specific content of the psychotic voices (I am not taking care of the children) came to be understood as a depressive turning back on the self of her accusation against the mother (filled with unconscious murderous impulses), who did not take care of her children, seeing them briefly in the evenings and leaving them in a dangerous place. The analyst's interpretation seemed to help the patient become aware that her acute anxiety about "forgetting" (her notebook) stemmed from the unconscious fear that this was the first sign of a psychotic break. In reality, her father's forgetfulness must have felt like a lack of protection and continuity of attention, which represented a real danger to the child, and her linking of anxiety with her experience of her father gives her a more integrated sense of self and history. The "clinical narrative" on change and no change began with the question as to whether the groups could observe any changes in the patient's symptoms, beliefs, and expectations about her problems and treatment ("Do I look like a bag lady?" meaning "Am I psychotic?"). After two years of analysis, the patient's symptomatic fear of loss of reality was undergoing a transformation. Her unconscious expectation that the treatment could cause another breakdown could be verbalised, linked to more ordinary childhood experiences of loss, and lightened.

### *Third anchor point: the patient's structure, the analyst's supportive interventions, and resonances in the group processes*

Given her prior psychotic episodes and hospitalisations, Mrs C was deeply frightened about how severe her troubles were and how the analysis would affect her. This made sense of the special resonance in the groups about certain "supportive" interventions of the analyst. Two questions from Level 2 guided the formulation of a third anchor point for observations: "Did conflicts prevail, which needed interpretation, or were structural problems [a dominance of primitive defences which weaken the personality structure] predominant, which needed other kinds of intervention?" [that is, what is most appropriate in a primitive state, support or interpretation] and "Is the patient able to adequately regulate her impulses, her affects, and her self-esteem?"

Linked in the end to questions about the patient's structure, there were several heated discussions about what were called "supportive" interventions by the analyst: ("Now we have time to deal with it", "We will talk more about this", and ". . . quite a difference in your reactions"). The observations and reflections explored what might be coming from the analyst's unconscious countertransference anxiety, and what from structural problems in the patient, which might be making these interventions effective in furthering the analysis. The groups asked if there was a better way to interpret, by naming Mrs C's anxieties rather than "reassuring" her about the continuity of the analysis, or encouraging her about her improvements?

By eight months into the analysis, the session material about the dangerous intersection suggested that the patient was more able to recall "time past" in "time present": ". . . something happened . . . I didn't tell you." The analyst was no longer making interventions to help sustain in Mrs C's mind that there was a past, present, and future for the analysis.

* * *

At twenty-two months into the analysis, the analyst continued to make interventions, which some called "supportive": "you want to be honest" or "more genuine". Others saw some of these interventions as restating the fundamental rules. Still others came back to wonder why encouragement was given rather than naming the patient's anxieties about dishonesty. Finally, the question was raised as to whether the analysts in the groups discussing the sessions were themselves caught up in some transmitted anxiety.

The patient's ongoing compliance with the analyst occurred even as Mrs C gained insight, revealing her intense fear of, and attachment to, dependency on the analyst as well as on her husband. In one of the early analytic sessions selected by the analyst, there could be heard the repeated expression of agreement: "Ya, ya. I feel that a lot" and "Ya, and the bag lady is about psychosis too." When the analyst said, "One worry is money but the main worry is not money," Mrs C says, "That's true." And her last comment in the session echoes a comment from the analyst in an earlier session: "I agree, ya, we'll talk more about it."

A hypothesis about structure was becoming more fleshed out with detail: Mrs C was unable, in the analytic sessions in the first week and still in the eighth month, to leave the analyst without feeling that their link was threatened, and so she tried to compensate with compliance. Her "echoing" the analyst's "we'll talk more" represented *both* a taking in of the analyst's internal analytic setting *and* a resistance through compliance. Reflection on a parallel process at work in the groups' repeated worry about the "supportive" interventions indicated that unprocessed anxieties and primitive defences against them had created ongoing "structural problems", which were "at times predominant", and which needed "other kinds of intervention". A clinical narrative was developing that the split-off traumatic experiences suffered by the patient, which had led to the hospitalisations and the delusional ideas that she was "not taking care of the children", were projected into the analyst, were being processed by the groups, and would take more time to be worked on in the analysis.

However, at other times in the analysis, the analyst could facilitate the patient's ability to make contact with anxieties about impulses she had acted on, rather than felt or thought about, in the past.

> *A*: I think that when you are talking about this document, you are telling me something else too.
>
> *P*: My birth date is very significant, it's part of me. (Pause.) I sometimes have dreams about rebirth. I especially remember a dream from a long time ago: I go along a beach and there are white houses and I call my mother. I'm nervous about travelling . . . because of sexuality and because of identity . . . I'm afraid of being caught.

In response to the analyst's intervention (". . . you are telling me something else"), the patient brings the dream of the beach, and, in her associations, she expresses anxiety about travelling, sexuality, being "caught". The analyst's interpretation that the patient was addressing an internal situation led the patient to think of identity and rebirth and to bring the dream: "on a beach with white houses, I call my mother". In the context of the dream representing anxiety, Mrs C elaborates old anxieties about losing control sexually and losing her sense of self when she travels (when she had had a brief sexual encounter in the past).

The patient's tolerance for the disturbing feelings and anxieties in associations to the dream were a mark of progress in the analysis; it was a dream that was turning a page in Quinodoz's (2002) sense that the disturbing dream and associations indicate underlying transformations through the "return" of split-off parts of the self during a phase of integration. The anchor point linked the issue of the "supportive" interventions to questions about the patient's structural problems (which were predominant in early sessions). These questions could be held in mind by the groups in order to observe repetition and change, as the analyst's interventions focused less on continuity of the setting and more on the patient's aggression, sexuality, and anxiety. Both groups agreed that the sessions at the end of the second year showed a growing capacity for representation and symbolisation in the patient.

### *Level 3: what kinds of therapeutic action were at work in the changes observed in the patient and in the analytic process?*

Both the analyst and the groups responded to the Level 3 question: "What are the analyst's hypotheses about change at an explicit and implicit level that can be inferred as present in the work of the analyst? Have they changed along different moments of the analysis?"

At the end of the second year, the analyst felt some change in the patient's use of her own bodily and mental resources, in that the patient no longer gave up on herself and was able to do work without both members of the analytic couple fearing a collapse of the process. The analyst experienced the patient as starting to fight to get something out of life, as hungry and feral. As a result of significant deprivation in the patient's childhood, the analyst had felt a pull "to provide", but is recently more able to pull back. The analyst is afraid (and potentially angry) that the patient may decompensate, as if at a dangerous intersection, but it seems to the analyst that Mrs C is more able to discover parts of herself that have been unknown, especially her anger with her husband and with the analyst.

* * *

Questions from Level 3 were taken up: "What other hypotheses about the patient's problems and the way to work on them could be formulated from other theoretical or technical approaches? What are the more convincing and less convincing aspects of these different hypotheses and how could they be refined so that they better match the clinical material?"

The kinds of therapeutic action at work in the changes in the patient that were discussed in both groups indicated a many-faceted approach in the analyst's interventions, some of them implicit. The patient was observed to be capable of more regulation of impulses and with a stronger core self at the end of the second year of analysis. The analyst needed to contain the patient's projected anxiety in the psychotherapy, to bear the endless repetitive worries about details in her life and obsessional thinking. In the early sessions of the analysis, the analyst facilitated insight in the patient by naming her fears of loss of mind and loss of control, making these fears more conscious, which reduced somewhat the patient's impulsivity, and sexualisation of anxiety. The analyst facilitated some greater subject object differentiation through naming the patient's anger towards the analyst and towards the husband. The analysis of projections on to the husband of herself as "villain" also helped with subject object differentiation, although much difficulty in this area remained. The analysis of the patient's harsh superego, her over-responsibility and repetitive self-reproaches, helped to begin to make conscious what had been unconscious aggression at deprivation and loss. However, there was still much to do in the analysis concerning her tendency to self-reproach for not visiting her mother as a child, or for not caring for her children or for her classes, which defended against experiencing her own dangerous anger with her mother and disappointment in her father. The analyst's way of listening to the patient's stories about current external situations of danger as repetitions of traumatic situations of childhood and aggression, without interpreting this yet, was facilitating Mrs C's ability to bear more difficult affects. The transference was interpreted tactfully, which was leading to a greater closeness in the analysis, helping the patient to know her own mind better. The question of whether unconscious resistance to unbearable anxiety states lead to the supportive interventions remained open.

## *Conclusions*

Two clinical observation groups from the same local IPA society explored the "text of analytic sessions" from different phases of the analysis, with the analyst present and contributing in selecting the sessions, answering questions, and giving her ideas on therapeutic action. Over a period of fourteen hours of work, the groups of analysts from different theoretical backgrounds selected similar symptoms, inhibitions, and anxieties in the patient's functioning as key anchor points and made complementary observations about change and no change in the patient and in the analytic process.

The three-level model guided the groups to take three consecutive approaches to the material. At the first level, group members listen with floating attention to the derivatives of the unconscious in the patient and the process, they infer subtle changes in the patient's functioning in the sessions, "but without formulating them yet", and they make initial hypotheses about "the dynamic trends and changes session to session" (Fleming & Benedek, 1964). Approaching the material with Level 2 questions, participating psychoanalysts explore diagnostic questions posed in ordinary language to help "estimate the degree of resistance and anxiety in the patient", to develop "empathy with the patient's regressive state", to grasp "at the greatest possible depth, reactions of transference and countertransference", and to recognise "dynamic trends" in the changes in later sessions, in order to formulate change and absence of change in the patient. With Level 3 questions on therapeutic action, groups reflect on how the observed changes were facilitated, to make a set of formulations about the transformational processes rooted in the details of the session material.

The three-level model for observing patients' transformations did facilitate the discussions, which resulted in complementary reports, with verbatim sessions from three stages of the analysis, showing specific kinds of change and absence of change in a patient who had suffered severe neglect, danger, and traumatic loss as a child. I would like to thank the presenting analyst, the reporters, and the members of the groups for their excellent work.

## *Acknowledgements*

I wish to thank Dr Grifone for her excellent presentation of the history and verbatim sessions, for her participation in the groups in clarifying important questions, and for her generosity in agreeing (with her patient's consent) to permit publication of this chapter.

Analyst/presenter: Rose Grifone, PhD.

Group I: Reporters: Dan Traub-Werner, MD, Stephen Leibow, MD; Members: Don Carveth, PhD, Rose Grifone, PhD, Mary Stewart, MD, Alex Tarnopolsky, MD.

Group II Reporter: Doron Almagor, MD; Members: Cathy Carmichael, MD, Geraldine Fogarty, PhD, Rose Grifone, MD, Gavril Hercz, MD, Akbar Rajabi, MD, Jane Thurley, MD, Klaus Wiedermann, PhD.

## *References*

Baranger, M., Baranger, W., & Mom, J. (1983). Process and non-process in analytic work. *International Journal of Psychoanalysis, 64*: 1–15.

Faimberg, H. (1996). Listening to listening. *International Journal of Psychoanalysis, 77*: 667–677.

Fleming, J., & Benedek, T. (1964). Supervision. A method of teaching psychoanalysis—preliminary report. *Psychoanalytic Quarterly, 33*: 71–95.

Grinberg, L. (1990). *The Goals of Psychoanalysis: Identification, Identity, and Supervision*. London: Karnac.

Norman, J., & Salomonsson, B. (2006). "Le tissage des Pensees": Une methode pour presenter et commenter une materiel clinique psychanalytique dans un groupe de pairs. *L'Annee Psychanalytique International*, 141–159.

Quinodoz, J.-M. (2002). *Dreams That Turn Over a Page. Paradoxical Dreams in Psychoanalysis*. London: Routledge.

Reith, B. (Ed.) (2011). *Initiating Psychoanalysis: Perspectives*. London: Karnac.

Tuckett, D. (1993). Some thoughts on the presentation and discussion of the clinical material of psychoanalysis. *International Journal of Psychoanalysis, 74*: 1175–1189.

Tuckett, D. (2008). *Psychoanalysis Comparable & Incomparable: The Evolution of a Method to Describe and Compare Psychoanalytic Approaches*. London: Routledge.

# PART IV

# THE 3-LM: A CASE, REPORT, AND DISCUSSION

CHAPTER NINE

# Transformations in Paula with "no history"

*Michael Šebek*

When I was invited to present the case material by the IPA Project Committee on Clinical Observation and Testing in order to study transformations by using expert work groups and Ricardo Bernardi's three-level model for observing patient transformations (3-LM) in the IPA Congress in Prague 2013, I was very pleased to have this extraordinary possibility to discuss my work with many respected colleagues from different parts of the psychoanalytic world. As for this 3-LM, I had no experience with its application before.

I decided to present the case of Paula because, during the time of treatment, I was aware of several interesting changes but I had done no work on their systematic conceptual elaboration.

## *Paula*

Paula was thirty years old when she asked for the first visit, after being referred by a colleague. She has an inconspicuous appearance, no make-up, various grey colours in her dress, quiet voice, signs of scopophobia, not very talkative. She slowly said that her life is not "juicy", that somatic problems took away all remaining self-esteem, that she is single and is afraid of serious relations with men, in fact, with anybody. She feels she has no value, and that she is the main cause of her troubles. She often has the feeling that what she is telling is not "true", or as if someone else were speaking instead of her. She conveys that she has "no history", "no emotions", and that "nothing really serious" happened in her childhood with her mother, father, and two younger brothers: "I cannot really complain". Then she describes, without any recognisable emotion, the "automatic" feel of her life: journeys to work and back home, each day the same, no excitation, no sex, no pleasures. Furthermore, she does social work in the town department dealing with homeless people.

Her way of thinking reminds me at first of "operational thinking" in psychosomatic patients, or an "empty depression". My feelings in the countertransference evoke questions: does she need some "resuscitation", or is she fearful and keeping me at a distance through her negations: "nothing happened", "it has no meaning", "no content", etc.? Some picture is being uncovered: her ego is again and again severely pressured by a sadistic superego, or both psychic agencies are merging into a unified "no", as if all her objects were totalitarian and she was imprisoned, existing behind the wall—cut off from life. Her drives seemed to be inhibited, repressed, and re-somatised. Silent shame is experienced: she saw herself as "nothing". She formulated that she used to use a social façade (false-self) for her survival in everyday situations. Her sense of life as "automatic" reminded me of novels of the Czech writer Vladimír Páral. (In his novels, people live like automatons, in a stereotyped life, partly promiscuous, depressed in the communist Czechoslovakia of the 1950s and 1960s.)

## *Biography*

To get a sense of Paula's life history was, for a long time, just barely possible. She said that she was giving me (and herself) "pieces" of history.

The following text presents the rough outline of her biography as it emerged step by step from dozens of sessions. Some other aspects of her history emerge in the sessions presented here.

She had nearly no information about the developmental history of her parents. She said this was never really talked about in her family. Therefore, for example, she did not know anything about her parents' political attitudes towards, or engagement in, the communist regime. For the most part, she was not informed about the life of her grandparents. Her mother had a problem with her own mother (the patient's grandmother), probably a lack of empathy. The father's mother more or less hated the patient's mother. There were noisy conflicts between the parents, conflicts that were reported not to have existed before the children were born. Both parents were felt to be distant towards Paula. It was revealed that Paula did not remember any really intimate relations with her mother or her father. When she cried as a small girl, her father usually told her that it was wrong to cry, that it would not help anything. Mother mostly assumed a critical attitude towards her when she wanted to share her problems in childhood and, later, in adolescence. So, Paula learnt to keep a withdrawn attitude towards them. In her school years, she was aware of her tendency to be like a boy, and this feeling remained unchanged until her adulthood. The most intense erotic fantasies she remembered were expressed to her teacher in high school, who rejected her, and this was experienced with "enormous shame". As an adult, she always doubted she could be an interesting person for anyone. Once, she brought a memory of her seeing her father masturbating; it was in her parents' bedroom during the night—she was of school age. She was shocked. From about ten years old, she enjoyed taking care of her younger brothers. Her adolescent years seem to her to have been the worst: she could not form any good, deep relationships, either with men or with women, and she did not know why. She thinks it was her fault. She thinks that she never really fell in love with anybody. Sexual life is "dead" for her: no wishes, no real excitation, no pleasure. Despite all of this, some signs of hidden positive emotional life appeared: she reads books, she likes art—but she very rarely talks about this with anyone.

## *Therapy*

I hesitated somewhat to start therapy with Paula. I had a feeling that her destructiveness was too large, or that the wall behind which she was hidden, full of shame and anxiety, was too high. However, as early as in the first interviews, she had moments when some of her internal thoughts and feelings briefly emerged, and she appeared as very sensitive, vulnerable, fragile, and shy. Finally, she evoked in me some curiosity by hiding and defending herself so much. I had learnt immediately, from the first sessions, that I had to be very cautious but also active: to my silent listening, when it happened, she responded with helplessness, anxiety, and long silences caused (as she said) by feelings of emptiness and despair.

Paula was very afraid to come more than twice a week (later three times), and she could only overcome her anxiety after three years of a preparatory stage for psychoanalysis (her first session at four times a week is presented as the fourth clinical illustration/session). She was afraid of meeting me with "emptiness", and I was discovering that in her self there was operating something like a totalitarian and persecuting "mafia" taking away all images and feelings. Some sessions were nearly dead, as if sucked dry of any content. In the transference in the first months of therapy, she was convinced that I would throw her away as a "useless thing" because she was "not able to make any progress". This sadomasochistic constellation dominated for a long time in dozens of sessions, and, although it diminished, it never completely disappeared. If I was silent, she felt rejected, started to accuse herself of being a bad patient, and her self-esteem fell rapidly. After my first long vacation (three weeks), she felt destroyed, again "empty". She said she withdrew from "friends" (during the time I was not present), did not go to meet them, stayed alone, felt desperately helpless. She could connect this with my absence, and felt even worse, because "things like someone's vacations are quite normal, and she should be able to stand it . . . and obviously she is not, and she feels guilty and is ashamed". I thought it was a mixture of "a lost helpless small girl" (an oral deprivation?), and "an angry jealous response": the first was more conscious, and the second unconscious.

## *Sessions*

I present four sessions from different periods of treatment. The following one is from the beginning of the therapy. Paula preferred to use the couch (scopophobia). At that time, I knew little about her, and the session illustrates some difficulties of our work.

## *The third session, frequency twice a week*

She is on time, she looks a bit anxious, goes quickly to the couch.

*P*: [Silence of more than a minute.] I should say something but I do not know what . . . [silence]. I have no idea . . . [a long silence].

*T*: Maybe you are afraid of something.

*P*: Perhaps yes . . . [sigh], what terrifies me is that I look here like incompetent . . . unable, there is nothing really important that would make some sense. [It is difficult to hear her hushed voice.]

*T*: It looks as if something has lost importance and meaning . . .

*P*: . . . [silence]. Perhaps yes, I do not know. . . . I remember that when I got the illness, a year ago, I said, it is the end of life, there is no future for me . . . but I do not want to return to it [silence lasting some minutes]. But already, before that, I have been living an uninteresting life.

*T*: Uninteresting?

*P*: Nothing was happening, nothing that could interest anybody [silence again, I feel she keeps me behind a wall, but also invites my curiosity].

*T*: How did it happen that you think like this . . .?

*P*: I do not know . . . When I meet people I always try to be OK, at least I try to pretend that everything is OK. I try to adjust to their expectations . . . [saying this in a more lively way].

*T*: Also to my expectations?

*P*: Here, I should talk about myself, I am not used to . . . I do not know . . . [silence lasting 1–2 minutes] it is so awkward. It would be better to escape from here . . . [she looks at her watch].

*T*: In order to save yourself . . .

*P*: Yes . . . before you kick me out of here. You only waste your time with me.

*T*: It sounds as if you value your place here and you are afraid of losing it.

*P*: . . . Unfortunately this is true, but I do not want to be dependent on anybody.

*T*: Why?

*P*: All relations I have had . . . they were one big disappointment . . . [a silence] but it was also my fault, I am sure I have caused it myself. My behaviour was impossible, and it is difficult to understand me, what I am saying. I do not express myself well.

*T*: You said "all relations" . . .

*P*: My parents . . . I do not know if a disappointment is a correct expression, they are living their life and I live my life. But I was and am disappointed by my mum, I am not a good daughter to her, and she always saw my faults and mistakes. In the past few years, we practically never talk about anything important, she does not ask me, and I do not tell her how I live. And my father . . . He was never really interested in me [sigh, silence].

*T*: So, now I understand some of the difficulties you have here, when talking about yourself, with me.

*P*: But maybe all I am saying here is false, my fiction. It was all my fault, probably I was also not a good daughter. I was too distant to them . . . I was not telling mum my private things.

[End of the session.]

### *Session (the fifty-sixth, in the middle of the week, after eight months since the beginning of the treatment, still twice a week)*

This session was very surprising and moving. It was the second session after my return from holiday. She dared to reveal much more than ever before, and at the end of the session I was unusually flooded with her need for relatedness.

She was on time, as almost always, a bit nervous as always, went quickly to the couch, and assumed her somewhat defensive position with her hands on her belly.

*P*: I think I am here blundering between drawing near, and distancing . . . I can't get out of it, and I am very busy with my work, so no time for anything for myself, which enables me not to feel injured . . . I feel as if I am divided psychically, I am able to weep for a whole day, but I am able to talk myself into saying: "that's nonsense!—it is better to plan something!" . . . I feel overloaded by tasks and think that the best thing would be to run away somewhere . . . without having to return.

[Short silence.]

*T*: Aha [I think she will bring something more].

*P*: [Silence for about ten seconds.]

*T*: You have said, "to weep for the whole day" [it was the first time she had mentioned her weeping].

*P*: No, no, hahaha, there is nothing to weep for . . . I could probably explain it as fatigue, and overwork, distress, anxiety . . . nothing really serious, it does not move me when talking about it . . . [a silence]. I do not understand it much, it is a matter of "last time, it was better, or worse", so it is with me . . . As if I am out of control of it, but it is also possible it is an illusion, maybe it was not better earlier, and I do not remember . . .

*T*: Hmm, you have said "out of control" [in many sessions she stressed her urge to control herself and situations around her sessions involved this].

*P*: I am not as efficient as I used to be . . . less responsible, I cannot fulfil what is expected from me . . . I mean in my work; it is most visible there; I think it will be a disaster when somebody discovers what I am doing; I do not believe that I fulfil what I promise . . . [pause].

*T*: Can you give me some examples?

*P*: What comes to mind is this "Educational Association", I do not communicate with them, I do not reply to their emails . . . and also, if I plan to meet some of their people whom I know, for instance, one friend who wants to meet me, I cancel appointments, then I felt guilty because he likes me, but I cannot force myself to act differently . . . [pause].

*T*: How do you understand this?

*P*: What I would do with him, when we meet? . . . Before I was functioning in a way that met his expectations, I did not want to disappoint him . . . this has disappeared. I feel nothing will happen when I cancel or postpone the meeting. But I do not understand what is going on with me . . . and I am terrified, and it does not make any sense. I feel indifferent, I cannot explain why . . . and I cannot change it. The only fear I have is that people will give up on me, if I go on this way.

*T*: Fear of desolation?

*P*: Perhaps yes . . . it goes this way inevitably, and it terrifies me . . . [silence].

*T*: It seems to me, that in spite of all negation of the relevance of the outside world, you come here and you give some value to it.

*P*: I come here, but it might be slap-bang into the water . . . now I feel as if I have lied; maybe all that I say is some internal theatre and none of it is true.

*T*: It looks as if you see me now as if I were a judge, and not a person who can understand you when you do not understand yourself . . .

*P*: I would be glad if you could understand me when I am confused . . . I think I need assurance that all is going in the right direction here . . .

*T*: Yes, maybe it is similar to children who do not understand many things but they rely on parents that nothing bad will happen.

*P*: It would be so nice if it were so [a longer silence] . . . I guess here is the safest place I have felt anywhere, and at the same time I am terrified by it, I do not know why it is so [in a very quiet voice].

*T*: If your safety is in danger, there must be some cause . . .

*P*: (quietly) I think it is . . . you will travel somewhere and I will break down . . . and therefore I need the idea "all is indifferent to me" and, connected with this, I am aware how much there is nobody around me, many people but no one close, some people I have known for years . . . I play with them all the time, the same plays about safety that do not really exist. When I am talking now I have feeling that something is disappearing, I say one thing, and think another one. Is this intelligible?

*T*: You need to talk about me and it is dangerous in some way?

*P*: Yes, and instead of talking about you I talk about others . . . You know I have got an idea of death, fear of death: all is only borrowed in life . . . all is childish and naïve.

*T*: I think you feel something strong towards me, and you are afraid now about what to do with it; you see it as naïve and childish.

*P*: Yes, it is so and I am grateful to you that you understand it.

### *The 110th session (three times a week, after sixteen months since the beginning of the therapy)*

The slow process of getting more frequent sessions reflects her diminishing fear of closeness and growing capacity to share her mental contents with me.

The next session shows in a condensed (dream) way the huge difficulties she was facing.

*P*: I have the feeling you have come here because of me [she has seen me coming to my office from outside], I have been thinking of what you said last time. That I can share feelings only with somebody who suffers ... in this sense I have chosen a good profession. At least in this way I can have some proximity ... Feeling of loneliness, and distance ... It is permanent! I have believed that I functioned somehow, especially in my job ... finally I feel I am tired, but I am not working so much. So why do I complain? But what do I get from all this? I have depression, it is a poor life and I seek some escape from it. I have an idea that I have cyclic dreams about water ... [silence].

*T*: Was there one or more?

*P*: I have one, it is a more visual ... I seek something on an embankment of the river. Suddenly, I see a very big machine that regulates the flow of the river and a big fortification is created before my eyes. This wall is bigger than necessary. [Silence] ... In reality I would think that the wall is too big. The fact is that I am far from people, such a horrible distance.

*T*: Aha.

*P*: In the dream I go along the wall and I wonder where it will finish. But I am not active enough. I should be striving more. When I try it, it finishes as something empty. No results. [She then repeats some self-criticism about how she is impossible ...]

*T*: In your dream, you move ahead.

*P*: But with no results [again some stereotyped remarks on her inadequacy].

*T*: The severe judge inside of you is governing now, and you are afraid I see your "no results".

*P*: Yeah, I feel steadily that I should be different from what I am. All I do is useless. But maybe I am blowing this up. It may be not so serious ... Maybe nothing serious, no problem. My problems are worthless.

*T*: As you were not born "worthless", I think you have seen something like this in the behaviour of your parents to you?

*P*: I do not know, I did not complain to my parents but sometimes I was afraid of something, and both my parents were saying "do not be mad or stupid", but it was so seldom that I talked about myself. Right now, mum would say to me that she never had any fear, that she does not know what fear is, and she is proud of it. Therefore, she could not see my fear. I was afraid to be afraid, strange, isn't it? It is better not to show fear. In this I am a perfect psychosomatic. Instead of feeling afraid to go to school, I used to have infections and physical injuries . . . I am now lost . . . How did it happen I started to talk about this? [She is confused by losing her ego control.]

*T*: Someone can be ill but not anxious.

*P*: Yeah, illness is objective [now a longer silence].

*T*: What is in your mind now?

*P*: I am speaking about things that I never talked about with anyone, but there is probably no other way. I am standing behind the wall and I do not know if I am allowed to tell such things and if it is understandable. In the dream, I am seeking for something and I must find it on my side of the wall but I am not yet very far advanced in this. There is a feeling of estrangement between words and feelings. I am saying something and it is not fitting with what I intend to say. So, I am losing myself in it. In relationships with people I am without history, without a persona, I cannot imagine that somebody could be interested in me. And here I try to keep some façade to be acceptable for you. That in reality I am foecal, which I should not or cannot show.

*T*: Not being unbearable here for me, not being unbearable for mother and father

*P*: Yeah, something like this. So, I should finish, I think?

*T*: There is still about five minutes

*P*: I do not hurry, only again my guilt, I should not interfere with your time.

[She is getting up, looking at my face, smiling and saying] But I thank you really.

### *The first session in the psychoanalytic setting four times a week (after three years of treatment)*

I was surprised by her quick shift from the present to memories and a courageous act to show she can do it four times.

She is on time. She looks a bit tense, and she quickly looks at me before lying down.

*P*: Such a short time from yesterday's session that I could not be sure we had just changed the frequency ... I was thinking about what is really changing, I guess it will be more about the past than what is going on in present time [saying it cautiously].

*T*: Have you been afraid?

*P*: Yes, it is a change, I am uncertain how it will work out, I left earlier from my work, at 1.00 p.m., I hope my boss will not punish me ...

*T*: Why?

*P*: I work from 8.00 a.m. to 1.00 p.m., anyway I cannot work for a longer time. Concretely, today was terrible. I had three clients, all of them were talking about dead mothers; one of them, she had long-lasting conflicts with her mother, both parents then made suicide attempts, she was trying to save her mother after this ... all three clients have been getting worse in the last while, and I had to call the psychiatric service to help with them. Just a feeling that one must act! I think somewhere it touched me. And more, my feeling of helplessness again. After this work I am so tired, and my chief thinks I should work more. I should be an automaton ... I feel angry when thinking about it.

*T*: I guess you were touched when comparing your problems with your mum with similar problems in your clients?

*P*: Yes, it is about me, but I should have some distance from these clients; instead I am mixing their realities with mine. Yes, I remember. We have been talking for a year about rescuing mothers, or my mother. I mean what I have learnt from my mum is that daughters live in order to make the life of mothers happier [saying it with some bitterness]. By the way, the marriage of my parents was not worthwhile, the same with my three clients: their mothers were depressive, one lived on drugs, and the second consumed alcohol.

*T*: And your mother?

*P*: Not alcohol, but some drugs, painkillers, and her bad marriage—for many long years she was deciding whether to leave my father or to stay with him [I was hearing this from her for the first time in this verbal form], there was no outcome ... Now I am returning to it, my parents were quarrelling more and more when I was school age, and breaks between open conflicts were shorter and shorter ... it is possible they were fine with it ... I remember that somebody, I do not know who, said about them that they were like Italians, arguing in order to be able to sleep with each other afterwards. But it is a question as to whether they had a sexual life: I did not see it . . . And now I am getting a memory that once my mum told me that all their conflicts started after their children were born, me and my brothers. Before they had—she said—a peaceful life. I understand that around bringing up children there are more disputes, but it is difficult to say . . .

*T*: Hmm . . . [I am surprised by this unexpected flow of memories.]

*P*: Logically, I have been functioning as self-caring child who did not need anything. They did not help me with anything for school, I did everything alone—except twice they did act: once when I was thrown out of the specialised maths class, and a second time, when I was nearly kicked out of high school because of a bad mark in class. Otherwise, all went smoothly for me. Therefore, I have no history, nothing special I need to remember.

T: A silent, non-disturbing child with "no memory", as you often were in many previous sessions.

*P*: Yeah, but it was not my intention, I simply did it. My father was never really interested in me, so I wondered how I could disturb him . . . through some noise? Perhaps. And mother? She always felt overwhelmed, everything was too much for her . . . perhaps I was too anxious that my mother would totally break down when I tore my trousers somewhere outdoors. I think I learnt to make things up or hide things as much as possible. Only if it was already a big scrape, then I had to say something.

*T*: A big scrape?

*P*: There were not very many of them. Once a broken window in the school—I was in a big group of classmates. Then some parents in the school complained of the bullying of one classmate: it was a girl, I was only present there, passively watching it, but I did not help her. I do not know what my parents said or did—I think I was forbidden to go to the cinema for a couple of days? But the biggest punishment from my mum was—in some other situations when I was nasty or something—she stopped talking to me. But I think generally my parents had no problems with me, I was daughterly, obedient, because of my fear. No protest.

*T*: Maybe, because of fear you hid in your "no protest" . . .

*P*: I must agree, more and more during my school age I felt like a boy, or closer to a boy and the boys around. At home, I was obedient, but outdoors, on the streets I was much wilder, but sincerely I do not remember it very well. As it is often with me: I do not remember anything. Maybe I was a bit more lively at home also? I think all this started when I was in the first grade. I hated skirts, but when I was three years old—I saw my photo—I had a skirt. My mum went crazy because it was "trousers all the time". When I was in the fourth and fifth grades, I had my first girlfriends.

*T*: As "a boy" with an imaginary penis, could you feel stronger than your mother?

*P*: It was something like this. Generally, I was happier among boys, and probably I was less endangered by mum. I had a world of my own where mum had no power. It is still like that today. My mother was quite upset that I was boyish. I think that she was the same in her childhood—she grew up with boys, too. Therefore, maybe, she had been pressuring me to be more a girl, but mostly among people outside of the family—at home she was more tolerant about it. Being a girl, I can see I have trouble even up to the present. I know what I should do as a woman, but I do it with an effort. I must push myself. Then I feel like a puppet that is driven by something from outside. Once, when I was small, I did not want to go on some trip in the countryside. My father took up a rod of some sort, and he was pushing me with this stick to go ahead until he was satisfied that we had walked quite a long distance. Better not to recall it . . . but maybe I was also lazy.

*T*: As if to go ahead is connected with father's "rod", man's force . . . and at the same time to be a girl or woman, to be like a puppet.

*P*: Haha, this submission . . . I go where the rod is directing me . . . and in order to exclude a physical father I am holding this rod above myself, pushing myself, here is my identification with my father, the only problem is that I do not know where I am going.

*T*: It was your way, your direction in this session, your material directed me.

*P*: [silence] Aha . . . My thoughts are now that today I was not forced to go ahead. Yeah, we have more sessions now and nothing has happened since yesterday's session, so I need not go ahead, I have felt free to look back, it is not a father's "go ahead".

*T*: Yeah, but you had a fantasy at the beginning of the session that you could be punished by your chief—the father figure—for being on your own today.

*P*: Hopefully I will not be [saying it playfully].

* * *

So far, my data on which some inferences about transformations should be done are as follows.

I was very impressed by the discussion of the case material by all participants in the panel "Tracking transformations in a psychoanalytic process: unconscious and explicit" held at the IPA Prague Congress: Ricardo Bernardi, Margaret Ann Fitzpatrick-Hanly, Marianne Leuzinger-Bohleber, and Judy Kantrowitz.

Ricardo Bernardi stressed, in Level 1 (phenomenological descriptions), "the depth of Paula's inhibition of her mental and emotional life" and also her positive response to the analyst's listening and interventions. He brought to the foreground "the wall" in the dream and its symbolic meaning. In Level 2, he sees the changes in the experience of illness (from no history, no emotions, to awareness of her problems and herself), patterns of relationship (her parents and other people enter into her memories and experiences), conflicts and defences (from "nothing really serious happened in my life" to "I feel like a puppet"), and structural functions: mentalization, affect regulation, communication and symbolisation, and attachment (from no excitation, no sex, no pleasures, to more lively emotional and symbolic expressions). I fully agree with Bernardi's inferences about Levels 1 and 2.

Level 3 is more difficult to answer: is Paula suffering more from a structural deficit, or is she more a neurotic case with conflicts and oedipal problems? I had this question in mind after the initial interviews. During that time, she appeared as having more a personality disorder or being a psychosomatic case. Later, during the treatment, I gradually discovered some attachment traumas and object-relational traumas. Even later, the neurotic (conflict) aspects started to come more to the surface. This successively unfolded complexity documents how it is relevant not to stick to one or two initial theories about a patient and to retain an open mind, not only during the listening, but also with regard to inferences originating as second or third thoughts. Bernardi considers the "wall" in Paula's dream as a central symbol, condensing in a complex way Paula's individual difficulties, familial difficulties, and possibly socio-political or cultural difficulties, too. I agree with that. The wall as a symbol for Paula's individual difficulties seems to be the most easily proved. The existence of "wall" or "walls" in her real family can be clearly seen from Paula's references to it (e.g., poor or eruptive family communication). The socio-political meaning of the wall is more speculative in its nature, but I am convinced it is present in the culturally determined part of the collective unconscious in the Czech Republic (Šebek, 2013) as a consequence of the transgenerational historical experience with oppressive (totalitarian) regimes in Central Europe (Habsburg monarchy, Hitler's occupation of Czechoslovakia, forty years of communist régime). There were real walls such as the "iron curtain" and the Berlin Wall, information "walls", different ideological segregations and persecutions which were, step by step, introjected in the form of totalitarian objects and transmitted to descendents through families and other external influences (Šebek, 1996, 1998, 2013). Some defences against totalitarian objects consist of the false-self organisations and denial (Paula, and probably also her family, denied political issues). All these qualities are present in Paula's psychic organisation (severe superego transforming the self to "nothing", false self trying to behave and feel as if "I am all right", always ready to adjust to others).

Margaret Ann Fitzpatrick-Hanly concentrated on the clinical narrative, using anchor points for tracking change. For instance, she selected "she has no value, no history, no emotions" which I understood at the beginning of the therapy as a "work of the negative" (Green, 2001), or a sign of negative narcissism (Green, 1999). If it were destructively (compulsively) repeated or malignant during the course of the therapy, there would most probably be "no progress" or "no therapy" in the transference and in the reality. Although negations were repeated in Paula's sessions, it was not at all a mechanical process, but a creative one, in which libidinal and object redistributions were happening (see de M'Uzan, 2013). Fitzpatrick-Hanly puts it in these words: ". . . the history of her childhood emerges with liveliness: she wanted to make noise, to disturb her father, she remembers tearing her trousers. . . . Now we see emerging from denial, dissociation, and self-reproach a lively instinctual child . . ." Furthermore, Fitzpatrick-Hanly makes a connection between my "curiosity" in the countertransference and transference interpretations, and she demonstrates convincingly their effectiveness by using vignettes from the clinical material. I am aware that beyond those effects demonstrated by Fitzpatrick-Hanly, I used interpretative work very often more for building and protecting a very thin link with Paula, who was very afraid of silence as a sign of her inadequacy. As the work with Paula went on, I gradually became more aware that my interest (curiosity) in her, which she felt as something new for her (a new object), was a prerequisite of some transformative effect of my interpretations.

Paula was probably severely deprived of empathy in the course of her personality development, and this was underlined by Marianne Leuzinger-Bohleber in making the reference (regarding Paula) to the trauma model based on object relations and their collapse, resulting in the breakdown of internal communication. It corresponds with my initial feelings that Paula needed "resuscitation". Paula's feeling of total abandonment came to the surface in many sessions. Leuzinger-Bohleber's opinion of Paula's transformations suggests using the following categories: appearance, states of self, object relations, superego–ego–id, indicators for central unconscious fantasies and conflicts, and relationship with the analyst. Although Bernardi's and Fitzpatrick-Hanly's conceptualisations are slightly different, there is a significant convergence in their inferences about Paula's transformations on the basis of the clinical data. In their findings, thoughts, and hypotheses, I can also find my thoughts—some of them elaborated by what Leuzinger-Bohleber calls an "expert validation". Different conceptualisations of Paula's transformations are not conflicting, but enriching each other, adding specific insights and emphasis—as Judy Kantrowitz indicated: ". . . this method (3-LM) will help decrease theory wars".

Judy Kantrowitz wrote very thoughtful comments on the 3-LM, Paula's transformations, my analytic work, and contributions by Bernardi, Fitzpatrick-Hanly, and Leuzinger-Bohleber. She also stressed the role of the group in observing clinical data, especially the potential to appreciate complexities and nuances in the process and changes that are occurring. She is convinced that multiple theories can be explored "to see how well they are supported by data". However, she is afraid that studying only the analyst's theories—conscious or unconscious—is "intellectualising and distancing ourselves from how very personal analytic work is". The role of empathy, "some inchoate aspect of identification" of the analyst, "dimensions of the analyst's character and conflicts"—all this and more influences the development of the patient and the analytic stance. As for me, as the analyst, she refers to several levels of my approach and a variety of my real and possible theories, adding an important personal factor that helped me in the work with Paula. This interpretation of my approach is, for me, inevitably the most difficult to comment on, but I feel that some personal factors (Kantrowitz is right) helped me to create and keep a good working alliance with Paula.

Group reports based on work during the Prague IPA Congress are the second part of how my clinical case was observed.

Here, there is no space to go into detail about their reports. Therefore, only a brief summary is presented.

1. It is right to say there was a general agreement that Paula had become livelier, less anxious, less defensive, and started to symbolise and associate the present with the past. Briefly, libidinal revivification and redistribution regarding her internal objects can be described. Nevertheless, her aggressive impulses are still blocked, repressed, or denied, or directed to herself. Here is the analyst's task for the future.
2. Groups could find a positive relation between the analyst's actions-interpretations—and progress of the patient. Groups also observed, for instance, that the analyst served for Paula as some sort of new object in her life. Only one group concluded that the progress in the patient was caused more by the analyst's presence than his actions. This group had no opportunity to discuss the material with the analyst, and it seems to be an important fact. Some other groups indicated that discussion with the analyst in the group helped them better understand the patient and the analytic actions. Simply, pure texts are not enough.
3. Each group formulated Paula's transformations on the 3-LM in their specific way, thanks to different schools, different experiences, and also different languages. Generally, there were difficulties in finding a proper diagnostic (nomothetic) category (borderline organisation, post traumatic constellation, hysteric features, psychosomatic organisation, self-disorder), but there was general agreement on the idiosyncratic diagnosis: Paula is the patient with the "wall" as a central problem of her internal and also external world—"wall" entering the transference and the countertransference.
4. Although analysts in groups represented the international community, consisting of different schools, different analytical backgrounds, and different languages, there is a surprising convergence in their assessment of the analytical process (mostly positive), and of Paula's psychic changes and lasting problems not yet touched.

## *Conclusion*

The 3-LM seems to be a useful tool for assessment of the patient's changes in the analytical treatment. The possibility to work directly with narrative materials fits with the character of clinical psychoanalysis, and, therefore, it is a promising method in psychoanalytic research. In Paula's case, there was prevailing agreement regarding her psychic transformation, and discussions served mostly to expand and deepen our views of what was happening in this therapeutic process through the lenses of four sessions.

## *References*

De M'Uzan, M. (2013). The same and the identical. In: *Death and Identity* (pp. 3–15). London: Karnac.

Green, A. (1999). *The Work of the Negative*, A. Weller (Trans.). London: Free Association Books.

Green, A. (2001). *Life Narcissism Death Narcissism*, A.Weller (Trans.). London: Free Association Books.

Šebek, M. (1996). Fates of totalitarian objects. *International Forum of Psychoanalysis, 5*: 289–294.

Šebek, M. (1998). Posttotalitarian personality—old internal objects in a new situation. *Journal of the American Academy of Psychoanalysis, 26*: 295–309.

Šebek, M. (2013). Psychoanalyse in Tschechien. *Psyche – Z Psychoanal, 67*: 209–237.

CHAPTER TEN

# A report on Paula with "no history"

*Robert S. White*

## *Clinical observation*

August 2–3, 2013, Prague IPA Congress: Marina Altmann de Litvann, moderator; Robert White, reporter. The group consisted of analysts from Germany, the UK, the USA, and Lithuania. The two moderators were from the USA and Uruguay.

We used clinical material by the Czech psychoanalyst Michael Šebek. We examined four hours, the third hour of psychotherapy seen twice weekly, a session in the seventh month seen twice weekly, a session seen three times weekly at fourteen months, and the first session in four times per week psychoanalysis after three years.

The patient was a thirty-year-old unmarried Czech woman who had no emotion, no life, no sexual feelings. She worked as a social worker for the homeless. She is the oldest sibling and has two brothers. Both parents were reported to be distant to the patient. They fought often with each other. She did enjoy taking care of her younger brothers. She does not remember making any deep attachments with men or women; she has never fallen in love.

## *Level 1: phenomenological description of the transformations*

The group picked three anchor points from the first session:

1. No juice: a metaphor used by the patient to describe herself. It captured her sense of having no feelings, no pleasure, no erotic feelings. She was an automaton or a puppet hiding behind a façade.
2. No history: another self-description. She could not remember large parts of her history or only in vague "pieces". She lacked a narrative.
3. To be like a boy: a fantasy from early childhood and persisting into adulthood. She wore grey colours with no make-up. The analyst described her as "a lost, helpless small girl".

Many other anchor points are possible in this clinical material. Another group chose the automaton image. Paula "often has the feeling that what she is telling is not 'true', or as if someone else were speaking, instead of her". Another possibility is guilt: "It was all my fault, probably I was not a good daughter. I was too distant to them". Still another group chose the wall as a metaphor. This image comes from a dream in the third hour presented, but it is present in the analyst's mind from the beginning. The anchor points often overlap with each other. No juice and being an automaton, for example, could be separate anchor points or combined.

### *No juice*

#### *Session one*

In the beginning of the hour, she describes herself as "no idea", "incompetent", "lost importance and meaning", "end of life", and an "uninteresting life". She speaks in fragments with long pauses. She alludes to a global sense of terror. In the transference, she is wasting the time of the analyst, who will kick her out. She feels she is a disappointment. The picture is one of psychic numbness with a free-floating and undifferentiated feeling of terror.

#### *Session two*

She speaks of "weeping for the whole day", a first. She is terrified now that she cannot control her feelings. Later in the hour, she states "I come here but it might be slap-bang into the water". Now we have some juices flowing, water in her tears. She is now sad. The terror is now more focused, a fear of losing control of her emotions. The slap-bang into the water is not very clear, but hints at some unknown violence. At the end, surprisingly, she expresses gratefulness to the analyst, a larger change. There is a slight transformation: she can now be sad and anger is hinted at.

### *Session three*

She presents a dream. The very fact of dreaming represents a transformation in the ability to portray emotion. However, the dream is barren of feeling and no person other than herself appears. In the dream, she is on the embankment of a river. There is a very big machine that regulates the flow of the river. Here we have even more juice, which must be regulated and controlled. Later in the hour, she reveals fear, "afraid to be afraid". She was afraid to go to school. In speaking of whether anyone might be interested in her, she is "faecal". All of these appear to be elaborations of affects not seen before, fear rather than terror, a river of juice, full of bad faecal smells. These represent positive transformations of affect. Yet, there is also the persistent negation of these affects: "I seek some escape from it", "it finishes as something empty", "all I do is useless" or "my problems are worthless". This persistent negative remains unchanged.

### *Session four*

She brings up a problem from work and reveals concern for her women clients. She feels "touched". Thinking of her tendency to be an automaton, "I feel angry when thinking about it". In speaking of her parents, she brings up the possibility of a "sexual life". She reveals she can be happier among boys, where she could be "wilder". At the end of the hour, the analyst notes a playful interchange. Affects continue to transform, now allowing hints of eroticism, aggression, and energy. However, the persistent negative remains untransformed, a "silent non-disturbing child with no memory" or "I feel like a puppet".

## *No history*

### *Session one*

She brings up her parents but there is no life, no detail in their images. She emphasised their disappointment in her. This is also enacted with the analyst; he will be disappointed and feel he is wasting his time.

### *Session two*

There is no mention of any history but it continues to be enacted. She is being "slapped", "judged", abandoned by the analyst, and "break[s] down", "no one close", and "disappearing". This seems to hint at some trauma. There is no transformation at this point.

### *Session three*

She talks about her parents. Her mother denies that she has any fear, so could not see the fear of her daughter. It is also enacted in talking to the analyst about things never talked about before. The negative continues to be enacted; she is interfering with his time. She again says she is "without history". There is a slight transformation in slowly revealing some details about her parents, but no transformation in the negative.

### *Session four*

She has more of a focus on her parents. Daughters live in order to make mothers happy. Her parents' marriage was not good and the children were blamed. Her mother used drugs and painkillers. She wonders if they had a sex life. She was a self-caring child. Her mother was always overwhelmed and she was anxious that her mother would break down. Her mother would punish her by not talking to her. Her mother did not like her playing with the boys, but the patient suspects mother was similar in her youth. For the first time, she brings up her father. She had a memory of father pushing her with a stick when she did not want to go on a trip in the countryside. Here we have a greater transformation, with much more detail. But the negative remains; she is a puppet or she does not know where she is going. The intensity of the negative does seem somewhat reduced—a small transformation.

### *A tendency to be like a boy*

#### *Session one*

She dresses in grey colours, with no make-up. There are several references to not being a good daughter.

#### *Session two*

There are no references to gender.

#### *Session three*

She has a dream in which there is a very big machine that regulates the flow of the river. It has the feel of a phallic symbol. She does not associate to this and there are no overt references to gender.

#### *Session four*

Suddenly, this becomes an alive issue. Daughters live to make their mothers happy. During her school years, she felt like a boy, or closer to a boy. Boys were associated with wildness and independence from mother. She remembered hating skirts and her mother's objections to trousers. "I was happier among boys." "I had a world of my own where mum had no power." She thought that her mum may have had similar boyish tendencies and thus was pressuring her to be a girl. She does not know what to do as a girl. There is again the image of a puppet. She had a memory of father pushing her with a rod to make her go ahead. Here, she reveals that her masculine side hides her energy, her rebellion, and her phallicness. The feminine is passive, submissive, and pulled by others.

## *Level 2: identification of the main diagnostic dimensions of change*

Given the time constraints of the group, it is usually not possible to use all the dimensions in any depth. The group must then choose to concentrate on those dimensions that seem more relative to the clinical case. In this case, we concentrated on structural aspects of mental functioning and type of disorder.

### *Perception of self and others*

In the first session, she presents herself as having no self, no affects, nothing inside. All is colourless. Likewise, she mentions no identifiable persons. She mentions her parents briefly, but they have no characteristics, no life. There is a very gradual transformation in the hours presented. While she is quick to negate herself or hide behind a false self, more details appear. In the second session, a man is interested in her and she runs away. She can start to feel dependent on the analyst. In the third session, she has a dream in which there is a large wall that leads to estrangement. She keeps herself hidden behind the wall. There continues to be very little reference to others. In the fourth session, she can describe her clients who have their own difficulties. She is worried that she mixes up her own conflicts with theirs. Her parents take on personality for the first time. Her mother is unhappy; her father pushed her to take a trip. She mentions her brothers for the first time. Her mother has a past. She has a wild side that she keeps hidden. So, by this point, we are starting to see self and object transformations, at the very beginning stages. Transformation of affects are similar. From the deadness of the first session, we traced the metaphor of juiciness. Gradually, affects appear: sadness, anger, gratefulness, empathy for others. She can hint at sexuality. Terror becomes fear of particular objects. She can now empathise with her female clients. There is some recognition that mother had her own difficulties. Integration with split states remains lacking. She can still swing from more differentiated affects and self-representations to the dead and empty state. She still has little sense of a self-directed life and the metaphor of the puppet still predominates. While she can begin to dream, the dream itself is mechanical and devoid of living objects.

### *Affective regulation*

In the beginning, there are no affects except a global terror. There is no sexual pleasure. It is better not to think about it. Relationships do not seem to exist. In the subsequent hours, affects emerge. Now there is the fear of being overwhelmed. So, control and dyscontrol become issues. She is weeping too much. She can move from global terror to a specific fear of deletion or abandonment. She is not yet at the stage where she can provide any self-security under pressure. If her analyst abandons her, she will break down. There is no mention of any personal relationship, except to flee from.

### *Internal and external communication*

We do see the beginning of dialogue with the analyst. There are several moments where she expresses gratitude. She is afraid of his abandonment and her dependency on him. A playful quality can appear. There is no indication of communication with anyone outside of the dyad.

### *Attachment with internal and external objects*

Any bonds with internal or external objects remain tenuous and fleeting. She fears abandonment, so quickly detaches and resumes a dead and detached defence against attachment. Much of this is not verbalised, but enacted in the transference. She appears largely incapable of starting new attachments and quickly severs any attachment interest of others. She is now showing the beginning of anger when she feels abandoned. With her parents, there appears the repetition of a deep attachment to terrible and abandoning objects. There is no sense of a third.

## *Type of disorder*

She appears to operate at a borderline level of organisation. Splitting and paranoid defences predominate. There is no evidence of psychotic functioning but she has a great fear of dissolution. Her personality type is best characterised as chronic trauma (PTSD).

She has the psychic numbing so characteristic of trauma, without the sensory disturbances (flashbacks, intrusive memories, visual disturbances). One might speculate that as she emerges from the deadened state, more of these disturbances may appear. Others in the group would characterise her as a developmental arrest or early attachment disorder. The analyst states that she operates at operational thinking.

## *Level 3: testing of explanatory hypotheses of change*

### *Therapeutic focus*

In the first hour, the analyst has a number of foci: affects, the here and now, references to transference and defence, and containment. He stays very close to the material. Most of his interventions are clarifications. He is interested in moving from global terror to fear of specific objects. For example, at the very beginning, he states, "Maybe you are afraid of something" and followed that up with, "It looks as if something has lost importance and meaning". Much of his work is to clarify which feelings belong to which person. This is summed up as: "So, now I understand some of the difficulties you have here, when talking about yourself, with me." The emphasis is in the separation of you and me. He is sensitive to awareness of his countertransference reactions, for example, when he notes to himself : "I feel she keeps me behind the wall, but also invites my curiosity."

The second session is seven months later. He starts with a similar focus on affects and clarifications. Then, he starts to tie together split-off states: "It seems to me, that in spite of all the negation of the relevance of the outside world, you come here and you give some value to it." Then his next intervention: "It looks as if you see me now as if I were a judge, and not a person who can understand you when you do not understand yourself." Finally, "I think you feel something strong toward me, and you are afraid now about what to do with it; you see it as naïve and childish." Now there is stronger push to transference and interpretation of unconscious fantasy. He is moving from a deficit model to a conflict model.

The third hour is fourteen months after the second hour. The patient brings in an important dream. The analyst then states, "The severe judge inside of you is governing now, and you are afraid I see your 'no results'." A little later, the analyst offers a construction: "As you are not born 'worthless', I think you have seen something like this in the behaviour of your parents to you." The patient brings up the estrangement between words and feelings, which continues to be a persistent focus. The patient can respond with much more detail about her guilt and feeling unacceptable. She thinks of herself as "faecal". The analyst then states, "Not being unbearable here for me, not being unbearable for mother and father." What we see in this hour is much more detail from the patient and her ability to talk about guilt. The analyst continues to point out transference and make interpretative statements.

The fourth hour is two years after the third hour, her first in a psychoanalytic setting. The patient brings in a number of new childhood memories. The analyst makes a transference interpretation: "A silent, non-disturbing child with 'no memory', as you often were in many previous sessions." She gives more history about feeling like a boy, then the analyst asks, "as a 'boy' with an imaginary penis, you could feel stronger than your mother?" The group found this a jarring interpretation, adding the imaginary penis, which seems unnecessarily theoretical and not supported by the clinical material. However, the patient seems to accept the interpretation and goes on with more material about femininity. As a woman, she feels like a puppet, driven from the outside. She uses a rod in describing her father and the analyst picks up on this metaphor: "as if to go ahead is connected with father's rod, man's force, and at the same time to be a girl or woman, to be like a puppet." Here we see the first focus on sexuality and the attempt to connect split off states.

### *Change in therapeutic focus*

In the first hour, the patient presents herself mainly in a deficit mode. The analyst works on very basic foci: attachment and non-attachment to the analyst, clarification of who feels what, and containment of terrifying affects. By the second hour, there is a marked change. Psychic conflict has appeared; now there are references to guilt and fear of infantile needs. There are more overt references to transference and attachment to the analyst. The global terrors can now be talked about as specific fears. By the third hour, the therapeutic focus remains the same, interest in transference, superego conflict. We see the first interpretation of a construction. What has changed is the level of detail that both patient and analyst bring to the discussion. In the fourth hour, the analyst makes his first sexual interpretation and the patient responds with material about her wish/fear not to be a girl.

### *Explicit and implicit models of the analyst*

The emphasis is on conflict of wish and defence, using the structural model (superego), staying close to the surface of the clinical material, use of constructions and carefully bringing up transference when it is in the preconscious. This speaks to a basic Freudian model. Attention to split-off states may speak of a Kleinian influence and the need to contain terror may speak of a Bionian influence. The group agreed that the analyst was working in an analytic frame from the beginning of treatment, even at twice weekly.

### *Change in models*

The most marked change was between the first and second hours. The first hour had a focus on containment and differentiation, working in a deficit mode, while the other hours were working in a conflict mode. Guilt, infantile dependence, and sexuality come into play in the analysis. The analyst uses a consistent model in these last three hours.

### *Other hypotheses and possible interpretative strategies*

Attachment theory—this would focus on her fear of attachment and the style of defending against attachment. This is certainly present in the material, but would seem to ignore many other rich developmental lines.

Object relations theory—this would focus more closely on the here and now transference and highlight aggressive derivatives and regression into paranoid states. This, too, is present in the material, but would go in a different direction than the present analysis.

New object theory—at times, the analyst does seem to offer himself as a new object. In the second hour: "Yes, maybe it is similar to children who do not understand many things but they rely on parents that nothing bad will happen", inferring that she can rely on him. In the third hour, he says, "Not being unbearable here for me, not being unbearable for mother and father", suggesting that he will be a better object than her family.

*CHAPTER ELEVEN*

# Discussion of Paula with "no history"

*Judy Kantrowitz*

Before this conference, I never participated in the groups that have been studying the transformational process. I was invited as an outsider to bring a perspective that might be different from those who have been immersed in the process. Both Marvin Hurvich and Margaret Ann Fitzpatrick-Hanly took time to explain to me what they were doing. At first, I was very doubtful that I could offer anything. I was admiring of the careful work they had done in constructing this project. I read Ricardo Bernardi's excellent chapter summarising the project. In the course of reading it, I had two thoughts. (1) Wasn't the initial interview time apt to be more structured, less likely to lead to free association, and so look better organised? (2) The fact that the analyst selected the material to be observed made the group totally dependent on which material the analyst chose. Might other hours offer a very different view? By the end of the chapter, Ricardo had cited both these factors as limitations in the method. It was only when I read the clinical material provided by Michael Šebek that I could find any place to expand on what this very sophisticated group of clinician–researchers already appreciate. If there is any contribution I can make to this project, I think it will be in expanding what can be revealed about the analyst in relation to the patient.

I begin my discussion by briefly talking about the project. Then I highlight how each of the discussants used Michael Šebek's case to illustrate the process. Finally, I present what I have seen that is not included in their descriptions.

## *The project*

Increasingly, the world outside of psychoanalysis asks us to be accountable in providing data to document progress in the work we do with our patients. However, most research methods are not suited to studying changes that can occur in psychoanalysis. For many years, what researchers primarily did was measure what was measurable, not capturing the aspect of treatments that were specifically psychoanalytic. Marianne Leuzinger-Bohleber has addressed this issue and stressed the importance of projects that study narrative material. I completely agree. Tracking transformation in psychoanalysis, I believe, is a method that can systematically trace change. It asks us to conceptualise the problem from the standpoint of the particular patient. What is the patient struggling with? This question is not posed at a level of theory, but, rather, at the level of observed phenomena. The patient is his or her own baseline. The model asks that we avoid jargon and document our perceptions with data from the sessions. It is theory neutral.

How do we know whether there is change? We understand that there needs to be evidence, but what kind of evidence? Too often, the answer to this question becomes polarised as life changes *vs.* analytic changes. One of the strengths of the current model is that it does not make this kind of choice necessary. It asks for evidence of change in the patient's life: in relationships, intimate, familial, and social, in work and leisure activities, in interests and creativity, and in symptoms and sense of well-being, not one's impressions or inferences, but using actual quotes from the patient's material, comparing them over time to support the presence of positive change, no change, or deterioration. Such changes are dimensions that we would consider in relation to every patient, though not every area would be the reason for their distress. These are the kinds of data we call life changes, the kinds of changes that people outside of our profession understand. Nevertheless, we, as analysts, are also specifically interested in psychic change. We believe that internal and external changes are related.

I wonder why the group has chosen to call these changes "transformations". What do they mean by this word? How is transformation different from change? Transformation sounds like a very big idea. Something structural? Unconscious? How is this manifest in the material? What criteria do we use to infer that this has occurred? These questions seem related to some of the project's aims. We care about these changes, and we also care about understanding how and why changes occur, if and when they do, for a given patient. I think we need to remain as clear as possible when our observations can be agreed to demonstrate internal change and when we are using data to support *inferences*. I think it is possible to agree about change, but transformation—if something bigger is meant—I think it will remain an inference, unless we can define what it means more precisely and provide clinical evidence to document that it has occurred.

A particular strength of this project is introducing the role of a group. It is a method that provides validation of the psychoanalytic work. The participants stimulate each other, expanding and deepening ideas. What we are able to see when we talk to each other is always more than when we work by ourselves. The participants may each perceive what transpires and what is the vehicle of change somewhat differently, focusing on different aspects of the material. These emphases do not need to be viewed as contradictory, though they might be, but they are also probably additive. A group process is likely to result in a greater appreciation of complexity and nuance in the process and changes that are occurring. Similarly, multiple theories can be explored to see how well they are supported by data. Often, these, too, need not be either/or choices. Many of us believe in partial theories. Perhaps this method will help to decrease theory wars.

To return to the specificity of this patient with this analyst: change can be perceived in Paula's increased availability of affect, while, for a patient who began by being flooded with affect, the change could be increased containment. The idea that Paula erected a wall to protect herself from being flooded is an inference; her inability to express affect, her emptiness and shutting herself down with self-criticism are data. By having four points of observation spread over time, we can observe if there is change and in what direction. We pick the dimensions we observe based on our original understanding of the patient's difficulties. Ricardo Bernardi has beautifully illustrated this process. Paula's depth of inhibition of mental and affective life are presented in the initial material and then tracked over the three subsequent points in time. Using Paula's words in the sessions, he traces where change has occurred. His conclusion that her experience of her illness is the best indicator of change is amply supported with illustrations of her expanded mental and affective content. The "wall" is lowered. Her increased ability to share these contents with her analyst indicates less fear of closeness with him, an indication of internal change. The markers of change are related, but he illustrates which aspects have developed most, as well as which do not so far have a sufficient indication of change. Note well, he does *not* make inferences. He uses data to support his conclusions.

Then there is the question of the patient's use of the analyst's interventions. Margaret Ann Fitzpatrick-Hanly skilfully traces Michael Šebek's work with Paula's transference: for example, his initial intervention, "My expectations", opens up expression of her fears of rejection and "indirect rebellion to trying" to communicate; in the second section, his saying, "See me as a judge, not someone who can understand"; "your safety is in danger" leads to increased openness with her acknowledging her fear of dependency as well as her wish to feel safe with her analyst and understood by him. The third section, where Šebek's saying "not being unbearable to me, not being unbearable to mother or father", stimulates "an unbearable contrast" for Paula, and yet she can take in how he is different and acknowledge this by thanking him. As she begins analysis, through his describing Paula as "a silent, non-disturbing child with 'no memory,' as you often were in many sessions", he links her behaviour in the past and her behaviour with him, facilitating her exploring these childhood memories.

Marianne Leuzinger-Bohleber gives an overview of this project in relation to clinical research, then traces changes in Paula and focuses on the changes concerning her traumatisation. Trauma is evidenced in absence: the empty circle, black hole, robot state, no memory. She identifies an attachment trauma and one that is transgenerationally transmitted. She shows how Šebek has carefully approached her "wall of trauma, understood and empathised with her, leading to evidence of her being on her way to a separate life and identity". She compares two models of trauma, the psycho-economic arousal and anxiety that cannot be contained and an object relations model in which both internal object relations and internal communication break down, resulting in an ability to integrate trauma through narrative, and she wisely concludes we need both theories. If a narrative can be restored, as has occurred, do we consider this structural change? Is this what is meant by transformation? Do we think of dissociation as representing an unconscious? Preconscious? Or a walled-off, separate conscious state? An unformulated experience? No question, if we bring parts together, no matter why they have been apart, something significant has changed. However, are we closer to knowing which theory fits?

Using the patient's and analyst's words in the session, each of the panelists has noted and connected the changes in Paula related to Šebek's interventions. They make explicit the positive changes that occurred in her increased openness with her analyst. Fitzpatrick-Hanly and Bernardi note how she remains self-critical, frightened of relationships, and Fitzpatrick-Hanly highlights her enormous, still unrecognised, fear of her own aggressive impulses that she has turned on herself; I would add that she has projected, thereby exacerbating her fear. Leuzinger-Bohleber illustrates Paula's increased ability to use narrative while noting that many areas, for example, her sexuality, have not yet emerged as a focus for her attention.

A third question: what has informed the analyst's interventions? What theory is the analyst using, explicitly or unconsciously? Can we discern this from what is said or not said? Can we connect changes, positive or negative, to the theories that the analyst is employing? Here I would ask: is it only theory, explicit or unconscious, that informs the analyst's interventions? While we hope a theory is selected because it fits the patient's problems, when analysts ally themselves with a particular theory overall, I think it is often related to something personal. Theories might serve as a kind of self-supervision—seeking something that compensates for a personal proclivity: for example, for a stance that might be too close or too distant, or theories might serve to support personal values or beliefs. Theories can alert us to things we do not automatically perceive and so are very useful to expand our work. However, I do not think theories are just theories. They are filtered through who we are as people.

You have all had a chance to read Šebek's sensitive and complex work with Paula. He enables us to understand what he is doing through his elaboration of his thoughts and feelings as, and after, he listens to her. He begins each of the four sections by alerting us to what he has found most compelling about the current session. After his first meeting with Paula, he offers many possible theories about the nature of her difficulties. All of them seem relevant and plausible. In the hours, it is possible to trace how his theories inform his interventions. However, the same theories that he described could lead to very different interventions. For example, he notes that sadomasochistic conflicts are present throughout the treatment. Early on, he notes to Paula how she anticipates demands and rejection while letting her know he understands her feeling of lack of safety. In the second session, he interprets her seeing him as a judge, but simultaneously offers her an alternative view, "a person who understands you", and later he indicates that her self-criticism is not innate, but learnt based on her understanding of her parents' behaviour that she assumed indicated how they saw her. Each time, he points to her self-criticism, but also simultaneously offers his understanding of why this is her view, so his observation is not itself experienced as criticism of how she reacts. The effect on her might be very different if he did not join his interpretation with his empathic understanding. Only in the fourth example, when she is out from behind the wall, explicitly anticipating criticism from another in current reality and talking about memories of being criticised in the past, does he address it directly as her "fantasy of being punished". His choices reflect his clinical sensitivity to her "silent shame" that has resulted in negation of all aspects herself and created a protective distance between herself and others. His interventions suggest he sees different levels. The negation, being behind a wall, and "silent shame" are the surface. How Paula consciously perceives herself, or the aspects of herself, which can easily become conscious, is where he starts. Her responses are confirmatory. He is a sensitive, talented analyst, patient and able to address her material in a way that does not frighten or shame this young woman who has become terrified of interactions with others, believing she can only expect criticism and ultimately disappointment if she lets herself care about another. He not only interprets her transference, he offers himself as what Hans Loewald calls "a new object", one who understands and provides empathy.

The group asks whether the analyst's interventions are formed by explicit or unconscious theories. I would say that it is not only theory that informs what an analyst does. Dimensions of the analyst's character and conflicts also influence his analytic stance, how close or distant he is, the sensitivity in his wordings, his timing of interventions, non-verbal communication, which is harder to appreciate from a transcription or summary of hours, but all of which are also influenced by what the particular character and conflicts of the patient stir in him. Of course, we do not know anything about Dr Šebek apart from what he tells us about how he thinks and works with this patient. Maybe what I will point to is what others are labelling unconscious theories, but I think of this as something much less cerebral.

Let us start with why he decides to treat Paula. He sees "her destructiveness [as] too big" or the wall to hide her shame and anxiety "too high". Yet, he saw in moments that some internal thoughts and feelings emerged "and she appeared as very sensitive, vulnerable, fragile, and shy". This latter perception could be a further caution for some about taking her into treatment, but it is not for Dr Šebek. He says she has stimulated his curiosity. He quickly realises he needs to be cautious, but active, or she will retreat to "emptiness and despair". He also indicates his awareness of his countertransference feeling that she needs "resuscitation". This way of describing his feelings seemed to mirror the patient's affect distancing. It is a contrast to what I have described about how close his words stay to her affect state. In the actual work, Šebek is not distant. So, how can we understand this? I think he lets us see that he can resonate with her need for distance, that he viscerally, as well as intellectually, has a feel for her state. We see how he is able to stay in contact with her, facilitating ever greater availability of her affect through his empathy, patience, and kindness, a willingness to go slowly, adjust his pace to hers, while gently leading her forward.

All of that is illustrated in the work, but I want to point to something he shows but is not specifically addressed. He recognises the places for access to her adaptive functioning, places where she has not retreated so totally. He notes, "she reads books, she likes art." Dr Šebek indicates he reads novels, too. Her "automatic life" has made him think of the novels of Vladimír Páral. They share an appreciation of representations of affect and conflict in art, a place where there can be recognition and resonance, but where it does not become too close or directly personal. We can see how he uses this awareness by working in displacement with her on many occasions. Over time, it can be acknowledged that what she is talking about is herself, and what she is feeling with Dr Šebek. His timing in helping her express her feelings in the transference indicates an exquisite attunement to her readiness to expose them. Similarly, his attunement to Paula's adaptive aspects are evidenced as he focuses on each forward step that she takes. Aware that she is frightened of being hurt and disappointed by how she is responded to, he highlights progressive steps that she can see as her own, such as in the last hour, when Dr Šebek notes that she, not he, has directed the course of the session, and she had introduced a fantasy about something that might happen in the present, not just focused on the past. He helps her see her strengths. Is this something Dr Šebek would do with every patient? Maybe, but I suspect it is also specifically a response to this patient and recognition of her need to experience someone recognising something positive about her. Is that an unconscious theory? Possibly, but I think it is also something more personal—something about Dr Šebek that is able to facilitate Paula's development, some inchoate aspect of identification that enables him to do this beautiful piece of work leading to a positive change in a very fragile, frightened woman. By calling what we unintentionally reveal in our work unconscious theories, I think we are intellectualising and distancing ourselves from how very personal analytic work is, from how much we use aspects of our personal selves that we have learnt to hone and contain, but that make what we each do as specific as that which each patient brings, as well as being influenced by the particular patient. Observation of this interdigitation between the characteristics of patient and analyst and its influence on facilitating or impeding the process of change is another variable to track.

# PART V

# CLINICAL CONCEPTS

CHAPTER TWELVE

# Some reflections on the three-level model: organising psychoanalytic knowledge through clinical observations and generalisations

*Marvin Hurvich*

The chapter begins with some preliminary comparisons between the three-level model (3-LM) and the key sources from which it was constructed: the *Diagnostic and Statistical Manual for Mental Disorders* (*DSM*) (American Psychiatric Association, 2013), the *Psychodynamic Diagnostic Manual* (PDM Task Force, 2006) and the *Operationalized Psychodynamic Diagnosis* (*OPD*-2) (OPD Task Force, 2008). Then the Prague contributions of Manfred Cierpka and Donna Bender are summarised. The question is raised as to how the 3-LM findings are being organised, and how this relates to methodological issues, especially, reliability and validity. Finally, the issue of definition of variables is illustrated, focusing on the concept of transformation, utilising a propositional method, to be described below.

A central goal of the *PDM*, accurately described as a "work in progress", was to provide a more clinically serviceable classification system. This was an alternative to the narrower, atheoretical, symptom/descriptive approach of the *DSM*. The *PDM* presents personality patterns and disorders as the *first* axis/dimension, while symptom patterns, the S axis, as the *third*. This reverses the *DSM* priority, which heavily emphasises symptoms over personality factors.

While following the descriptive nomenclature of the *DSM*, the *PDM* authors also introduced a *subjective* dimension that includes both clinical vignettes and vivid depictions of how patients experience their symptoms. Bernardi and his group (of which I was a member) likewise began with the patients' subjective experience as the first level of the 3-LM.

*PDM* additionally includes an axis on mental functioning, which is based on psychostructural components. These have most frequently been referred to as ego and superego functions, which are central to psychic structure and structural change, and consist of adaptive, defensive, and organisational components. They are anchored to clinical manifestations and fit into the 3-LM at Levels 2 and 3. The *PDM* includes additional important sections, such as conceptual and research foundations for a psychodynamically based classification system of mental health disorders. This critical component merits a consideration of its own, but cannot be directly addressed here.

The *OPD-2* is a detailed, psychodynamically based, operationally defined guide for diagnosis, treatment, and research, which also highlights both subjective experience and structural considerations. The five axes of the *OPD* multi-axes system are: Experience of the illness and Prerequisites for Treatment, Interpersonal Relations, Conflict, Structure, and Mental and Psychosomatic Disorders. The authors have worked out Focus Selection and Treatment Planning, Change Measurement, and much more.

The 3-LM is a clinical guide which facilitates tracking the psychoanalytic process from the perspective of change on three levels: (1) the patient's experiential vantage; (2) identification of the main diagnostic dimensions of change; (3) elaboration on the explanatory hypotheses of change as formulated by psychoanalytic theorists. The 3-LM centres on change/transformation for the patient over the course of the analysis, with two guiding foci: an *anchor point*, describing problem areas and diagnostic/dynamically related dimensions that can be discerned early in analysis, and a *transformation point* which reflects a change in the earlier anchor point. Illustrations and questions were developed and adapted from the other instruments to orientate an evaluator in formulating these changes, and exploring their underpinnings.

In developing the 3-LM, the operative strategy was to begin studying individual cases, leaving definitions of change and their relation to transformation relatively open and unelaborated, while accumulating clinical data, and offering clinical guidelines that would particularise these issues. This inductive approach was expected to allow the clinical data organised through the 3-LM criteria to highlight what was changing, and what factors were associated with it. Colleagues who had the opportunity to attend one of the 3-LM clinical workshops reported that they were especially clinically rich, while transformations regarding relevant areas of change were being noted, explored, and summarised.

Ricardo Bernardi, Chair of the Prague Congress Panel, "Observing transformations in patients: the assessment of mental functioning", invited Manfred Cierpka and Donna Bender, major contributors to the *OPD-2* and to the *DSM-5* Personality and Personality Disorders Work Group, respectively, as well as myself, to participate on the panel.

Cierpka's contribution to the symposium was titled, "Operationalising structural change based on the *OPD-2*". He described how the *OPD* group has recently developed an instrument that delineates four levels of differentiation and integration criteria which allows a mapping of levels of personality functioning on to the defined levels of structural integration. The instrument is called the Levels of Structural Integration Scale (LSIS). In his report of a study on structural change, findings were that at the end of treatment, patients valued positive alterations in their symptoms and in their interpersonal difficulties. However, in later follow-up evaluations, the patients' emphasis was on structural change. The latter was assessed with the Heidelberg Structural Change Scale (Grande et al., 2006, 2009), which evaluates the patients' willingness and ability to work with the problematic issues central to their psychopathology. In the *OPD-2*, change is both carefully defined, with two foci (symptom change, and structural change), and operationally described. This is one of the most comprehensive and well-researched diagnostic systems based on psychodynamic principles, and new studies continue to be published.

Bender centred her presentation on the development of the Level of Personality Functioning Scale (LPFS; American Psychiatric Association, 2013). She described how the Personality and Personality Disorders Work Group of the *DSM-5* constructed a new model of personality disturbance by adding to the categories of personality type and disorder a severity of personality functioning impairment dimension that assesses various capacities such as tolerance of multiple perspectives, reflective functioning, and sense of personal uniqueness. The group adopted the basic principle that levels of personality functioning could be established by dimensionalising impairments, and that these would reflect the degree of severity of all personality disorders. They embraced a research and clinically based view that levels of *self* and *interpersonal* functioning were key variables associated with the general constitution of personality. It was from these considerations and assumptions that the LPFS was constructed. For a description of the development and validation of LPFS, see Bender, Morey, and Skodol (2011) and Morey and colleagues (2011). The LPFS self domain is comprised of identity and self-direction components and the interpersonal domain consists of empathy and intimacy. Each of the four components is systematically defined across five levels ranging from 0 (little or no impairment) to 4 (extreme impairment).

Zimmermann and colleagues (2012) have summarised the achievement of the *DSM-5* Personality and Personality Disorders Working Group as follows:

> From our perspective, assessing the severity of PD (Personality Disorder) along a continuum of self and interpersonal functioning is a major step forward in the classification of PD, as it brings the DSM-5 toward what psychodynamically oriented clinicians have done successfully for many years. (p. 9)

This achievement is further enhanced by the fact that there was considerable resistance to this approach in *DSM-5* circles. Interestingly, the *OPD* group has accomplished a related integration. Their mapping levels of personality functioning on to the levels of structural integration, using the Levels of Structural Integration Axis, has similar components to the LPFS: a levels/dimensional view of personality functioning, based on a severity variable, that is, levels of structural integration. Indeed, Zimmerman and colleagues (2012) report eight studies already completed comparing the *OPD-2* LSIA with the *DSM-5* LPFS. The authors of both of these instruments have provided interrater reliability and various kinds of validity, and spelled out the instrument's psychometric properties. These are significant achievements.

### *A recommendation for assessing the core conflict*

The issues of reliability and validity can be illustrated in relation to a suggestion for a specific refinement of the 3-LM variables. For example, the manual for the 3-LM states that Level 2 is the place to delineate conflicts. It may be useful in this regard to specify the patient's *key core conflict* as an anchor point. Here is an illustrative example from Michael Šebek's illuminating case report (see Chapter Nine). The key core conflict being proposed here is supported by a number of different items from the clinical record as well as the central role it can be seen to play in the transference. First, the patient reported feeling greater safety in the early sessions, which later also frightened her. For the first three years of the treatment, there was the related fear of coming more than twice a week, and the feeling of inauthenticity, as well as describing herself as being behind a protective wall. There was also a countertransference component: the analyst's hunch that the patient wanted *resuscitation*, or (here I would guess "and") that her defensiveness stimulated his curiosity. The hypothesised core conflict can now be stated as follows: the increased sense of safety stimulated deep wishes for merger in this maternally deprived patient, that carries the threat, especially because she is poorly integrated with less than optimal boundaries, of loss of a separate sense of self experienced by the patient as a threatening fear of breakdown. Another indication of the centrality of this conflict, highlighted by Margaret Ann Fitzpatrick-Hanly (see Chapter Eight), is the patient's need to keep distance from others because she experiences herself as an unbearable faecal product and that she also expects painful criticism. So, the distance protects her parents, analyst, and others, and is associated with the fantasy of being destroyed by close contact with her. This fantasy of her toxic qualities suggests Fairbairn's (1940) clinical observation of the schizoid patients' fear that their needy love would destroy the object (3-LM Level 3). Šebek's sensitive handling aspects of this core conflict are hypothesised to be central to the reported progress made.

Again, from a methodological standpoint, it would be useful to add to the 3-LM criteria for the reliable identification of one or more core conflicts in clinical cases. Once these criteria are developed, particular core conflicts can be explored more reliably in relation to transformational criteria.

It is relevant to point out that a considerable body of psychoanalytically based empirical research has been devoted to a version of the patient's core conflict. Over a number of years, Lester Luborsky, and his colleagues developed the concept of the Core Conflictual Relationship Theme (CCRT) as a major indicator at the heart of the patient's psychodynamic centre (Luborsky & Crits-Christoph, 1990). When concepts such as the core conflict can help clarify a key anchor point in the application of the 3-LM to clinical cases, and are also amenable to operational definition suitable for empirical research, they are a gain both for clinical psychoanalysis and for psychoanalytically based research methodologies. A similar advantage for developing operational definitions of the variables included in the 3-LM Manual for potential research purposes has already been illustrated by Cierpka and Bender in their presentations.

## *Basis for establishing agreement*

With regard to methodology, the question may be raised as to how much agreement might there be in a clinical group as to what is the core conflict, and how much agreement is found on the other issues being evaluated with the 3-LM. A thus far undecided question is whether the 3-LM authors want to craft careful definitions, as operational as possible, for the terms/variables included in the 3-LM, as both the *OPD* group and the *DSM-5* Personality and Personality Disorders group did. Additionally, there is the question of whether the 3-LM authors want to develop methods to establish and assess interrater reliability. This would additionally require more detailed illustrations and specific criteria for the items included in each of the three Levels. It would require more specificity of the operations to be utilised for identifying the relevant criteria at all three levels.

At this time, reliability could be based on group consensus, as criteria are refined that could lead to adequate independent interrater reliability guidelines. The "expert validation" approach developed by Leuzinger-Bohleber and her colleagues (Leuzinger-Bohleber & Fischmann, 2006) constitutes a version of "consensus" reliability. Independent interrater reliabilities might be a next methodological goal.

After substantial success in running clinical groups that discussed psychoanalytic cases as described above, and which resulted in summaries of the transformations and their underpinnings, the work produced so far has brought to light numerous thought-provoking hypotheses and interrelationships. A summary of each case presentation has been prepared by a reporter, who attempts to include the major formulations of participants based on 3-LM guidelines. Since, typically, two groups have met simultaneously but separately to discuss the same case material, two reports are available for comparison. However, as of now, little work has been done on the criteria for assessing the degree of agreement of the two reports. More recently, attempts have been made to have each member of the group summarise independently their views of the case. A consideration of this issue, and various alternatives for dealing with it, appear to be a justified priority to enhance further tightening for the methodology of the 3-LM. As will be described below, a propositional method is already proposed as a way to organise the case discussions and to compare findings across cases, as well as to systematise definitional features of the key concepts that are being described.

## *Assessing 3-LM results across cases*

Another and related consideration for dealing with central concepts is to devote effort to their definition. The widely held view that psychoanalytic concepts can only be understood when they are embedded in a detailed review of their historical origins necessarily lacks succinctness. These issues have constituted a challenge to the clarification of psychoanalytic concepts, and to a systematic exploration of their interrelationships.

The 3-LM shares with these other two instruments a focus on diagnostic considerations that are centrally based on psychoanalytic concepts. The 3-LM, a more recent entry into the field, has not thus far developed operational definitions. In this regard, Bucci (2010) wrote the following:

> I would argue that the central scientific problem for psychoanalysis is not whether the concepts of the theory have or have not been refuted but that they are not well defined. You can't refute concepts that are ill defined. The concepts of psychoanalysis need to be defined systematically and consistently in terms of one another and in terms of observable events.

Neither has enough thought and space up to this point been devoted to issues of reliability and validity by the 3-LM group, as already discussed. These issues have been integral to the LSIA and to the LPFS scales.

Below, I will offer some illustrative definitional components of transformation, a key variable for the 3-LM. Since these are set forth in propositional form, I shall first provide some orientation, which is currently being utilised by the Clinical Observation Group.

## *The propositional method*

A major focus of the 3-LM is on change/transformation. Based on experience with a number of cases over the past several years in different countries and languages, organised and sponsored by the IPA Clinical Observation Group, ably chaired by Marina Altmann de Litvan, one can observe that assessment of the kinds of change found in a variety of patients demonstrated that transformations showed a range of individual differences, both in kind and quality. While more detailed and careful definition of terms has been recommended above, here I shall illustrate a method for delineating definitional components of the transformation concept.

This approach to concept definition, in the present framework focusing on the related constructs of change and transformation, is what Norbert Freedman and I have called the propositional method (Hurvich & Freedman, 2011a). The term "proposition" indicates a relatively succinct declarative statement about clinical observations and clinical generalisations, following Waelder (1962). Wherever possible, propositions should be stated in plain language, with effort devoted to formulations that are refutable and empirically testable. This method complements dictionary definitions and review articles, and would add clarity and succinctness to what already has been learnt from the historical review approach.

From a methodological standpoint, the focus is on *clinical observations* and *clinical generalisations* that are experience-near. The aim of such an approach is to bring into focus the cumulative clinical knowledge found in the literature regarding central concepts, based on clinical observations made in a psychoanalytic setting. The method aims to highlight what is central about a concept (coreness), what the psychoanalytic dimensions and attributes of this concept are seen to be, and how any given proposition may be modified (i.e., limited by the given context in which it appears or is meant, or expanded in particular ways not specified by the initial proposition). Modifiers illustrate the view that concepts tend to be, as Rubinstein pointed out (cited in Holt, 1985) *probabilistic*, rather than *totalistic*. Modifiers, therefore, limit the generalisability of the proposition by specifying the conditions under which it holds and which it does not. The propositional method is an open system with room for added propositions and modifiers based on new contributions to the literature and on the given analyst's ongoing clinical observations. As an open system, it can accommodate the tendency over time for concepts to be elastic (Sandler, 1983), and involves a series of successive approximations with increasing delineation of the defining features of a concept. The propositional method is treated in more detail in Freedman, Hurvich, and Ward (2011, pp. 91–104). The process of setting aside the historical context, and focusing on those aspects of clinical observations and clinical generalisations that are currently useful, stating them clearly and applying modifiers where appropriate, constitutes an additional methodological feature that can increase the systematic explication of clinical psychoanalytic understanding.

### *Manifestations of transformations*

The propositions below on transformation are illustrative with no claim to completeness. As Wallerstein wrote in 1988, "'Psychic structure' and 'structural change' are among the most central and, at the same time, most problematic concepts within psychoanalytic theory" (p. 241). We are dealing with a challenging issue. While the term *change* refers to a modification and a shift, the term *transformation* implies a metamorphosis, a change in inner character and/or external form (Schachtel, 1959).

- Transformations may be positive or negative: a prominent example of the former has been the detailed elaboration of the components of "the therapeutic action of psychoanalysis" and the related "structural change" (Greenspan & Cullander, 1973; Lear, 2003; Loewald, 1960). Noteworthy negative examples have been designated as "malevolent transformation" (Sullivan, 1953) and "catastrophic change" (Bion, 1965).

- Transformations, positive and negative, may constitute an organising and reorganising influence on the psychic sphere, and show "ripple" effects. To what extent in any given case do the transformations constitute organisers, and what are the specific ripple effects?
- Transformations, both positive and negative, may be permanent to varying degrees. Some relevant modifiers here include: ego strength, superego severity, the pull of the repetition compulsion, and a host of contextual factors. The question can be raised as to what are the conditions that probably lead to permanence *vs.* reversion, regression, and oscillation?
- The clinically observed tendency to repeat maladaptive patterns constitutes an inhibiting force against positive transformations. Especially important here is the pull of UCS guilt leading to the conviction and requirement that the patient not have a better life. What are the conditions, in the patient, in the therapeutic ambience (therapeutic trust) and in the transference/counter-transference that facilitate or inhibit transformations?
- One way to characterise the transformation of repetition is via working through. Thus, successful working through may be seen as *repetition transformed* (Freedman & Ward, 2011).
- Beebe and Lachmann (2002) have emphasised that transformations are co-created in the interaction between the analyst and patient.
- The concept of transformation may be contrasted with the notion of *invariance* (Bion, 1965).
- Hurvich and Freedman (2011b) illustrated how aggression may be transformed by the concurrently active availability of the symbolising processes. A modifier here would be the extent, stability, and the conditions for a generalisation of the effect.
- A transformation principle found to be repeated throughout an analysis and beginning in the middle phase of treatment: the patient was repeatedly able to remember previously repressed and dissociated aspects and details of childhood sexual intimacy with her father following a current situation in which she had experienced a rise of self-esteem associated with the successful outcome of a task or challenge. Factors underscoring interference

with remembering these details were their inherently conflictual and traumatic nature, and that it was anxiety arousing when she was faced with the image of herself as an ordinary girl growing up with a father and a mother, and the self-image of her as a sexual partner with her father.

- Regarding some examples of positive transformations: there may be changes in the background of safety, the balance between positive and negative moods, the resumption of interrupted development, the lessening of symptom pain, the decrease of superego severity, the utilisation of more adaptive defences, the decrease of the power of maladaptive old self and object bonds, the development of a more cohesive self, with more mature forms of self-esteem regulation and more mature levels of narcissism, the development of a more coherent personal narrative, higher levels of object constancy, and more adaptive internal object and external interpersonal ties associated with changes in the internal object world, the decrease in the extent of inner and interpersonal conflict, the levels of, and disruptions from, anxiety, depressive affect, guilt, shame, anger, envy, and frustration, the increase of trust and optimism, and the level of active engagement with the challenges of life and personal and professional productivity and creativity.
- Negative organising influences are most clearly reflected in massive and also in chronic psychic trauma with well-known sequelae, in an increase in disorganising, regressive tendencies including self-destructive trends, consolidation of fear and hatred of reality, increases in interpersonal vengeful behaviours, hatred and prejudice, increases in the depth and extent of malignant narcissistic trends and progressive withdrawal into passivity, somatisation, excessive sleep, addiction, and negativism.
- There is space only to summarise transformations experienced by a substantively traumatised patient described elsewhere (Hurvich, 2011). A decrease in both guilt and shame led to dramatic improvements in her mood, increased work and artistic productivity, and in her significant relationship.

> "I have more of a self now. I feel more three-dimensional, a separated, moving body in the world, rather than an amorphous thing that was both too open and too closed to the world. There was not

> enough boundary there. A sea change has occurred in my expectations. The catastrophic element is gone. I now no longer feel that I will be destroyed by the situation or my choices. A bad day no longer leaves me with the feeling of suffocation or chaos. I feel I can sustain a loss without losing myself. Avoiding mistakes is no longer my prime motive. When I make a mistake, I feel more relaxed about it and behave more realistically and look for a way to repair it. There is much less fear of punishment. Saying yes and getting involved with other people is less frightening. I more often now expect good things to happen. The belief that good things will be ruined is losing power. That when things do not work out I can try again. This change feels related to the self-confidence that came from making clearer decisions and good choices. My tolerance for good feelings of accomplishment is greater. The old pattern of guilt and anxiety following success used to bring on headaches and nightmares, but no longer."

There was a noticeable shift from passivity to an active engagement with both outer and inner challenges. That has influenced a wide range of areas in her life.

- Finally, for now, transformation processes can be seen to occur in cycles:

> Psychoanalytic process always entails events before and after, moment to moment, within a session, across sessions, and across the course of treatment. Analytic process always has a cyclic aspect, and recognizing this leads us to define transformation *cycles* which function as organizers of the course of treatment. (Freedman, Lasky, & Hurvich, 2001, my italics)

In the course of treatment, one can observe transformation cycles where a desymbolising phase is regularly followed by a symbolising phase and *vice versa*. As an example of transformation cycles with regard to one specific variable, annihilation anxiety, a transformation cycle is facilitated when, through affirmative interventions (Killingmo, 1995) and increases in therapeutic trust (Ellman, 2007), in conjunction with therapeutic interventions, it becomes possible to lower annihilation anxiety, so that the annihilation content is less disruptive, less terrifying, allows for a reversal of ego regression and reinstates higher levels of ego functioning, especially increases in reflective function

(Fonagy & Target, 1997) and affect modulation. Under these conditions, there is a decrease in the likelihood of secondary anxiety reactions, where the initial anxiety triggers threatening anticipatory fantasies, which lead to more anxiety and disruption.

In closing, I will illustrate how the propositional method, in conjunction with the 3-LM, may be used as the basic methodology for indexing the commonalities and divergences in a range of transformations across cases in sample of any number of cases. These guidelines are only preliminary and illustrative.

1. Cast the main features of the case findings, at each of the three levels into propositional form. An illustration provided above is the specification of the core conflict of Šebek's case.
2. What are the major areas of transformation for any given patient?
3. Are there any discernable components in the description of these cases which are associated with high positive transformations compared with cases high in negative transformations compared with cases which have shown a preponderance of little change one way or the other?
4. Some likely relevant variables at each level are as follows:
   *Level 1*: Optimism, trust, positive sources of self-esteem, interest in others, self-acceptance, self-confidence, self-expression, capacity for love and sexuality, positive family and social relationships, satisfaction in work and interest in leisure activity and hobbies.
   *Level 2*: Ego strength, reality testing/reflective capacity, impulse control and affect regulation, referential activity, capacity for integration, tolerance for intrapsychic conflict, patterns of interpersonal relationships, core conflict and other major conflicts, flexibility *vs.* rigidity of defences and their adaptive/maladaptive implications, identity integration/disintegration.

These examples, many taken from the 3-LM, are illustrative of how they can be used by the propositional method. It is expected that across a series of cases, patterns and sub-patterns will be discernible, which will allow for preliminary and tentative generalisations regarding what factors appear to be associated with transformations, especially positive, negative, and minimal. With regard to the relatively few cases presented in committee workshops thus far, some general psycho-diagnostic implications appear to be affirmed. Near the top would be the presence of limited positive transformations occurring in patients who could be judged to have substantially compromised ego strength, poor impulse control, problematic and conflictual interpersonal relations, and major difficulties with self-integration. It is anticipated that a utilisation of the propositional method across a larger range of cases will yield many modifiers and nuances and a combination of a range of relevant patient, analyst, interactional, contextual, and environmental factors. This way of organising findings would be complemented by addressing the reliability and validity issues. At the Prague meeting, it was mentioned that the Cierpka and Bender presentations reflected a "building of bridges" to an instrument like the 3-LM. My sense of the bridge is an expanded discussion of methodological considerations as highlighted in this chapter and as illustrated by the two guest presentations.

## *References*

American Psychiatric Association (2013). *Diagnostic and Statistical Manual of Mental Disorders* (5th edn). Washington, DC: American Psychiatric Association.

Beebe, B., & Lachmann, F. M. (2002). *Infant Research and Adult Treatment: Co-Constructing Interactions*. Hillsdale, NJ: Analytic Press.

Bender, D. S., Morey, L. C., & Skodol, A. E. (2011). Toward a model for assessing level of personality functioning in DSM-5, part I: a review of theory and methods. *Journal of Personality Assessment*, *93*(4): 332–346.

Bion, W. R. (1965). *Transformations: Change from Learning to Growth*. London: Heinemann, 1984.

Bucci, W. (2010). Re: Defining before refuting. *Psychodynamic Research Listserv*, October 18.

Ellman, S. J. (2007). Analytic trust and transference: love, healing ruptures and facilitating repairs. *Psychoanalytic Inquiry*, *27*: 246–273.

Fairbairn, W. D. (1940). Schizoid factors in the personality. In: *Psychoanalytic Studies of the Personality* (pp. 3–27). London: Tavistock, 1952.

Fonagy, P., & Target, M. (1997). Attachment and reflective function: their role in self-organization. *Development and Psychopathology*, *9*: 679–700.

Freedman, N., & Ward, R. (2011). A very broad concept seen through a very narrow lens. In: N. Freedman, M. Hurvich, & R. Ward, with J. Geller & J. Hoffenberg (Eds.), *Another Kind of Evidence: Studies on Internalization, Annihilation Anxiety, and Progressive Symbolization in the Psychoanalytic Process* (pp. 191–202). London: Karnac.

Freedman, N., Hurvich, M., Ward, R., with Geller, J., & Hoffenberg, J. (Eds.) (2011). *Another Kind of Evidence: Studies on Internalization, Annihilation Anxiety, and Progressive Symbolization in the Psychoanalytic Process*. London: Karnac.

Freedman, N., Lasky, R., & Hurvich, M. (2001). Transformation cycles as organizers of psychoanalytic process: the method of sequential specification. Paper presented to the Annual Meeting of the Rapaport–Klein Study Group, Stockbridge, MA.

Grande, T., Dilg, R., Jakobsen, T., Keller, W., Krawietz, B., Langer, M., Oberbracht, C., Stehle, S., Stennes, M., & Rudolf, G. (2006). Differential effects of two forms of psychoanalytictherapy: results of the Heidelberg–Berlin study. *Psychotherapy Research, 16*(4): 470–485

Grande, T., Dilg, R., Jakobsen, T., Keller, W., Krawietz, B., Langer, M., Oberbracht, C., Stehle, S., Stennes, M., & Rudolf, G. (2009). Structural change as a predictor of long-term follow-up outcome. *Psychotherapy Research, 19*(3): 344–357.

Greenspan, S. I., & Cullander, C. C. H. (1973). A systematic metapsychological assessment of the personality: its application to the problem of analyzability. *Journal of the American Psychoanalytic Association, 21*: 303–327.

Holt, R. R. (1985). The current status of psychoanalytic theory. *Psychoanalytic Psychology, 2*: 289–315.

Hurvich, M. (2011). New developments in the theory and clinical application of the annihilation anxiety concept. In: A. Druck, C. Ellman, N. Freedman, & A. Thaler (Eds.), *A New Freudian Synthesis: Clinical Process in the Next Generation* (pp. 65–95). London: Karnac.

Hurvich, M., & Freedman, N. (2011a). The propositional method for the study of psychoanalytic concepts. In: N. Freedman, M. Hurvich, R. Ward, J. Geller, & J. Hoffenberg (Eds.), *Another Kind of Evidence: Studies on Internalization, Annihilation Anxiety, and Progressive Symbolization in the Psychoanalytic Process* (pp. 91–104). London: Karnac.

Hurvich, M., & Freedman, N. (2011b). Three pathways towards the modification of annihilation anxiety. In: N. Freedman, M. Hurvich, R. Ward, J. Geller, & J. Hoffenberg (Eds.), *Another Kind of Evidence: Studies on Internalization, Annihilation Anxiety, and Progressive Symbolization in the Psychoanalytic Process* (pp. 183–189). London: Karnac.

Killingmo, B. (1995). Affirmation in psychoanalysis. *International Journal of Psychoanalysis, 76*: 503–518.

Lear, J. (2003). *Therapeutic Action: An Earnest Plea for Irony*. New York: Other Press.

Leuzinger-Bohleber, M., & Fischmann, T. (2006). What is conceptual research in psychoanalysis? *International Journal of Psychoanalysis, 87*: 1355–1386.

Loewald, H. W. (1960). On the therapeutic action of psychoanalysis. *International Journal of Psychoanalysis, 41*: 16–33.

Luborsky, L., & Crits-Christoph, P. (1990). *Understanding Transference, the CCRT Method (The Core Conflictual Relationship)*. New York: Basic Books.

Morey, L. C., Berghuis, H., Bender, D. S., Verheul, R., Krueger, R. F., & Skodol, A. E. (2011). Toward a model for assessing level of personality functioning in DSM-5, part II: empirical articulation of a core dimension of personality pathology. *Journal of Personality Assessment, 9*(4): 347–353.

OPD Task Force (2008). *Operationalized Psychodynamic Diagnosis OPD-2: Manual of Diagnosis and Treatment Planning*. Cambridge, MA: Hogrefe & Huber.

PDM Task Force (2006). *Psychodynamic Diagnostic Manual (PDM)*. Silver Springs, MD: Alliance of Psychoanalytic Organizations.

Sandler, J. (1983). Reflections on some relations between psychoanalytic concepts and psychoanalytic practice. *International Journal of Psychoanalysis, 64*: 34–45.

Schachtel, E. G. (1959). *Metamorphosis*. New York: Basic Books.

Sullivan, H. S. (1953). *The Interpersonal Theory of Psychiatry*. New York: Norton.

Waelder, R. (1962). Psychoanalysis, scientific method, and philosophy. *Journal of the American Psychoanalytic Association, 10*: 617–637.

Wallerstein, R. S. (1988). Assessment of structural change in psychoanalytic therapy and research. *Journal of the American Psychoanalytic Association, 36S*: 241–261.

Zimmermann, J., Ehrenthal, J. C., Cierpka, M., Schauenburg, H., Doering, S., & Benecke, C. (2012). Assessing the level of structural integration using Operationalized Psychodynamic Diagnosis (OPD): implications for DSM-5. *Journal of Personality Assessment, 94*: 522–532.

CHAPTER THIRTEEN

# The assessment of changes: diagnostic aspects

*Ricardo Bernardi*

## *Introduction: dimensions of patient changes*

The three-level model for observing patient transformations (3-LM) presented elsewhere in this book (see Bernardi, Chapter One) aims to observe and describe patient changes by examining the clinical material from diverse angles or perspectives. While the first level of observation (phenomenological) gets closer to the material by taking advantage of the analyst's participant position in the process, Level 2 requires a "second look". Thereby, the analyst, as an observer, attempts to specify the dimensions of change based on categories that facilitate a systematic comparison both between different moments in the treatment of that patient and among different patients. Level 3, in turn, discusses hypotheses about change and its nature, including the analyst's explicit and implicit theories as well as alternative hypotheses. Clinical judgement usually combines the three levels, but the 3-LM attempts to transitorily separate them, seeking first an empathic understanding of the patient, and then conceptualising the main dimensions discerned and discussing their theoretical explanation.

Level 2 addresses the following question: what has changed, and how much? Psychoanalysis aspires to go beyond modifying symptoms or anxiety. Consequently, it involves a more substantial conceptualisation of the relevant dimensions of psychic change. How we assess these dimensions clinically is, essentially, a diagnostic question. Diagnosis and psychoanalysis have always been problematic allies. Freud's entire work shows a constant interaction between his clinical observations, his diagnostic conceptualisations, and the development of new theories at a metapsychological level (Wallerstein, 2006). However, Freud was not primarily interested in developing a diagnostic system.

In the following decades, we witness a double movement. On one side, several authors attempt to advance toward the diagnostic use of psychoanalytic concepts (e.g., the "Hampstead Psychoanalytic Index", 1981, and the structured interview proposed by Kernberg and colleagues (Kernberg, 2006)). Freedman and Hurvich have put forth a propositional method that allows us to identify the core of a psychoanalytical concept, its dimensions, and the contextual modifiers that grant specificity to its clinical use (Freedman, Hurvich, & Ward, 2011; Hurvich, 2003).

On the other side, the use of diagnostic categories has been strongly criticised for not respecting patients' singularity and uniqueness (Hoffman, 2009; Walls, 2006). The controversy around this subject (see, for example, Eagle & Wolitzky, 2011) shows how difficult it is to establish a common ground for dialogue. None the less, there is no substantial reason for viewing the acknowledgement of the patient's singularity and the use of diagnostic categories as opposites. In fact, they are different sides of the same problem, which is complex and leaves no room for simplistic solutions. Underscoring each patient's uniqueness and conceptualising shared features among different patients are complementary steps that improve our clinical understanding. The divorce between diagnosis and psychoanalysis did not benefit either. Psychoanalysis casts out concepts that could help to understand long-term changes, considering them as psychiatric or research terms. Clinical diagnosis, for its part, loses many potential contributions of psychoanalysis.

The 3-LM combines a phenomenological approach, intended to capture the uniqueness of each analytic experience, with a conceptualisation of the dimensions of patients' changes, which allows a better description of patients' transformations over the course of the analysis. The diagnostic categories contained in *DSM-IV* or *ICD-10* are, indeed, of very limited use in this case. Yet, at the same time, metapsychological concepts are too general and abstract to serve as tools for describing changes or transformations. In addition, current theoretical pluralism adds complexity to the situation in as much as the same theoretical terms can be used to describe diverse clinical phenomena, while the same facts can be named differently. Level 3 of the 3-LM aims to explore the potential richness of these concepts as well as their power to shed light on the clinical material and help analysts see new sides of it. Levels 1 and 2 entail a clinical approach that seeks to identify markers of change.

To select the questions that would guide the description and tracking of changes at Level 2, the 3-LM drew from the most currently influential psychodynamically orientated diagnostic systems, the *PDM* and the *OPD-2*. These systems provide operationalised definitions of their concepts, definitions whose goal is to link these concepts to the procedures used for assessing them. A shared meaning is then guaranteed, but the question is how much of the original theoretical content can be kept. The operationalised diagnostic system *OPD-2* (see below) answers this question by recognising the need for a compromise between conflicting meanings. Such compromise can be designated as the "smallest common multiple" of the diverse theoretical meanings rather than as a "consensus" (*OPD-2*, p. 14). The 3-LM does not include operational definitions but, inspired by them, formulates comprehensive questions in a language close to experience. These questions are expected to be self-explanatory for trained clinicians, even if their theoretical backgrounds differ. The sources of the questions are current psychodynamic diagnostic systems, especially the *OPD-2*.

## *The* OPD-2 *and* PDM *diagnostic systems*

The appearance of the *Operationalized Psychodynamic Diagnostic Manual*, version 2 (*OPD-2*) and the *Psychodynamic Diagnostic Manual* (*PDM*) represented considerable progress in the field of psychoanalytic diagnostics. Both systems attempt to provide categories with a high degree of systematisation, validity, and reliability by gathering and building on previous advances in this field. The *OPD-2* emerged as a result of the joint work of German psychoanalysts, psychotherapists, and psychiatrists, with Manfred Cierpka as their reference figure. The first version (*OPD-1*) appeared in 1996, and the second (*OPD-2*) in 2006. The *PDM* is a diagnostic system for children, adolescents, and adults published in 2006 in the USA by the American Psychoanalytic Association, the International Psychoanalytical Association, the Psychoanalysis Division of the American Psychological Association, the American Academy of Psychoanalysis and Dynamic Psychiatry, and the National Committee of Psychoanalysis in Clinical Social Work. The task force was chaired by S. I. Greenspan and composed of N. McWilliams and R. S. Wallerstein. The *OPD-2* has gone further than the *PDM* toward operationalising its definitions and assessing the reliability and validity of its diagnostic concepts (Cierpka, Grande, Rudolf, von der Tann, & Stasch, 2007; Doering et al., 2013; Zimmermann et al., 2012).

The *PDM* and the *OPD-2* are multi-axial systems. They combine the categorial and dimensional approaches, meaning that they define various types of phenomena and intend to specify their degree or magnitude as well. The *PDM* takes into account three dimensions: (1) personality patterns and disorders (P Axis), (2) profile of mental functioning (M Axis), and (3) symptom patterns: the subjective experience (S Axis). The *OPD-2*, in turn, includes the following axes: (1) experience of illness, (2) relational patterns, (3) conflicts, (4) structure, and (5) disorders (according to the *CIE-10*). The 3-LM borrowed these axes and added the *PDM*'s formulation of defences.

The "experience of illness" dimension explores the ways in which patients experience and give meaning to their suffering, including their beliefs about the nature and origin of their problems and about how treatment might help them. It is expected that, over the course of the analysis, patients will acquire a greater awareness about their difficulties. Although it may be painful and confusing at first, such awareness is expected to guide them towards new ways of experiencing themselves and their relationships with others.

Relational patterns may be observed in two different ways. One is directly in the analysis through the transference–countertransference relationship, the other through repetitive relational episodes narrated by patients where they describe their perceptions of others and of themselves. These relational episodes reflect the ways in which conflicts and structural problems are expressed in patients' relationships. The *OPD-2* outlines diverse types of typical conflicts. The 3-LM complemented this aspect with the *PDM*'s description of prevailing defences and the distortions or restrictions they impose on psychic processes.

The fourth axis of the *OPD-2* refers to the structural characteristics of mental functioning. Given its similarity to *PDM* and the scale of personality functioning of *DSM-5* and its usefulness for tracking changes, I examine this axis more thoroughly below.

### *Convergences among systems: structural aspects of mental functioning*

The most remarkable convergences among these diagnostic systems occur between Axis 4 of the *OPD-2* (structure) and the M dimension of the *PDM* (mental functioning), which are also in agreement with the levels of personality functioning scale (LPFS) of the *DSM-5*. While keeping the traditional definition of personality disorders, the fifth version of the *Diagnostic and Statistical Manual of the American Psychiatric Association* (*DSM-5*) (American Psychiatric Association, 2013) proposes an alternative model for the evaluation of the personality and its disorders in Section III ("Emerging measures and models"). This section defines personality disorders as disturbances in personality functioning in the self and in interpersonal domains. The "level of personality functioning scale" (LPFS) provides a dimensional assessment of core capacities of the personality in both domains. This scale allows practitioners to evaluate overall severity, which is the most important predictor of concurrent and prospective dysfunction. (Hopwood Malone, et al., cited in Bender, Morey, & Skodol, 2011; Skodol et al., 2011a,b,c; Tyrer, 2005).

The LPFS shows significant correspondences with Axis 4 (structure) of the *OPD-2* and the M Axis (mental functioning) of the *PDM*, even if the organisation of the items is not the same. Axis 4 (structure) of the *OPD-2* includes four dimensions that are important for tracking patient changes: (1) the capacity to adequately perceive the self and objects, (2) the regulation of the self (impulses, affects, and self-esteem) and the regulation of relationships with others, (3) emotional internal and external communication, and (4) attachment to internal and external objects. These four dimensions, in turn, include several sub-dimensions: for instance, the capacity for self-perception implies self-reflection, affect differentiation, and identity. The M Axis of the *PDM* contains nine dimensions, among them, the capacity for regulation, attention and learning, the capacity for relationships and intimacy (including depth, range, and consistency), and the quality of internal experience (level of confidence and self-regard). The LPFS of the *DSM-5* is based on personality functioning in relation to the self (identity and self-direction) and to the interpersonal realm (empathy and intimacy).

The LPFS rates personality functioning on a scale from 0 (little or no impairment) to 4 (extreme impairment). The *PDM*, in turn, propounds eight levels, from "Optimal age- and phase-appropriate mental capacities with phase-expected degree of flexibility and intactedness" to "Major defects in basic mental functions". This system also describes three levels of personality organisation: healthy, neurotic, and borderline. Finally, the *OPD-2* proposes a scale of levels of structural integration ranging from 1 (high level of integration) to 4 (disintegrated), with intermediate scores. There are two classes of structural failures. "Structural disorder" refers to the absence of certain structural differentiations and integrations (developmental deficits). "Structural vulnerability", by contrast, indicates that the structure was able to develop but can collapse under internal or external stress (*OPD-2*, p. 82).

To learn how comparable these different scales are, we must examine the content of mental functioning indicators, which shows an amazing concordance. The similarities between the *OPD-2* and the *DSM-5* that emerge from their conceptual comparison (Bernardi, 2010) have been empirically corroborated. Zimmermann and colleagues (2012) found a very high correlation between *DSM-5* descriptors of mental functioning level and *OPD-2* levels of structural integration ($r = 0.93$, $p < 0.001$). In the levels with greater disturbance, it is possible to find some divergences between indicators of both systems, especially in *OPD-2* axes associated with internal and external communication and attachment. The authors remark that certain dimensions are less represented in the LPFS, such as the capacity to elaborate internal experiences with the help of fantasies, bodily experiences, emotional communication, and the capacity to internalise representations of others and use them for self-regulation and for the establishment of triangular relationships (p. 7). At the same time, they note that the *DSM-5* includes some important dimensions, such as the capacities to self-direct and to guide oneself by moral standards, which are less represented in the *OPD-2* (p. 7, 8).

The sub-dimensions of the *OPD-2* structure axis are highly intercorrelated (< 0.8), suggesting the existence of an underlying common factor such as Kernberg's concept of identity diffusion. This notion refers to the lack of integration of concepts of the self and of significant others (Doering et al., 2013; Kernberg, 2006).

Structural change can also be assessed with the Heidelberg structural change scale (HSCS). At the end of their treatment, patients value changes at the level of their symptoms and interpersonal problems. Longer follow-ups, however, show that they appreciate structural changes even more in the long term, since these changes have a greater influence on their personal and interpersonal life (Grande, Dilg, Jakobsen, Keller, & Krawietz, 2009).

The comparison among the three diagnostic systems was discussed in two panels at the 47th (Mexico 2011) and 48th (Prague, 2013) IPA congresses. Panel members were analysts involved in the development of these systems: Manfred Cierpka (*OPD-2*), Marvin Hurvich (*PDM*), and John Oldham (*DSM-5*) at the Mexico Congress, and Donna Bender (*DSM-5*) at the Prague Congress. These panels were organised at the suggestion of the IPA Committee on Clinical Observation and were chaired by the author. The Prague panel, "Observing transformations in patients: the assessment of mental functioning", focused on the usefulness of this assessment for psychoanalysis. Panellists presented advances in their field and their potential use in the evaluation of patient transformations during analysis from a psychoanalytic perspective.

Table 13.1 compares the criteria used by the three systems to evaluate personality functioning.

The table confirms the remarkable convergence among criteria used by the three diagnostic systems. The *PDM* appeared somewhat earlier than the *DSM-5* draft, and they probably have influences in common, many of them from psychoanalytic literature. The first version of the *DSM-5* manuscript included the evaluation of self-representations (their complexity, differentiation, and integration) and of representations of others (their cohesion, complexity, and integration, as well as the use the self makes of them), which emphasised the

*Table 13.1.* Comparison of the levels of personality functioning in *OPD-2*, *PDM*, and *DSM-5*.

| *OPD-2* Axis IV: Structure | *PDM* M axis: mental functioning profile | *DSM-5** Levels of personality functioning: 1. Self; 2. Interpersonal |
|---|---|---|
| *Axis IV.1. Self perception* Reflect and differentiate self-image. Differentiate one's own affects. Design and further develop one's own identity. | M8. Self-observing capacity ("psychological mindedness"). M3. Quality of internal experience (level of confidence and self-regard). M6. Capacity to form internal representations. M7. Capacity for differentiation and integration. M5. Defensive patterns and capacities (**). | *1.i: Self: Identity* Experience of oneself as unique, with clear boundaries between self and others. Stability of self-esteem and precision in self value. Capacity and ability to handle a variety of emotional experiences. [*1.iii: Self. Integrity of the concept of self*: (a) regulation of self-esteem and respect for oneself; (b) the feeling of being an autonomous agency; (c) the valuing or appreciation of oneself; and (d) the quality of the representations of the self (complexity, differentiation, and integration)*. |
| *IV.1. Perception of the object* (capacity to perceive others totally and realistically). Self–object differentiation: distinguish one's own thoughts, needs, impulses from those of others. | M6. Capacity to form internal representations (**) M4. Affective experience, expression, and communication. | *2.i: Interpersonal. Empathy*: Comprehension and appreciation of others' experiences and motivations; tolerance of different perspectives; understanding of the effects of one's behaviour on others. |

(*continued*)

*Table 13.1. (continued)*

| *OPD-2*<br>Axis IV: Structure | *PDM*<br>M axis: mental functioning profile | *DSM-5**<br>Levels of personality functioning: 1. Self; 2. Interpersonal |
|---|---|---|
| Perceive others in their various aspects, that is, as whole persons.<br>Ability to design a realistic picture of others. | | |
| *IV.2: Self regulation*<br>Distance oneself from impulses, controlling and integrating impulses.<br><br>Distance oneself from affects, regulate affects<br>Distance oneself from emotional hurts, regulate self-worth. | M1. Capacity for regulation, attention and learning.<br>M9. Capacity to construct or use internal standards and ideals: sense of morality.<br>M3. Quality of internal experience (level of confidence and self-regard) (**). | *1.i: Self: identity* (**)<br>*1.ii: Self-direction*<br>Pursuit of coherent, meaningful short- and long-term goals.<br>Use of internal, constructive, pro-<br>Use of internal, constructive, pro-social standards of behaviour.<br>Capacity for productive self-reflection. |
| *IV.2. Regulation of object relationship*<br>Protect the relationship from one's own disturbing impulses; intrapsychic instead of interpersonal defence.<br>In relationships, maintain one's own interests and take due account of the interests of others.<br>Ability to develop a realistic picture of others. | M2. Capacity for relationships and intimacy (including depth, range, and consistency)<br>M4. Affective experience, expression and communication (**).<br>M6. Capacity to form internal representations (**). | *2.i: Interpersonal. Empathy* (**)<br>*2.ii: Interpersonal. Intimacy*<br>Depth and duration of positive bonds with others.<br>Wish and capacity to be close.<br>Mutuality of regard, reflected in interpersonal behaviours. |

(*continued*)

*Table 13.1.* (*continued*)

| *OPD-2*<br>Axis IV: Structure | *PDM*<br>M axis: mental functioning profile. | *DSM-5**<br>Levels of personality functioning: 1. Self; 2. Interpersonal |
|---|---|---|
| *IV.3. Emotional internal communication. Symbolisation*<br>Generate and experience one's own affect.<br>Create and use one's own fantasies.<br>Emotionally animate the perception of one's own body, or bodily self. | M4. Affective experience, expression, and communication (**)<br>M6. Capacity to form internal representations (**). | *1.i: Self: identity* (**).<br>*1.ii: Self-direction* (**). |
| *IV.3. Emotional communication with the external world*<br>Make emotional contact: allow feelings towards others, dare to make emotional investments, achieve "we" feeling (reciprocity).<br>Express one's own affects, let oneself be reached by the affects of others.<br>Experience empathy. | M2. Capacity for relationships and intimacy (including depth, range, and consistency) (**).<br>M4. Affective experience, expression and communication (**). | *2.i: Interpersonal. Empathy* (**).<br>*2.ii: Interpersonal. Intimacy* (**). |
| *IV. 4. Attachment capacity to internal objects*<br>Internalisation: positive self-representations, positive object-representations, ability to build and maintain positive object-related affects.<br>Positive introjects: ability to care for oneself, to calm, console, help, protect oneself,to stand up for oneself. | M6. Capacity to form internal representations. (**) | *1.i: Self: identity*<br>*2.ii: Interpersonal. Intimacy* (**)<br>[*2.iii: Interpersonal. Complexity and integration of representations of others;*<br>(a) Coherence, complexity, and integration of the mental representations of others; |

(*continued*)

*Table 13.1. (continued)*

| *OPD-2*<br>Axis IV: Structure | *PDM*<br>M axis: mental functioning profile. | *DSM-5**<br>Levels of personality functioning: 1. Self; 2. Interpersonal |
|---|---|---|
| Variable and triangular attachments: different internal object qualities; attachment to one does not mean turning away from another. | | (b) use of the representations of others to regulate the self. |
| *IV.4. Attachment capacity to external objects*<br>Ability to make attachments: attach to others emotionally (gratitude, loving care, guilt, sadness).<br>Accept help: ability to accept support, care, concern, guidance, apologies from others.<br>Ability to sever attachments and tolerate farewells. | M2. Capacity for relationships and intimacy (including depth, range, and consistency) (**).<br>M4. Affective experience, expression, and communication (**). | *2.II: Interpersonal. Intimacy* (**) |

* The *DSM-5* was consulted on the website of the American Psychiatric Association on 28 July 2010 and 30 June 2012. Text fragments that were found in the first consultation but had been removed before the second one have been placed between square brackets, with one asterisk [*]. There are slight wording variations in the different versions of the *DSM-5* that do not alter the meaning.

** When a single item of one system is associated with several items of the other systems, repetitions are marked with (**). In the case of the *PDM*, patterns and defensive capacities should be mentioned in practically every row.

systems' convergence. These indicators, and the use of terms such as "mentalization", were eliminated in later versions due to their complexity and the difficulties they presented for current psychiatric evaluation. Convergences between the *DSM-5* and the *OPD-2* are noteworthy, since these systems were formulated by independent groups of researchers.

It is important to mention that the LPFS represents a bridge between the *DSM* system and psychoanalysis that was absent during the decades of *DSM-III* and *DSM-IV* dominance. Luyten and Blatt (2011) state that dimensional perspectives mark the beginning of a new era in psychiatric diagnosis that could bring radical changes in the conceptualisation, classification, and treatment of mental disorders. These authors consider that viewing personality development and its psychopathology from the dual perspective of the self and the interpersonal domain will lead to increasing convergence with neurobiological and psychosocial investigations.

## *Discussion*

The 3-LM intends to translate the core concepts of the three diagnostic systems into comprehensive, friendly questions. We can use as an example the *OPD-2* "Internal communication" dimension. The 3-LM formulates this dimension as follows: "How rich is the patient's dialogue with himself or herself based on affective experiences, bodily self, fantasies, dreams, sexuality, symbolic representations, and capacity to play and creativity?" The *OPD-2* discriminates among the following capacities: "1) to generate and experience one's own affects; 2) to create and use one's own fantasies, and 3) to emotionally animate the perception of one's own body or bodily self". If we consider the other systems, we can relate these capacities to those of the *PDM*, especially to the following sub-dimensions: "Affective experience, expression, and communication" and "Capacity to form internal representations". Turning now to the *DSM-5*, we find similar capacities in the self-functioning areas of identity and self-direction. Identity includes: "Experience of oneself as unique, with clear boundaries between the self and the others; Stability of self-esteem and precision in self value; and Capacity and ability to handle a variety of emotional experiences", This last one is the more directly linked to internal communication. Capacities associated with self-direction are "Pursuit of coherent, meaningful short- and long-term goals; Use of constructive, pro-social standards of behaviour; Capacity for productive self-reflection". The third one is also closely related the same dimension of the *OPD-2*.

This comparison shows that there is an overlap among these diverse formulations but there are also clear differences. The *OPD-2* and the other diagnostic systems favour clearly defined functions, while the 3-LM prefers to combine them in a general question and let participants explore them according to their own clinical perspective. Doing so opens the door for analysts with different theoretical backgrounds to introduce their own nuances. We know that theoretical influences on clinical observation are inevitable (see Leibovich de Duarte, Chapter Seven). Still, the crucial issue is whether these influences saturate and restrict observation or are used to widen it, thus encouraging new questions and perspectives. In this sense, explicit or implicit personal theories can facilitate a more subtle exploration of the clinical material. Such an exploration, however, is only possible if theoretical concepts are continuously connected to the clinical material to which they refer. This material, rather than the theoretical notions as such, constitutes the basis for discussion.

The extent to which the evaluation stemming from the 3-LM questions matches that of the original diagnostic systems must be empirically determined. Some 3-LM groups added questionnaires to study the interrating agreement among group participants, but these have not yet been compared with the mentioned diagnostic systems. Participants' opinions about the degree of overall change could also be collated with changes in the evaluation of the level of mental functioning, according to the *OPD-2* or LPFS, both at the beginning and over the course the analysis. This comparison could enrich analysts' observations and provide useful information for the diagnostic systems.

Some differences among the requirements of these systems and that of the 3-LM have to be considered here. As a research tool, the *OPD-2* demands special training, and the clinical interview must combine associative and exploratory instances. Patients have to narrate one relational episode, describe people close to them, and add descriptions of themselves as persons (Cierpka, communication at Prague's panel, 2013). The LPFS of *DSM-5*, by contrast, achieves an acceptable interrater reliability without extensive clinical experience or training (Zimmermann et al., 2013). The 3-LM, in turn, is supposed to be used by trained analysts, and the extensive material discussed usually includes descriptions required by the *OPD*-2.

Should the 3-LM incorporate more rigorous operational definitions, or make use of those of the *OPD-2*, or of other diagnostic systems? Would this be advantageous? Hurvich (see Chapter Twelve) has pointed out the benefits of moving in that direction. Contrariwise, some working group participants are interested in favouring a different path. They consider the first level especially useful and have suggested giving more room to analysts' free associations. The 3-LM strikes a balance between both directions; there is no actual contradiction between them, and working groups could explore any of them according to their interests.

The 3-LM adopted the *OPD-2* distinction between conflict and structure. This is a controversial issue. While some authors highlight the clinical and theoretical significance of failures in the development of the ego structure (Killingmo, 1989; Stolorow & Lachmann, 1981, p. 308), others, such as Kernberg (2005), consider that these deficits are defensive and determined by unconscious intrapsychic conflicts. Concepts such as Marty's "essential depression" and "operational thinking", in turn, stress that traumatic internal or external conditions can overwhelm the defensive process, leading to the production of negative phenomena in mental functioning (Marty, 1985). The careful observation of therapeutic changes regarding both conflicts and structural functions proposed by the 3-LM can shed light on this debate.

In what order do conflicts and structural sub-dimensions change throughout the therapeutic process? Do they change simultaneously, since they are highly intercorrelated? Or, depending on the patient, do some modifications precede others, supporting or triggering them? These are questions the 3-LM can help explore. For example, in Leticia's case (see Chapters One and Two), her marked inhibition and fear revealed a certain structural vulnerability of her mental functioning. As she was gradually able to use the analyst as a containing external/internal object, she could enhance her reflecting function, which was stimulated by the analyst's interventions. She was, thus, able to improve affect and anxiety regulation. Changes in self-perception, regulation, and communication led to increased processing and awareness of internal experiences. Such strengthening of the patient's functions was achieved mostly through the analyst's non-interpretative interventions. It is interesting to note that only once Leticia's mental functioning had been enhanced was it possible to start exploring conflicts that might have contributed to her inhibition.

The process described above shows the usefulness of supplementing moment-to-moment observation in the session with a more careful exploration of processes that unfold over long periods of time and lead to changes in patients' mental functioning.

## *References*

American Psychiatric Association. (2013). *Diagnostic and Statistical Manual of Mental Disorders, 5th Edition: DSM-5*. Arlington, VA: American Psychiatric Association.

Bender, D. S., Morey, L. C., & Skodol, A. E. (2011). Toward a model for assessing level of personality functioning in DSM-5, Part I: A review of theory and methods. *Journal of Personality Assessment, 93*(4): 332–346.

Bernardi, R. (2010). DSM-5, OPD-2 y PDM: convergencias y divergencias entre los nuevos sistemas diagnósticos psiquiátricos y psicoanalíticos. *Rev Psiquiatr Urug, 74*(2): 179–205.

Cierpka, M., Grande, T., Rudolf, G., von der Tann, M., & Stasch, M. (2007). The Operationalized Psychodynamic Diagnostics System: clinical relevance, reliability and validity. *Psychopathology, 40*: 209–220.

Doering, S., Burgmer, M., Heuft, G., Menke, D., Bäumer, B., Lübking, M., & Feldmann, M. (2013). Assessment of personality functioning: validity of the Operationalized Psychodynamic Diagnosis Axis IV (Structure). *Psychopathology*. doi: 10.1159/000355062.

Eagle, M., & Wolitzky, D. (2011). Systematic empirical research versus clinical case studies: a valid antagonism? *Journal of the American Psychoanalytic Association, 59*(4): 791–818.

Freedman, N., Hurvich, M., & Ward, R., with Geller, J., & Hoffenberg, J. (2011). *Another Kind of Evidence: Studies on Internalization, Annihilation Anxiety, and Progressive Symbolization in the Psychoanalytic Process*. London: Karnac.

Grande, T., Dilg, R., Jakobsen, T., Keller, W., & Krawietz, B. (2009). Structural change as a predictor of long-term follow-up outcome. *Psychotherapy Research, 19*(3): 344–357.

Hampstead Psychoanalytic Index (1981). *Bulletin of the Anna Freud Centre, 4*: 217–220.

Hoffman, I. Z. (2009). Doublethinking our way to "scientific legitimacy": the desiccation of human experience. *Journal of the American Psychoanalytic Association, 57*: 1043–1069.

Hurvich, M. (2003). The place of annihilation anxieties in psychoanalytic theory. *Journal of the American Psychoanalytic Association, 51*: 579–616.

Kernberg, O. F. (2005). Unconscious conflict in the light of contemporary psychoanalytic findings. *Psychoanalytic Quarterly, 74*: 65–81.

Kernberg, O. F. (2006). Identity. Recent findings and clinical implications. *Psychoanalytic Quarterly, 75*: 969–1003.

Killingmo, B. (1989). Conflict and deficit: implications for technique. *International Journal of Psychoanalysis, 70*: 65–79.

Luyten, P., & Blatt, S. J. (2011). Integrating theory-driven and empirically-derived models of personality development and psychopathology: a proposal for DSM V. *Clinical Psychology Review, 31*: 52–68.

Marty, P. (1985). *L'ordre psycho-somatique*. Paris: Payot.

Skodol, A. E., Bender, D. S., Morey, L. C., Clark, L.A., Oldham, J. M., Alarcon, R. D., Krueger, R. F., Verheul, R., Bell, C. C., & Siever, L. J. (2011a). Personality disorder types proposed for DSM-5. *Journal of Personality Disorders, 25*(2): 136–169.

Skodol, A. E., Clark, L. A., Bender, D. S., Krueger, R. F., Livesley, W. J., & Morey, L. C. (2011b). Proposed changes in personality and personality disorder assessment and diagnosis for DSM-5, Part I: Description and rationale. *Personality Disorders: Theory, Research, and Treatment*, 2: 4–22.

Skodol, A. E., Clark, L. A., Bender, D. S., Krueger, R. F., Livesley, W. J., & Morey, L. C. (2011c). Proposed changes in personality and personality disorder assessment and diagnosis for DSM-5. Part II: Clinical application. *Personality Disorders: Theory, Research, and Treatment*, 2: 23–40.

Stolorow, R. D., & Lachmann, F. M. (1981). Two psychoanalyses or one? *Psychoanalytic Review, 68*: 307–319.

Tyrer, P. (2005). The problem of severity in the classification of personality disorders. *Journal of Personality Disorders, 19*(3): 309–314.

Wallerstein, R. S. (2006). Psychoanalytically based nosology: historic origins. In: *Psychodynamic Diagnostic Manual (PDM)* (pp. 385–402). Silver Spring, MD: Alliance of Psychoanalytic Organizations.

Walls, G. (2006). On being willing to sell your grandmother short: a reply to Wolitzky. *Psychologist–Psychoanalyst (Newsletter of Division 39 of the American Psychological Association), XXVI*: 20–22, 26.

Zimmermann, J., Benecke, C., Bender, D. S., Skodol, A. E., Schauenburg, H., Cierpka, M., & Leising, D. (2013). Assessing DSM-5 Level of Personality Functioning from videotaped clinical interviews: a pilot study with untrained and clinically inexperienced students. *Journal of Personality Assessment*, doi: DOI:10.1080/00223891.2013.852563.

Zimmermann, J., Ehrenthal, J. C., Cierpka, M., Schauenburg, H., Doering, S., & Benecke, C. (2012). Assessing the level of structural integration using operationalized psychodynamic diagnosis (OPD): implications for DSM-5. *Journal of Personality Assessment, 94*(5), 522–532.

# PART VI

# AN APPLICATION OF THE 3-LM AT THE END OF ANALYTIC TRAINING

CHAPTER FOURTEEN

# The three-level model in psychoanalytic training

*Beatriz de León de Bernardi and Marina Altmann de Litvan*

The purpose of this chapter is to recount an experience of partial application of the three-level model in the field of psychoanalytic training. This initiative, conducted by Marina Altmann de Litvan and Beatriz de León de Bernardi, emerged as a response to concerns expressed by the Teaching Committee of the Uruguayan Psychoanalytical Association's (APU) Training Institute. The Committee's concerns were tied to the difficulties experienced by a large number of graduating candidates in writing their final paper, the Associate Member Paper, which constitutes a requirement for membership in APU and the IPA. Their inability to write this paper is felt by many graduates as an outstanding debt and poses an obstacle to their professional and scientific development. Furthermore, it also constitutes a loss for both the psychoanalytic institution that trained them and the International Psychoanalytic Association, as these candidates cannot hold local or international institutional positions that are reserved for members.

The Uruguayan Training Model, which was recognised by the IPA in 2006 as one of its three educational models, has three requirements. Candidates must undergo personal psychoanalysis, pass supervisions and seminars, and write a paper on an analytic process that shows ability to use major psychoanalytic concepts and an adequate articulation between theory and clinical practice. For their essay to be accepted, candidates must discuss it with five analysts. If approved, it may be submitted to the General Scientific Meeting (as long as confidentiality is respected).

The Uruguayan Psychoanalytical Association and its training institute were founded in 1955. In 2003 the Uruguayan Ministry of Education officially recognised the Institute as a Graduate Institute, its curriculum as equivalent to that of a Master's programme in psychoanalysis, and the Associate Member Paper as tantamount to a Master's thesis. Training focuses on Freud's founding concepts, but the Association and its institute have always been open to incorporating the whole range of psychoanalytical schools of thought (de León de Bernardi, 2010).

Both promoters of this project are full members of the Uruguayan Psychoanalytic Association, and have participated in various instances of application of the three-level model with working groups discussing clinical cases. As Chair of the Project Committee on Clinical Observation and Testing, Marina Altmann de Litvan took part in the development of the model and its application in different IPA regions. Beatriz de León de Bernardi, in turn, participated in and co-ordinated initiatives that applied this model in Uruguay and other Latin American countries. We believe that the three-level model created by the Project Committee on Clinical Observation and Testing may be useful in assisting candidates with writing the Associate Member Paper.

The three-level model proposes a thorough exploration of changes undergone by patients during the analytic process based on the study of sessions chosen by the analyst. Some sessions correspond to the initial moments of the analysis and others to later stages, to enable the group to identify transformations by comparing both. We thought that this approach would help candidates choose and contrast the most significant aspects of their clinical case and, thus, show transformations in the analysis or the lack thereof. Progressively considering different levels of observation of clinical experience—the phenomenological level of the session, the level of dimensions of change, and the level of explanatory hypotheses—might help candidates to visualise the scope of these transformations and conceptualise them. In this way, it would facilitate candidates' communication of their findings to the psychoanalytic community through their writing.

We were well aware from the start that, since we were working with a group of graduating candidates, we should not use the model systematically. Rather, it should act as an inspiring guide to favour the development of a group work process that would also involve each group member's ability to find his or her own work dynamics. Furthermore, as our institution is open to different theoretical perspectives, we would need to maintain an open, flexible, and neutral attitude in order to respect, and help clarify and display, participants' own viewpoints.

## *Material and methodology*

The working group comprised two co-ordinators and twelve graduating candidates, who had finished their training from one to fifteen years earlier. Hence, the group was heterogeneous. Members had not had much prior contact with each other because they belonged to different generations.

At the first meeting, we introduced the methodology, which involved monthly three-hour sessions. This frequency would allow participants time for reflection between meetings. We asked group members to choose the case that would serve as the basis for their papers. Some had already chosen it, while others did so during the first stages of the process. Candidates had to present both the initial interviews and sessions from a later stage that, in their view, illustrated changes produced in the patient. We asked participants to identify the different thematic lines that stood out in the material from the first interviews, and left the selection process open. The latter would be completed as group members progressed in their individual work in parallel with the work of the group.

We also posed some questions as triggers that could facilitate both the first stages of individual work with the clinical material, and the start of group work. Some of the questions we asked were as follows. What did analysts think about what the patient brought to the session? What were the patient's beliefs about his or her problems? How did the patient convey what was happening to him or her and why? What were the patient's explicit or implicit expectations regarding the treatment? What had been the analyst's impressions of the first contact with the patient? From the analyst's perspective, what were the most outstanding aspects of the patient's problems?

Group work consisted of an in-depth discussion of one piece of clinical material that was chosen by lottery. Planned in different stages, this work progressed simultaneously with group members' individual efforts with their own clinical materials. Participating candidates could send their work in progress to the co-ordinators and request feedback on it. The latter was delivered occasionally outside group sessions and focused on specific points.

We attributed particular significance to participants' reports, which they took turns to write. After each meeting, one of the candidates must record the topics discussed and group members' various perspectives on the material presented. This report was read and commented upon at the beginning of the next meeting in order to allow candidates to reconnect with the work done previously and with their own thoughts about it.

Clinical materials were shared in such a way as to preserve confidentiality.

## *Work process*

The group met for two years to study two cases in depth, one during the first year and the other during the second. We held six monthly meetings in the first year (the first one was an introductory meeting) and five in the second.

### *Phenomenological level*

#### *Selection and presentation of the clinical material*

The selection of the clinical material for their papers gave rise to questions and concerns among participants. Concerns referred mainly to changes achieved in the analysis, the nature of these changes, and whether or not this process could be considered psychoanalysis. Questions such as, "Is this an analytic process?" and "Is this a psychoanalysis?" emerged at various times and must be explored in order to realistically confront the material presented with institutional requirements. Manifold factors could generate doubts, among them, personal insecurities, the nature of the transference relationship, and psychoanalytical ideals reinforced by the institution that might sometimes become removed from actual practice. Candidates expressed these doubts even when they believed that transformations had occurred in the analysis that were beneficial for the patient. Their concern hindered the selection of the clinical material, for it led them to belittle their own experience and, in short, prevented them from observing, pondering, and recapturing this experience in a written work. We will come back to this issue in the final discussion.

### *Presentation of the clinical material*

Presentations followed the three-level model, which considers it indispensable that analysts read the clinical case. Reading the material facilitates a more vivid transmission of their experience with their patients. In the act of reading, they convey patients' emotional tones and their own emotional response to these tones, thus enriching group observation. The presentation includes a brief summary of patients' history and their current situation, analysts' communication of their internal image of their patients, the latter's physical appearance, gestures, and emotional tone, and, perhaps involuntarily, also analysts' reactions to them. Non-verbal aspects of the relationship also come up during the first presentation and allow us to infer rudimentary aspects of the transference and countertransference.

In this sense, the point was not to ask candidates to provide an "objective", detached account of their experience; group observation also entails observing analysts' participation in the process. At the same time, analysts presenting the material follow the associations of the other group members, who may ask for clarifications or make comments, especially at the end of the reading. Analysts then present their own point of view, in agreement or in contrast with the others' viewpoint.

### *The group's listening attitude towards the material: from "observation" to "resonance"*

We should also ponder the group's listening attitude towards the clinical material presented. This is not a supervision process, which performs both teaching and institutional evaluation functions. Neither is it an analytic session. In the session, analysts follow patients' associations and empathically resonate with them moment by moment. It is only afterwards that they can engage in a reflexive exploration of what took place. In the working group sessions, the group's listening work travels a reverse path. We start by carefully examining and listening to the clinical material, which includes patient and analyst, from outside the scene of the session. In this context, our listening may easily bring to mind various psychoanalytic theorisations of a general, abstract nature, as happens sometimes in scientific discussions. In this case, the co-ordinators' role is to leave these associations on hold as questions, since at this stage we cannot ascertain if they are consistent with the material.

For instance, in the presentation of the first case, the analyst changed the expression "flower holder" (*florero*) to "vase" (*jarrón*) in her answer to her young male patient. This doubtless led the group to make manifold associations about the patient's sexual identification and difficulties. Yet, in the end, we were able to set this issue aside for the time being as an open-ended question. Instead, participants focused on "group resonance" phenomena that guided the observation towards other aspects of the session that were generally deemed more relevant. These aspects displayed the patient's current anxiety more directly and allowed group members to infer underlying unconscious problems that were distant from consciousness and must be investigated.

### *Phenomenological level and metaphors*

Group resonance phenomena emerge not only from the reading of the material, but also from the communication and prioritisation of certain aspects of it. In this way, in the first case, the analyst highlighted the particular way in which the patient made contact with her. She felt that he experienced "a kind of whirlwind anxiety" that was expressed from the first interview in the accelerated pace of his discourse and his inability to fall into thoughtful silence. The patient claimed that he felt he was in a "quicksand", an expression that particularly resonated with the group as an indication of instability and vulnerability. This feeling of instability surfaced when discussing topics related to his body and identifications.

Authors such as Aulagnier (1986) have stressed the pictorial and figurative nature of analysts' interpretations, favoured by the process of formal regression that guides suspended attention at certain times during the session. In many opportunities, the group's reflection stemmed from the impregnation of certain images present in the clinical material. At other times, instead, it hinged on images emerging from the discussion that condensed key aspects of the patient's life stage and set of problems. For example, the image of a puzzle appeared after listening to the interviews of the second case, where different aspects of the patient's personality and conflicts seemed to suggest scant integration. Images such as *the whirlpool, the quicksand,* or *the puzzle* arose as metaphors expressing patients' various life situations and subjective experiences (Altmann, 2008).

Such images influenced the group's thoughts both during the first reading of the interviews and during the unfolding of the analytic material and its subsequent conceptualisation. The first patient's feeling of being in a quicksand was later connected to painful emotional and physical sensations that had been heralded in the preliminary interviews. The image condensed the patient's feelings of insecurity with regard to certain physical limitations and his fears in relation to the future of his sexual, emotional, and professional life. In addition, it was linked to his insecurity and conflicts concerning his primary bonds. Metaphors arising from group work were the product of the interweaving of presenters' communication of their experience with their patients, the impact of the reading on participants, and the group's emotional and intellectual processing of the material. In this sense, these metaphors also facilitated the creation of a common ground for dialogue among participating analysts.

We might question the validity of these group resonance phenomena and their value as clues in our enquiry into patients' problems. None the less, we need to keep in mind that such processes of group selection are based on the various experiences of group members, that is, on their personal analysis and clinical and theoretical training. In this sense, these first observations are laden with implicit theorisations, as Sandler (1983) points out, and open the way for potential conceptualisations. Metaphors emerging in analysis have been viewed as a bridge between bodily experience and the mind (Modell, 2005), and are at the service of the expression and recontextualisation of emotional non-verbal memories, some of them traumatic. The metaphorising process would facilitate the passage from concrete observation to symbolisation and conceptualisation (Wurmser, 1977; de León de Bernardi, 2013) at the level of both individual and group work. In this way, the analyst's visualisation of her patient's anxiety as a whirlwind in the first case, or the image of the puzzle in the second case, evoked in group members their differing experiences and partial theorisations in relation to anxiety or to deficiencies in early development.

### *Level of dimensions of change*

Group members spontaneously identified these dimensions, but formulated them in different theoretical languages. In the first case, the topic of anxiety led to the question of difficulties in the containment of affects and emotional regulation. The group pointed out changes produced between the first and second interviews. In the second interview, the pace of the patient's discourse slowed down, and he was occasionally able to think about himself and his problems. This transformation led participants to think that his anxiety stemmed from neurotic conflicts rather than deficiencies related to identity problems.

Reflection and discussion concerning whether the material showed the prevalence of structural deficiencies or neurotic conflict started as a question and resurfaced at different stages of group work. In this context, the presentation of the second patient, who showed disorganised aspects, as a *puzzle*, led the group to hypothesise the existence of significant deficits in her primary bonds, a feature that came up again at subsequent times in the analysis. Participants also considered the dimension referred to changes that might have taken place in patients' perception and appropriation of their own problems (how they perceive their "illness" according to the model).

On occasion, the group also addressed obstacles that candidates might have encountered in the psychoanalytic treatment of their patients. Work on these obstacles promoted their incorporation as material for reflection and analysis in candidates' papers and the discussion of their potential negative impact on the analysis. Participants also considered the mode of the transference and obstacles arising in connection with it. The first patient was marked by experiences of physical pain. Consequently, in the first stages of the analysis, the analyst took on a holding function without interpreting the transference. Taking on this function, however, generated in her doubts about her position as an analyst as well as a feeling of insecurity.

Yet, was explicit transference work necessary for patient or analyst, or was it rather an institutional requirement? Or, was the possibility of establishing a different relationship with a new object what was at stake at the time? Candidates advanced different hypotheses on this issue. Some referred to the appositeness of resorting to explicit transference interpretation in the first stages of the analysis in cases such as this one, where the patient must confront his illness. Participants also considered that the analyst's feeling of powerlessness and constraint might express countertransference responses that supplemented the patient's powerlessness and insecurities in relation to his present and future. The patient defended himself against these insecurities with omnipotence and personal neglect, which increased his anxiety. In addition, the group discussed how to work with hostility at the level of the transference.

At the end of the analysis, the patient showed transformations tied to an increased modulation of affects and a greater ability to reflect and symbolise (dreams and associative richness). Changes included anxiety reduction, the deepening of his transference bond with his analyst, and a shift in his relationship with his family. He can now change his subjective position with regard to his illness, thus reducing his omnipotent defences and accepting his limitations in a different way.

### *Level of explanatory theoretical hypotheses*

This chapter does not aim to narrate the evolution of a clinical case in detail but to thoroughly describe the stages of group work. In the last stage of our discussion of the first case, we tackled the third level of analysis, that is, we explored the analyst's implicit and explicit theoretical hypotheses in a dialogue with the group's ideas.

The analyst had considered hypotheses that attributed a psychological meaning to her patient's physical illness—explanations that were used by the patient himself. Yet, as the analysis progressed, she had been led to think that these explanations were a defence against the various kinds of difficulties experienced by her patient due to his physical limitations. Participants suggested several theoretical approaches, among them Pierre Marty's ideas in relation to psychosomatic patients. The analyst, however, did not feel that this perspective suited her patient's characteristics. Neither did she think that he handled his illness in the manner of a hysterical neurotic. On the contrary, the conflicts he displayed alluded to fear of submission and dependence, for he reacted with attitudes of omnipotence and exaggerated narcissistic affirmation.

We hoped candidates would be able to explore the specificities of each case. How is this patient different from other patients? Such exploration would lead to an enquiry into different theoretical developments that suited these specificities. We did not encourage a thorough analysis of the theoretical ideas arising from the discussion of both cases. Rather, our purpose was to advance a methodology that favoured the examination of different explanatory hypotheses based on the experience and perspectives of group members in relation to their own cases. These hypotheses would stem from their training and their singular internalisation of psychoanalytic theories.

### *Organising the clinical material discussed in the group in order to write and conceptualise each participant's material*

At the end of the first year and during the second one, group work started focusing on the writing process. After the analyst had read the sessions she had chosen, we invited participants to describe how they would develop and put together a table of contents for their papers. This activity involved a new way of organising and prioritising different thematic lines and moments in the analysis, concentrating more directly on the writing work and its challenges. To do so, the co-ordinators promoted autonomous individual work. On occasion, several group members got together outside of the group meetings to work on their papers on their own.

Participants mentioned their difficulty in choosing the thematic lines and material that best suited their papers. Generally speaking, they had collected a lot of material and had a hard time selecting the most significant fragments, choosing required setting aside sessions that they deemed important. Taking a more detached attitude regarding the material was challenging because they felt very invested in it. How could they translate the space of the intimate scene of analysis into the space of writing and public exposure, even if confidentiality were preserved? Such translation entailed conceptualising what they had experienced and thought, which was hard for them to do.

### *Different paths toward conceptualising the clinical material*

One participant suggested a different use of the notion of suspended attention, not in the presence of the patient or in contact with the group, but in a second moment, while reading the clinical material in solitude. She thought that this practice would bring to the surface the thematic lines to be tackled in her paper. Another group member mentioned that she needed to reread the clinical material she had chosen and rethink it in light of various authors' ideas on psychic change, a topic that interested her at the time.

The ways in which participants search for the central thread (or threads) of their papers differ, and they find this thread at different stages in their writing. In some cases, they do so at the beginning, in others, during the writing process, and in others yet, once they have finished and are able to resignify *a posteriori* some aspects of the early stages. Once they complete it, they have a clearer view of the paper as a whole.

An essential component of the Associate Member Paper, stressed by the co-ordinators, is candidates' personal reflection on their experience and the ways in which this reflection develops. Yet, this is not an easy task; besides being subject to evaluation, the paper mobilises fantasies related to the meaning of analytic identity and institutional belonging.

## *Evaluation and discussion*

The group work we carried out for two years affected participants (both candidates and co-ordinators) in different ways. Two recently graduating group members wrote their papers during the first year, and two who had graduated more than five years earlier, during the second year. Five candidates have made significant progress, and two have just started. One participant gave up writing. The co-ordinators would ask about each member's writing process, which accompanied the various stages of group work.

Reports read to the group significantly contributed to the step-by-step evaluation of group and individual work. In addition, these reports played a major role in the conceptualisation process; they resumed earlier discussions, making it possible to rethink the issues discussed. Over time, reports went from simple "minutes" of the exchanges to true syntheses that also included theorisations explored by the group.

This undertaking has led us to reformulate our question as follows: What are the reasons that lead candidates to delay writing their Associate Member Paper, and to what extent did our work, inspired in the three-level model, facilitate the writing process?

In relation to problems arising in psychoanalytic education, some have described how the influence of personal ideals is enhanced by institutional ideals associated with the essential components of psychoanalysis and psychoanalytic identity (Garza Guerrero, 2002; Kernberg, 2000). Explicitly or implicitly conveyed institutional ideals can sometimes have an impact on candidates. These ideals may generate an excessively self-demanding behaviour, or lead candidates either to conform too much to institutional thinking (de León de Bernardi, 2010) or to believe that their paper must include theoretical developments that largely exceed institutional requirements.

The three-level model contributed significantly to candidates' ability to observe, reassess, and appreciate the richness of the clinical material. This result was achieved by working at the phenomenological level, very close to experience, and by distinguishing this level from the tracking of implicit theories and reflection upon alternative hypotheses. Furthermore, the careful and comparative observation of different moments in the analytic process suggested by the model helped bring to the fore one of the major goals of analysts' task and role: patients' transformations.

Consequently, narcissistic aspects of institutional belonging and psychoanalytic identity shifted to the background. They were doubtlessly present, but recovered their trophic nature and were put at the service of group work. In this sense, the richness of collective work acted as a catalyst and container for candidates' anxiety by helping them reconnect with the curiosity typical of clinical researchers and with the playful side of our endeavour.

Working progressively from clinical experience towards more abstract theorisation levels also promoted group conceptualisation and theorisation. Tuckett (1994) has pointed out the difficulties experienced by analysts in conceptualising and communicating clinical facts, especially since the observer is always included in these "facts". This characteristic of psychoanalysis poses an obstacle for analysts in general. Still, its negative effects are enhanced in the case of candidates who are writing the Associate Member Paper, which is often experienced as an initiation rite. We believe that raising group members' awareness of these aspects by constantly striving to focus on exploring the features of analytic work, the reasons for analysts to intervene in certain situations and moments of the analysis, and the impact of such interventions on the patient contributed to candidates' working-out process and to the formulation of hypotheses of a more general nature.

By promoting an honest debate on analytic work in a small group in pace with the writing process, we sought to help participants appropriate their personal experience and develop individual perspectives. In addition, writing enables the transmission of ideas in the broader context of the local and international scientific communities (Kantrowitz, 2006).

As co-ordinators, we found the experience challenging because we had to be particularly alert to transformations in the analytic process without losing track of other relevant matters: questions raised by the contact between analyst and patient, singular modes of the transference–countertransference interplay, and varying explanatory hypotheses about the psychic functioning of a patient in a specific analytic process. In this sense, group work also had an impact on us; it constituted an enriching learning process for both co-ordinators.

## *References*

Altmann, M. (2008). Cómo se da el nacimiento del paciente en la mente del analista. XVI Jornadas de Psicoanálisis de APU. Desafíos del psicoanálisis contemporáneo. Montevideo, Uruguay, Asociación Psicoanalítica del Uruguay (APU).

Aulagnier, P. (1986). *Du langage pictural au langage de l'interprète. Un interprète en quête de sens* [From Pictorial Language to the Language of the Interpreter: An Interpreter in Search of Meaning]. Paris: Payot.

De León de Bernardi, B. (2010). La formación psicoanalítica en un contexto de pluralismo teórico y técnico [Psychoanalytic Training in a Context of Theoretical and Technical Pluralism]. *Revista Latinoamericana de Psicoanálisis, 9*: 119–138.

De León de Bernardi, B. (2013). Field theory as a metaphor and metaphors in the analytic field and process. *Psychoanalytic Inquiry, 33*: 247–266.

Garza Guerrero, C. (2002). Organisational and educational internal impediments of psychoanalysis. *International Journal of Psychoanalysis, 83*: 1407–1433.

Kantrowitz, J. (2006). *Writing about Patients: Responsibilities, Risks and Ramifications*. New York: Other Press.

Kernberg, O. (2000). A concerned critique of psychoanalytical education. *International Journal of Psychoanalysis, 81*: 97–120.

Modell, A. (2005). Emotional memory, metaphor and meaning. *Psychoanalytic Inquiry, 25*: 555–368.

Sandler, J. (1983). Reflections on some relations between psychoanalytic concepts and psychoanalytic practice. *International Journal of Psychoanalysis, 69*: 335–345.

Tuckett, D. (1994). The conceptualisation and communication of clinical facts in psychoanalysis—Foreword. *International Journal of Psychoanalysis, 75*: 865–870.

Wurmser, L. (1977). A defense of the use of metaphor in analytic theory formation. *Psychoanalytic Quarterly, 46*: 466–498.

*CHAPTER FIFTEEN*

# The use of the 3-LM to teach candidates to observe transformations in clinical cases

*Liliana Fudin de Winograd and Adela Leibovich de Duarte*

Finding new tools to train psychoanalysts at our training institutes is certainly a goal shared by many IPA societies. Two members of the Argentine Psychoanalytic Society (SAP), Dr Adela Leibovich de Duarte, member of the Project Committee on Clinical Observation and Testing and institute instructor andLiliana Fudin de Winograd, director of the Institute, who are familiar with the three-level model for observing patient transformations (3-LM), thought it would be useful to conduct a workshop with our institution's candidates following this model.

SAP's psychoanalytic training project states that psychoanalytic training must take into account the general difficulties posed by any training process as well as some that are specific to psychoanalytic training. Among the latter are the difficulty in distinguishing different observational levels in psychoanalytic sessions, the distance between clinical practice and explanatory concepts, the variety of theoretical models that may inform clinical practice, the relevance of the artisanal–emotional–creative aspect in the "dynamic field" of the analytic relationship, the need for conceptual rigour and formalisation, and the inclusion of the ethical dimension.

For this reason, as established in the 2012 Analyst Training Project, seminars and other educational activities conducted at our training institute seek to promote a comprehension and reflection process with the following objectives.

- Identify, clarify, and articulate concepts developed by Freud and other psychoanalytic authors through a critical, systematic reading of their ideas.
- Guide candidates in their articulation of theory and clinical practice.
- Relate the models studied to problems arising in current clinical practice, both at mental health facilities and in private practice.
- Strengthen psychoanalytic training in clinical work, thence the significant role of referenced clinical practice in the curriculum.
- Enrich psychoanalysis with contributions from other disciplines.
- Develop favourable attitudes toward research and written production. (SAP, 2012, translated for this edition)

"Referenced clinical practice" constitutes a critical aspect of candidates' training. The Institute promotes their interest in reflecting on clinical work and conceptualising experience by way of various theoretical models. We shall refer briefly to the referenced clinical practice seminars to facilitate readers' understanding of the context in which our interest in the three-level model was aroused. Referenced clinical practice constitutes the focal point that articulates most of SAP's training seminars. The basic idea is to promote and solidify an itinerary that goes from clinical practice to theory, and *vice versa*. The point is not to conduct collective supervisions (these have their own space in the institution). Rather, it is to explore clinical procedures and inferential and theoretical–clinical generalisation processes. The collective nature of the seminar allows participants to share their experiences and confront them with others. In this way, they can delve into diverse clinical materials that enrich their training.

Clinical materials discussed with candidates come from different sources. They are drawn from classic cases, provided by instructors or analysts in training, or taken from SAP's clinical discussion sessions or scientific presentations. The goal of this work is to analyse the observational and narrative dimensions, the inference process, the analyst's interventions, and the explanatory and contextual dimensions. As we pointed out earlier, this theoretical–clinical work is founded on clear ethical principles that candidates start applying at the beginning of their training.

In this context, we considered that the three-level model would be a very useful practice for candidates. They could apply it in sessions with a patient under treatment and focus their detailed attention on transformations occurring over the course of the analytic process. The main goal was to test the effectiveness of this model in further developing candidates' observation skills in clinical practice. Level 1, in particular, encourages participants to focus on observation and description, which are very hard to address with other methodological approaches.

We decided to carry out a pilot test with analysts in training, who studied clinical material provided by a SAP member. The experience was carried out at SAP headquarters on 31 May and 1 June 2013. We worked from 2.00 p.m. to 8.00 p.m. on the first day and from 9.00 a.m. to 6.00 p.m. on the second day, taking one break on Friday and two on Saturday. There were two groups, two co-ordinators (Dr Adela Leibovich de Duarte and Liliana Fudin de Winograd), and two summarisers (Graciela Cervato and Ana Fleischer de Trenes). The psychoanalyst in charge of the case, Gabriela Cassoli, visited both groups to answer questions on the material.

Twenty candidates at different stages of their training made up the two groups. Participants received the material and the observation model ahead of time and were instructed to print them out. In this way, they could decide whether or not to read the material in advance. The latter consisted of sessions from three different moments in the analytic process: preliminary interviews, two sessions from the first year of treatment, and two sessions that had taken place after two years of analysis. The patient was a forty-year-old professional woman and mother of three children who had just divorced her husband when she sought help due to an anxiety crisis. She saw her analyst three times a week.

### *Level 1*

We worked on the first level most of the time because, at first, participants found it hard to limit their contributions to describing what they observed, that is, to a *phenomenological description of the analytic process*, as they had been instructed to do. A tendency to "supervise" prevailed in both groups. Based on the patient's discourse, group members were inclined to offer opinions on the analyst's interpretations and suggest other options. Then they replaced this approach with rapidly formulated explanatory hypotheses. Co-ordinators had to repeat the instructions and explain that the goal was to identify transformations arising from the observable aspects of the material, and to detect problems based on what participants had observed. These problems, which were specific to the patient, would be traced in sessions from different stages in the analytic process as dimensions of observation. In this way, candidates would be able to identify observable data that made it possible to determine whether transformations had occurred or not. Repeated explanations helped them focus on the set goal.

Co-ordinators devoted a long time to this level because one of the objectives, as mentioned above, was precisely to help build candidates' capacity for clinical observation. It is very clear that the group's ability to delve into the clinical material in depth for many hours led to the broadening of each participant's range of observation. Moreover, the group effect facilitated the incorporation of different perceptual registers—linguistic, gestural, and rhythmic, among others. Comments made by the treating analyst during the meetings made it possible to integrate information on visual, inflection, and tonal aspects, as well as the analyst's emotional countertransference experience.

### *Level 2*

The purpose of this level is to identify the main dimensions of psychic functioning along which transformations do or do not occur. Questions posed organise the articulation between observation records and categories that, despite involving a greater level of abstraction, remain close to experience. The questions suggested for this level and the order in which they were asked were very useful to reach this end. While some of them were not answered, they opened interesting paths of enquiry that could be explored in depth during the rest of the teaching process. Out of all the categories provided, both groups focused mainly on the subjective experience of illness, patterns of interpersonal relationships, and main intrapsychic conflicts.

### *Level 3*

Finally, the groups succeeded in connecting this level—the analyst's theoretical hypotheses about change—with the previous ones. They could, thus, formulate the kind of hypotheses suggested by the model. This constituted a significant achievement; when participants had started working on Level 1, they had spontaneously offered this type of hypotheses, yet with scant observation to support them. The main aspects discussed in this level were therapeutic foci, explicit or implicit hypotheses of the analyst, other hypotheses, and possible interpretative strategies.

To conclude:

1. The three-level model and its application are congruent with our institution's psychoanalytic training objectives and methodology. Indeed, this method of working with clinical material promotes a clear discrimination among observational and narrative dimensions, the inference process, and the explanatory dimension. In addition, it attributes great significance to the notion of field (Baranger & Baranger, 2008) by incorporating the treating analyst into the process.
2. This model interconnects and categorises questions among and within the three levels. In this way, it helps participants organise their thinking process to formulate hypotheses. This feature makes the 3-LM an excellent teaching resource.
3. Group work helps candidates widen their channels of observation, whether by attending to other group members' perceptions or through the emotional effect of sustained group work. It is worth highlighting here that candidates' enthusiasm grew over the course of the activity; they became much more involved at the end than they had been at the beginning.
4. A survey administered to participating candidates yielded the following results:
    (a) Participants rated the activity as very positive and expressed great satisfaction for having taken part in it. They underscored that (i) generally speaking, it had helped them realise the importance of conducting a detailed clinical examination during the analytic process, and (ii) they had learnt a lot by listening to other group members and sharing observations.

They could, thus, identify transformation "indicators" they would have missed without the help of the group.

(b) Regarding the three-level model in general, while it was hard for them to answer the questions posed, candidates mostly agreed that these questions served to organise their thoughts and furnished them with parameters to detect transformations. Moreover, the model was a good tool to reflect on their practice.

As co-ordinators, we coincided with participants' assessment. We think that it will be very useful to incorporate this activity into our institute's training process.

## *References*

Baranger, M., & Baranger, W. (2008). The analytic situation as a dynamic field. *International Journal of Psychoanalysis, 89*: 795–826.

Sociedad Argentina de Psicoanálisis (SAP) (2012). Proyecto de formación psicoanalítica [Psychoanalytic training process]. In-house document.

# PART VII

# FURTHER DEVELOPMENTS OF THE 3-LM IN CHILD ANALYSIS

CHAPTER SIXTEEN

# Three-level model for observing child patient transformations

*Marina Altmann de Litvan, Delfina Miller, and Ricardo Bernardi*

Child analysis has its own special characteristics. Since children are undergoing an accelerated process of development and, hence, are constantly changing, analysts have to enter into this process in order to to guide their patients towards a healthy growth.

Child analysts work on a reconstruction sustained by regression and conflict, but, more particularly, on a construction based on certain development patterns and influenced by external factors which interact with phantasies and defences (dynamic unconscious). Previously or simultaneously with the analysis of conflicts, we must often work with aspects that are still not sufficiently structured and whose development conditions conflicts (Olesker & Lament, 2008).

In this way, changes and transformations will gradually take place that cannot be predicted. They are new creations generated between patient and analyst that are specific to this encounter and lead to a particular maturation process. The various aspects of child organisation acquire a new configuration, combining to form the developmental lines described by Anna Freud (1965). A sense of self is gradually built by way of a discontinued, non-linear, and unpredictable process.

How will analysts, then, be able to determine whether they are producing these transformations, how they are achieving them, and what consequences such transformations have for the child? To answer these questions, we have developed the three-level model for observing child patient transformations. This model starts with a careful characterisation of patients and their problems and abilities (capacities, relationships, emotional patterns, behaviour tendencies), then asks what changes occurred during treatment and what are their causes. It is inspired in the work of the IPA Clinical Observation Committee and the model for adult patients developed by Dr Ricardo Bernardi (2011) as well as influenced, in reference to the clinical observation of children, by the proposals of the Hampstead Psychoanalytic Index (Bolland & Sandler, 1965). Its aim is to track transformations that take place as a result of a psychoanalytic process, seeking evidence in the clinical material.

## *What do we look for in the clinical material?*

We look for positive or negative changes, or the absence of change in the child. To do so, we take into consideration the child's expected level of development, the environment in which (s)he is growing, and his/her parents' perspective and parenting skills.

In its application to child patients, the model emphasizes *play* because the latter is a natural form of expression in children as well as a privileged means of exchange with the analyst. Through play, patients display their wishes, anxieties, phantasies, defences, and object relations. Play, therefore, enables us to assess level of development, abilities, and personality organisation, but mainly to promote growth and emotional development (Kernberg, Chazan, & Normandin, 1996).

From the Freudian perspective, play is anchored in sexual drives, curiosity, and the child's wish to know about its origins. These will lead to the production of infant sexual theories that are expressed through the body by way of play and actions that cause pleasure (Freud, 1905d).

Play allows us to understand the dynamic levels of conflict and the structural aspects of the organisation of the psychic apparatus through children's pleasurable display of their phantasies (Freud, 1908e).

Moved by desire, they play and unfold unconscious dynamics without losing the self's commitment to reality. Thus, they may shift from the hallucinatory realisation of desires to the figuration of their satisfaction by examining and modifying reality (Volinski de Hoffnung et al., 1986). Later, Freud (1920g) will connect play to repetition compulsion, which is linked, in turn, to the death instinct (the peek-a-boo game).

According to Klein (1962, 1964), there is a close connection between unconscious and conscious that is expressed through play—anxieties, phantasies, and early defences. She posits the existence of unconscious phantasies that are expressed in infancy. In her formulations on play technique, she equates children's games with adults' verbal associations; during the analytic session communication occurs through play and actions that may or may not be accompanied by words, but allow access to the unconscious. This unconscious scene, always present, active, and in constant interaction with reality, explains children's mental functioning.

While actions and games involve different levels of symbolisation than do words (much more primitive), we may find in them a road to unconscious phantasies, going from bodily modes of expression, linked to discharge and exploration, towards greater degrees of symbolisation. This "doing" (comparable to adults' words or dreams) is a precursor of thought. Furthermore, it is precisely this display by means of actions and games that will enable analysts to observe children's functioning and detect change.

Behind play, then, we discover a whole process of projection, working through, and discharge that leads us to emphasise the need to interpret children's play by playing with them and for them in the transference. Thus, we may facilitate the symbolic reparation of internal objects and self-representation. This close relation between phantasy and structuration is exactly what will enable us to affect mental organisation through analysis. By playing with our patients and interpreting their play, we can modify phantasies about internal and external objects as well as anxieties and defences linked to these phantasies. This process will generate transformations in children's mental functioning.

To conduct a child analysis, therefore, analysts certainly need to know how to play and patients must be able to do so, as was remarked by an exceptional child analyst, Donald Winnicott (1958, 1971). According to him, play carried out in the analysis, in the transitional space between analyst and patient, gives rise to a creative process that is enriching for both. Analyst and patient should freely undergo an experience of trust that is framed in the shared goal of understanding, relief, growth, and maturation.

We can then prove the structuring condition of play, especially when it unfolds in analysis. Consequently, we focus on the observation that may be conducted by the analyst, not only in order to understand the child, but also, in this case, to assess the analytic process and the patient's development. The chosen material, therefore, must include meaningful fragments where we may see not only how and where children have developed and how they behave and express themselves, but also how they play and how they act during their playing and how analysts think, interpret, and play. This approach will allow us to study the analytic process as a whole.

In addition, this model introduces the evaluation of *sensory and affective regulation*. Sensory regulation is highly relevant for children because it influences their ability to achieve and maintain an optimal range of performance and adaptation to ordinary challenges. Regulatory–sensorial processing reveals the capacity for sensory modulation, the degree of control, intensity, and nature of responses to a sensory stimulus (*Psychodynamic Diagnostic Manual* (*PDM*), 2006).

Sensory regulation constitutes the first step towards affective regulation because the latter is gradually developed by way of the processing of stimuli, sensations, perceptions, and experiences that children will gradually transform into emotions and feelings. This capacity to represent sensations and modulate affective states in order to generate adaptive responses is acquired in the bond with others and becomes the basis for the organisation of the self (Fonagy, 1995).

Before infants develop the ability to observe and respond to affects as a mental fact, affect regulation is performed through behaviour. Spitz (1965) notes a series of behaviours that lead to states of disintegration and to tantrums. These are avoiding the gaze of the mother because it leads to painful mental representations, reversing aggression and turning it into acts of self-punishment, immobilisation, and fighting with the mother.

Infants can learn a lot from dyadic interactions. Mother and child are simultaneously developing inner experiences in a mutual feedback system, which gives the child opportunities for interactive regulation and self-regulation (Emde, 1999; Sander, 1977; Silverman,

1998). In this way, children intuit ways to preserve their experience of safety in the future.

From this link between the personal and the interactive system emerges a pattern of unique and distinctive regulation for a particular dyad (interactive model) and a particular form of self-regulation characteristic of each infant. Children, thus, learn and develop forms of interactive regulation and self-regulation that are tolerable for both mother and child (Silverman, 1998). This interactive behavioural system is internalised, and relationship models are instated over time as mental models, or what, in psychoanalysis, we call "mental representations". Internal models demonstrate the existence of adaptive and defensive features (Silverman, 1998). The interactive attachment system acts as a regulator of affects and is established through expressions and emotional responses to a positive or negative tone that develop between mother and infant.

## *The implementation of this model*

### *How should clinical material be presented in order to enable observation to be made?*

We will start presenting meaningful material from the first interviews with the child and his parents in order to be able to evaluate the mentioned aspects as well as the dimensions of the child's psychic functioning in which transformations will be observed.

We include in this presentation basic data (age, sex, school performance, reason for consultation and demand, framed by family constitution, meaningful events in the patient's history, acute or chronic stressors, traumatic situations, somatic illnesses, medication), patterns of development in relation to the chronologic age of the child (psyche–soma integration, dream, feeding, sphincters control, psychomotor development, cognitive tools, performance, emotions) and the libidinal stage (representation of self, relationships), as well as an evaluation of the organisation of his personality and its level of functioning (conflicts and structure).

Then we wonder:

- Who is this child and how is he?
- What and who motivated consultation at this moment?

- What is his level of functioning and which disorders does he present in regard to the expected development stage for his age?
- How does the child feel what is happening? How do his parents live it? What do parents and child do in this regard?
- What do they expect from treatment?

Then we present later moments of the analysis (for example, after six months, one year, two years, etc.) chosen by the analyst to show those transformations that he considers meaningful (positive or negative) in some of the initially presented dimensions.

The clinical presentation must be useful to the analyst for monitoring his work, or to the group of colleagues for discussing whether there are positive or negative changes, or no changes at all.

These vignettes should be described through sufficiently meaningful material that can give support both to the phenomenological evaluation and to the inferences about the underlying unconscious processes and the transformations at stake.

The analyst will make a presentation paying special attention to transference and countertransference, providing a good and detailed description of what happens in the child during the session, in himself, and, eventually, in his parents. In order to do this, the analyst will have to register what is related to play, but also his memory of the sequence of facts, the child's behaviour, his impressions, the specific dialogues, and the emotions that are displayed in their meeting. Special consideration will be given to the relation between these aspects and the symptoms that generated the consultation. In an optional way, other complementary methods could be used, such as filming, recordings, etc.

The description of these meetings will allow the focusing of analysis and discussion on the value of transformations that took place in each of the meetings as well as along the therapeutic process, emphasising the interaction between patient and analyst.

## *Level 1: phenomenological description of transformations*

### *Aims of group discussion at Level 1*

We expect the listening to clinical vignettes that describe transformations in the child (regarding his behaviour, emotions, performance, relationships, personality organisation) and in his relationship with the analyst, as well as the comments that promote these changes, help participants improve their listening and observation capacity, favouring the identification of new subtleties in the clinical material, as well as possible blind spots of the process, from the patient or the analyst.

*Questions that give orientation to evaluation at this level*

(A) Which aspects of the material (supplied by the child, his parents, teachers, or other informants) suggest the existence of positive or negative transformations, or the absence of transformations?

(B) Which of these changes may be attributed to the growth of the child in regards to the development patterns that were highlighted in the material presentation? (For example, dream, feeding, sphincters control, psychomotor development, relationships.)

(C) Which may be attributed to changes in the environment? (Family events such as separations, divorce, death, newborns, accidents, moving, etc.)

(D) As we mentioned before, we shall give a special place to the child's play. First, we observe whether his play is in agreement with his age and gender, and which phase of the libidinal development it refers to.

Regarding these aspects, we shall note transformations or the absence of them, taking as a model the evaluation of play proposed by Kernberg, Chazan, and Normandin (1996):

- Type of play (sensory-motor, exploration, construction, phantasy).
- Narrative (originality, elaboration, organisation, sequence).
- Subjects (presentation, elaboration, and processing).
- Affects (which and how many, with which intensity and adequacy, level, and way of regulation).
- Expressed relationships (with the analyst, among characters within the game).

(E) Which transformations can be observed in the course of one session? And through different moments in time?

(F) In which of these areas are meaningful changes perceived which show transformations in the general functioning and well-being of the child?
   (a) Symptoms and subjective well-being.
   (b) Relationship within his family, and out of it (peers, teachers, etc.).
   (c) School performance and interests.

(G) Changes in treatment regarding:
   (a) How does the child accept it? (For example: attitude regarding the setting.)
   (b) How does the child use the therapist?
   (c) How does the child use the therapist's interventions?
   (d) How does the child use his own mind and body during the session?
   (e) How does the child use the mind and body of his care-givers?

(H) How have therapist and patient participated in the transformation process? Which is the perspective of each of them about transformations? What is the perspective from the child's care-givers and teachers in this regard? What relations can be established between the transformations and the characteristics of the analytic process?

(I) Which parts of the clinical material have a special resonance in participants regarding the transformation process?

## *Level 2: identification of the main diagnostic dimensions of change*

### *Aims of group discussion at Level 2*

The aim at this level is helping the analyst and, at the same time, training participants in the group discussion, in the identification of the main dimensions along which transformations may occur or not.

Transformations should be identified in relevant dimensions from a psychoanalytic point of view (for example, not only if patients have a better performance, but mainly in which aspects we can support or accompany this change: patterns of relationship, capacity for empathy, sense of self, self-esteem, etc.). A systematic and valid description of change requires that the different points of reference are compared along the same dimension, or, at least, comparable dimensions. For this, the analyst's report has to offer a perspective about the child's problems that is sufficiently wide and, especially, of his mental and interpersonal functioning.

Taking into account the multiplicity of theoretical languages, it is convenient at this level to begin the discussion using a phenomenological language and seeking to operationalise concepts.

Once transformations are analysed in the patient, in a language close to experience and theoretically non-saturated, we will contextualise the specific transformations according to a more comprehensive description of the child's problems and of other transformations that should be considered. This level should prepare and strengthen the observational basis for discussion at Level 3, in which the understanding of transformations from different theoretical perspectives will be studied further.

### *Questions that give direction in the identification of the main dimensions of change*

The following questions seek to identify the dimensions along which transformations could occur. They are mainly based on *OPD-2* (OPD-2 Task Force, 2008) and *PDM* (2006) proposals.

#### *1. Subjective experience of illness*

1A. Which are the main problems and symptoms of the patient according to the analyst's judgement? What subjective experience does the child have of them? Which are his beliefs regarding what occurs and his expectations regarding treatment? How much is the patient aware of his problems? Which is the parents' perspective about the child's problems? Which is the teachers' perspective about them? How much does the child see the ways that could lead him to a change? And his parents? How much do analyst, patient, and parents (other informants could correspond, too) agree about the expected transformations?

1B. How did these aspects change? How much has changed the understanding of problems in the child and the expectancy of transformation possibilities? How has this been modified in parents (or other relevant informants)?

1C. Do contextual factors which affect the therapeutic process exist? (E.g., crisis situations, traumatic experiences, somatic illnesses, etc.) How capable is the patient of facing these situations?

*2. Patterns of interpersonal relationships*

*Relational patterns outside analysis*

2A. How are the patient's interpersonal relationships, especially in those bonds which imply closeness and intimacy? Do they have depth, range, and consistency?

2B. How does the child experience others? How does he experience himself in relation to others? (E.g., does the child feel comfortable and relaxed in the presence of the adult? Is he friendly, evitative, or does he seek for excessive attention? How is his visual, verbal, and bodily contact? How do others (mother, father, siblings, peers) experience the child and themselves in relation to the child? How is his relationship with them?

How are these aspects observed in the sessions?

*Relational patterns with the analyst*

2C. What characteristics does the transferential–countertransferential relationship have? (E.g., how is the relationship with the therapist? Is it comfortable and relaxed? Does the child show hesitancy to connect at the beginning? Is his play isolated and solitary in the analysis? Are his bonds in the play reciprocal, of co-operation? Of competence? Is there inhibition?) Do they manage to relate in a close and intimate way? Can this relating be expressed through words?

2D. How have these aspects changed (2A, 2B, 2C)?

*3. Main intrapsychic conflicts*

3A. Which are the main conflicts and affects related to them? (E.g., individuation, self-esteem, guilt, oedipal conflict, identity conflict). Which are the prevailing unconscious phantasies that can be inferred from conflicts? How much consciousness does the child have of them?

And his parents? Do they have the capacity to calm down and provide adequate measures for containment and facing of the conflict? To regulate anxiety, to acknowledge, to tolerate and to soothe, helping to encode conflicts with the internal and external reality as enduring resolution?

3B. Are defences against conflicts adequate and flexible or mainly dysfunctional (distortioning or restricting internal and external experiences)?

3C. Which affects accompany this dynamics? For example, does he manifest aggression? Caution? Fear? Pleasure? Joy? Reactions of frustration? Anger? Rage? Surprise? Uneasiness? Sadness? Feeling lost? Is he able to control himself? Is he worried about the effects of these on others?

3D. How have these aspects changed.

*4. Mental or personality functioning: structure*

4A. What is the level of the child's mental functioning in the following areas?

### *4A1. Self-perception and perception of others: identity*

How capable is the child, taking into account the expected level of development, to adequately perceive his own internal states and those of the others? Can he feel empathy, tolerating and understanding different points of view? Does he have an integrated sense of his own identity that corresponds to the expected level of development? Can he integrate in his identity his own past and especially the traumatic experiences in the way that would be expected considering his level of development? Which are the characteristics of the prevailing identifications?

How is his self-perception and self-representation? (Integrated/contradictory, adequate/inadequate, dystonic/syntonic).

How are his affective states in this regard? Does he feel disdain, appreciation, shame, pride for himself?

How are his object representations? (E.g., enabling, persecutory, idealised, devaluated, fragile . . .)

How are his manifestations regarding the dependency and autonomy expected for his level of development? (E.g., does he show good will and want to do things by himself? Does he insist on things being done as he wants? Does he get angry if it is not like that? Does he get angry if he does not achieve what he wants?)

Does he act freely according to his desires and obligations? Does he act reactively? (E.g., does he present oppositional manifestations?) Does he show flexibility or stubborness and obstinacy?

Does the child show pleasure in his success only when approval is shown to him?

How have these aspects changed?

### *4A2. Sensory regulation*

Taking into account the expected level for his development, how is his ability to control the degree, intensity, and nature of his responses to sensory stimuli? (E.g., excessive response with fear, anxiety, negativism, stubborness, self-absorption?) How does he react to the different stimuli (sounds, lights, touch)? (E.g., lack of response, excessive response, etc.) Does his father/mother have the capacity to provide a feeling of vitality and enthusiasm? Does his father/mother have the capacity to regulate physiological states (sleep, hunger, activation, sedation, pain, temperature). How much do parents manage to understand what is happening to the child and have an answer that helps him?

What is the child's general level of activity? How much does it vary?

Does he have the capacity to keep the focus of his attention on one activity or interaction? What average time does he devote to one specific toy or activity? Is he frequently distracted?

Regarding the psyche–soma integration, we can wonder: How does he feel his body? Does he feel he likes it? Are there signs in his bodily posture that call one's attention? And in his way of walking? Does the child have organic illnesses? Does he frequently become ill? Which are his manifestations and experiences about them? What are his parents' experience about his illness? Has this incidence of somatic factors revealed any situation? If so, has he been able to discover in analysis the factors that precede his psyche–soma disorganisation, for example, apathy, depression, withdrawal?

How strong is the influence of factors depending on the context (e.g., changes linked to development, somatic illnesses, medication, acute or chronic stressors, traumatic situations, etc.) and how capable is the patient of facing these difficulties? How do parents influence these aspects?

### *4A3. Affective regulation*

We will begin by asking ourselves certain general questions that will give us direction regarding the development of the capacity for affective regulation.

Which attachment style and reflexive capacity does the child show? And his parents? What regulation model was suggested and approved? (For example, we consider the following aspects regarding his father/mother: does (s)he have the capacity as an adult for tenderness, for erogeneity inhibited in its end? Does (s)he have the capacity to take into consideration the reasons behind actions from others? To take into account the feelings, mental states, and desires of his/her child? To anticipate danger and neglect? To regulate his/her child's anxiety and anguish? Does the father/mother have the capacity for building a bond of safe attachment, including tolerance of both early dependence and growing autonomy?

Taking the above into account, we define the following.

How does the child feel in himself and perceives in others the wide range of affects expected at his age? How much does he manage to process his impulses and emotional experiences in a way that favours his adaptation and satisfaction?

Do his norms and ideals help him in acknowledging and tolerating his emotional experiences in the face of adversities, keeping a stability in accordance with his level of emotional development?

Can he regulate his self-esteem when facing internal and external demands? Does he have the capacity to balance his own interests and those of the others protecting him and his bonds?

Is he capable of regulating the relationships with others (capacity of intimacy, reciprocity, taking care of himself and the other in relationships)?

How much is the child able to integrate positive and negative feelings towards himself and others?

How would you place him with regard to the level of development expected for his age? And regarding the model received from the family?

How have these aspects changed?

### *4A4. Internal and external communication and symbolisation*

In this regard, we ask: how rich is the dialogue of the child with himself and others, based on affective experiences, phantasies, dreams, sexuality, bodily self, and symbolic representations? How would you place it regarding the level of development expected for his age?

Does the child count on the necessary tools and has he adequately developed them? (E.g., is his vocalisation and speech production adequate for his age? Does he understand others' speech well? Is the primary thought process and/or his verbalisations in the play expected for his age? How does he use the information for the resolution of problems?)

Does his father/mother have the capacity to help in this process?

How have these aspects changed?

### *4A5. Bonds with internal and external objects*

How deep and stable are the child's relationships with internal and external objects? How much can he create relationships of intimacy and reciprocity based on stable representations and on representations differentiated between himself and others? How does he handle the relationships that imply the existence of a third?

How capable is the child of initiating and finishing relationships and facing separations?

How would you place him regarding the expected level of development for his age?

How have these aspects changed?

## *Level 3: testing of explanatory hypotheses of change*

Aims of group discussion at Level 3: at this level we shall propose the theoretical perspectives that might explain change or no change in the patient.

*3A. Therapeutic foci*

3A1. Which are the aspects that have received special attention from the analyst in his interventions, and that one can suppose he considers play a central psychodynamic role in the clinical case, originating or maintaining conflicts? How much do analyst, child, care-givers, and teachers coincide about the need to work around them?

3A2. Have these foci of the analytic work changed through time? Why?

*3B. Level and type of disorder*

3B1. Do the child's symptoms integrate in one syndrome? Is it possible to identify a type of development disorder, personality disorder, or any other kind of disorder?

3B2. Is the level of personality organisation orientated towards a functioning that is healthy, neurotic, border, or psychotic? Could the therapeutic work be centred in neurotic conflicts, or was it necessary to previously, or at the same time, attend to structural failures in the functioning and psychic integration that affected the stability of conflicts and therapeutic work?

How have these aspects changed?

*3C. Explanatory hypotheses of change*

3C1. Which are the main theories and hypotheses from the analyst (explicit or implicit) that can be seen in his/her work? Have they changed through treatment?

3C2. Which other explanatory hypotheses of change could be suggested from different theoretical perspectives? Which are the most and least convincing aspects of each of these different hypotheses and how could they be refined in order to better adjust to the clinical material?

The three levels of analysis and discussion could rightly be seen as a contribution of an expert validation of our clinical inferences (in this regard, see Marianne Leuzinger-Bohleber's contribution in Chapter Five).

## *References*

Bernardi, R. (2011). Three-level model for observing patient transformations. Internal document.

Bolland, J., Sandler, J., & the Hampstead Child Therapy Clinic (1965). *The Hampstead Psychoanalytic Index: A Study of Psychoanalytic Case Material of a Two-year-old Child*. New York: International Universities Press.

Emde, R. (1999). Moving ahead: integrating influences of affective processes for development and for psychoanalysis. *International Journal of Psychoanalysis, 80*(2): 317–339.

Fonagy, P. (1995). Playing with reality: the development of psychic reality and its malfunction in borderline personalities. *International Journal of Psychoanalysis, 76*: 39–44.

Freud, A. (1965). *Normality and Pathology in Childhood*. New York: International Universities Press.

Freud, S. (1905d). *Three Essays on the Theory of Sexuality*. *S.E., 7*: 123–246. London: Hogarth.

Freud, S. (1908e). Creative writers and day-dreaming. *S.E., 9*: 141–154. London: Hogarth.

Freud, S. (1920g). *Beyond the Pleasure Principle*. *S.E., 18*: 7–64. London: Hogarth.

Kernberg, P., Chazan, S., & Normandin, L. (1996). *Cornell Play Therapy Scales*. New York: New York Hospital Cornell University Medical Center.

Klein, M. (1962). *The Psycho-analysis of Children*. The International Psychoanalytical Library, 22. London: Hogarth Press.

Klein, M. (1964). Infant analysis. *International Journal of Psychoanalysis, 7*: 31–63.

Olesker, W., & Lament, C. (2008). Conceptualizing transformations in child and adult psychoanalysis. *Psychoanalytic Study of the Child, 63*: 273–279.

OPD 2 Task Force (2008). *Operationalized Psychodynamic Diagnosis OPD-2. Manual of Diagnosis and Treatment Planning*. Cambridge, MA: Hogrefe & Huber.

*Psychodynamic Diagnostic Manual* (*PDM*) (2006). Classification of child and adolescent mental health disorders (pp. 175–369). Silver Spring, MD: Alliance of Psychoanalytic Organizations.

Sander, L. (1977). The regulation of exchange in the infant-caretaker system and some aspects of the context-content relationship. In: M. Lewis & L. Rosenblum (Eds.), *Interaction, Conversation, and the Development of Language* (pp. 133–156). New York: Wiley.

Silverman, D. (1998). The tie that binds: affect regulation, attachment, and psychoanalysis. *Psychoanalytic Psychology, 15*(2): 187–212.

Spitz, R. (1965). *The First Year of Life: A Psychoanalytic Study of Normal and Deviant Development of Object Relations*. New York: International Universities Press.

Volinski de Hoffnung, P., Medici, C., Sapriza, S., Altmann, M., Braun, S., Cuttinella, O., Ihlenfeld, S., López, C., Vallespir, N. (1986). El juego en psicoanálisis de niños. In: *El juego en psicoanálisis de niños*, Volume I (pp. 129–194). Laboratorio de Psicoanálisis de niños. Asociación Psicoanalítica del Uruguay.

Winnicott, D. W. (1958). *Through Paediatrics to Psychoanalysis*. London. Hogarth Press.

Winnicott, D. W. (1971). *Playing and Reality*. 1–156. London: Tavistock.

*APPENDIX I*

# Brief guidelines: IPA clinical observation groups

*Marina Altmann de Litvan*
*(On behalf of all the members of the Project Committee on Clinical Observation)*

## *Introduction*

In 2009, the members of the Project Committee on Clinical Observation started working from different points of views and in different directions. We agreed, however, that intensive clinical observation and the communication of insights gained working with our patients is still the heart of our discipline. Therefore, we are convinced that, for the future of psychoanalysis, it will be essential to improve our clinical observations again and again and to show that psychoanalysis is capable of initiating long-lasting psychic changes in our patients. After working groups within the EPF and the IPA have impressively studied the minds of psychoanalysts in great detail for a decade and contributed to a greater understanding of differences between implicit and explicit theories of analysts in different IPA cultures, our Project Committee—in addition to these groups—would like to focus on the individual patients and their transformations during psychoanalyses.

After a period of development, the Committee has created a model called the three-level model for observing patient transformations, which is presented in these guidelines.

Currently, there are different methods being developed in the IPA to study the psychoanalytic process. We suggest that before choosing one, you should study all of them in order to work with the one that best fits your needs.

The Project Committee on Clinical Observation welcomes all analysts who are interested in the creation of one or more IPA clinical observation groups in their own psychoanalytic societies, and encourages them to follow the steps described in this guide.

The guidelines presented here aim to give groups of analysts a method to apply the three-level model for observing patient transformations to psychoanalytic clinical material. Should your group find any difficulty, please do not hesitate to contact us through our public Google site: https://sites.google.com/site/clinicalobservation/ or our email address: ipa.clinical.observation@gmail.com

The three-level model for observing patient transformation is a heuristic, or a guide, for refining, conceptualising and systematising clinical observations about patient transformations. It aims to enhance clinical observations, making them more accurate and more useful for the evaluation of theories and theory building through the sustained analysis of clinical material. The term "transformation" is used here in its most common sense, meaning a change or an alteration.

"Observation" includes listening to unconscious communication (analyst as participant) and the observation of clinical facts (analyst as observer, taking a "second look" at the material).

The three-level model for observing patient transformation:

- is focused on the patient (in the context of his/her relationships);
- is focused on transformations;
- observes the same clinical material from three different levels:
    - phenomenological description of the analytical process;
    - the main dimensions of change;
    - the analyst's theoretical hypotheses about change.

Please contact us and ask us for our latest version of the three-level model for observing patient transformations (3-LM).

The model itself is self-explanatory, but here we present several practical aspects that need to be considered.

One strategy to improve the quality of clinical observation and its communication is the so-called "psychoanalytical expert validation". It can be applied in the 3-LM.

## *Psychoanalytical expert validation*

Psychoanalysis has developed a rich tradition of supervision and peer-group supervision in order to cope productively with the drawbacks of clinical research. These range from the arbitrary status of clinical observations for buttressing a given theoretical stance or hypothesis; the hazard of hermetically closed viewpoints; narcissistic confirmation, in lieu of the (self) critical reflection of an observation; a gravitation towards "positively resolved" star cases, in contrast with the absence of poorly performed treatments; the danger of (unconscious) "fabrication" (especially in cases of training); repetition or conformity to mainstream discussions within the psychoanalytic community and, as a consequence, the disappearance of innovative, unconventional ideas, and much else. But we should not throw out the baby with the bathwater.

The psychoanalytical expert validation takes up this tradition and tries to systematise it. There are different forms of psychoanalytical expert validation, which create opportunities for clinical research by psychoanalysts working either in private practice or engaged in institutions, hospitals or universities. The aim of all forms of psychoanalytical expert validation is to critically reflect on the influence of unconscious adulteration or limitation of our understanding of complex clinical material due to interfering countertransference reactions or other (unconscious) disturbances of our professional functioning. See Chapter Five by Marianne Leuzinger-Bohleber.

## *Steps for starting systematic clinical working groups*

The chart on pages 323–326 is a proposal, a sort of starting point, to understand group functioning and the way in which different roles come into play. It is complemented by the "Suggested questions for group discussion" that you will find in the following pages of this appendix. Steps one, two, and three correspond mainly to the phenomenological level of the 3-LM, while steps four, five, and six take the 3-LM's third level, "Testing explanatory hypotheses of change", with some dimensiones which correspond to 3-LM's Level 2 (e.g., conflict, how have the experience of illness and expectations changed?, etc.).

## Steps for starting systematic clinical working groups

| | Moderator | Presenter | Group | Reporter |
|---|---|---|---|---|
| 1 | 1.1) Explains procedure | 1.2) Presents a short summary of some of the patient's biographical | Ask clarifications about patient's history in the external world, analysis, and inner world | 1.1) Explains procedure |
| | | 1.3) Presents assessment interviews in detail illustrating what (s)he thinks is wrong with the patient and why (s)he looked for analysis (written and oral transmission) | | |
| | | 1.4) Presents a psychoanalytic diagnosis | | |
| 2 | 2.1) Introduces group discussion | 2.3) Follows associations of group members | 2.2) Psychoanalytical discussion of assessment interviews | Summarises the gained insights of the session |
| | | 2.4) Presents own view in addition or in contrast to the group | Ask diagnostic information that is missing | Summarise alternative hypotheses, critics |

| | Moderator | Presenter | Group | Reporter |
|---|---|---|---|---|
| 3 | | | | 3.1) Brings summary of last session |
| | 3.2) Reads summary, asks for modifications, additions, agreements | | | |
| | 3.4) Introduces group discussion | 3.3) Presents the detailed summary of one or two of the sessions illustrating the transformation processes | 3.5) Psychoanalytical discussion of process interviews | Summarises the gained insights of the session |
| 4 | | 4.1) Presenter summarises first "hypotheses" concerning the transformation | | |
| | 4.2) Reads summary, asks for modifications, additions, agreements | | | |
| | 4.3) Introduces group discussion | | 4.4) Psychoanalytical discussion of transformation process and presenter's hypothesis | Summarises the gained insights of the session |

| Step | Moderator | Presenter | Group | Reporter |
|---|---|---|---|---|
| 5 | 5.1) First conceptual considerations (close to the clinical material, including implicit theories of the analyst, etc.) are discussed | | | |
| | | | | Summarises the gained insights of the session |
| 6 | 6.1) The group goes back to the material of assessment interviews and tries to understand the anchor point (the starting point of the transformation in greater detail. Includes detailed diagnostical information | | | |
| | | | | Summarises the gained insights of the session |
| 7 | 7.1) Reads summary, asks for modifications, additions, agreements | | | |
| | | 7.2) The process continues until the presenter thinks that (s)he has deeply understood the transformation process | | |
| | | 7.3) Summarises gained insights (2–5 pages) | | |

| | Moderator | Presenter | Group | Reporter |
|---|---|---|---|---|
| 8 | | | 8.1) Expert group validates presenter's summary. Convergences and divergences are documented. | |
| 9 | | 9.1) Writes a case study on the transformation process of the patient | 9.2) Help by reading different versions of the paper in the sense of the above mentioned "psychoanalytical expert validation". One aim would be to combine a summary of the whole treatment with the summary of the sessions analysed by the Clinical Observation group. | |
| 10 | | 10.1) The presenter does not write a case study on the transformation process of the patient | 10.2) The group continues the work with other cases and collects the summaries systematically. The documentation of the gained insights of the different cases may be a valuable clinical (research) material in itself that could be used by the group as a whole or by some members of the group for future publications. | |

In our experience, this proposal is adjusted according to the aims and scientific culture of the region to which it belongs. In this way, we find that the different regions have privileged different questions.

## *Clinical material*

The 3-LM has been designed to evaluate the transformations of the patient and, therefore, proves to be especially interesting and useful when it is applied to clinical material that presents some kind of doubt regarding the nature and/or degree of the changes in the patient. It is important that the analyst who chooses the material bears in mind these doubts. Even if these doubts about the transformations of the patient have to be present at the moment of choosing the material, it is better that the analyst does not make them explicit at the beginning, and relates them while the group discussion is taking place.

The clinical material is chosen in such a way that allows a good description of the situation at Level 1 and that shows transformations along time.

We suggest presenting a brief biography of the patient, the first session (and second, if necessary), and two later moments of analysis, for example at six months and a year and a half later, or the interval that the analyst believes to be convenient for the purpose.

It is of great importance that the presenter of the clinical material takes the responsibility to respect the confidentiality rule, deleting or changing any biographical information that could enable the patient's identification in any way (names of people, educational institutions, enterprises, etc., but also any participation in well-known events, or other identifiable situations). This is the presenter's responsibility. Participants will not use or disseminate the material without the presenter's explicit consent.

In order to decide on the length of the clinical material, the presenter will need to consider the time (s)he will have to present it (not more than 10–15% of the total time).

The clinical material will be read aloud in one go at the beginning of the first group meeting. As the focus will be on transformations of the patient along time, a complete reading of the material is necessary before starting the activity. As it is also of interest to observe the transformations in one session, it is useful that the material shows the interaction between analyst and patient.

To summarise:

1. It is important to prepare the clinical material in a way that provides the necessary information for the discussion.
2. Respect the confidentiality rule. As we have already mentioned above, the presenter will have to be careful to modify all the information that could serve to identify the patient.
3. Take at least three different moments of analysis where transformations can be observed.
4. The clinical material will be the result of the transcription, or the notes taken by the analyst, and it will include interventions of the patient and interpretations from the analyst, differentiating them clearly through fonts or symbols.

APPENDIX II

# Clinical observation group, San Francisco (CO-SF1), May–August 2012

*William Glover*

The reporter plays a major role in the conceptualisation process. S/he summarises alternative hypotheses, critics, and resumes earlier discussions, making it possible to rethink the issues discussed. S/he summarises the insights gained from the session, as shown in this example.

## *Report 24 August 2012*

### *1. Subjective experience of illness*

We changed this to "subjective experience"

*1A. What are the patient's symptoms, beliefs and expectations about her/his problems and treatment? What is the patient's experience of her mind?*

Anchor hours:

- Patient (pt) feels empty and persecuted, flooded by primitive anxiety (i.e., initial dream about spores growing through the wall of her house).

- Analyst (A) describes pt as "tumbled". In anchor hour 2 (A2) (p. 8) pt says "I think I'm going along fine and then the rug's pulled out and I'm completely upended . . . I can't stop the free fall!"
- Pt uses word "shimmery" to describe an anxious, dissociated state the group thought of as a prodromal state indicating the degree of threat the pt experiences.
- Pt is not an interpreting subject. Her mind is undifferentiated and she has difficulty distinguishing her thoughts from reality. A1 (p. 6), "I'm having a hard time reconciling the idea of the dream being how I *think* about myself, *vs.* that really *being* the case."
- In the A1 dream, something wrong is covered up and pt wants it to show, hoping it can really be repaired, not just spackled over.
- Alternative view: pt primitive but also able to symbolise, communicate, and use A. That is, first dream represented her situation well and she could think about it. Pt's primitiveness may be defensive regression.

*1B. How have these aspects changed?*

Transformation hours:

- Pt's mind is coalescing. Difference between earlier being a mind (undifferentiated) and now having a mind (differentiated). Now there's a self that you can talk to about things. Pt's mind isn't shimmery now, she's wobbling between self attack and thinking but not as tumbled and empty.
- Pt has greater capacity for self-reflection. Developing her own thoughts, not just saying what A is saying. For example, in transformation hour 1 (T1) she sees herself as excluding A, "I disconnect and go off by myself" and can reflect "why would someone do that?" (p. 10)

- Pt sees multiple points of view (p. 13): "I don't know if I was attacking my insight . . . or you for not being receptive, or for being receptive."
- Pt says "How I want to be" (p. 15)—a statement of coming into being. Her desire is activated. Opening paragraph of last hour, she says "in here the open-heartedness, the back and forth, is so real, or *could* be" (top p. 13).

- Final meeting: Pt's primitiveness might be conceptualised as regression in face of a pathological organisation that leads her to eschew pleasure or knowing what she wants. Her development makes it possible for A and her to see her pathological organisation and for her to begin to recognise the internal aspect of her problems.

### *2. Patterns of interpersonal relationship*

### *3. Main intrapsychic conflicts*

*3A. What are the main conflicts (and their related affects)?* Are defences adequate and flexible or predominantly dysfunctional, distorting, or limiting internal and external experiences?

*3A1. Is the psychopathology focused mainly on relatedness or on self-definition?* How consistent and enduring are the conflicts? Are they a predominant factor in patient's disturbances or are conflicts inconsistent and erratic due to structural conditions that affect mental functioning?

Anchor hours:
We saw the pt's issues as primarily pre-oedipal. Her secret is about the integrity of the self and there is a psychotic or annihilation level of anxiety. Some in the group didn't find the concept of conflict useful with such a primitive mind. There is not enough of a self for conflict, pt too split to experience conflict. Conflict between agencies is not developed. In this view experiencing conflict is a developmental achievement. Others felt conflict exists at all levels of psychic structure as a basic phenomena of mental life. The primitive conflicts are between need for help and terror of annihilation. Wishes for reassurance and merger coexist with wishes for separateness and self preservation.

### *3B. How have these aspects changed?*

In later hours we observed that instead of just feeling her world breaking apart, the pt felt others were attacking her and that she might be attacking them. The development of this "paranoia" along with the beginning recognition of her pathological internal organisation (attacking good objects) were thought to reflect increased mental structure. We also observed more differentiated, oedipal type conflicts emerging over longing for and pleasure of being with the analyst. In a recent dream, there was a reference to a primal scene.

### *4. Mental or personality functioning. Structure*

*4A. What is the level of mental functioning in the following areas?*

*4A1. Perception of self and others*. How capable is the patient of perceiving and reflecting on her/himself and others productively, differentiating thoughts and affects and perceiving others adequately, empathising with them, tolerating and understanding different perspectives? Can the patient adequately discriminate him/herself from others, and have an integrated feeling of her/his identity and personal history?

Anchor hours:

- Negative perceptions of self and others predominate, alternating with moments of idealisation and merger.
- Lots of collapsing identifications; pt–Mo, pt–son, son as part of herself. Badness and doubt expressed through son.
- Threats to self seemed more global annihilation than paranoid projection. Things are breaking up *vs*. others are breaking them up. Paranoia would be more organised.

*4B1. How have these aspects changed?*
Transformation hours:

- Differentiation from parents. T1 (p. 10). "I grew up with things that had nothing to do with me suddenly becoming my fault. Blame had to be put somewhere—they put it *into* me! . . . it makes me mad I now do it to myself!"
- Pt sees multiple points of view (p. 13). "I don't know if I was attacking my insight . . . or you for not being receptive, or for being receptive."
- Pt owing projections, that is, she starts out in T2 talking about having nothing to offer—something the analyst experienced in the countertransference early on when she felt she had nothing to

offer the pt. Pt now recognises this as her own experience (owning projection = structural change?).

- In T2, pt tells about a maternal figure in a film she saw who has boundaries, judgement, a mind of her own.
- Alternative view: Drama in film material may indicate a lack of change. Pt seducing the A with, "I dramatically trust you". She has such an idealised Mo, her anxiety about not trusting the A isn't present.

*4A2. Regulation. Is the patient able to adequately regulate impulses, affects, and self-esteem?* Is self-direction based on coherent internal standards and meaningful short-term and life goals? Has he or she the capacity for balancing the interests of self and other and for protecting relationships?

Affect regulation.
Anchor hours:

- A perceives pt as brittle, pent up.
- Pt's explosiveness and anger is manifest in her throwing a chair in anger at her kids. (A2) This preceded pt asking the A if there is an error on the bill—being charged for days she was on vacation. The A offers to take the charges off the bill. Some in the group thought the pt had really known about the policy and it was a disagreement, not a misunderstanding. Therefore, throwing the chair was also an expression of anger at the analyst and the pt's breakdown may have been defensive, to avoid her anger at the A. A careful not to blame pt or provoke aggression.
- Pt fears retaliation for her aggression. After daring to confront a teacher about giving kids sweets, the pt is worried it will be held as a "black mark" against her. A2 (p. 8). There is confusion where the black marks reside. Does the pt also hold black marks against the A? Pt can assert herself in an accusatory way but is then terrified of retaliation.

*4B2. How have these aspects changed?*
Transformation hours.

- A allowing more silences, doesn't feel need to demonstrate her presence as much. Pt seems sad and besieged, settles into feelings, less brittle.

- Developing capacity for ambivalence *vs.* only black marks before.
- T2, (p. 15) "My experience as Mother of my kids—how I want to be . . . And what I didn't get." Same themes from first session but not so attacking of herself. Able to explore similar theme without masochistic self-recrimination. Affect regulation better. Can now look at something difficult without being overwhelmed.
- Film. They've faced her destructiveness. It's now symbolised in this way. They're operating within the law that recognises damage. She knows she's already been stabbing.
- Winnicott, with the antisocial boy, puts him out of the house, "this is not acceptable", but boy rings bell and W still lets him back in. Consequences to aggression but didn't abandon him.
- Alternative view: The film material contains a seductive idealisation of the analyst that may be a Trojan horse, hiding the pt's distrust and aggression. Pt's ability to really damage A is glossed over.
- Alternative view: In A's effort to be a new, good object, A may collude with pt's wishes for merger and to remain in a compliant relationship that denies aggression and separateness.

*4A3. Communication.* How rich is communication (internal and/or external), based on affective experiences, fantasy, sexual and bodily self, and symbolic internal representations?
*4A4. Attachment.* How deep and stable is the bond or attachment with internal and external objects and the capacity of making, separating, and severing relationships? How capable is the patient of intimacy and reciprocity based on cohesive, complex, and integrated representations of self and others?

Anchor hours

- Pt seeks merger with the A: that is, in first hour the pt fits in by bringing a dream, getting A to explain, and using the A's language. Pt can't tolerate movement between two people and it becomes very dangerous when this merged state is lost. In this view, the breakdown over the bill in A2 is because the merger was threatened when they weren't on same page.

  Alternative view. Some saw a lack of differentiation and separation as dangerous but not a wish for merger.
- Anxious attachment configuration. Pt's Mother described as an anxious, empty alcoholic who demanded pt comply with a false

picture of a happy family. A's image of a Norman Rockwell diorama. Problematic object relationship of an anxious, empty child looking to a Mo who is also anxious and empty. This is where pt goes to deal with separation.

*4B4. How have these aspects changed?*
Transformation hours

- Indications of more secure attachment. Pt more differentiated, able to go off and play to some degree and come back to A with her own thoughts. Rapprochement.

### *5. Type of disorder*

*5A. Is it possible to identify a type of personality disorder or other kind of disorder?*
*Is the level of organisation of the personality healthy, neurotic, or borderline?*
*5B. How have these aspects changed?*

### *6. Therapeutic foci.*

*6A. What are the findings that play a central role in the psychodynamics of the clinical picture, causing or maintaining the disturbances, and which need special attention from the analyst?*
*6A1. Do conflicts prevail (needing interpretation) or are structural problems predominant (needing also other kinds of intervention)?*
*6A2. What are the main problems and changes the interpretations of the analyst aim to, and how have they evolved?*

*Developmental trajectory*

Anchor hours:

- Arrested development, pt not a person yet. A speaks to the pt as someone quite young. Time stopped in childhood and starts again in treatment.

Transformation hours:

- Consolidation of maternal function. Main emotional connection in treatment is Mo who sticks with the child no matter what.

Pt hasn't fully internalised maternal function yet but is learning to play with analyst, who has a maternal function. Trying to play by herself but she doesn't yet fully believe Mo is there. Struggle to establish a safe dyad.

- Is there a full triadic level? Not lived yet. What's missing?—Interpretative, paternal function; understanding her internal world in addition to corrective emotional experience.
- Emergence of paternal function. In film, the woman's phone call to the police is anticipation of interpretative function, that things can be faced. Announcing that the paternal law of the Father can now be approached. A has triadic function, even if pt not there yet.

  Alternative view—it's also something they've already achieved.

## *Level 3*

Analyst's hypotheses at an explicit and implicit level? Have they changed during analysis?

What other hypotheses could be considered? Which aspects of the hypotheses are more or less convincing?

We addressed Level 3 by looking for the therapeutic action that accounted for the changes observed.

Containing the patient's primitive anxiety was seen as primary. In an early hour, the pt described a scene from a James Bond film that conveys this aspect—Bond's love interest has had a terrible experience and is huddled on the floor of a shower with water pouring over her. Bond joins her there, sitting silently, helping her process the terrible experience, like the A being with the pt understanding and containing the anxiety without forcing interpretations. Later, the group emphasised that containment also includes addressing things. A—"In the early hours I was addressing her unspeakable anxiety, trying to think her experience for her and to put that into words." Additional aspect: the terrible experience involved extreme violence and we learn that the woman later tried to kill Bond. The scene was also a harbinger of aggression to come.

The analyst invites the pt to explore her thoughts and anxieties in a direct way: that is, in the first hour the A asks about the dream and later points to a relational aspect (nonchalant care-takers); later, the A identifies the anxious mother, anxious child formulation; later yet, in T1, the A says, "I think your inclination is to go out and play today." Given the patient's wishes for merger, these direct interpretations were felt to be necessary but also to run a risk of triggering the patient's compliance and becoming reassurances that might cover things over rather than open them up.

This risk was countered by the analyst's extensive use of gentle, descriptive, non-blaming or analyst-centered interventions that diminished the pt's fears in the transference. "Right now I look dangerous and you aren't solid", or "Something I just said scared you more." The A is careful not to tell the pt more than she thinks she is ready to hear, unlike the patient who, in an Anchor hour, interpreted her son's experience prematurely. The A crafts her interpretations carefully so as not to trigger pt's persecutory anxiety, making comments like "things are neutralized" that avoid placing blame. These are what Ferro describes as "weak", "unsaturated" interpretations that give the pt space to work with them.

Progress is reflected in the evolution of the interpretations. Early on, the A couldn't say anything about the pt's defensive operations as the cause of her suffering because it would feel persecutory. In the later hours, the A's interventions opened up multiple possible levels of meaning. The work has progressed to point that the pt is now capable of considering that, out of her own anxiety, she is breaking things up, not just that things are breaking up or that others are attacking and breaking things up. The A can make resistance interpretations, ". . . you're going inside, stopping short" (p. 14). Interpretation of internal conflict also becomes possible. "The very thing you do to keep it alive kills it" (p. 14).

The A's sensitivity when the pt felt encroached on or expected to comply with the A's interpretations seemed meant to allow the pt to develop as a separate, autonomous person. It was unclear if this was an explicit or implicit hypothesis of the A. The "inclination is to go out and play today" interpretation may have been unconsciously intended to correct the pt earlier experiencing the A as an authoritarian parent, "I can't have any conflicting feelings about this space. I better take advantage of it" (p. 10). But when the A indicates there are two subjectivities present, the pt is threatened by too much separateness and starts to doubt the A's presence (p. 11). The A is aware of the effect of her interventions, and when the pt is disturbed she follows up with sensitively attuned interpretations: "Are you saying the connection is broken off and doesn't exist?" (p. 11).

There was a developmental, structure-building aspect to the interpretations. Providing a new object experience led to pt developing object constancy and object usage. Pt identified with A's ability to think (Bion). As two people became present in the room, conflict and aggression could begin to be talked about. A question deserving further investigation is how the patient internalised the thinking capability of the A, moving from compliance and merger to being more her own person.

## *Group process*

The group consisted of twelve members; a presenter, two moderators, a recorder, and eight members from the two IPA institutes in San Francisco, ranging from recent graduates to senior analysts, including several training analysts. We met for a full day in May followed by evening sessions in June, July, and August for a total of twelve hours over four meetings.

We got off to a great start on 12 May. The group liked the work and saw clear evidence of significant change. Members were very enthusiastic about the experience. The follow-up meetings had not been scheduled in advance and it is testimony to the group's commitment that, except for two absences, everyone attended all the sessions.

### *Methodological issues*

Some methodological issues were significant in our group: our inexperience with this new method, the group's ambivalence about the dimensions of change categories, and the function of the report. Each of these issues will be discussed.

The three-level model is an evolving, flexible method. The Clinical Observation Project Committee created a useful methodology, but has had limited opportunity to train moderators. Our recorder had attended two demonstration meetings and our moderators had attended one each. The Project Committee anticipates the method will be adapted in each locale, but our lack of experience led us to reinvent the method as we went.

From the beginning, the group felt the dimensions of change categories (what we called "the grid"), did not adequately encompass what we were observing. Variations of the statement, "I can't find a place for my idea in the grid" became a refrain. At the initial session, we agreed to follow our own path, referring to the grid when it seemed useful. During the first meeting, various categories were brought up but not systematically elaborated.

Given the difficulty of finding a time we could all attend, it turned out that six weeks transpired before our second meeting. The facilitators proposed we proceed to Level 3, therapeutic action, and backfill our thinking about dimensions of change, but the group had lost touch with the material and we were uncertain how to proceed. The reporter had distributed a report on the first meeting, including several dimensions of change that the group resonated with, but we did not use the report to rekindle our discussion as the three-level protocol calls for. Instead, after muddling around for a bit, we decided to read through the first hour closely to get back in touch with the material and look for mechanisms of change. We had a very interesting discussion of the hour and some hypotheses about therapeutic action were generated, but we did not follow them longitudinally. We noted that meeting in the evening for only two hours was less satisfactory than the initial all-day session.

In the second meeting, this writer felt we had one foot in the clinical observation method and another in a more familiar free-style case discussion. The leaders did not want to dampen the enthusiasm of the group and, given the resistance to the grid, were hesitant to stick with the three-level protocol. Instead, we tried to stimulate and guide discussion by example. The moderators and recorder became the most active group members, trying to prime the pump by taking the lead in the discussion and in proposing hypotheses of change. In doing so, we might have inadvertently inhibited the very discussion we wished to facilitate. Some group members, experienced analysts, were surprisingly quiet. The group still worked well together and this may have been a necessary step in finding our way, but, without being clear about our method and the roles of the moderators and recorder, this writer felt we veered towards becoming a basic assumption dependency group.

Formulating and identifying change in a case is a daunting task and, in a free discussion, the most articulate, confident voices are likely to dominate. A pecking order can assert itself. Dividing the task and speaking to a specific dimension of change, as the three-level model calls for, that is, "What about change in regulation of affect, or attachment?", is much easier and can encourage group participation, building a better group product. At moments, there seemed to be a parallel process with the A's dilemma over when to put words to the pt's experience and when to allow her to develop her own thinking.

Making more use of the report could have helped us. In the three-level method, the recorder's report provides continuity between meetings. After the initial session, each meeting begins with reading and correcting the report to launch further discussion. We experienced an example of this in the final session in the very interesting discussion of conflict. As described previously, given the group's reaction to the grid, we were hesitant to use the report to follow up systematically even with the categories we found useful. Putting observations into categories can be confining, but also can facilitate thinking longitudinally about change along a particular dimension, rather than looking for change globally or sequentially, hour by hour. In future, each member could be asked to track their own observations and hypotheses as the group progresses and then contribute to the report. Hypotheses about therapeutic action could be developed as we proceed and then reviewed when we get to Level 3.

### *Group process*

Parallel processes are frequently observed in case conferences. Each of the working parties sponsored by the IPA, including clinical observation, have found that the work group is a container where the material presented resonates with the group's dynamics, creating a situation where unconscious dynamics in the analytic dyad find expression in the group. While we cannot know from the transcript what happened in the room, the group can know its own experience, which will be a displacement and diffraction of the case discussed, and that data is as useful as the material presented.

In our final meeting, we discussed our group process. We asked ourselves why we liked the experience so much. "We looked at the material closely in a collegial, generative way, thinking together instead of fighting for turf." "The group held the analyst in similar way to how the analyst worked with her difficult pt." The presenter reported feeling on the first day that the dyad of her and her pt was like "a little boat at sea now being supported by a larger group."

One group member felt we were building something valuable together, but very carefully and cautiously, and that this reflected something about the case. Another felt we had quieted aggression in the group and tiptoed around each other. There was relatively little divergence of opinion in the group. In the case material, the A had said something to the pt about her fear that no one is "robust" enough to tolerate disagreement without holding "black marks" against the other. Were we a robust enough group to risk disagreeing with each other? When the topic of aggression in the group was brought up, we quickly went into a general discussion of disagreement in clinical groups, indicating our difficulty with talking about aggression in our own group.

The question was raised as to whether there were things that had not changed in the case, or where we felt further change was desirable. We agreed there was more to be done, but we did not go into specifics. We recognised we had been protective of the analyst and avoided criticising her technique. Did this protectiveness and the harmonising tendency in the group affect the expert validation?

We discussed how it worked to mix the two institutes in the group. We were new to this group, the method, and the case, but come from the same analytic community and have overlapping histories. Someone said it was exciting to hear different voices in depth and appreciate how they think. There was general agreement that we worked well together and that mixing institutes may have lessened aggression in the group. One member disclosed that another member had been part of his progression committee and that he enjoyed hearing them express views different to those they had held back then. This comment indicated something of the depth of history between the members and the institutes. This history is long, complex, with much collaboration, but not without significant competition, hurts, resentments, and, one might even say, elements of violence. In the group, we were strongly motivated to have a good experience with each other and this contributed to our carefulness. The group might have feared aggression and that disagreement would lead to destructive fragmentation, echoing the danger in the case that separateness and aggression would be annihilating.

Why was the group so quick to dismiss the grid? The group might have sought to unify and define itself against the IPA and the Project Committee. We quickly revised the first category, "Subjective experience of illness", to "Subjective experience". This was both creative and a declaration of independence from the Project Committee. At one point, there was a direct expression of anxiety: "the IPA wants to find out what we think in San Francisco". In objecting to the grid, it was said, "we don't think that way in San Francisco", as though there is a unified way of thinking here. Perhaps we were avoiding possibilities of disagreement amongst ourselves by disagreeing with the grid. The reaction to the grid is also a reflection of the longstanding controversy within psychoanalysis between empirical and hermeneutic views of evidence. Clinical observation, with its attempt to evaluate change, has an empirical aspect that many analysts are sceptical about.

At our final meeting, one member said that going over the material again and again is like looking at a painting again and again—it becomes an aesthetic experience. The research product of the group remains to be determined. The educational experience achieved was valuable in its own right.

*APPENDIX III*

# Suggested questions for group discussion

## *Questions about Level 1*

### *Phenomenological description of transformations*

1. What aspects of the material suggest the existence of positive changes, negative changes, or the no existence of changes? Which prevail?
2. Are there changes that may be noticed in the course of one session? And, through time, between different sessions? In which areas is it possible to observe changes? (E.g., (a) capacity to love and sexuality; (b) family and social relationships; (c) occupation and leisure; (d) interests and creativity; (e) symptoms and subjective well-being.) Which is the patient's perspective regarding his changes?
3. Do changes exist in the analytic process regarding (a) how the patient uses the analyst and her interventions; (b) how the patient uses his/her own mind and body during the session?
4. Which parts of the clinical material had a special resonance for the participants of the group and can be considered as anchor points that make it possible to track changes in the patient? What

is the relation of these anchor points with the foci of the analyst's interpretations?

## *Questions about Level 2*

### *Dimensions of change*

1. Subjective experience of illness and contextual factors
1A. What are the patient's subjective experience, beliefs, and expectations about his/her problems and treatment? How much does (s)he recognise his/her problems? How much does (s)he foresee possibilities of change? To what extent do patient and analyst agree regarding the expected transformations?
1B. Do contextual factors exist which affect the therapeutic process? (For example, crisis situations, traumatic experiences, somatic illnesses, drugs, etc.? How capable is the patient of facing these situations?)
1C. How have these aspects changed? How much has the patient's understanding of his/her problems and therapeutic possibilities modified?
2. Patterns of interpersonal relationship
2A. How are the interpersonal relationships of the patient, especially in the bonds which imply closeness and intimacy?
2B. How does the patient experience others and how does (s)he experience him/herself in relation to others? How do others experience the patient and how do they experience themselves in relation to the patient? (Both in transference–countertransference and in the other meaningful bonds.)
2C. To what extent can I relate the patient's current relational patterns to the experiences lived in his/her childhood and with the bonds that (s)he establishes with the analyst?
2D. How have these aspects changed?
3. Main intrapsychic conflicts
3A. What are the main conflicts (e.g., individuation *vs.* dependency; submission *vs.* control; need for care *vs.* self-sufficiency; self worth, guilt, oedipal conflict, identity conflict). Which are the dominant unconscious fantasies that can be inferred from conflicts and relational patterns?

3B. The prevailing defences are adequate and flexible, or dysfunctional, distorting, or limiting internal and external experiences?

3C. How have these aspects changed?

4. Structural aspects of mental functioning

4A. What is the level of mental functioning in the following areas?

### 4A1. *Perception of self and others: identity*

How capable is the patient of adequately perceiving his/her own internal states and those of others? Is (s)he able to empathise, tolerating and understanding the existence of different points of view? Does (s)he have an integrated feeling of his/her own identity, open to the possibility of unconscious aspects? What are the characteristics of identification (especially pathological ones)? Does (s)he manage to connect with his/her past and give direction to his/her life, with a sense of agency and short- and long-term wishes and goals?

4A2. *Affective regulation*: Is the patient able to adequately regulate his/her impulses, affects, and self-esteem? Do his/her ideals and values help him/her to handle his/her emotions? Does (s)he manage to regulate his/her need of self-esteem when facing internal and external demands? How much does (s)he achieve an adequate balance between his/her own interests and those of the others?

4A3. *Internal and external communication. Symbolisation.* How rich is the dialogue with him/herself and the others, based on affective experiences, bodily self, fantasies, dreams, sexuality, symbolic representations, and capacity to play and creativity?

4A5. *Attachment with internal and external objects.* How deep and stable and differentiated are the relationships with internal and external objects? How much can (s)he start and finish relationships and tolerate separations? How does (s)he handle relationships which imply the existence of a third one?

4B. How have these aspects changed?

### *5. Type of disorder*

5A. Is it possible to identify a type of personality disorder or other kind of mental or bodily disorder?

5B. How severe are the disturbances of personality functioning? How much is analytic work conditioned by the structural vulnerabilities of mental functioning?

5C. How have these aspects changed?

### *Questions about Level 3: explanatory hypotheses of change*

1. On which aspects did the interventions of the analyst mainly focus? Has his/her explicit or implicit hypotheses and interventions changed along treatment?
2. Could there be other theoretical hypotheses or interpretative strategies? In what are each of them convincingly adjusted to the material?
3. What is the nature of the observed changes, their depth and expected stability?

*APPENDIX IV*

# Forms to be used before and after the group discussion

*Survey 1*

**Name:** ................................................... **Date:** ......................

Please be so kind to give us your opinion.

**FORM TO BE FILLED BEFORE BEGINNING THE GROUP ACTIVITY:**

| Comparison of initial interviews with later moments of analysis | 1. No change or worsening | 2. Slight positive changes | 3. Moderate changes | 4. Important changes |
|---|---|---|---|---|
| 1) Global change of the patient | | | | |
| 2) Changes in the patient's "use" of the analyst and his/her interpretations | | | | |
| 3) Changes in the patient's use of his/her own mental and bodily resources for the analysis | | | | |
| Comments: | | | | |

## *Survey 2*

**Name:** ................................................... **Date:** .......................

**FORM TO BE FILLED AFTER THE GROUP ACTIVITY:**

We will highly appreciate that you give us your opinion again, after the group discussion.

### *Level 1: phenomemonological. global description of changes*

| Comparison of initial interviews with later moments of analysis | 1. No change or worsening | 2. Slight positive changes | 3. Moderate changes | 4. Important changes |
|---|---|---|---|---|
| 1) Global change of the patient | | | | |
| 2) Changes in the patient's "use" of the analyst and his/her interpretations | | | | |
| 3) Changes in the patient's use of his/her own mental and bodily resources for the analysis | | | | |

### *Level 2: main dimensions of change*

0. No data/Doesn't answer.
1. Extreme disturbances. Non-integrated functioning.
2. Important disturbances. Severe limitations in functioning
3. Moderate disturbances, with some limitations in functioning
4. Minimum or imperceptible disturbances and limitations

Note: Intermediate values can be marked with half a point (for example 1.5; 2.5; etc.)

| Dimensions moments | Initial moment | Later |
|---|---|---|
| 1. Experience of illness: understanding of difficulties and hints of possible changes | | |
| 2a. Relational patterns outside the analysis | | |
| 2b. Relational patterns with the analyst | | |
| 3. Defences and conflicts | | |
| 4.1.a Self-perception, sense of identity and integrity of the self | | |
| 4.1.b. Perception of others. Empathy | | |
| 4.2.a. Regulation of impulses, affects, and self-esteem | | |
| 4.2.b. Regulation of the relationship with others (self-care and care of the other, reciprocity) | | |
| 4.3.a. Internal communication and symbolisation (bodily and mental self) | | |
| 4.3.b. Communication with others (depth and richness of affects and representations) | | |
| 4.4.a. Bonds with internal objects | | |
| 4.4.b. Bonds with others. Capacity to establish and end bonds, to face separation, and the existence of a third | | |

## *Level 3: explanatory hypotheses*

| Adjustment of theoretical hypotheses to the material | Very little or nothing | Something | Quite | Very much |
|---|---|---|---|---|
| 1) Was the group able to discuss different theoretical hypotheses examining their adjustment to the material? | | | | |

## *Evaluation of group discussion*

| Usefulness of the model to observe and understand changes | Very little or nothing | Something | Quite | Very much |
|---|---|---|---|---|
| 1. How useful did you find the group activity to refine the observation of the material? | | | | |
| 2. How useful did you find it to conceptualize the dimensions of change? | | | | |
| 3. How satisfactory do you feel the discussed theoretical explanatory hypotheses to understand changes? | | | | |
| *Other comments you would like to add:* .................... | | | | |

*APPENDIX V*

# Clinical observation work groups (2011–2013)

| Date | City | Activity/ institution | Moderators | Groups/ participants |
|---|---|---|---|---|
| 8–9 Nov 2013 | Lima, Perú | | Mayela Falvi | 1g/8p |
| 24–25 Sept 2013 | Campo Grande, Brazil | FEBRAPSI Congress | Bruno Salesio<br>Andrea Quiroga | 1g/12p |
| Aug 2013 | Prague, Czech Republic | IPA Congress | Margaret Ann Fitzpatrick-Hanly<br>Robert White<br>Nancy Delpréstitto<br>Luis Villalba<br>Juan Baena<br>Adela Leibovich de Duarte<br>Liliana Fudin<br>Andrea Quiroga<br>William Glover<br>Louis Brunet<br>Tamara Fischmann<br>Ulrich Bahrke<br>Ricardo Bernardi | 10g/70p |

(*continued*)

| Date | City | Activity/ institution | Moderators | Groups/ participants |
|---|---|---|---|---|
| | | | Marina Altmann de Litvan<br>Marvin Hurvich | |
| July 2013 | Prague, Czech Republic | IPA Pre Congress | Marianne Leuzinger-Bohleber<br>Siri Gullestad<br>Marina Altmann de Litvan<br>Ricardo Bernardi | 2g/34p |
| July 2013 | Montevideo, Uruguay | APU | Beatriz de León de Bernardi<br>Marina Altmann de Litvan<br>Luis Villalba<br>Nancy Delpréstitto<br>Ricardo Bernardi | 3g/40p |
| 8–9 June 2013 | Sao Paulo, Brazil | Soc. psic. de sao paulo | Marina Altmann de Litvan | 1g/22p |
| 6–7–8 June 2013 | Santiago de Chile, Chile | Sociedad Psicoanalítica de Chile | Beatriz de León de Bernardi<br>Nancy Delpréstitto<br>Luis Villalba<br>Ricardo Bernardi | 3g/36p |
| 3–4 May 2013 | Lima, Perú | | Mayela Falvi | 1g/8p |
| May 2013 | Pelotas, Brazil | Sociedad Psicoanalítica de Pelotas | Silvana Hernández<br>Nancy Delpréstitto<br>Luis Villalba | 1g/15p |
| 2013 | Tel Aviv, Israel | Ongoing group | Meir Winocur<br>Irene Melnick | 1g12p |
| May–June 2013 | Buenos Aires, Argentina | SAP, group of candidates | Adela Leibovich de Duarte and<br>Liliana Fudin | 1g/10p |
| March 2013 | Montevideo, Uruguay | Uruguayan Psychoanalytic Association | Marina Altmann de Litvan<br>Ricardo Bernardi | 1g/10p |

*(continued)*

| Date | City | Activity/ institution | Moderators | Groups/ participants |
|---|---|---|---|---|
| 18–19/1/2013 | New York | | Margaret Ann Fitzpatrick-Hanly | 1g/20p |
| Oct 2011– July 2012 | Toronto, Canada | | Margaret Ann Fitzpatrick-Hanly | 1g/6p |
| 1 Dec 2012 | Frankfurt, Germany | Congress of the DPV (German Psychoanalytical Association) | Marianne Leuzinger-Bohleber | 1g/30p |
| 23–24/11/2012 | Lima, Peru | Sociedad Psicoanalítica Peruana | Mayela Falvy | 1g/8p |
| Oct 2012– Apr 2013 | New York | Lucy Daniels Foundation Project | Margarete Ann Fitzpatrick-Hanly | 1g/7p |
| Sept 2012 | Buenos Aires, Argentina | Ongoing group working on analytic training | Andrea Quiroga de Pereira | 1g/4p |
| 9–10 Oct 2012 | Sao Paulo, Brazil | Sociedade Brasileira de Psicanálise de Sao Paulo FEPAL Pre Congress | Marina Altmann de Litvan<br>Virginia Ungar<br>Ricardo Bernardi | 3g/40p |
| 21–22 June 2012 | Frankfurt, Germany | | Marianne Leuzinger-Bohleber<br>Siri Gullestad | 2g/20p |
| June 2012 | Toronto, Canada | | Margaret Ann Fitzpatrick-Hanly | 2g/15p |
| 8–9 June 2012 | Montevideo, Uruguay | Asociación Psicoanalítica del Uruguay | Nancy Delpréstitto<br>Beatriz de León de Bernardi<br>Mercedes Gallinal | 3g/40p |
| June 2012 | Buenos Aires, Argentina | APdeBA | Virginia Ungar | 1g/5p |

(*continued*)

| Date | City | Activity/ institution | Moderators | Groups/ participants |
|---|---|---|---|---|
| May 2012–Dec 2013 | Montevideo, Uruguay | Candidates working their final paper | Marina Altmann de Litvan<br>Beatriz de León de Bernardi | 2g/12p |
| May–Aug 2012 | San Francisco, USA | | William Glover | 1g/12p |
| May–June 2012 | San Francisco, USA | | William Glover, Steven Goldberg, Maureen Murphy | 1g/12p |
| 23 May 2012 | Mendoza, Argentina | Argentinian Psychoanalytic Congress | Juan Baena<br>Andrea Quiroga de Pereira<br>Silvia Reznisky | 3g/43p |
| 24 Apr 2012 | Tel Aviv, Israel | | Marina Altmann de Litvan | 1g/12p |
| 30 Mar 2012 | Panamá | | Adela Leibovich de Duarte | 1g/20p |
| 14–15 Jan 2012 | New York | | Margaret Ann Fitzpatrick-Hanly<br>Marianne Leuzinger-Bohleber<br>Siri Gullestad<br>Marvin Hurvich<br>Ricardo Bernardi<br>Marina Altmann de Litvan | 3g/25p |
| 5–6 Nov 2011 | Buenos Aires, Argentina | | Adela Leibovich de Duarte<br>Ricardo Bernardi<br>Virginia Ungar | 3g/30p |
| Sept 2011 | Buenos Aires, Argentina | | Andrea Quiroga de Pereira | 1g/5p |
| 3 Aug 2011 | Mexico DF, Mexico | IPA Congress | Ricardo Bernardi<br>Marina Altmann de Litvan<br>Margaret Ann Fitzpatrick-Hanly<br>Marianne Leuzinger-Bohleber<br>Marvin Hurvich | 1g/20p |

*(continued)*

| Date | City | Activity/ institution | Moderators | Groups/ participants |
|---|---|---|---|---|
| 13 May 2011 | Montevideo, Uruguay | Montevideo Focus Group | Marina Altmann de Litvan<br>Ricardo Bernardi | 1g/10p |
| | | | Total number of participants (approx.) | 660p |

Moderators belong to psychoanalytic societies from different countries: Argentina, Brazil, Canada, Germany, Israel, Norway, Peru, United States, and Uruguay.

# INDEX

For Product Safety Concerns and Information please contact our EU representative GPSR@taylorandfrancis.com
Taylor & Francis Verlag GmbH, Kaufingerstraße 24, 80331 München, Germany

www.ingramcontent.com/pod-product-compliance
Lightning Source LLC
LaVergne TN
LVHW021116300926
849160LV00010B/754

* 9 7 8 1 7 8 2 2 0 1 8 1 6 *